Decentralized AI Networks and Blockchain Integration

Building secure, transparent AI ecosystems with blockchain technology

Ashish Manohar Jadhav

www.bpbonline.com

First Edition 2027

ISBN: 978-81-69619-134

Dedicated to

My late father

Prof. Manohar Ramchandra Jadhav

and

my late mother

Rekha Manohar Jadhav

Your sacrifices, wisdom, and love made everything possible.

You live on in every page of this work.

About the Author

Ashish Manohar Jadhav is a senior technology leader with 30+ years of experience shaping enterprise-scale digital transformation, AI-driven platforms, and blockchain-based regulatory systems operating at national and hyperscale levels. He currently serves as senior vice president and head of technology for the Digital Business Group of India's largest private sector conglomerate (Fortune 500), where he steers mission-critical platform strategy across complex, regulated domains.

Ashish is widely recognized for his ability to convert business strategy, regulatory mandates, and risk considerations into resilient, cloud-native platforms, including systems processing 100+ million transactions. As chief architect for large-scale B2B, B2C, and G2C ecosystems, he has led the adoption of Azure Cloud, Kubernetes, event-driven architectures (Kafka), microservices, APIs, AI-driven decision intelligence, and open-source technologies to deliver scalability, reliability, and governance.

A defining achievement of his career is leading the blockchain-based **Distributed Ledger Technology (DLT)** platform implementing India's telecom regulations (TCCCPR, 2018) to combat unsolicited SMS and voice communications. Delivered as part of a telecom operators' consortium, this nationwide RegTech platform enabled digital consent governance, real-time message scrubbing, and regulator-grade compliance reporting. This established a landmark blockchain deployment at national transaction scale and reinforced trust across enterprises, consumers, and regulators.

Ashish has also led enterprise AI platform strategy, embedding predictive analytics, anomaly detection, and intelligent automation into high-volume transactional platforms to support both commercial outcomes and regulatory compliance.

He brings deep expertise in technology governance, risk, and compliance, with his leadership further extends to HRMS, procurement digitization (Source-to-Pay), RFID-enabled supply chains, and large-scale workforce ecosystem platforms.

Ashish holds a bachelor of engineering and a master of technology, along with executive education in strategy and leadership from IIM Indore. He is certified in Azure cloud, blockchain architecture, Agile (Scrum Master), DevOps, and API design and architecture.

An active industry thought leader, Ashish is a trusted advisor to advisory and governing boards navigating AI adoption, cloud transformation, blockchain-driven regulation, and hyperscale digital ecosystems.

About the Reviewer

Nandish Dave is the director of technical support at BitGo, a global leader in digital asset custody, wallets, trading, staking, and blockchain infrastructure serving institutional clients worldwide. He leads global technical support operations for high-availability, security-critical systems that power custody, wallet, API, and trading platforms across the digital asset ecosystem.

His work focuses on applying artificial intelligence and machine learning to real-world production environments, where he has led initiatives involving AI-driven support automation, **retrieval-augmented generation** (**RAG**) systems, intelligent triage, workflow orchestration, and operational analytics. These efforts have improved operational efficiency, reduced manual workload, and accelerated response and resolution times across enterprise support organizations.

With deep expertise in blockchain infrastructure, distributed systems, APIs, incident management, and customer operations, Nandish plays a key role in launch readiness, operational risk management, incident governance, and cross-functional coordination for new products and platform enhancements. He collaborates closely with engineering, product, security, and executive leadership teams to establish support standards and operational excellence practices for mission-critical systems.

Beyond his professional responsibilities, Nandish serves as a technical reviewer for books and publications focused on artificial intelligence, machine learning, blockchain technologies, decentralized AI networks, and blockchain integration. He is passionate about emerging technologies and their practical application in building scalable, reliable, and customer-centric systems.

Acknowledgement

I want to express my deepest gratitude to my family for their unwavering support and encouragement throughout the writing of this book, especially to my wife, Dipti Jadhav, and my sons, Parth Jadhav and Saksham Jadhav. Your patience, understanding, and belief in me provided the strength to see this project through to completion.

I am also grateful to BPB Publications for their guidance and expertise in bringing this book to fruition. It was a long journey of revising this book, with valuable participation and collaboration of reviewers, technical experts, and editors whose sharp eyes and deep knowledge made this a far better work than I could have produced alone.

I would also like to acknowledge the valuable contributions of my colleagues and co-workers during my many years in the technology industry, who have taught me so much and provided valuable feedback on my work. I extend special mention to Joydeep Mukherjee, Babu Jayaraj, Abhijeet Mahajan, and many other outstanding professionals whose collaboration, insights, and camaraderie have been instrumental in shaping my thinking. The real-world experiences we shared are woven into every chapter of this book.

I would also like to express my heartfelt gratitude to my sisters Ashwini Satralkar and Shweta Kadam for always supporting me and motivating me through every step of this journey. Your belief in me has meant more than words can express.

A special acknowledgment goes to my manager and mentor, Mr. Anish Shah, President at Jio Platforms Limited, for always challenging and motivating us to go the extra mile on technology. Your relentless pursuit of excellence and your faith in our abilities have been a constant source of inspiration.

Finally, I would like to thank all the readers who have taken an interest in this book and for their support in making it a reality. Your encouragement has been invaluable. It is my sincere hope that the knowledge and insights shared in these pages will be of genuine value as you build the next generation of AI systems.

Preface

Artificial intelligence and blockchain are no longer technologies of the future; they are reshaping industries, economies, and societies today. Yet despite their individual maturity, the convergence of these two domains remains one of the most underexplored and consequential frontiers in modern computing. Having spent over three decades leading enterprise technology transformations, including a landmark national-scale blockchain deployment for India's telecom regulatory framework, I have witnessed firsthand both the immense promise and the very real limitations of centralized AI systems. This book is born out of that experience: a practitioner's guide to building the next generation of AI, one that is decentralized, transparent, and governed by communities rather than gatekeepers.

Decentralized AI Networks and Blockchain Integration is designed to be a comprehensive, hands-on companion for engineers, architects, and technology leaders who want to understand and implement the convergence of AI and blockchain at production scale. The book is structured across six thematic sections and twelve chapters, each building on the last to take you from foundational concepts to real-world deployment:

Chapter 1: Introduction to Decentralized AI and Blockchain — Establishes the conceptual framework by exploring the limitations of centralized AI, the principles of Web3, and how blockchain addresses fundamental challenges of transparency, ownership, and equitable access in AI systems.

Chapter 2: Fundamentals of Blockchain Technology for AI — Provides the essential technical foundation (consensus mechanisms, smart contracts, tokenization, and distributed storage) and explains how blockchain's properties of immutability and programmability unlock new AI paradigms.

Chapter 3: Decentralized AI Network Architecture — Dives deep into network topology, node coordination, data distribution strategies, and communication protocols for designing resilient, scalable networks that support distributed AI computation.

Chapter 4: Smart Contracts for AI Applications — Teaches you to write, test, and deploy smart contracts for AI use cases, covering Solidity design patterns, AI model registration, automated payment systems, and Oracle integration for external data.

Chapter 5: Federated Learning with Blockchain — Explores privacy-preserving distributed training, blockchain-based coordination, differential privacy, and secure multi-party computation, with practical implementations using TensorFlow Federated.

Chapter 6: Model Deployment and Management – Covers the complete lifecycle of AI model deployment in decentralized networks, including versioning, distribution strategies, A/B testing, runtime management, and monitoring.

Chapter 7: Tokenomics, Incentive Mechanisms and Decentralized Governance— Focuses on designing sustainable token economies that incentivize participation, covering utility vs. governance tokens, staking models, reward distribution algorithms, and economic security. The chapter further explores democratic governance for AI networks, covering voting systems, DAO implementations, proposal mechanisms, delegation models, and dispute resolution for community-driven AI evolution.

Chapter 8: Privacy-preserving AI Techniques — Covers advanced cryptographic techniques including homomorphic encryption, zero-knowledge proofs (zk-SNARKs), trusted execution environments, and privacy-preserving data sharing with practical implementations.

Chapter 9: Security and Threat Detection — Addresses the full security threat landscape of decentralized AI, including attack vectors, defense mechanisms, smart contract auditing, anomaly detection systems, and incident response procedures.

Chapter 10: Building Production Ready Systems — Provides hands-on guidance for enterprise adoption, covering production architecture, CI/CD strategies, monitoring and observability, disaster recovery, scaling, and cost management.

Chapter 11: Case Studies and Future Trends — Examines real-world decentralized AI deployments across healthcare, financial services, supply chain, and scientific research, and concludes with emerging trends, regulatory developments, and future opportunities.

Whether you are an AI engineer seeking to eliminate centralization risks, a blockchain developer looking to extend smart contracts into the AI domain, or a technology leader charting your organization's path into Web3-powered intelligence, this book is written for you. Familiarity with either AI/ML concepts or blockchain technology is beneficial, but the book is structured to be accessible to practitioners who are expert in one domain and newer to the other.

I hope that the technical depth, real-world context, and practical guidance in these pages help you not only understand decentralized AI, but actually build it. The future of AI is open, collaborative, and democratically governed. Let us build it together.

Code Bundle and Coloured Images

Please follow the link to download the
Code Bundle and the ***Coloured Images*** of the book:

https://rebrand.ly/934be6

The code bundle for the book is also hosted on GitHub at **https://github.com/bpbpublications/Decentralized-AI-Networks-and-Blockchain-Integration.** In case there's an update to the code, it will be updated on the existing GitHub repository.

We have code bundles from our rich catalogue of books and videos available at https://github.com/bpbpublications. Check them out!

Errata

We take immense pride in our work at BPB Publications and follow best practices to ensure the accuracy of our content to provide an indulging reading experience to our subscribers. Our readers are our mirrors, and we use their inputs to reflect and improve upon human errors, if any, that may have occurred during the publishing processes involved. To let us maintain the quality and help us reach out to any readers who might be having difficulties due to any unforeseen errors, please write to us at: **errata@bpbonline.com**

Your support, suggestions and feedback are highly appreciated by the BPB Publications' Family.

Piracy

If you come across any illegal copies of our works in any form on the internet, we would be grateful if you would provide us with the location address or website name. Please contact us at business@bpbonline.com with a link to the material.

If you are interested in becoming an author

If there is a topic that you have expertise in, and you are interested in either writing or contributing to a book, please visit www.bpbonline.com. We have worked with thousands of developers and tech professionals, just like you, to help them share their insights with the global tech community. You can make a general application, apply for a specific hot topic that we are recruiting an author for, or submit your own idea.

Reviews

Please leave a review. Once you have read and used this book, why not leave a review on the site that you purchased it from? Potential readers can then see and use your unbiased opinion to make purchase decisions. We at BPB can understand what you think about our products, and our authors can see your feedback on their book. Thank you!

For more information about BPB, please visit www.bpbonline.com.

Join our Discord space

Join our Discord workspace for latest updates, offers, tech happenings around the world, new releases, and sessions with the authors:

https://discord.bpbonline.com

Table of Contents

CHAPTER 1
Introduction to Decentralized AI and Blockchain

Introduction

Artificial intelligence (**AI**) has historically been developed and deployed in centralized silos, cloud platforms, proprietary data centers, and isolated research labs. While this model accelerated progress, it also entrenched the concentration of control, exacerbated privacy risks, and limited collaborative potential. Decentralized AI reframes these paradigms by leveraging blockchain's immutable ledger, native token economics, and consensus-driven governance to distribute every layer of the AI lifecycle, ranging from data ingestion and model training to inference and reward allocation.

Importantly, this distribution employs a hybrid architecture; computationally intensive operations like model training and inference remain off-chain or on Layer 2 scaling solutions for performance and cost efficiency, while blockchain anchors critical verification points, data provenance hashes, model checkpoints, governance decisions, and reward distributions for security and auditability. Full on-chain AI training remains infeasible due to current computational and economic constraints, making this pragmatic hybrid approach essential for practical deployment.

This chapter lays the conceptual groundwork for understanding how blockchain's core attributes are immutability, transparency, programmability, and decentralization. Thereby, natively complementing AI's need for secure, auditable, and incentive-aligned networks.

Structure

The chapter covers the following topics:

- Centralization problem in AI
- Web3 principles and decentralization
- Overview of blockchain technology
- Benefits of decentralized AI

- Key challenges and solutions for decentralized AI networks
- Industry landscape and key players
- Regulatory considerations
- Future vision and opportunities

Objectives

By the end of this chapter, readers will be able to explain, why blockchain is essential for decentralizing AI, addressing data silos, governance opacity, and single points of failure, identify key Web3 principles such as permissionless access, trustless consensus, and tokenized ownership as well as how they enable distributed AI collaboration, describe blockchain's core components (ledger, consensus, cryptography) and smart contracts as the programmable substrate for AI networks, assess benefits of decentralized AI: transparent model provenance, resilient architectures, data sovereignty, and aligned incentive structures, recognize major challenges such a scalability, privacy, incentive exploits, governance complexity as well as blockchain-based solutions such as Layer 2 scaling and zero-knowledge proofs, map, the stakeholders of decentralized AI ecosystem (protocols, compute providers, data marketplaces) and their roles in a token-driven economy, understand regulatory considerations (privacy, securities, IP) and how on-chain proofs and modular governance ensure compliance, and envision: future decentralized AI paradigms: autonomous AI economies, edge-blockchain integration, and AI governance **decentralized autonomous organization** (**DAOs**). This foundational knowledge directly prepares readers for the advanced technical concepts, architectural patterns, and implementation strategies explored in subsequent chapters. The principles, challenges, and solutions introduced here form the conceptual scaffold upon which practical decentralized AI network design, development, and deployment depend. The emphasis of this chapter is on how blockchain enables, enhances, and transforms decentralized AI. Thereby, ensuring that every technical detail and design consideration remains anchored to real-world applications and measurable benefits for AI practitioners, researchers, and organizations seeking to leverage distributed intelligence networks.

Centralization problem in AI

The AI landscape today is dominated by a handful of powerful technology corporations that control the infrastructure, data, and tools necessary for AI development and deployment. This centralization has created a precarious ecosystem where the decisions and limitations of a few dominant players increasingly constrain innovation, competition, and equitable access to AI capabilities.

Leading providers like **Amazon Web Services** (**AWS**), Microsoft Azure, and Google Cloud Platform collectively hold over 60-65% of the AI cloud computing market, while NVIDIA commands 92% of the AI GPU market for data centers. Proprietary large language models from companies like *OpenAI*, *Google*, and *Anthropic* further solidify this control across the

AI value chain from cloud infrastructure and specialized hardware to massive datasets and state-of-the-art models. This vertical integration creates formidable barriers to entry for new participants, concentrates economic value among incumbents, and establishes dependency relationships that limit the autonomy of developers, researchers, and organizations seeking to leverage AI technologies.

The concentration of AI capabilities within a small number of entities raises fundamental concerns about accountability, transparency, and democratic governance of technologies that increasingly shape critical decisions across healthcare, finance, criminal justice, and public policy. When a handful of corporations determine which AI applications are permissible, what data can be used for training, and how algorithms are designed and deployed, for instance, in opaque content moderation systems, credit scoring models, or automated hiring algorithms, society becomes vulnerable to unchallengeable outcomes without public scrutiny or meaningful recourse.

The lack of alternative infrastructure forces individuals and organizations to accept terms and conditions they may find objectionable or to forgo access to transformative technologies entirely.

Defining centralization in modern AI

Centralization in modern AI concentrates data, computation, model ownership, and decision-making within a few entities. This creates systemic risks, including single points of failure, opaque governance, biased incentives, and uneven access, limiting transparency, accountability, and equitable participation across the AI value chain.

Data silos and monopolies

Large AI corporations accumulate vast proprietary datasets behind closed systems, creating competitive moats that prevent data sharing, limit model diversity, and exclude smaller players from accessing the information resources necessary for competitive AI development. This concentration manifests in several critical ways:

- **The data advantage**: Large technology companies have accumulated vast datasets through their consumer-facing platforms, search engines, social networks, and cloud services. Major search platforms process billions of queries daily, leading social networks collect data from billions of active users, and dominant e-commerce platforms monitor purchasing patterns across millions of customers. This data concentration creates significant structural advantages for training sophisticated AI models.

- **Proprietary data moats**: These companies guard their data assets zealously, creating what economists call **data moats**, competitive advantages that become stronger over time. As users interact with AI services, they generate more data, which improves the models, which attracts more users, creating a self-reinforcing cycle that smaller competitors cannot match.

- **Access inequality**: Startups and academic researchers face significant barriers in accessing comparable datasets. While some companies offer limited APIs or datasets, even these external access channels are constrained by rate limits, data filtering, and abstraction layers that prevent the quality, completeness, and real-time nature available to internal teams. This disparity fundamentally limits the ability of smaller players to compete in developing state-of-the-art AI systems.

Vendor lock-in and platform dependence

AI developers become trapped within proprietary ecosystems through specialized **application programming interfaces** (**APIs**), custom frameworks, and integrated toolchains that make migration costly and technically complex, reducing innovation and creating unhealthy dependencies on single platform providers. This entrapment occurs through multiple mechanisms:

- **Infrastructure reliance**: Modern AI development increasingly depends on specialized cloud infrastructure such as high-performance GPU clusters, dedicated AI accelerators, and fully managed intelligence platforms. The comprehensive ecosystems built around these offerings make it technically challenging and financially prohibitive to migrate workloads to alternative environments.
- **API and service integration**: When applications are built around specific AI service interfaces such as large language model endpoints, vision processing APIs, or managed machine learning pipelines, the effort required to re-architect code for different providers imposes prohibitive switching costs.
- **Proprietary formats and standards**: Each major platform defines its own model serialization formats, training frameworks, and deployment conventions. For example, Google's TensorFlow models optimized for TensorFlow Serving or TPU deployment require significant rework to run on AWS SageMaker's PyTorch endpoints or Azure ML pipelines, while PyTorch's TorchScript models face compatibility challenges when ported to TensorFlow's ecosystem. This fragmentation forces developers to invest significant time in custom converters and integration layers, further raising barriers to interoperability and platform migration.
- **Economic lock-in**: Pricing models often include significant discounts for volume commitments or ecosystem integration, making it economically challenging for organizations to maintain multi-vendor strategies or switch providers.

Risks and failures of centralized architectures

Centralized AI systems concentrate critical operations in single entities, creating pronounced vulnerabilities: a single breach can compromise data and models, service outages halt entire platforms, opaque governance fosters unaccountable decisions, and market dominance stifles competition and innovation.

Single points of failure

Centralized AI services such as APIs for inference or model hosting clusters present attractive targets for **distributed denial-of-service** (**DDoS**), ransomware, or regulatory takedown. A single data-centric outage can cripple global services. The key risks to this include:

- **Service unavailability**: Latency spikes or complete downtime when critical nodes fail or lose connectivity.
- **Data tampering**: While centralized systems implement internal access controls and monitoring, malicious insiders or sophisticated attackers may still alter training corpora or model weight checkpoints without public verifiability or external accountability. This can poison model behavior undetected by outside stakeholders, compromising system integrity.
- **Censorship vulnerability**: Central authorities can unilaterally disable or throttle AI capabilities based on jurisdictional or policy edicts.
- **Cascading business impact**: Modern businesses increasingly rely on AI services for critical operations, including customer service chatbots, fraud detection, content moderation, and automated decision-making. When these services fail, the business impact extends far beyond the immediate technical disruption.
- **Geographic and regulatory risks**: Centralized platforms face region-specific risks, including government censorship, regulatory changes, and geopolitical tensions. Services can be banned or restricted in entire countries, instantly cutting off access for millions of users and businesses.

Algorithmic opacity and black-box models

Opaque, proprietary AI models obscure decision logic, making it impossible for users or regulators to understand or trust outputs. This black-box nature hinders accountability, bias detection, and transparent validation of AI-driven results. The key concerns include:

- **Lack of transparency**: Centralized AI providers typically offer their models as black-boxes, providing little to no insight into training data, model architecture, decision-making processes, or potential biases. This opacity makes it impossible for users to understand why specific decisions are made or to verify the appropriateness of AI recommendations for their use cases.
- **Audit impossibility**: Without access to model internals, training data, or decision logs, external auditors cannot verify that AI systems comply with regulatory requirements, ethical guidelines, or industry standards. This is particularly problematic in regulated industries like healthcare, finance, and legal services.
- **Debugging and improvement challenges**: When AI models produce incorrect or biased results, users have limited recourse for understanding the root cause or

implementing improvements. They must rely entirely on the platform provider to identify and fix issues.

Biased training data and lack of accountability

Unrepresentative datasets embed systemic biases into AI outcomes, and without transparent audit trails or clear provenance, tracing errors or assigning responsibility for discriminatory results becomes nearly impossible. This manifests through several critical issues:

- **Embedded biases**: Centralized AI models trained on large unfiltered datasets frequently replicate societal biases, perpetuating discrimination in critical domains such as hiring, lending, and criminal justice. Examples include facial recognition systems with higher error rates for women and darker-skinned individuals, language models associating certain professions with specific genders, and resume screening tools disadvantaging candidates from particular educational backgrounds.
- **Limited recourse**: Users facing biased or harmful AI behavior have little ability to alter underlying models, retrain with more balanced data, or implement bias correction, forcing them to either accept flawed outputs or discontinue use.
- **Accountability gaps**: The complexity and opacity of centralized AI providers create significant challenges for establishing responsibility when harms occur, complicating efforts to enforce liability or enact remediation measures.

Economic and social impact

Centralized AI funnels the vast majority of economic value to a handful of dominant platforms, marginalizing data providers, developers, and emerging innovators. High expenses for data, computational resources, and specialized talent create barriers that shut out startups and reinforce incumbent dominance. This concentration of power enables pervasive surveillance practices that erode privacy and informed consent, while central entities command excessive influence over information flows and decision-making processes, posing significant threats to competition, innovation, and democratic governance.

Key consequences

These key consequences illustrate how concentrated control over AI resources creates systemic barriers, stifles innovation, and threatens privacy and democratic processes. Addressing these issues requires decentralization to redistribute power, foster competition, and protect individual rights in AI development and deployment.

The economic and social impacts include:

- **Wealth extraction**: Platform owners capture most AI-driven economic gains, sidelining contributors and smaller developers. This value concentration means that those providing raw materials, computational resources, or specialized expertise receive minimal compensation relative to the value they generate, while dominant corporations accumulate vast profits without corresponding risk exposure or accountability to stakeholders.

- **High entry barriers**: Rising costs for essential inputs, including cloud infrastructure, specialized hardware, and proprietary training datasets, deter new market entrants.
- **Innovation suppression**: Dominant players can stifle or acquire rivals, steering development toward their interests rather than broader societal needs. Monopolistic practices such as predatory pricing, exclusive licensing, and acquisitive strategies that eliminate competitors reduce the diversity of AI approaches, technologies, and business models available to users and applications.
- **Surveillance and privacy threats**: Centralized data hoarding facilitates expansive monitoring, undermining user privacy. When corporations control massive datasets without meaningful oversight or consent mechanisms, they can extract behavioral patterns, predict personal preferences, identify vulnerabilities, and sell insights to third parties without accountability to those whose data has been harvested.
- **Power imbalances**: Control over AI-powered services consolidates in a few entities, risking democratic institutions and individual autonomy. When critical AI systems are controlled by private corporations with profit motives, democratic societies lose the ability to ensure that AI systems serve public interests or remain transparent to elected representatives and affected citizens.

Web3 principles and decentralization

The emergence of Web3 represents a fundamental reimagining of how digital systems operate, moving from centralized, platform-controlled architectures to decentralized, user-sovereign networks. These principles, when applied to artificial intelligence, offer transformative possibilities for creating more equitable, transparent, and democratic AI ecosystems.

Core tenets of Web3

Decentralization of authority, native digital ownership through tokens, trustless consensus, permissionless participation, and composable open protocols that collectively empower users and applications with sovereignty, interoperability, and transparent governance.

Permissionless systems

Permissionless architectures significantly broaden access to AI infrastructure and innovation by eliminating gatekeepers and central authorities, though participants still face economic barriers such as capital requirements, hardware costs, and gas fees. Unlike traditional platforms that require approval for participation, permissionless blockchain systems enable anyone to contribute, compete, and create without intermediaries by following publicly stated protocols. This paradigm shift redistributes power from centralized providers to a global community of developers, researchers, and organizations, cultivating an open AI ecosystem where talent and innovation can emerge from anywhere worldwide. The following aspects define permissionless systems:

- **Definition and characteristics**: Permissionless systems allow anyone to participate without requiring approval from a central authority. In the context of blockchain networks, this means that individuals can join the network, validate transactions, deploy smart contracts, or build applications without needing permission from gatekeepers.
- **Technical implementation**: Permissionless systems achieve this openness through cryptographic proof mechanisms rather than identity verification. For example, Bitcoin's proof of work system allows anyone with computational resources to participate in network security, while Ethereum's smart contract platform enables anyone to deploy decentralized applications without platform approval.
- **Implications for AI**: In permissionless AI networks, researchers, developers, and organizations can contribute models, data, or computational resources without requiring approval from centralized platforms. This dramatically lowers barriers to entry and enables innovation from unexpected sources. A researcher in India can contribute a breakthrough algorithm, a healthcare provider in rural Ethiopia can share anonymized patient data, and a startup in the Middle East can deploy AI services, all without requiring permission from *Silicon Valley* gatekeepers.

Trustlessness and peer-to-peer validation

Trustlessness does not mean the absence of trust; rather, it explicitly shifts trust from institutions to the correctness of cryptographic protocols and well-designed incentive mechanisms. Participants place confidence in mathematical proofs and verifiable code that any node can independently validate, eliminating reliance on specific individuals or centralized authorities. This foundation enables transparent systems where cooperation emerges through aligned incentives rather than institutional guarantees:

- **Cryptographic foundations**: This trustlessness is enabled by several cryptographic primitives:
    - Digital signatures that prove authenticity without revealing private keys.
    - Hash functions that create tamper-evident records.
    - Merkle trees that enable efficient verification of large datasets.
    - Zero-knowledge proofs that allow verification without revealing underlying data.
- **Consensus mechanisms**: Trustless systems rely on consensus mechanisms to ensure all participants agree on the state of the system without trusting any single party.

Different consensus algorithms offer various trade-offs:

- Proof of work provides security through computational difficulty.
- Proof of stake achieves consensus through economic incentives.
- Delegated proof of stake balances efficiency with decentralization.
- Proof of authority optimizes for known validator sets.

- **AI applications**: In trustless AI systems, model training, validation, and inference can occur without participants needing to trust each other. Smart contracts can automatically verify that contributors have provided legitimate data or computational work, distribute rewards fairly, and ensure that AI models behave as specified—all without human intervention or centralized oversight.

Native digital ownership

Native digital ownership represents a fundamental paradigm shift that empowers individuals to own, control, and monetize digital assets directly without intermediaries. Web3 enables true ownership through cryptographic guarantees and smart contracts, replacing platform dependence with user agency. This transformation allows creators, data providers, and AI contributors to capture value directly from their work and maintain sovereign control over digital assets. The following dimensions define native digital ownership:

- **Programmable property rights**: Web3 introduces the concept of native digital ownership through tokens and smart contracts. Unlike traditional digital assets that exist at the discretion of platform providers, Web3 assets are owned directly by users and protected by cryptographic guarantees.
- **Token standards and interoperability**: Various token standards enable different types of digital ownership:
  - ERC-20 tokens represent fungible assets like currencies or utility tokens.
  - ERC-721 (NFTs) represent unique, non-fungible assets like digital art or identity.
  - ERC-1155 enables both fungible and non-fungible tokens in a single contract.
  - ERC-4626 standardizes tokenized vaults for yield-bearing assets.
- **Self-custody and control**: Native digital ownership means users maintain direct control over their assets through private keys, rather than depending on platform providers to honor their ownership claims. This fundamental shift in control has profound implications for how value is created, captured, and distributed in digital ecosystems.
- **AI asset tokenization**: AI asset tokenization transforms core components of the AI lifecycle into tradable digital tokens on blockchain platforms. Training datasets become fractionalized ERC-20/721 tokens representing data ownership shares; trained models are licensed as NFTs with embedded royalties; compute resources are pooled

as fungible GPU-hour tokens; and contributor reputation scores serve as soulbound tokens for verifiable credentials.

- **A typical workflow**: Data providers tokenize datasets and stake them in liquidity pools. Model trainers access data via smart contract collateral, train models, and mint NFTs. Inference providers deploy models and earn query fees. Smart contracts auto-distribute royalties to data owners, trainers, and compute providers across the AI supply chain.

From Web2 to Web3

The shift from Web2's centralized platforms to Web3's decentralized protocols marks a fundamental change in digital power structures and economic relationships. In Web2, AI applications are dominated by gatekeepers who control user data and model development, limiting transparency and innovation. Web3 leverages blockchain and peer-to-peer networks to restore data ownership, enable self-sovereign identities, and tokenize contributions, fostering privacy, auditability, and equitable participation. This transition transforms the AI ecosystem into a transparent, incentive-aligned network where users directly benefit and democratic innovation flourishes.

Centralized platforms vs. decentralized protocols

The fundamental difference between centralized platforms and decentralized protocols reshapes how value is created, controlled, and distributed in digital ecosystems. Centralized platforms consolidate authority, data, and economic benefits in the hands of a few corporations, while decentralized protocols distribute power across network participants through transparent governance and cryptographic trust. This distinction profoundly impacts AI development, creating vastly different incentive structures, ownership models, and innovation dynamics. The key contrasts include:

- **Platform dynamics**: Web2 platforms concentrate power by controlling user data, imposing unilateral terms, and extracting economic value through advertising or fees while creating monopolistic network effects. Companies like *Facebook* and *Google* exemplify this model, dictating content policies and monetization without transparency or user agency.

- **Protocol architecture**: Web3 protocols invert this dynamic through transparent, immutable smart contracts that enable peer-to-peer interactions without intermediaries. Users own their data via cryptographic keys, participate permissionlessly, and benefit from equitable value distribution. Composable protocols like MakerDAO and Uniswap demonstrate how modular systems can interoperate to create complex financial services without centralized control.

- **Technical implementation**: Protocols leverage blockchain platforms like Ethereum for transparent governance, decentralized storage solutions like IPFS for user-controlled data, and permissionless validator networks for censorship resistance. This architecture replaces gatekeepers with cryptographic trust and consensus mechanisms, fostering resilient, equitable AI ecosystems where innovation thrives without monopolistic constraints.

User sovereignty and self-custody

Transitioning from Web2's custodial frameworks to Web3's self-sovereign model empowers individuals to fully control their data, identities, and digital assets. In the Web2 era, centralized platforms manage user credentials, restrict data portability, and monetize personal information without direct user benefit. Web3 upends this dynamic by placing private keys and verifiable credentials directly in users' hands, ensuring that only they can authorize data sharing, AI model access, or token transfers.

Self-custody extends beyond wallets to include decentralized identity wallets and encrypted data vaults, enabling users to grant or revoke permissions at any time. This model fosters true data portability: individuals can move their preferences, reputations, and usage history across AI services without gatekeepers. By combining user-held cryptographic keys with on-chain access controls and zero-knowledge proofs, decentralized AI platforms can deliver personalized, privacy-preserving experiences while preserving user autonomy and reducing reliance on intermediaries.

Applying Web3 to AI

The application of Web3 principles to artificial intelligence creates entirely new possibilities for how AI systems are developed, governed, and monetized. Harnessing Web3 principles empowers AI systems with enhanced decentralization, transparency, and user-centric control. By integrating blockchain-based identity, data sovereignty, and token economies, AI transitions from siloed platforms to open, collaborative networks. This approach unlocks new paradigms for trustless model training, fair value distribution, and privacy-preserving data sharing, catalyzing a more equitable and innovative AI ecosystem.

Token incentives for data and model contribution

Token-based incentives transform AI data scarcity from exploitation to equitable participation. Traditional AI development requires massive datasets often acquired through unfair extraction, while tokenization rewards contributors proportionally and sustainably by aligning economic incentives with network growth and quality improvement. This creates transparent value capture mechanisms where data providers, model developers, and AI validators share in protocol success.

The Incentive design principles and model monetization include:

- **Proportional rewards**: Contributors earn tokens reflecting their data's actual utility and value.

- **Quality assurance**: Smart contracts automatically validate data provenance and integrity before rewards.
- **Privacy preservation**: Cryptographic techniques enable compensation without exposing sensitive information.
- **Sustained engagement**: Long-term contribution models align network health with participant incentives.
- **Usage-based tokens**: Pay-per-inference models create direct economic flows.
- **Staking mechanisms**: Collateral systems guaranteeing model quality and reliability.
- **Governance rights**: Successful model tokens grant protocol decision-making power.
- **Market liquidity**: Tradeable tokens enable flexible valuation and investment.
- **Technical implementation**: Smart contracts automatically authenticate data quality, quantify individual contributor impact on model performance, distribute rewards transparently based on validated contributions, and resolve disputes autonomously. This creates self-sustaining ecosystems where data providers, model developers, and consumers interact through aligned economic incentives rather than extractive relationships.

Decentralized identity and reputation systems

Self-sovereign identity gives users complete control over digital credentials, vital for trust in decentralized AI networks. This approach enables participants to build verifiable reputation profiles that follow them across protocols and platforms, creating portable trust scores independent of centralized authorities:

- **Emerging standards**: Emerging standards and technologies support this infrastructure:
    - **W3C verifiable credentials**: Interoperable, cryptographically signed digital attestations that comply with global standards, enabling credentials to be recognized across disparate systems.
    - **Decentralized identifiers (DIDs)**: Globally unique, resolvable IDs independent of central registries, allowing individuals to maintain sovereign control over their identity across networks.
    - **Zero-knowledge proofs**: Validate credentials without revealing private data, enabling trust verification while preserving privacy and confidentiality.
    - **Soulbound tokens**: **Soulbound tokens (SBTs)**, an experimental concept, are non-transferable tokens representing unique qualifications, achievements, and credentials permanently bound to individual blockchain identities. Despite promising standards like EIP-4973 gaining traction, they face unresolved challenges in revocation mechanisms, privacy protections, and decentralized governance models.

- **Reputation building**: Participants earn reputation by delivering reliable AI models, contributing high-quality data, validating peers' work, and engaging in governance. Reputation aggregates from multiple network activities and becomes increasingly valuable as contributors demonstrate consistent performance.
- **Cross-network portability**: Reputation scores move seamlessly across AI networks, preventing siloed identities and preserving trust profiles. This portability enables contributors to leverage their established reputation when entering new protocols and ecosystems.
- **Technical architecture**: Identities are anchored on blockchain ledgers with credentials issued by trusted authorities or decentralized algorithms. Reputation aggregates from multi-network activities, while privacy-preserving cryptographic protocols enable verifiable claims without exposing personal details, balancing trust, privacy, and interoperability.

Community governance of AI services

Community governance promotes vibrant participation from a diverse body of contributors, including model developers, data providers, subject matter experts, and end users, who collectively shape the platform's roadmap. Committees or DAOs can form to focus on specialized issues such as privacy policy updates, maintenance of open-source model repositories, or strategic partnerships with other protocols. Delegated voting and quadratic funding incentivize minority voices and support grassroots initiatives, fostering greater inclusivity.

Accountability mechanisms, such as transparent proposal histories, dispute resolution systems, and open audit trails, further enhance trust and legitimacy. By decentralizing decision-making, community governance helps prevent undue concentration of power, mitigates the risk of censorship, and ensures that the evolution of AI services remains aligned with the broader interests of the participant community.

Ultimately, this governance approach empowers stakeholders to prioritize transparency, innovation, and adaptability, turning decentralized AI ecosystems into living, community-driven platforms able to address evolving technical and societal challenges.

Decentralized AI platforms replace centralized product teams with on-chain, stakeholder-driven governance. Token holders can propose and vote on:

- **Protocol enhancements**: Upgrading consensus mechanisms, integrating privacy tools like **zero-knowledge succinct non-interactive arguments of knowledge (zk-SNARKs)**, or adding cross-chain bridges.
- **Incentive rebalancing**: Tweaking reward structures to uplift underrepresented data domains or reduce environmental impact.

- **Ethical safeguards**: Smart contracts enforce quantifiable ethical rules on-chain, such as data provenance requirements, consent verification, and reward distribution fairness. Complex constraints like model bias evaluation or fairness metrics require off-chain oracles for assessment, with automated smart contract actions (pausing deployment, slashing stakes) triggered only when oracle-verified thresholds are breached.

This community-led model ensures protocols evolve in step with stakeholder priorities, uphold ethical standards, and swiftly counter new security threats, laying the groundwork for scalable, transparent, and resilient decentralized AI ecosystems.

Overview of blockchain technology

Blockchain technology fundamentally transforms how AI systems manage trust, transparency, and coordination by replacing centralized intermediaries with distributed, cryptographically secured networks. The decentralized architecture of blockchain and its programmable logic directly resolve the transparency, reliability, and incentive misalignment issues endemic to centralized AI platforms by embedding provenance tracking, secure coordination, and trust at scale into the very infrastructure of AI development and deployment.

At its core, blockchain provides verifiable, tamper-resistant records via hashes, Merkle proofs, and metadata stored on-chain, with raw data and full model parameters in off-chain systems like IPFS. This enables independent verification of contributions, computations, and decisions without storing voluminous raw content on-chain.

The integration of blockchain with AI addresses longstanding challenges around data provenance, model versioning, contributor attribution, and fair compensation. Smart contracts automate complex multi-party agreements, ensuring that data providers receive proportional rewards, that model updates follow agreed-upon governance rules, and that dispute resolution occurs transparently according to predefined protocols. This automation reduces friction, eliminates intermediaries, and creates economically sustainable ecosystems where participants trust the protocol rather than centralized administrators.

The core components that enable blockchain's transformative impact on AI include:

- **Distributed ledger**: An append-only, cryptographically linked record of every AI event from raw data submissions to model checkpoints, which ensures an immutable audit trail. Each transaction is hashed and linked to previous blocks, creating a chain of custody that cannot be retroactively altered without detection. This persistent, verifiable history enables stakeholders to audit AI system behavior, trace errors to their source, identify malicious contributions, and establish accountability for AI outcomes. The distributed nature means that no single party controls the historical record, preventing censorship or manipulation of past events.

- **Model lineage auditing**: Block hashes anchor each training round and validation metric, allowing stakeholders to trace a model's evolution from initial data shards to final parameters. This granular provenance tracking records which datasets contributed to training, what hyperparameters were used, how validation scores changed over time, and which governance decisions influenced model development. Researchers can reproduce training runs, regulators can verify compliance with ethical guidelines, and users can assess whether models were trained on appropriate data. This transparency builds trust and enables continuous improvement by making model development processes visible and reviewable.

- **Global state consistency**: Identical ledger copies across participating nodes guarantee that data providers, trainers, and validators operate on the same authoritative model snapshot, eliminating inconsistencies common in centralized or federated setups. Consensus mechanisms ensure all participants agree on the current state of training progress, reward distributions, and governance decisions before proceeding. This shared source of truth prevents synchronization errors, duplicate payments, conflicting model versions, and divergent interpretations of protocol rules. The result is a coherent, coordinated AI development process that functions reliably despite involving geographically distributed, potentially untrusted participants operating independently.

Consensus mechanisms

Decentralized AI protocols leverage tailored consensus models to secure and coordinate distributed workflows, such as:

- **Proof of work (PoW)**: Computational puzzles anchor high-stakes events—such as final model checkpoints, providing strong censorship resistance and Sybil attack mitigation through economic cost.
- **Proof of stake (PoS)**: Token-based validator collateral reduces energy consumption, accelerates finality for model-update transactions, and aligns incentives for honest parameter aggregation.
- **Delegated proof of stake (DPoS)**: Elected block producers deliver sub-second block times ideal for latency-sensitive training loops, enabling rapid gradient commits while preserving decentralized oversight via periodic elections.

  By tuning stake weightings, slashing conditions, and validator rotations, these consensus frameworks balance security, efficiency, and speed to support diverse AI training and inference requirements.

The following table is an overview of consensus trade-offs:

Mechanism	Security	Latency	Energy use	AI suitability
PoW	High (proven)	High (10-60 min blocks)	Very high	Low (compute-intensive, slow for training data)
PoS	Moderate (maturing)	Low (seconds)	Low	High (efficient for frequent updates)
DPoS	Moderate	Very Low	Low	High (scalable inference)

***Table 1.1**: Consensus trade-offs*

Cryptographic primitives

Cryptographic primitives are foundational tools in blockchain that ensure security, data integrity, authentication, and efficient verification for trustless decentralized AI systems.

The core blockchain tools ensure secure, trustless operation with:

- **Hash functions**: Hash functions take arbitrary input data and produce a fixed-size output (digest) with several crucial properties. Deterministic, one-way, collision-resistant (e.g., SHA-256), used for model fingerprinting and data integrity.
- **Digital signatures**: Digital signatures provide authentication and non-repudiation, ensuring that messages come from claimed senders and have not been modified. Authenticate messages via elliptic curve cryptography, enabling model attestation and identity verification.
- **Merkle trees**: Efficiently verify data subsets, ensuring dataset integrity and federated training validation. Merkle trees enable efficient and secure verification of large data structures without requiring the complete dataset.

Smart contracts and programmability

Smart contracts enable autonomous execution of AI protocols on the blockchain, embedding logic for transparent, reliable deployment, operation, and upgrades without intermediaries.

However, they face key limitations: strict determinism for consensus, gas limits capping computation (e.g., Ethereum's ~30M per block), and the inability to handle heavy AI tasks like model training on-chain, requiring off-chain compute with on-chain verification.

Contract lifecycle

Smart contract lifecycles automate AI protocol management through immutable, on-chain deployments that govern training, staking, rewards, and dispute resolution. Deterministic executions ensure transparent and consistent enforcement, while upgrade mechanisms maintain adaptability by integrating new features without sacrificing historical data or provenance. The contract lifecycle encompasses three critical phases:

- **Deployment**: Immutable bytecode modules governing training workflows, staking mechanisms, reward distribution, and dispute resolution are deployed at known on-chain addresses. These serve as the immutable foundation for protocol operations, creating permanent records of initial contract specifications.
- **Execution**: Deterministic contract invocations allow participants to register data fragments, submit gradient updates, validate model integrity, or claim token rewards, ensuring transparent and consistent protocol enforcement across all network nodes. Each function call creates an auditable transaction record accessible to all network participants.
- **Upgradability**: Proxy design patterns and decentralized governance enable seamless contract enhancements, such as introducing new privacy safeguards, consensus rule adjustments, or incentive recalibrations, while retaining historical data and model provenance. This allows protocols to evolve and respond to emerging needs without erasing the complete audit trail of prior operations.

State management

Contract state management balances persistent and transient data handling through storage slots for durable key-value data, with memory, stack, and calldata managing temporary computational needs. Efficient state handling is critical for maintaining integrity, auditability, and performance across decentralized AI operations. Smart contracts utilize multiple data storage mechanisms optimized for different use cases:

- **Storage slots**: Persist key-value pairs with associated gas costs for reads and writes. These permanent records form the foundation of the contract state, storing critical AI protocol data such as model parameters, contributor profiles, reward distributions, and historical audit trails.
- **Memory and stack**: Temporary spaces allocated for function execution and computation during contract calls. These volatile storage areas optimize for speed during contract execution, enabling complex AI calculations and validations without the high costs of persistent storage.
- **Calldata**: Immutable inputs supplied to functions upon invocation. This read-only data contains function parameters and submitted information, creating permanent records of all contract interactions and requests submitted by network participants.

Oracles and cross-chain interoperability

Oracles securely connect on-chain contracts to external data, enabling real-world inputs for AI models and metrics verification through both centralized and decentralized networks.

Advanced computation oracles provide off-chain calculation with verifiable proofs. Cross-chain bridges facilitate seamless token transfers and federated learning across diverse blockchains, supporting AI model migration and multi-chain inference in a scalable, interconnected ecosystem. This interoperability infrastructure includes:

- **Oracles**: These bridge on-chain contracts to external off-chain data sources, employing centralized providers or decentralized networks like Chainlink to securely fetch and verify real-world information such as market feeds or AI model performance metrics. Decentralized oracles use consensus mechanisms to validate data accuracy, preventing single points of failure and data manipulation.
- **Computation oracles**: They perform complex off-chain calculations within trusted execution environments or employ optimistic verification proofs, feeding verified results back on-chain. These enable resource-intensive AI computations to execute efficiently while maintaining on-chain verification of correctness.
- **Cross-chain bridges**: Enable movement of tokens via lock-and-mint or burn-and-mint schemes and facilitate federated learning workflows spanning multiple blockchains, supporting seamless AI model migration and multi-chain inference deployment. This allows AI networks to leverage diverse blockchain ecosystems while maintaining unified governance and asset liquidity.

This programmable foundation underlies trustless coordination of AI network operations from micro-transactions to collective governance, crafting scalable, interoperable, and resilient decentralized AI ecosystems.

Infrastructure challenges

Blockchain throughput limits AI workloads requiring high-volume, low-latency processing. Layer 2 rollups (Optimism, Arbitrum), sidechains (Polygon), and sharding (Ethereum Danksharding) balance the scalability trilemma while preserving security/decentralization.

Cloud lock-in: AI relies on proprietary GPU clusters and managed platforms (AWS SageMaker, GCP Vertex), creating migration barriers through specialized APIs and ecosystem dependencies that inflate decentralization costs.

Scalability solutions

The blockchain scalability trilemma requires balancing throughput, security, and decentralization to support AI workloads such as model training and inference. Layer 2 rollups inherit L1 security while delivering 100x TPS gains, whereas sidechains provide customization at the cost of bridge risks, and sharding achieves linear scaling through parallel processing.

The following table is an overview of the scaling approaches comparison:

Approach	Key mechanism	AI benefits	Trade-offs
Layer 2 rollups	Off-chain batching + L1 proofs (optimistic/ZK)	100x+ TPS for inference; low latency	Dispute periods (optimistic); proof costs (ZK)
Sidechains	Pegged independent chains (e.g., Polygon)	Custom gas/ consensus for training	Bridge risks; liquidity splits
Sharding	Parallel shards + beacon (Ethereum, Near)	Linear capacity growth	Cross-shard complexity; DA sampling

Table 1.2: Scaling approaches

Multiple scaling approaches address these constraints through different architectural tradeoffs:

- **Layer 2 scaling**: Off-chain channels and rollups (both optimistic and zero-knowledge) batch transactions or gradient updates, settling compressed proofs on the main chain. This approach boosts throughput and reduces latency while preserving on-chain security guarantees. Optimistic rollups assume transactions are valid unless challenged, enabling faster settlement, while zero-knowledge rollups use cryptographic proofs for instant finality and enhanced security.
- **Sidechains**: Independent blockchains linked via cryptographic bridges offer customizable consensus and higher transaction capacity at lower cost. However, they inherit distinct security models and introduce bridge attack vectors and liquidity fragmentation, requiring careful security architecture to prevent token loss or network attacks.
- **Sharding**: Dividing the network into parallel shards, each processing a subset of transactions or model updates, multiplies overall capacity. A beacon chain coordinates cross-shard communication and finality, though designers must address data availability, cross-shard consistency, and equitable security distribution. This approach enables near-linear scalability improvements as the network grows.

By combining these techniques and carefully tailoring bridge designs, shard assignments, and rollup parameters, decentralized AI protocols can create infrastructures that are scalable, secure, and fully decentralized, capable of supporting both complex model training and real-time inference.

Throughput vs. decentralization trade-offs

Achieving high transaction throughput often means reducing the number of validators, which can weaken decentralization and security, while maximizing decentralization with many validators typically lowers throughput due to consensus overhead. In decentralized AI, this trade-off applies not only to simple transactions but also to complex operations like federated learning updates and data exchanges. High throughput is essential for real-time inference and rapid model training coordination, whereas broad validator participation ensures trust and fairness.

Emerging solutions such as dynamic validator pools that adjust participation based on network load, hybrid consensus algorithms blending PoS and **proof of access (PoA)**, and Layer 2 rollups that offload computation while anchoring security on the main chain, which enable AI protocols to balance speed with distribution.

Traditional blockchain metrics must be reassessed through the lens of AI-specific requirements such as real-time model training, low-latency inference, and continuous data validation. Understanding these metrics enables practitioners to select appropriate blockchain platforms and design architectures that meet both AI operational needs and decentralization principles:

- **Transactions per second (TPS)**: Raw throughput (reported under optimal conditions): Bitcoin ~7 TPS, Ethereum ~15 TPS, Solana ~65,000 TPS. Real-world performance varies significantly due to network congestion, block sizes, and validation overhead. Solana typically achieves 1,500-4,000 TPS during normal operation.
- **Latency**: Confirmation time, finality time, and network propagation delay.
- **Decentralization**: Measured by validator count, geographic distribution, operator diversity, and ease of entry/exit.
- **AI requirements**: Sub-second consensus for gradient commits, millisecond inference responses, burst capacity, and global edge deployment.

Designing decentralized AI infrastructures requires adaptive architectures that evolve consensus parameters, validator incentives, and off-chain mechanisms in line with technological advances and governance objectives. This flexibility enables networks to optimize for emerging AI use cases while maintaining security and decentralization principles.

Gas fees and cost management

Gas fees dynamically price computational work on blockchain networks, directly influencing operational costs, user behavior, security, and overall network health, which is especially critical for AI workloads. While market-driven pricing efficiently allocates scarce resources, the resulting cost volatility can exclude smaller participants from accessing the network and its services.

Effective approaches combine protocol-level optimizations and economic incentives such as adaptive fee schedules that reduce costs during off-peak times, batching AI inferences to distribute expenses, and offloading frequent transactions to Layer 2 solutions or sidechains secured via cryptographic proofs.

Gas fee models also reflect governance and tokenomics frameworks that shape network participation and growth. Designing transparent, fair, and scalable fee structures aligned with AI's computational demands is essential to promote inclusivity, efficient resource utilization, decentralization, and security within sustainable AI-enabled blockchains.

Gas quantifies network computational effort, discouraging denial-of-service attacks and rationing limited resources. Transaction fees use market bidding, where higher bids prioritize inclusion, and congestion inflates costs. Ethereum's EIP-1559 innovated with an algorithmically adjusted burning base fee and validator priority tips, stabilizing price predictability.

Migrating to Layer 2 dramatically reduces costs. As of February 2026, Polygon cuts fees by roughly 100x versus Ethereum mainnet (post-Dencun upgrade and Polygon zkEVM optimizations), Arbitrum reduces them by 10-20x with near-instant finality, and optimism offers comparable savings through rollup technology. Fee levels fluctuate with network congestion, base gas prices, and upgrades, underscoring scaling solutions' role in balancing costs, throughput, and decentralization.

Benefits of decentralized AI

Blockchain technology fundamentally enables, enhances, and transforms decentralized AI systems, delivering a range of benefits that directly address the inherent challenges of traditional AI frameworks. These advantages span operational, economic, governance, and societal dimensions, creating AI ecosystems that function with greater transparency, equity, security, and inclusivity than centralized alternatives.

Transparency improves through immutable audit trails documenting every training decision and model update. Economic equity advances via token-based compensation that rewards data providers, trainers, and validators proportionally. Security is strengthened through cryptographic verification and distributed consensus that prevent unauthorized manipulation. Data privacy increases through zero-knowledge proofs and federated learning that enable AI development without centralizing sensitive information. Resilience improves by eliminating single points of failure across distributed infrastructure. Innovation accelerates as reduced barriers enable diverse participants to contribute novel approaches. Democratic governance ensures stakeholders collectively shape protocol evolution rather than having decisions imposed by profit-driven corporations. As illustrated in *Figure 1.1*, the multi-faceted benefits are driving the adoption of decentralized AI workflows. They are systematically categorized across security, trust, economic models, and interoperability layers, and decentralized architectures eliminate single points of failure and democratize network access to drive the adoption of AI workflows.

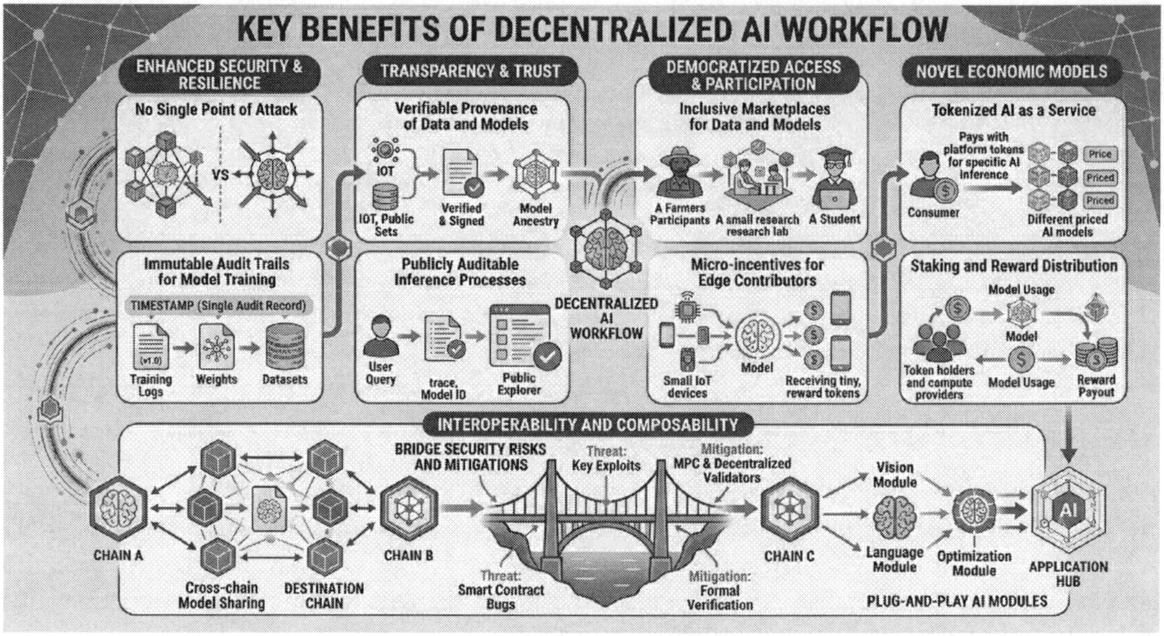

***Figure 1.1**: Key benefits of decentralized AI workflow*

Enhanced security and resilience

Decentralized AI systems deliver superior security through distributed architectures that eliminate single points of failure, Byzantine fault tolerance mechanisms that protect against malicious actors, and cryptographic protocols that ensure data integrity. Blockchain technology creates immutable audit trails for complete transparency, while peer-to-peer networks provide inherent resilience against attacks and system failures.

No single point of attack

Centralized AI infrastructures are vulnerable to catastrophic failures from attacks, outages, or censorship. The distributed ledger and consensus protocols of blockchain eliminate single points of attack by dispersing data and model governance across numerous nodes. This architecture hardens decentralized AI systems against adversarial disruption and censorship, enhancing uptime and integrity.

Immutable audit trails for model training

Every data contribution, model update, and parameter change is cryptographically recorded on an immutable ledger. This guarantees tamper-resistant provenance, allowing stakeholders to verify the exact lineage of any AI model version and detect any unauthorized modifications or poisoning attempts, improving overall system trustworthiness.

Transparency and trust

Decentralized AI systems foster transparency and trust by recording every aspect of data usage, model creation, and decision-making on immutable blockchains. This enables anyone to independently verify AI model origins, training processes, and outcomes, cultivating confidence among stakeholders and ensuring accountability throughout the AI lifecycle.

Verifiable provenance of data and models

Blockchain records link datasets, training epochs, and model checkpoints transparently via cryptographic proofs (hashes, signatures), enabling rigorous assessment of authenticity and origin.

Data quality evaluation, however, often requires supplementary off-chain validation (e.g., statistical tests) or decentralized reputation systems, as provenance confirms source integrity but not inherent accuracy or bias.

Publicly auditable inference processes

By integrating blockchain with smart contracts, inference requests and responses can be logged on-chain or via decentralized oracles. This transparency allows third parties to audit AI decisions, promoting accountability and compliance with regulatory requirements for explainability. This transparency mechanism proves particularly valuable in high-stakes applications such as financial services, healthcare diagnostics, and legal decision support, where algorithmic accountability is paramount. Third-party auditors can reconstruct inference scenarios, validate model performance claims, and ensure that AI systems operate within established ethical and legal boundaries. The immutable nature of blockchain records prevents tampering with audit trails, establishing a foundation of trust that supports regulatory compliance and public confidence in AI-driven decision-making processes.

Democratized access and participation

Decentralized AI networks eliminate traditional gatekeepers and lower barriers to participation by enabling anyone from individual smartphone users to small organizations to contribute data, computational resources, or expertise in exchange for fair token-based compensation. This creates inclusive global marketplaces where participants worldwide can access advanced AI capabilities regardless of their geographic location or institutional affiliation.

Inclusive marketplaces for data and models

Blockchain-enabled token economies foster open marketplaces where diverse participants contribute, share, and monetize datasets and AI models. This inclusivity breaks down monopolistic barriers, empowering startups, independent researchers, and community contributors to engage in AI innovation on an equitable footing.

Micro incentives for edge contributors

Layer 2 micropayments (Polygon, Arbitrum) enable token rewards for small-scale data providers and edge devices validating models or supplying local computations. This democratizes AI contributions, fostering data diversity and localized intelligence, which is impractical on mainnet due to high gas costs.

Novel economic models

Blockchain-enabled token economies transform AI services by introducing automated, programmable pricing and reward mechanisms. Utility, governance, staking, and reward tokens align incentives among data providers, model developers, validators, and users—enabling dynamic pricing, fair revenue sharing, and economic security that traditional centralized models cannot achieve.

Tokenized AI as a service

Blockchain protocols enable AI services to be offered as tokenized products where users pay via native tokens for access to inference APIs, model fine-tuning, or dataset licenses. This creates transparent and programmable economic interactions without dependence on centralized intermediaries.

Staking and reward distribution

Data contributors, validators, and compute providers lock tokens as collateral and earn proportional rewards for their contributions verified on-chain. These staking mechanisms align incentives, foster honest participation, and establish automated, trustless compensation pipelines.

Interoperability and composability

Cross-chain interoperability and modular architectures enable AI applications to leverage specialized capabilities from multiple blockchains, such as governance on Ethereum, training on Polygon, and inference on Cortex. At the same time, composable AI modules allow rapid assembly of tailored intelligence pipelines, maximizing performance, efficiency, and innovation.

Cross-chain model sharing

Interoperable blockchain bridges enable AI models, data proofs, and reputation tokens to move between chains like Ethereum, Solana, and Cosmos. This cross-pollination lets specialized AI modules collaborate across platforms, expanding network effects beyond siloed ecosystems.

Bridge security risks and mitigations

Bridges remain prime attack vectors—$2B+ stolen since 2021 via smart contract bugs, validator compromises (Ronin), and oracle manipulation. Mitigations include light-client verification, threshold signatures (2/3+ honest validators), formal audits, and emerging trustless designs like BitVM.

Plug-and-play AI modules

Blockchain-based smart contracts and standardized token interfaces promote composable AI architectures. Developers can mix and match pre-trained models, data oracles, and governance modules from diverse sources, building sophisticated AI pipelines with modularity, reusability, and extensibility at their core.

Through these benefits, blockchain transforms decentralized AI from a conceptual vision into a resilient, transparent, equitable, and globally accessible reality, empowering an open AI economy driven by community participation and cryptographic trust.

Key challenges and solutions for decentralized AI networks

Blockchain fundamentally transforms decentralized AI systems but also introduces distinctive challenges and complexities. Thereby, successfully harnessing its benefits requires carefully designed technical architectures, governance models, economic incentives, and legal frameworks.

Technical hurdles

Decentralized AI faces inherent performance constraints (limited blockchain throughput and high latency), privacy challenges on public ledgers, and the need to balance on-chain verification with off-chain computation. These hurdles must be addressed to enable scalable, privacy-preserving AI workflows.

Throughput and latency constraints

Public blockchains impose transaction rate ceilings and confirmation delays that conflict with the high-frequency updates demanded by AI training and inference. Model gradient commits and inference micropayments can overwhelm on-chain capacity, creating bottlenecks that hinder real-time responsiveness. This fundamental mismatch between blockchain performance characteristics and AI operational requirements necessitates careful architectural considerations:

- **The performance gap**: Traditional centralized AI systems can process hundreds of thousands of requests per second with millisecond latency. In contrast, most blockchain networks struggle with significantly lower throughput and higher latency, creating fundamental performance constraints for AI applications.
- **Quantitative performance analysis**: The performance disparity becomes evident when examining specific blockchain implementations. Bitcoin operates at approximately 7 transactions per second with 10-minute block confirmation; Ethereum achieves approximately 15 transactions per second with 1-to-5-minute finality; Polygon delivers 7,000 transactions per second with 2-second finality; and Solana reaches 65,000 transactions per second with 400ms finality. In comparison, centralized systems consistently exceed 100,000 transactions per second with 1- to 10-millisecond latency.
- **Impact on AI workloads**: Federated learning across distributed edge devices demands sub-second synchronization cycles to aggregate model updates effectively. If blockchain consensus and transaction finality are slow, it increases training time and reduces model freshness. Similarly, real-time AI inference platforms suffer if blockchain-mediated data validation or access controls introduce prohibitive delays, undermining user experience and decision accuracy.

Addressing these constraints involves layering solutions that decouple AI workload processing from core blockchain bottlenecks. Layer 2 rollups accelerate transaction throughput, sidechains offload specialized computations, and sharding enables parallel processing, all of which are vital for scaling AI on decentralized networks while meeting stringent performance demands.

Data privacy on a public ledger

Data privacy on public ledgers presents a significant dilemma for decentralized AI, as the inherent transparency of blockchain conflicts with stringent data confidentiality needs. Directly storing raw training datasets or sensitive AI model parameters on transparent blockchains exposes proprietary information to all network participants, risking privacy breaches and intellectual property theft.

This *transparency privacy paradox* highlights the fundamental incompatibility between blockchain's open, auditable nature and the privacy essential for many AI applications. Even if training data remains off-chain, metadata logged on-chain can inadvertently disclose sensitive insights, revealing usage patterns or model behavior that compromise privacy.

Addressing these challenges requires advanced privacy-preserving techniques such as zero-knowledge proofs, secure multi-party computation, and differential privacy, alongside architectural designs that separate data storage from computation transparency. Balancing the benefits of verifiable trust with the imperative of confidentiality is critical to unlocking decentralized AI's full potential without sacrificing privacy or security.

On-chain vs. off-chain compute balancing

Blockchain platforms are inherently designed for consensus validation and transaction verification rather than intensive computation. Running resource-heavy AI workloads entirely on-chain is cost-prohibitive and slow, necessitating a nuanced distribution of tasks.

Core AI computations such as gradient evaluations, extensive model training, and hyperparameter optimization exceed on-chain capacities. However, fully outsourcing these tasks to off-chain, potentially untrusted nodes risks compromising verifiability and the integrity of the AI pipeline. Decentralized AI architectures use zkML proofs (zk-SNARKs/STARKs), optimistic verification, and TEE attestation to make off-chain computations (training/inference) provably auditable on-chain via compact proofs. On-chain validation handles critical checks like model hashes and signatures, while off-chain resources manage heavy compute, balancing decentralization's trust guarantees with scalable performance.

This hybrid model enhances security and trust through on-chain anchoring of results, while optimizing performance and reducing costs via scalable off-chain compute.

Governance and coordination

Decentralized AI systems necessitate sophisticated governance frameworks to manage complex technical decisions while safeguarding against collusion, Sybil attacks, and manipulation. Multi-layered DAO architectures must balance broad democratic participation with the inclusion of technical expertise, embedding robust safeguards to uphold legitimacy and network security.

DAOs play a pivotal role in stewarding AI infrastructure, managing parameter update votes, and guiding economic policies. Effective governance design requires reconciling inclusivity with voter competence, resolving disputes transparently, and overseeing upgrade proposals without central authorities.

However, governance mechanisms face challenges: token-based voting systems are vulnerable to plutocratic control and Sybil attacks, where actors create numerous fake identities or pool tokens to dominate decision-making. Such vulnerabilities threaten honest consensus, potentially enabling malicious manipulation of AI models and undermining network integrity. Designing resilient, transparent, and fair governance structures is essential for the sustainable advancement of decentralized AI networks.

Economic and incentive design

Token-based incentive frameworks are fundamental to aligning contributions for spanning data provision, computational power, and validation with proportional economic rewards. Mechanisms like staking, slashing, and dynamic pricing foster fairness, network stability, and sustainable growth while deterring malicious actors.

Token value volatility poses significant challenges due to sharp price swings, creating economic unpredictability for AI service providers and users, undermining confidence and participation. Furthermore, speculative trading or market manipulation threatens the integrity of staking economies, making long-term commitments to data quality and computational reliability fragile.

Designing a *fair reward distribution* is equally complex. Compensation must reflect genuine contribution quality rather than mere volume or token accumulation. This requires nuanced micro-incentive models that empower smaller, edge contributors without diluting security or enabling disproportionate influence by large stakeholders, thereby ensuring an inclusive and resilient decentralized AI ecosystem.

Regulatory and legal uncertainty

Decentralized AI systems operate across diverse global jurisdictions, each governed by varying privacy laws such as GDPR and CCPA, which complicates data sovereignty and cross-border compliance. Right-to-erasure (GDPR Article 17) directly conflicts with blockchain immutability, as personal data cannot be deleted from distributed ledgers without breaking consensus. Common mitigations store sensitive data off-chain (IPFS / Arweave) with on-chain content hashes / pointers—erasure destroys off-chain access while preserving verifiable ledger integrity.

Verifying consent, lawful usage, and cross-border transfers on transparent chains demands additional mechanisms like zk-proofs and automated compliance oracles.

Liability attribution for autonomous decentralized AI decisions is another complex issue. When such systems cause harm or produce biased outcomes, pinpointing legal responsibility among numerous decentralized contributors becomes difficult. Traditional accountability models relying on identifiable vendors falter in decentralized contexts, necessitating new frameworks that fairly allocate liability while preserving the benefits of distributed governance and innovation.

Proposed solutions

Addressing the multifaceted challenges of decentralized AI demands an integrated approach that balances scalability, security, privacy, and governance. Combining architectural, cryptographic, and organizational innovations is essential to building resilient, efficient, and trustworthy networks.

Hybrid on-chain/off-chain architectures

Hybrid on-chain / off-chain architectures offer a compelling path to resolving scalability and cost issues by combining the strengths of both domains. These systems offload intensive computations to trusted execution environments or federated nodes while anchoring cryptographic proofs or checkpoints on-chain, balancing resource efficiency with verifiable trust and auditability.

Zero-knowledge proofs and MPC for privacy

Zero-knowledge proofs (ZKP) and **multi-party computation** (MPC) enhance privacy by enabling verification of data or computation correctness without exposing sensitive inputs. ZKPs prove transactions or model validity on public ledgers privately, while MPC distributes computation among participants to prevent any single node from accessing complete sensitive data.

Layered governance frameworks

Layered governance frameworks address decentralization challenges by balancing competing needs: scalability vs. security, privacy vs. transparency, expertise vs. democratic participation, and innovation vs. stability. Mechanisms like quadratic voting, delegated staking, reputation-weighted governance, and dispute-resolution DAOs mitigate risks of collusion and Sybil attacks. Parameterized smart contracts enable adaptive governance rules that evolve with ecosystem demands.

This integrated approach across technical, governance, economic, and legal dimensions is pivotal to unlocking decentralized AI's transformative potential, ensuring networks remain scalable, secure, equitable, and compliant.

Industry landscape and key players

Blockchain acts as the enabling substrate on which a diverse ecosystem of decentralized AI initiatives, protocols, enterprises, and research efforts flourishes, each transforming how AI models are created, governed, and monetized. This landscape encompasses protocol developers optimizing blockchain for AI workloads, decentralized data networks monetizing datasets, model governance platforms enabling collective decision-making, inference networks distributing execution across nodes, and computational resource markets tokenizing GPU and TPU capacity. Major platforms, including Ethereum, Polygon, and Solana, serve as foundational layers, while specialized AI-focused blockchains emerge to address machine learning-specific requirements. Traditional technology companies and venture capital increasingly recognize decentralized AI's potential, driving partnerships and innovation across the ecosystem.

Major blockchain protocols in AI

Four major blockchain protocols for AI integration have emerged as foundational layers for AI integration, each offering distinct trade-offs in security, scalability, and programmability:

- **Ethereum**: As the pioneering programmable blockchain, Ethereum underpins a vast AI ecosystem of smart contracts, token-driven incentives, and decentralized governance. Its extensive developer community and mature **decentralized finance (DeFi)** infrastructure offer reusable components for AI marketplaces and staking models, though scalability remains an ongoing challenge.

- **Polygon**: Functioning as Ethereum's Layer-2 accelerator, Polygon dramatically boosts transaction throughput and slashes costs, enabling rapid, low-fee AI model updates and micropayment flows. Its seamless interoperability with the Ethereum mainnet ensures composable AI contracts and scalable deployment.
- **Solana**: Renowned for blazing-fast finality and minimal fees, Solana excels at latency-sensitive AI tasks, where frequent model retraining and data exchanges demand near-real-time performance. Its parallelized runtime optimizes federated AI across numerous edge nodes.
- **Cortex**: Designed specifically for AI workloads, Cortex embeds on-chain inference directly into smart contracts. Developers can submit model artifacts and execute machine learning predictions natively, merging blockchain consensus with AI computation in a single layer.

Leading decentralized AI projects

Pioneering decentralized AI initiatives are redefining trust, transparency, and collaboration in artificial intelligence. These projects harness blockchain and distributed computing to enable secure data sharing, verifiable model training, and democratic governance. By innovating in scalability, privacy, and incentive design, they showcase the transformative potential of decentralized AI to create open, resilient, and equitable intelligent systems.

Several open networks and consortia are at the forefront of advancing decentralized AI applications:

- **SingularityNET**: It operates a decentralized marketplace where AI algorithms and services interconnect, enabling AI agents to monetize capabilities via native tokens. Its protocol supports composability and modularity, allowing developers to create multi-agent workflows governed transparently.
- **Fetch.ai**: It establishes an open economic framework for autonomous AI agents empowered by blockchain-based identity and reputation systems. It emphasizes decentralized data exchange, predictive analytics, and edge computing incentivized through native tokens.
- **Ocean protocol**: Ocean protocol leads decentralized data marketplaces, enabling providers to retain sovereignty while monetizing assets via tokenized data tokens and smart contracts. By unlocking diverse, privacy-preserving data pools through compute-to-data and on-chain provenance verification, it enhances AI model training with high-quality, verifiable datasets.

Enterprise and consortia initiatives

Collaborative enterprise and consortium efforts are accelerating decentralized AI adoption by pooling resources, expertise, and governance. These initiatives focus on creating interoperable standards, scalable infrastructure, and compliant frameworks to integrate AI with blockchain securely and efficiently. Through collective innovation and shared objectives, they address practical challenges such as data privacy, regulatory compliance, and economic incentives, driving real-world decentralized AI deployments that balance innovation with enterprise-grade reliability and trust.

Large technology companies and industry consortia are integrating blockchain with AI for enterprise use cases:

- **IBM and Microsoft Azure confidential computing**: Enterprise giants are developing secure enclaves fused with blockchain verifiability to enable privacy-preserving AI workloads. These solutions underpin trusted federated learning that harnesses sensitive data without exposing raw inputs, extending blockchain's trustworthiness into hybrid cloud environments.

- **Hyperledger and enterprise DAOs**: The Hyperledger project of the Linux Foundation delivers modular blockchain frameworks that support permissioned ledgers for enterprise AI governance. Coupled with emerging enterprise DAOs, these tools empower distributed decision-making on shared AI assets while maintaining regulatory compliance and operational transparency.

Academic and research efforts

Cutting-edge academic and research initiatives are pioneering the theoretical foundations and practical implementations of decentralized AI. Collaborative research across institutions accelerates innovation, validates new architectures, and addresses real-world scalability, security, and ethical challenges, establishing a robust scientific bedrock for the future of decentralized AI networks. Key research domains include:

- **Federated learning platforms**: Academic consortia pioneer privacy-preserving AI training methods aligned with blockchain's decentralized ledger properties. Research focuses on the synergy between federated learning protocols and blockchain-based incentive mechanisms that ensure secure contribution tracking and model update validation.

- **Open-source privacy frameworks**: Initiatives like OpenMined develop open-source libraries integrating multi-party computation, differential privacy, and zero-knowledge proofs with blockchain oracles. These frameworks provide reference architectures that enable transparent, confidential model training and validation in decentralized AI systems. Open-source libraries like ZKP toolkits (zkSNARK libraries), MPC frameworks (MPyC, ZenGo), and differential privacy toolkits (Opacus) are being integrated into blockchain-orchestrated AI pipelines, allowing rigorous privacy guarantees alongside transparent audit trails.

Regulatory considerations

The integration of blockchain with decentralized AI networks raises complex regulatory and compliance challenges, requiring attention to both global and local legal frameworks. Innovators must address emerging standards for algorithmic transparency, data privacy (such as GDPR), smart contract liability, and token governance, all of which may differ by jurisdiction. Navigating these evolving obligations is essential to ensuring that decentralized AI systems remain both innovative and compliant as the regulatory landscape continues to develop worldwide.

Data protection laws

Decentralized AI ecosystems, which often handle personal or sensitive information from globally distributed nodes, must navigate stringent regulations such as the European Union's GDPR and California's CCPA. These mandates emphasize user privacy, informed consent, the right to erasure, and transparency. The immutable nature of blockchain poses unique challenges to compliance, especially regarding data deletion and user control. To address this, decentralized AI projects leverage cryptographic on-chain proofs of consent, off-chain data storage paired with on-chain access logs, and selective encryption or anonymization methods to safeguard privacy while maintaining auditability.

In parallel, evolving AI-specific regulatory frameworks from governments and global bodies focus on accountability, transparency, fairness, and bias mitigation. Decentralized AI models benefit from blockchain's verifiable audit trails and on-chain governance, which facilitate compliance with requirements around explainability and risk assessment, supporting ethical and transparent AI deployments.

Smart contract legal status

The legal status of smart contracts is an evolving domain, merging traditional contract law with automated execution. Challenges around enforceability, jurisdiction, and liability arise as smart contracts increasingly govern AI-driven processes and transactions. Clarifying these issues is vital to building trust, encouraging widespread adoption, and ensuring compliance, allowing smart contracts to integrate cohesively with existing legal frameworks while unlocking new opportunities in decentralized AI:

- **Enforceability and jurisdiction**: Despite streamlining governance, payments, and compliance in decentralized AI, smart contracts face inconsistent legal recognition worldwide. Key questions remain about their enforceability, the applicable jurisdiction, and how disputes are resolved when contracts operate autonomously without human intervention. Addressing these uncertainties necessitates hybrid solutions that combine on-chain automation with off-chain legal systems, arbitration mechanisms, or regulatory sandboxes tailored for decentralized AI environments.

- **Code as law principle**: Treating code as law underscores the importance of rigorous formal verification and transparent smart contract design in decentralized AI ecosystems. This approach minimizes risks from unintended contract behaviors or vulnerabilities that could cause systemic failures or regulatory penalties, thereby fostering trust and resilience in AI-powered blockchain systems.

Financial compliance for tokens

Tokens integral to decentralized AI ecosystems face rigorous regulatory scrutiny aimed at protecting investors and upholding market integrity. Navigating this complex landscape requires meticulously crafted tokenomics and compliance frameworks to enable innovation within legal boundaries.

- **Securities regulation**: Governing bodies like the U.S. **Securities and Exchange Commission** (**SEC**) and the **Markets in Crypto-Assets** (**MiCA**) of the European Union closely evaluate tokens used for governance, staking, or incentives. To mitigate classification as securities, tokens are often structured as utility tokens with explicit functional roles, avoiding investment contract characteristics. Decentralized governance models further reduce central control risks to support compliance.
- **Stablecoin oversight**: Stablecoins facilitating AI service payments attract stringent oversight regarding reserve backing, transparency, and **anti-money laundering** (**AML**) compliance. Decentralized AI networks employing stablecoins implement transparent reserve audits alongside decentralized compliance mechanisms to meet these global regulatory standards effectively.

Ethical frameworks and standards

Decentralized AI harnesses blockchain to embed ethics such as fairness, transparency, and privacy by design. Global guidelines from organizations like the **Organization for Economic Co-operation and Development** (**OECD**) and the **International Organization for Standardization** (**ISO**) provide responsible AI standards that decentralized governance and immutable audit trails can enforce through on-chain policies and continuous compliance monitoring.

With rising regulatory demands for AI auditability and accountability, the immutable ledgers of blockchain supply transparent, trustless records of data provenance, model training, and inference decisions. This establishes robust accountability frameworks enabling community or regulator-led audits while safeguarding user privacy, ensuring ethical AI deployment aligns with evolving societal and legal norms.

Future vision and opportunities

Decentralized AI networks are poised to intersect with complementary technologies, governance innovations, and advanced privacy techniques, creating transformative opportunities for global inclusion and collaborative discovery. As blockchain frameworks mature and AI capabilities rapidly expand, these networks offer the promise of more equitable data stewardship, transparent algorithmic governance, and borderless access to advanced machine learning tools. Widespread adoption of decentralized AI could enable new models for participatory data ownership, fair compensation to contributors, and robust privacy, even as collective intelligence scales across industries. Integration with technologies like secure multi-party computation, zero-knowledge proofs, and cross-chain interoperability will further empower individuals, organizations, and underserved communities to collaborate and innovate with trustless, censorship-resistant platforms.

Ultimately, decentralized AI stands to redefine the landscape of innovation, unlocking resilient infrastructure for shared scientific advancement while creating new pathways for economic participation and digital sovereignty worldwide.

Convergence with emerging technologies

The integration of decentralized AI with IoT and edge computing addresses latency and privacy by enabling localized inference and federated learning at the network edge. For instance, smart factories deploy thousands of sensors in federated learning setups, using blockchain to anchor model updates and coordinate token-based incentives, fostering a circular industrial AI economy.

Simultaneously, AI transforms DeFi by automating risk management, portfolio rebalancing, and market operations through autonomous AI agents. Tokenized AI services introduce *AI-as-Asset* paradigms, where investors stake tokens in dynamic, yield-generating AI models, merging financial innovation with AI-driven economic activity.

Next-generation governance models

Reputation-weighted voting moves beyond mere token holdings, assigning voting power based on verified expertise and past contributions. Utilizing on-chain data like model accuracy, data quality, and governance engagement, this approach ensures that critical decisions reflect informed judgment, reducing plutocratic influence and boosting technical integrity in protocol evolution.

Liquid democracy empowers fluid governance where participants choose between direct voting and delegating power to trusted experts, with delegation revocable at any time. This dynamic model allows specialized stakeholders such as data scientists or cryptographers to represent community interests appropriately, scaling participation while maximizing the use of distributed knowledge and expertise.

Advanced privacy techniques

Fully homomorphic encryption (**FHE**) enables secure AI operations by allowing computations on encrypted data without exposing sensitive information. This end-to-end data confidentiality is crucial for decentralized AI workflows. However, current FHE implementations face performance trade-offs that continual hardware and algorithmic improvements aim to overcome, making encrypted blockchain-based AI increasingly feasible.

Decentralized identity utilizing verifiable credentials empowers users with self-sovereign control over authentication, reputation, and access in AI networks. By leveraging cryptographically signed attestations and zero-knowledge proofs, individuals can validate qualifications or permissions without divulging private data, supporting GDPR compliance, combating Sybil attacks, and fostering trust in pseudonymous decentralized communities.

Societal impact and inclusion

Decentralized AI offers transformative potential to reduce global inequality by making advanced AI technologies accessible to communities in underserved regions that lack traditional centralized infrastructure. By combining mobile-optimized platforms, local computing at the network edge with micropayment systems, and portable open educational credentials, individuals in underserved areas can actively participate as data providers, AI developers, and technology consumers. Token-based reward structures ensure that value generated through participation flows directly back to contributors, creating pathways to economic participation and prosperity for geographically dispersed communities.

In the research domain, decentralized AI accelerates collaborative breakthroughs by uniting researchers, academic institutions, and citizen scientists across diverse fields, including pharmaceutical development and environmental science. Shared data repositories, collaborative training protocols using federated learning, and immutable audit trails enable rapid progress while maintaining data privacy and research integrity. Token economies that compensate contributions in data sharing, computational resources, and validation services dissolve organizational silos and historical barriers, enabling expansive, inclusive research ecosystems capable of addressing humanity's most pressing challenges.

Practical guidelines

Building effective decentralized AI systems requires careful integration of technical infrastructure, economic incentive mechanisms, and governance structures to achieve scalability, establish trust, and ensure regulatory compliance. Adopting thoughtfully designed hybrid computation models, well-crafted incentive schemes, privacy-centric architectural decisions, and multi-layered governance frameworks forms the essential foundation for constructing resilient, inclusive AI ecosystems.

The following strategies capture core lessons and approaches for developing resilient, inclusive AI ecosystems:

- **Design hybrid architectures**: Move resource-intensive operations such as model training and inference execution to off-chain environments or Layer 2 scaling solutions, while anchoring critical validation points on the primary blockchain layer for transparency and immutability. Leverage state channels and rollup technologies to manage frequent interactions efficiently, while maintaining the primary blockchain as the authoritative source for governance decisions and protocol evolution.

- **Balance decentralization and performance**: Align consensus mechanisms with specific computational requirements, such as employing proof of stake or delegated proof of stake for high-volume training operations, and proof of work or proof of stake for governance participation. Distribute workloads intelligently across multiple blockchain networks to achieve an optimal balance between operational costs, response times, and security guarantees.

- **Develop robust incentives**: Compensate data contributors and validators proportionally according to the quality and impact of their contributions through token rewards. Implement staking requirements combined with penalty mechanisms for misbehavior and offer reputation-adjusted compensation to maintain sustainable network economics. Establish token burn mechanisms and supply controls to maintain economic stability and discourage speculative behavior.

- **Integrate privacy and compliance**: Deploy cryptographic techniques such as zero-knowledge proofs and secure multi-party computation to substantially reduce sensitive personal data exposure on public blockchains. Implement self-sovereign identity systems that give individuals control over consent and compliance verification. Build a modular compliance infrastructure that can adapt to varying regulatory requirements across different jurisdictions.

- **Implement layered governance**: Establish multi-tiered DAO structures incorporating token holders, elected delegates, specialized committees, and experienced core teams to balance community participation with technical expertise. Employ cryptographic voting mechanisms like commit-reveal schemes, establish minimum participation thresholds, and implement Sybil resistance protocols to prevent concentrated voting power and manipulation. Use reputation-weighted voting and liquid democracy models to enable flexible, merit-based governance allocation.

By adhering to these comprehensive guidelines and implementing privacy as a core architectural principle, utilizing smart contracts for transparent and trustless coordination, achieving scalability through Layer 2 solutions and network sharding, maintaining complete transparency through immutable audit trails, embedding compliance requirements directly into protocol design, fostering seamless interoperability across platforms, empowering community participation in governance decisions, and establishing continuous monitoring and adaptation mechanisms—decentralized AI networks can achieve sophisticated, secure, and efficient systems that advance innovation while upholding rigorous ethical standards and legal compliance.

Conclusion

This chapter has laid a comprehensive foundation for understanding the transformative impact decentralization can have on AI. By unveiling the systemic challenges of centralized AI, such as concentration of control, lack of transparency, and privacy vulnerabilities, it made the case for integrating Web3 principles and blockchain technology as catalysts for change. The discussion navigated the core benefits of decentralized AI networks, including enhanced trust, security, and equitable participation, while also weighing the inherent technical, economic, and governance challenges. Practical guidelines distilled here serve as a blueprint for designing effective decentralized AI ecosystems, emphasizing the delicate balance between innovation, scalability, privacy, and ethical governance.

In the next chapter, we will focus on the technical bedrock underpinning these systems: the fundamentals of blockchain technology. This chapter will delve into consensus mechanisms, smart contract architectures, and Layer 2 scaling solutions, equipping readers with the technical insights necessary to architect scalable, secure, and privacy-preserving decentralized AI infrastructures.

CHAPTER 2
Fundamentals of Blockchain Technology for AI

Introduction

The convergence of blockchain technology and artificial intelligence marks a transformative milestone in computing evolution. While **artificial intelligence** (**AI**) has advanced automation, data-driven insights, and predictive capabilities, its centralized architectures suffer from fragility (e.g., OpenAI's 2023 ChatGPT outages disrupting millions of users), single points of failure, opaque governance, privacy vulnerabilities like the 2024 *Clearview AI data scraping* scandal, and limited collaborative scope. Blockchain counters these through decentralized, transparent, and tamper-resistant infrastructures that enable trustless, collaborative AI ecosystems.

Central to this transformation is **decentralized AI** (**DAI**), where AI models, data, and computational resources are distributed across blockchain-enabled networks without central oversight. Unlike federated learning, which coordinates model training across siloed data providers through a trusted central aggregator, or traditional distributed AI that relies on centralized infrastructure for orchestration, DAI harnesses blockchain's core features: immutability, decentralized consensus, and programmability. This enables secure, trustless collaboration, cryptographically verifiable contributions, aligned economic incentives, and fully autonomous AI workflows that operate without any single point of control or failure.

A solid grasp of blockchain fundamentals is indispensable for architects and developers building scalable DAI systems. This chapter delves into blockchain's layered architecture, consensus algorithms, smart contracts, tokenization, and decentralized storage, each contextualized for AI applications. This foundation is vital to democratize AI infrastructure, ensuring transparency, trust, and economic sustainability in decentralized ecosystems.

The interplay between blockchain and AI creates complementary strengths, addressing each other's limitations. AI excels at interpreting complex data and automating decisions, but struggles with provenance, transparency, and secure multi-party collaboration. Blockchain provides immutable data lineage, transparent model governance, decentralized coordination, and verifiable computation. Conversely, AI optimizes blockchain networks by enhancing consensus efficiency, automating smart contract security and gas optimization, enabling adaptive network scaling, and providing advanced, real-time anomaly detection, results that deliver a powerful, symbiotic advancement of both fields.

Structure

The chapter covers the following topics:

- Blockchain architecture and components
- Consensus mechanisms
- Smart contracts and virtual machines
- Tokenization and digital assets
- Distributed storage for DAI
- Scalability solutions for DAI
- Development tools and frameworks
- AI-specific case studies

Objectives

This chapter establishes a practical foundation in blockchain technology tailored specifically for DAI systems. Readers can expect to learn how blockchain's core tenets, including immutability, consensus, and smart contracts, directly resolve critical AI challenges regarding data provenance, multi-party coordination, and trustworthy automation. The curriculum moves beyond abstract theory to cover essential technical competencies. Readers will learn to select energy-efficient consensus mechanisms, design gas-optimized smart contracts for federated learning, and architect robust tokenomics for AI assets. Additionally, they will gain hands-on expertise in integrating decentralized storage solutions like IPFS and Filecoin, as well as implementing scalability solutions such as Layer 2 rollups. By the end, practitioners will be equipped with the DevOps strategies and architectural insights necessary to build, deploy, and scale production-grade decentralized AI ecosystems.

Blockchain architecture and components

The integration of blockchain technology with AI systems creates unique opportunities to solve longstanding problems in artificial intelligence. This includes a lack of transparency in model development, difficulty in verifying model performance claims, challenges in collaborative training across organizational boundaries, and the need for immutable audit trails in high-stakes AI decision-making scenarios. The core components are as follows:

- Transparency in model development is achieved through the application layer, where smart contracts encode and execute auditable model governance rules, making every decision and parameter change permanently visible and immutable.
- Verification of model performance claims relies on the data layer, where Merkle trees and cryptographic hashes provide efficient, scalable proofs of model integrity, training data provenance, and performance metrics without requiring recomputation.
- Collaborative training across organizational boundaries is enabled by the consensus layer, where protocols like proof of stake coordinate distributed learning rounds and validate contributions from untrusted participants without centralized orchestration.
- Immutable audit trails for high-stakes decisions are guaranteed by the network layer, where distributed nodes maintain a tamper-proof ledger of all AI activities, ensuring permanent, decentralized records accessible to all stakeholders.

This architectural mapping demonstrates how blockchain's components, nodes, ledgers, blocks, transactions, hash functions, and Merkle trees collectively resolve AI's trust and coordination challenges, creating resilient, verifiable, and collaborative intelligence ecosystems. Key infrastructure elements, such as computational nodes, shared ledgers, chained blocks, and recorded transactions, serve as the backbone for collaboration without central authority, verifiable AI workflows, and permanent data lineage. Foundational cryptographic tools like one-way hash functions and hierarchical Merkle trees ensure model authenticity and support efficient integrity checks at scale.

Modern blockchain architectures for AI applications must address specific requirements, including efficient verification of large datasets used in model training, coordination of distributed learning processes across multiple parties, immutable recording of model versions and performance metrics, and transparent governance mechanisms for collaborative AI development. Understanding the core components and their specific adaptations for AI workloads is essential for building robust decentralized AI systems that can operate at scale while maintaining integrity and trust. Together, these building blocks demonstrate how blockchain creates resilient, transparent, and self-sustaining AI networks that overcome the constraints of traditional centralized systems. The core layers and components of this trustless AI blockchain architecture are systematically presented in *Figure 2.1*, highlighting how decentralized consensus, cryptographic verification, and smart contract automation interface with machine learning models.

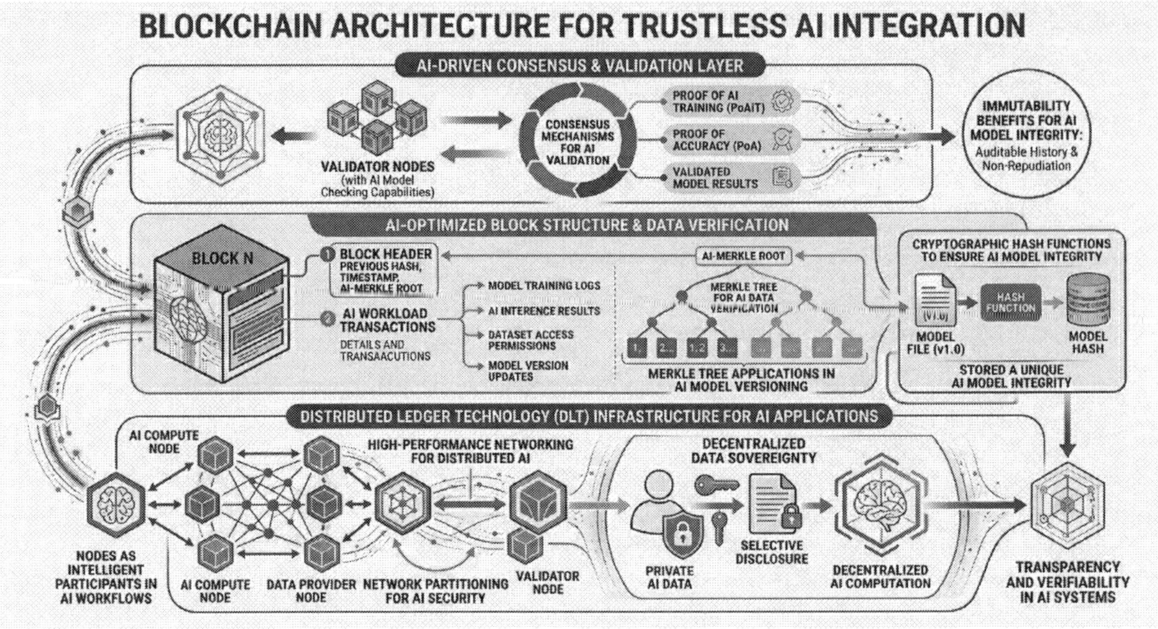

Figure 2.1: *Blockchain architecture for trustless AI integration*

Building blocks of trustless AI blockchain integration

The foundation of DAI networks rests upon a sophisticated architecture of interconnected blockchain components, each serving critical functions in enabling trustless AI collaboration, model integrity, and transparent governance. Unlike centralized AI systems that rely on single points of control, blockchain components create a distributed infrastructure where AI agents, data providers, and model validators can interact securely without intermediaries.

Nodes as intelligent participants in AI workflows

Nodes in DAI serve as active contributors rather than passive validators. They participate in federated learning rounds, validate model updates, and provide decentralized storage for datasets and weights, all while maintaining blockchain integrity. Equipped with diverse compute capabilities from powerful GPU clusters to lightweight IoT devices, these nodes collectively enable robust, scalable, and tamper-proof AI training and inference without centralized oversight.

Trust assumptions vary by threat model: honest-but-curious nodes follow protocol rules but may attempt to infer private training data from updates, while adversarial nodes could submit poisoned gradients or collude to manipulate consensus. Robust cryptographic commitments, stake-slashing mechanisms, and reputation systems mitigate these risks, ensuring reliable participation across diverse node capabilities.

Transactions as immutable records of AI operations

In DAI, blockchain transactions extend far past value transfer to record complex AI workflows transparently and securely. Transactions encode model parameter updates, dataset quality attestations, and automated payments for AI services. Smart contract-driven transactions enable autonomous AI agents to negotiate licensing, access data marketplaces, and coordinate distributed training, creating auditable trails for accountability and reproducibility.

Together, these components form the foundational infrastructure that guarantees data provenance, secure multi-party collaboration, and verifiable computations, enabling advanced AI systems to operate reliably on a decentralized, trustless network.

DLT fundamentals for AI applications

Distributed ledger technology (**DLT**) provides the foundational infrastructure that transforms traditional AI development from centralized, opaque processes into transparent, collaborative networks. The core principles of DLT: consensus, immutability, and decentralization, address fundamental challenges in AI systems, including trust, reproducibility, and fair value distribution.

Consensus mechanisms for AI validation

Traditional AI model validation suffers from subjective evaluation criteria and potential bias in centralized review processes. DLT consensus mechanisms enable objective, algorithmic validation of AI models through cryptographic proofs and economic incentives. Proof of learning protocols, an emerging research area, validate that participants have genuinely contributed to model training by requiring cryptographic evidence of computational work performed on specific datasets. Early implementations and academic proposals, such as those from *Stanford's Center for Blockchain Research* and the *OpenMined* initiative, demonstrate feasibility through techniques like verifiable gradient computation and dataset-specific proof systems. While promising for preventing sybil attacks and ensuring honest contributions, these mechanisms remain experimental and face challenges in computational overhead and standardization.

The consensus layer integrates seamlessly with AI validation workflows by encoding quality metrics, performance benchmarks, and adversarial testing results directly into the blockchain state. This integration ensures that only models meeting predefined quality thresholds gain network acceptance, while malicious or low-quality contributions are automatically rejected through consensus mechanisms.

Decentralized data sovereignty

DLT fundamentally restructures data ownership and access patterns essential for AI development. Rather than centralizing datasets in corporate silos, DLT enables data owners to maintain sovereignty while selectively granting access for AI training through smart contracts. This paradigm preserves privacy and intellectual property rights while facilitating collaborative AI development across organizational boundaries.

The distributed nature of DLT ensures that AI training data remains available even if individual participants leave the network, creating robust, censorship-resistant datasets that support long-term AI research and development. This resilience is particularly crucial for scientific AI applications where data continuity spans decades.

Hash functions, block structure, and Merkle trees

This delves into cryptographic building blocks that ensure data integrity, transparency, and scalability within decentralized AI networks.

Hash functions generate unique digital fingerprints for AI models, datasets, and training updates, enabling tamper-evident verification essential for trustless collaborative learning. Block structures organize these transactions with cryptographic linking, creating an immutable chronological record of all AI workflow activities.

Merkle trees enable efficient, scalable verification by allowing participants to confirm inclusion of specific model updates or data contributions without downloading entire datasets, critical for bandwidth-constrained nodes in global federated learning networks.

Figure 2.2 is a structural overview, which allows a client to verify that a specific chunk of the AI model (e.g., Layer A update) is legitimate without needing to download or verify the entire model at once:

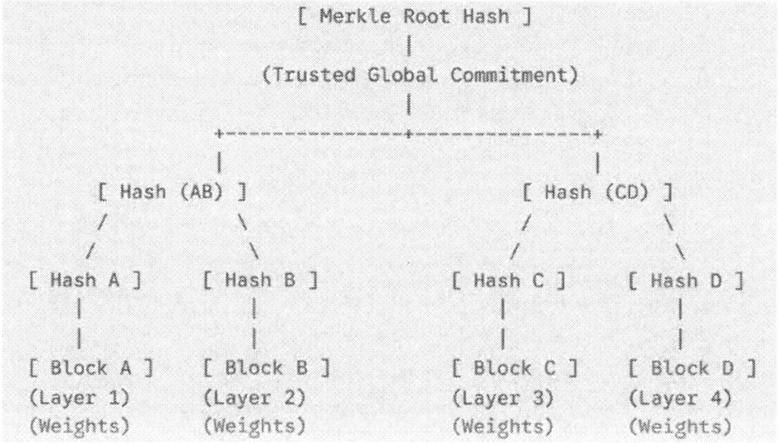

***Figure 2.2**: Merkle tree for model updates*

These block hashes serve as the leaves of a binary Merkle tree, which aggregates them upward into a single, trusted root hash. This structure enables efficient, piecemeal verification: a user can authenticate a specific model chunk without downloading the entire file by combining the chunk's hash with a **Merkle path** of sibling hashes. If the recomputed sequence matches the trusted root hash, the specific model update is confirmed to be authentic and uncorrupted.

Cryptographic hash functions to ensure AI model integrity

Cryptographic hash functions underpin the trustworthiness of AI models throughout decentralized learning by creating unique digital fingerprints for models, datasets, and training updates. These hashes enable verification of authenticity without exposing sensitive data, which is critical in privacy-focused settings like medical AI. In federated learning, participants prove ownership of local datasets by submitting cryptographic hashes to the blockchain, allowing coordinators to validate data diversity and quality securely. The collision resistance of hash functions prevents malicious substitution of models, safeguarding integrity and maintaining trust in AI marketplaces where authenticity directly influences adoption and valuation.

Block structure optimized for AI workloads

Blockchain blocks in decentralized AI networks require a specialized structure to accommodate the unique characteristics of AI data and computations. Traditional transaction blocks are optimized for financial transfers, but AI blocks must efficiently encode model parameters, training metrics, and validation results.

AI optimized blocks include dedicated fields for:

- Model version identifiers and lineage tracking.
- Cryptographic commitments to training datasets.
- Performance benchmarks and validation scores.
- Gradient aggregation summaries for federated learning.
- Incentive distribution records for AI contributors.

This specialized block structure enables efficient querying of AI-specific information while maintaining compatibility with standard blockchain protocols. The enhanced metadata facilitates automated discovery of compatible models and datasets, essential for dynamic AI collaboration networks.

Merkle trees for scalable AI data verification

Merkle trees provide an elegant solution for verifying the integrity of large AI datasets without requiring participants to download complete datasets. In DAI networks, Merkle trees enable efficient verification of dataset consistency, model parameter correctness, and training result authenticity.

For federated learning applications, Merkle trees allow aggregator nodes to verify that all participant contributions are genuine without accessing individual training data. Each participant generates a Merkle tree representing their local dataset, with the root hash serving as a compact commitment. The aggregator can verify contributions using Merkle proofs while preserving participant privacy.

The logarithmic verification complexity of Merkle trees scales efficiently with dataset size, making them practical for large-scale AI applications involving millions of training samples. This scalability is crucial for computer vision and natural language processing applications that require massive datasets for effective training.

Merkle tree applications in AI model versioning

AI models evolve continuously through training updates, creating complex versioning challenges in collaborative environments. Merkle trees enable efficient tracking of model evolution by representing each version as a leaf node, with parent nodes capturing relationships between versions. This structure facilitates rapid identification of model branches, merging of parallel development efforts, and verification of model lineage.

Architectural design for scalable AI networks

Designing blockchain networks for AI requires balancing high-throughput data transfers with low-latency consensus. Optimized topologies, such as fat tree or dragonfly, support parallel model synchronization and transaction propagation. Dedicated AI subnets handle compute-intensive tasks like gradient aggregation, while separate consensus subnets maintain finality and security. Network partitioning isolates privacy-sensitive workloads, and proximity-aware peer selection minimizes latency for model updates. Together, these strategies ensure scalable, responsive, and secure AI training and inference within decentralized networks.

High-performance networking for distributed AI

DAI networks demand specialized network architectures that balance the competing requirements of blockchain consensus and AI computation efficiency. Traditional blockchain networks optimize for transaction throughput and finality, but AI workloads require high-bandwidth, low-latency communication for model synchronization and data sharing.

Fat tree and dragonfly network topologies emerge as optimal solutions for AI blockchain hybrid networks, providing multiple paths for data transmission while maintaining the connectivity required for consensus protocols. These topologies support both the frequent, small transactions typical of blockchain operations and the large, periodic transfers characteristic of AI model updates.

Network partitioning for AI security

AI blockchain networks implement sophisticated partitioning strategies to isolate sensitive AI computations from public blockchain operations. Dedicated AI fabric networks handle model training and inference using high-performance interconnects like *InfiniBand*, while consensus operations utilize standard Ethernet networks for broader compatibility.

This partitioning approach prevents AI workloads from overwhelming consensus mechanisms while ensuring that blockchain operations cannot interfere with time-critical AI computations. The separation also enables different security models for AI and blockchain components, with AI networks implementing additional privacy-preserving protocols.

Consensus layer integration for AI model validation

Integrating consensus mechanisms with AI validation introduces innovative protocols that reward authentic training contributions and deter fraudulent activities. Proof of learning consensus requires participants to cryptographically prove computational work on AI tasks, transforming training into an economically incentivized process that aligns security with genuine model development.

Automated quality assessments become part of the consensus, leveraging standardized benchmarks to allow nodes to evaluate and vote on model performance objectively. This approach eliminates the reliance on subjective judgments, preventing low-quality models from infiltrating the network and encouraging meaningful improvements. Consequently, DAI networks maintain high standards and trust without centralized oversight.

Immutability benefits for AI model integrity

Blockchain's immutability introduces unparalleled transparency to AI development by creating tamper-evident records for every model update, training iteration, and performance metric. This immutable audit trail addresses critical concerns in AI safety, bias detection, and regulatory compliance, enabling researchers to trace complete model lineage, from data sources through algorithmic transformations.

The cryptographic guarantee that data on the chain cannot be altered prevents malicious actors from injecting backdoors or manipulating models undetected. This level of integrity is vital for AI applications with high stakes, such as autonomous vehicles, medical diagnostics, and financial decision-making, where trustworthiness directly impacts human safety and systemic stability.

Transparency and verifiability in AI systems

Traditional AI systems operate as black-boxes, making it impossible for users to understand how decisions are reached or to verify that systems behave fairly. Blockchain integration introduces unprecedented transparency by recording every aspect of AI system operation on an immutable, public ledger.

Blockchain transforms opaque AI black boxes into transparent systems by recording every operational aspect, including training procedures, dataset compositions, hyperparameters, and performance metrics on immutable ledgers. This comprehensive transparency enables stakeholders to independently verify AI behavior and compliance, building trust through verifiability rather than blind authority.

DAI governance becomes verifiable through permanent blockchain records of stakeholder votes on model updates and protocol changes, preventing governance manipulation. This creates AI systems accountable to users rather than centralized controllers, democratizing AI governance and ensuring equitable distribution of benefits and risks.

Advanced cryptographic techniques, particularly zero-knowledge proofs, enable verification of AI computations while protecting sensitive data and intellectual property. This cryptographic verifiability supports new business models where AI service providers guarantee computational integrity without exposing proprietary algorithms, balancing transparency, privacy, and commercial viability in decentralized AI markets.

Consensus mechanisms

Consensus mechanisms are critical to blockchain networks because they enable decentralized agreement on the validity of transactions and the state of the distributed ledger. For decentralized AI systems, the choice of consensus mechanism influences security, scalability, efficiency, and the ability to handle AI-specific workloads such as federated learning, model training, and autonomous agent coordination.

This section offers a comprehensive technical exploration of the three major consensus mechanisms: PoW, PoS, and DPoS, analyzing their principles, strengths, weaknesses, AI workload implications, and simplified pseudocode samples.

PoW

PoW is the original consensus mechanism popularized by Bitcoin. Nodes called miners compete to solve a cryptographic puzzle, typically finding a hash below a target value by altering a nonce in the block header. The first to find a valid solution gains the right to add the next block to the chain and earns a reward.

While energy-intensive and slow, making it unsuitable for high-frequency AI workloads like real-time model updates, PoW remains valuable in niche AI scenarios requiring maximum security guarantees, such as low-frequency audit logging, archival model provenance, or securing high-value AI asset registries where computational cost serves as a strong anti-collusion barrier.

A simplified pseudocode is as follows:

```
python
def proof_of_work(block, difficulty):
    nonce = 0
```

```
    while True:
        block_hash = hash(block + str(nonce))
        if block_hash.startswith('0'*difficulty):
            return nonce, block_hash
        nonce += 1
```

The technical insights are as follows:

- **Security**: High; requires substantial computational power to attack, making double-spending or rewriting history prohibitively expensive.
- **Energy trade-offs**: PoW is energy-intensive due to brute-force puzzle solving.
- **Throughput**: Limited by block time and network propagation delays.
- **Suitability for AI**: PoW's high energy cost and slow finality can hinder real-time or high-frequency AI tasks such as real-time federated learning or AI model updates. It is better suited for immutable timestamping or audit trails rather than active AI compute coordination.
- **AI workload example**: Some projects explore converting PoW cycles into useful computation, like training deep learning models, but general use remains inefficient.

PoS

PoS replaces computational puzzles with a deterministic selection of validators based on token stake. Validators lock up their tokens as collateral to gain the right to propose and validate blocks.

A validator selection pseudocode is as follows:

```
Python
import random
def select_validator(validators, stakes):
    total_stake = sum(stakes.values())
    pick = random.uniform(0, total_stake)
    cumulative = 0
    for v in validators:
        cumulative += stakes[v]
        if cumulative >= pick:
            return v
# Example usage
validators = ['node1', 'node2', 'node3']
stakes = {'node1': 150, 'node2': 300, 'node3': 50}
selected_validator = select_validator(validators, stakes)
print("Selected Validator:", selected_validator)
```

The technical insights are as follows:

- **Efficiency**: PoS vastly reduces energy consumption compared to PoW.
- **Validator selection**: Proportional to stake, with randomness/bias reduction mechanisms to maintain fairness.
- **Security**: Economic penalties for malicious behavior (slashing) incentivize honesty.
- **Scalability**: Higher throughput and faster finality enable more frequent AI model update blocks.
- **Suitability for AI**: PoS's efficiency suits decentralized AI with frequent transactions such as federated learning updates, microtransactions in AI marketplaces, and decentralized compute resource coordination.
- **AI workload example**: Validators can be AI training nodes or data contributors who stake tokens to participate in collaborative model building.

DPoS

DPoS enhances PoS by adding a layer of representative democracy. Token holders vote for a small set of delegates (or witnesses) who validate transactions and produce blocks on behalf of the network.

Delegate voting and block production pseudocode is as follows:

```
Python
class DPoS:
    def __init__(self):
        self.votes = {}  # delegate: votes
        self.delegates = []  # elected delegates

    def vote(self, voter, delegate, weight):
        self.votes[delegate] = self.votes.get(delegate, 0) + weight

    def elect_delegates(self, k):
        # elect top k delegates by votes
        self.delegates = sorted(self.votes, key=self.votes.get, reverse=True)
[:k]

    def produce_blocks(self):
        for delegate in self.delegates:
            print(f"{delegate} producing block")
# Example
network = DPoS()
```

```
network.vote('user1', 'delegate1', 100)
network.vote('user2', 'delegate2', 300)
network.vote('user3', 'delegate1', 50)
network.elect_delegates(k=2)
network.produce_blocks()
```

The technical insights are as follows:

- **Governance**: Delegates act as elected validators, improving decentralization in a scalable manner.
- **Performance**: DPoS can achieve higher throughput than both PoW and PoS by limiting the number of active validators.
- **Rewards**: Delegates receive rewards distributed among voters proportional to their stake.
- **Security**: Risks include potential centralization if the delegate election becomes dominated by wealthy stakeholders.
- **Suitability for AI**: Well-suited to AI workloads requiring rapid consensus, such as real-time AI inference on-chain, coordination of autonomous AI agents, and governance of AI **Decentralized Autonomous Organizations** (**DAOs**).

Use cases: Systems like **Enterprise Operation System** (**EOS**) and TRON showcase DPoS powering scalable AI and **decentralized application** (**dApp**) infrastructures.

Comparative analysis

Consensus mechanisms play a critical role in shaping the performance, security, and efficiency of DAI ecosystems. Each approach, PoW, PoS, and DPoS, offers distinct advantages and trade-offs that influence scalability, energy efficiency, and governance models. Understanding these differences is essential for selecting the right framework for AI-driven networks.

The features of PoW are:

- PoW remains valuable for establishing foundational immutability and security guarantees, but is hampered by cost and latency for active AI processes.
- PoW secures blockchain networks through computationally intensive mining, but is unsuitable for dynamic AI workloads due to its high energy consumption, latency, and inefficient handling of frequent model updates.

The features of PoS are:

- PoS delivers strong security with scalability and operational efficiency, supporting federated AI environments and marketplaces.

- PoS offers a more balanced solution, combining security with cost-effective, rapid finality, ideal for federated learning where timely aggregation and economic incentives are crucial.

The features of DPoS are:

- DPoS excels in applications demanding high throughput, rapid consensus cycles, and flexible governance, underpinning real-time AI agent coordination and DAO-managed AI ecosystems.
- DPoS further optimizes scalability and governance, making it well-suited for decentralized AI networks with numerous participants requiring fast consensus and collaborative decision-making. Emerging hybrid consensus algorithms and AI-inspired protocols, such as proof of learning, seek to align blockchain security rigor with the computational demands of AI training, providing eco-efficient and purpose-driven consensus frameworks.

Smart contracts and virtual machines

Smart contracts are pivotal to unleashing the full potential of decentralized AI systems by automating workflows, enforcing policies, and enabling trustless coordination without intermediaries. These self-executing programs, deployed on blockchain virtual machines, allow the codification of AI operational logic, governance, data sharing, and economic incentives, transforming static AI processes into dynamic, transparent, and secure decentralized applications.

Smart contracts as autonomous orchestration engines for AI workflows

Smart contracts are blockchain-hosted programs that autonomously enforce predefined rules once triggered. Within DAI systems, they serve as critical automation engines orchestrating workflows like federated learning coordination, model licensing enforcement, AI data marketplace transactions, and autonomous agent interactions. This automation eliminates dependency on centralized intermediaries susceptible to tampering or downtime, ensuring trustless, transparent, and tamper-proof execution essential for verifying AI provenance, regulating incentives, and enabling adaptive AI process management.

The key benefits are:

- **Trustless coordination**: AI parties can interact securely and transparently without trusting a single entity.
- **Transparent governance**: Protocol rules and tokenomics baked into smart contracts enable decentralized decision-making and incentives.

- **Immutable execution**: Contract code and executions are tamper-proof and auditable, essential for verifying AI model provenance and contributions.
- **Programmability**: Allows embedding adaptive AI logic such as updating permissions, automating payments based on model performance, or triggering re-training cycles.

Ethereum Virtual Machine and other VMs

Most smart contracts currently run on the **Ethereum Virtual Machine** (**EVM**), a turing-complete bytecode interpreter that executes contract code deterministically on every full node. The EVM enables developers to write contracts in languages like Solidity or Vyper, which compile down to EVM bytecode.

The alternative VMs supporting DAI are:

- **WebAssembly (WASM)**: Offers a faster, more flexible execution environment compatible with multiple blockchains and languages, enabling efficient AI-related computations.
- **Neon EVM**: Bridges Ethereum smart contracts to high-performance blockchains like Solana for scalable AI workflows.

The choice of VM affects AI contract performance, interoperability, and developer ecosystem access.

Automating federated learning with smart contracts

Smart contracts act as decentralized automation engines for federated learning by handling critical workflow stages without reliance on trusted intermediaries. They manage participant registration through whitelisting trusted data providers and compute nodes, orchestrate training rounds by triggering aggregation phases, and enforce contribution verification by logging cryptographic hashes of submitted model updates as tamper-evident proofs. Further, smart contracts facilitate automated, proportional incentive distribution based on the validated quality of contributions. This framework ensures impartial governance, fairness in rewards, and robust defenses against collusion or data manipulation, enabling scalable, transparent, and secure decentralized AI training.

In DAI training, smart contracts can automate:

- **Participant registration**: Managing whitelists of trusted data holders or compute nodes.
- **Round coordination**: Triggering each federated learning epoch and controlling aggregation.
- **Contribution verification**: Logging cryptographic hashes of model updates for tamper-evident records.

- **Incentive distribution**: Automatically rewarding contributors proportionally to their validated input quality.

Technical challenges and optimizations

On-chain deployment of AI workflows faces multiple critical challenges. High gas costs arise from executing complex smart contract logic and storing large AI metadata, demanding efficient contract design and strategic off-chain computation paired with on-chain cryptographic verification for scalability. The challenges are as follows:

- Storage limitations necessitate offloading bulk AI model weights and datasets to decentralized off-chain systems like IPFS, recording only essential metadata on-chain.
- Upgradability is addressed via proxy patterns and modular contract architectures, enabling seamless evolution alongside changing AI models and governance without loss of state.
- Security remains paramount; thus, rigorous formal verification and exhaustive testing processes are essential to safeguard immutable, irreversible smart contract code from vulnerabilities.

Emerging AI-enhanced smart contracts

Emerging as crucial automation engines, smart contracts facilitate DAI workflows by autonomously executing programmable tasks such as federated learning coordination, model licensing enforcement, and AI data marketplace operations.

AI-enhanced smart contracts distinguish between on-chain AI inference (lightweight, deterministic models embedded directly in Solidity for simple predictions) and off-chain AI decision support (complex models running externally with cryptographic commitments verified on-chain). Unlike static rule enforcers, these contracts leverage both approaches to adaptively execute terms, autonomously optimize resource allocation through reinforcement learning, and support intelligent dispute resolution within on-chain governance structures.

Beyond static rule enforcement, AI-enhanced smart contracts incorporate machine learning components to enable:

- **Adaptive contract execution**: Contracts can adjust terms dynamically based on real-time data patterns or predictive analytics from trusted oracles.
- **Autonomous decision making**: Integrating reinforcement learning for optimized bidding, resource allocation, or anomaly detection, with results attested via zero-knowledge proofs.
- **Intelligent dispute resolution**: AI models can evaluate conflicts and support automated settlements within on-chain governance frameworks, ensuring finality and auditability.

Programming examples of smart contracts for AI

This section presents concrete programming examples demonstrating how smart contracts are designed and implemented to automate AI workflows, enforce model licensing, model registry contracts, batch processing for multiple AI operations, model compression, payment and reward distribution, and manage federated learning coordination. They also handle tokenized AI assets on the blockchain, using languages like Solidity and leveraging frameworks such as Hardhat and Brownie for efficient development.

AI model licensing automation

The following is a Solidity contract demonstrating AI model licensing automation, typical of DAI marketplaces. It allows the owner to grant usage licenses to users programmatically and verify permissions:

```
// SPDX-License-Identifier: MIT
pragma solidity ^0.8.0;
contract AIModelLicense {
    address public owner;
    mapping(address => bool) private licensedUsers;
    event LicenseGranted(address indexed user);
    event LicenseRevoked(address indexed user);
    modifier onlyOwner() {
        require(msg.sender == owner, "Caller is not the owner");
        _;
    }
    constructor() {
        owner = msg.sender;
    }
    function grantLicense(address user) public onlyOwner {
        licensedUsers[user] = true;
        emit LicenseGranted(user);
    }
    function revokeLicense(address user) public onlyOwner {
        licensedUsers[user] = false;
        emit LicenseRevoked(user);
    }
    function checkLicense(address user) public view returns (bool) {
        return licensedUsers[user];
    }
}
```

Model registry contracts

Model registry contracts act as on-chain catalogs that encode how AI models are identified, priced, governed, and discovered across a decentralized ecosystem, linking each model's lifecycle to verifiable, transparent, and tamper-resistant states.

Model registry contracts serve as the foundation for DAI ecosystems, implementing sophisticated patterns that balance functionality, security, and gas efficiency. Use the following example to illustrate how a model registry can be represented and optimized in Solidity for DAI marketplaces:

```
struct ModelInfo {
    bytes32 modelHash;          // IPFS hash of the model
    address owner;              // Model owner
    uint128 price;              // Price in wei (packed for gas efficiency)
    uint64 createdAt;           // Creation timestamp (packed)
    uint32 version;             // Model version (packed)
    uint32 downloads;           // Download count (packed)
    bool isActive;              // Active status
}
```

Batch processing

Batch processing enables contracts to handle multiple AI operations in a single call, amortizing fixed gas overhead and reducing latency for high-throughput inference or training workflows. By looping over input batches inside the contract, developers minimize transaction count while preserving deterministic and auditable execution. Batch processing combines multiple AI operations into a single transaction to amortize fixed transaction costs, as shown in the following:

```
function batchPredict(int256[][] memory inputBatches)
    public view returns (int256[][] memory) {
    int256[][] memory results = new int256[][](inputBatches.length);

    for (uint i = 0; i < inputBatches.length; i++) {
        results[i] = predict(inputBatches[i]);
    }

    return results;
}
```

Model compression

Model compression reduces the on-chain and off-chain footprint of AI models through techniques such as quantization and pruning. Representing compressed layers in Solidity structures lowers storage costs, decreases computation requirements, and makes decentralized deployment of resource-constrained models more practical.

Model compression uses quantization, pruning, and related techniques to reduce model size and computational requirements, enabling lighter on-chain representations:

```
// Using 8-bit quantized weights instead of full precision
struct QuantizedLayer {
    int8[][] weights;
    int256[] scales;
    int256[] biases;
}
```

Payment and reward distribution

Payment and reward distribution logic turns training and inference participation into programmable economic flows. Contracts can allocate rewards proportionally to measurable contributions, enforce fair compensation without intermediaries, and plug into broader tokenomics schemes that sustain decentralized AI ecosystems.

Payment contracts implement advanced distribution mechanisms that incentivize participation while ensuring fair compensation:

```
function distributeRewards(bytes32 _jobId) external {
    TrainingJob storage job = trainingJobs[_jobId];
    uint256 totalContributions = _calculateTotalContributions(_jobId);
        for (uint i = 0; i < job.participants.length;) {
        address participant = job.participants[i];
        uint256 contribution = job.contributions[participant];
                if (contribution > 0) {
            uint256 reward = (job.
totalReward * contribution) / totalContributions;
            paymentToken.transfer(participant, reward);
        }
                unchecked { ++i; }
    }
}
```

The following are the technical insights:

- The contract enforces ownership and authorization via onlyOwner.

- Licensing state is immutable and auditable on-chain, ensuring transparent rights management.
- Events allow off-chain listeners to track license changes efficiently.
- This simple pattern can be expanded with pay-per-use models, subscription logic, or integration with oracles for off-chain data fees.

Note: **Smart contracts and VMs form the programmable backbone of decentralized AI infrastructures. They enable secure, transparent, and scalable AI systems by automating workflows from licensing and federated learning coordination to tokenomics and governance.**

Tokenization and digital assets

The fusion of blockchain and DAI networks rests significantly on the concept of tokenization, i.e., the transformation of AI models, datasets, compute resources, and governance rights into blockchain native digital assets. These tokens facilitate secure ownership, transferability, incentivization, and governance within DAI ecosystems. Understanding token types, AI-specific tokenization approaches, and tokenomics design for AI-centric DAOs is pivotal in architecting sustainable, scalable, and efficient decentralized AI platforms.

Token types relevant to DAI

In DAI ecosystems, tokens serve distinct and critical functions aligned with technical and economic requirements. These functions are:

- **Utility tokens**: They grant access or usage rights within an AI ecosystem or platform. For instance, users may stake utility tokens to access AI services, pay for compute cycles, or unlock specialized AI models. These tokens act as the fuel that drives platform interactions and incentivizes resource sharing among decentralized participants.
- **Governance tokens**: They empower holders to influence decisions such as protocol upgrades, model curation, or economic parameter changes within an AI DAO. Token holders propose and vote on initiatives, aligning incentives and promoting community-led evolution of decentralized AI networks.
- **Non-fungible tokens (NFTs)**: They uniquely represent singular AI assets, including proprietary AI models, datasets, training results, or intellectual property. Tokenization through NFTs provides immutable proof of ownership, provenance, and usage licensing, critical for intellectual property rights in AI marketplaces.

AI-specific tokenization approaches

DAI leverages specialized tokenization methods to unlock new economic and collaborative potentials. These methods are:

- **Model and dataset tokenization**: AI models and datasets become digital assets minted as tokens, enabling fractional ownership and flexible monetization. Fractionalized AI models allow widespread investment, collaborative refinement, and shared access, democratizing otherwise centralized intellectual properties.
- **Compute resource tokenization**: Scarce compute resources, such as **graphics processing unit** (**GPU**) or **tensor processing unit** (**TPU**) time, are tokenized to facilitate dynamic leasing and auctioning. Tokens represent access rights, temporal or priority-based, aligning incentives for compute providers while optimizing utilization in DAI training or inference tasks.
- **Token-curated registries (TCRs)**: TCRs employ token holder voting to curate and validate lists of AI assets, such as verified models or high-quality datasets. TCRs sustain ecosystem integrity and trust at scale through community-driven vetting by decentralizing quality control.

Tokenomics design for AI DAOs

Tokenomics design for AI DAOs must explicitly connect technical mechanisms with the real economic behaviors of contributors, model consumers, and governance participants. The following dimensions highlight how well-crafted token policies translate protocol objectives into concrete incentives and safeguards.

Tokenomics defines the following economic frameworks underpinning token issuance, utility, distribution, and governance within AI DAOs, serving as the linchpin for ecosystem sustainability and participant alignment. The approaches are as follows:

- **Issuance mechanisms**: Carefully architect initial supply, inflation or deflation schedules, and vesting protocols to balance network growth with token scarcity and fair access.
- **Incentive structures**: Design rewards proportional to meaningful contributions such as model training, data provisioning, validation, and governance activities, encouraging active participation and quality inputs.
- **Governance models**: Implement voting systems, such as stake-weighted or quadratic voting, to allocate decision rights while mitigating concentration risks and promoting equitable stakeholder influence.
- **Economic sustainability**: Integrate transactional fees, royalties on AI model usage, and fractional sales revenue that flow back into the DAO treasury, ensuring continued funding for development and operational costs.
- **Security and compliance**: Enforce tokenomics rules via smart contracts, apply slashing penalties for malicious behavior, and leverage AI-driven analytics to automate adherence to regulatory standards and detect anomalies.

This holistic tokenomics approach balances economic incentives, governance integrity, and regulatory compliance, fostering robust and self-sustaining DAI organizations.

Synergistic role of AI in tokenomics

Artificial intelligence enhances tokenomics by enabling more adaptive, secure, and efficient ecosystems. AI technologies further optimize tokenomics through the following:

- **Predictive analytics**: AI models forecast market demand for tokens and AI services, allowing dynamic adjustment of rewards and emission rates to maintain ecosystem stability and incentivize participation.
- **Automated compliance**: AI-driven monitoring systems ensure compliance with multi-jurisdictional regulations, automatically detecting anomalies or violations within token transactions and governance activities.
- **Smart contract optimization and security**: Machine learning tools scrutinize smart contract code during development, identifying vulnerabilities and optimizing logic to reduce gas costs and enhance security before deployment.
- **Governance support**: AI agents assist DAO stakeholders by summarizing proposals, community sentiment, and voting histories, promoting informed and transparent decision-making.

Programming example

An example Solidity smart contract fragment illustrates basic AI model fractional ownership through ERC20 tokens, enabling token holders to have proportional rights over an AI model asset. The programming example is as follows:

```
// SPDX-License-Identifier: MIT
pragma solidity ^0.8.0;
import "@openzeppelin/contracts/token/ERC20/ERC20.sol";
contract AIModelToken is ERC20 {
    address public modelOwner;
    event ModelUsagePaid(address indexed user, uint256 amount);
    constructor(uint256 initialSupply) ERC20("AIModelToken", "AIM") {
        modelOwner = msg.sender;
        _mint(msg.sender, initialSupply);
    }
    // Pay to use AI model
    function payForUsage(uint256 amount) public {
        _transfer(msg.sender, modelOwner, amount);
        emit ModelUsagePaid(msg.sender, amount);
    }
}
```

The explanation of the example is as follows:

- The contract mints a fixed supply of tokens representing fractional ownership or access rights to an AI model.
- Users pay for usage by transferring tokens to the model owner, automating micropayments via token transfers.
- This pattern can be extended with staking, DAO governance voting, or integration with licensing smart contracts.

Note: **Tokenization empowers decentralized AI networks by converting intangible AI assets and governance rights into secure, tradable digital tokens. Whether fractionalized AI models, compute resources, or governance voting power, tokens align stakeholder incentives and enable transparent, trustless participation. Coupled with AI-enhanced tokenomics that adaptively optimize the economic ecosystem, tokenization forms the foundation of sustainable and scalable DAI Autonomous Organizations.**

Distributed storage for DAI

DAI systems require storage solutions that match the scale, privacy, and resilience needs of large-scale model training and collaborative workflows. Traditional cloud storage introduces central points of failure, high costs, and data control concerns that conflict with DAI's core principles. Distributed storage protocols like IPFS, Arweave, and Filecoin provide content addressing, censorship resistance, and economic incentives crucial for AI workloads. As illustrated in *Figure 2.3,* which maps out the distributed storage ecosystem designed specifically for decentralized AI workloads, the transition away from centralized cloud infrastructure mitigates single points of failure while introducing robust content-addressing mechanics and this infrastructure which maps out the distributed storage ecosystem designed specifically for decentralized AI workloads:

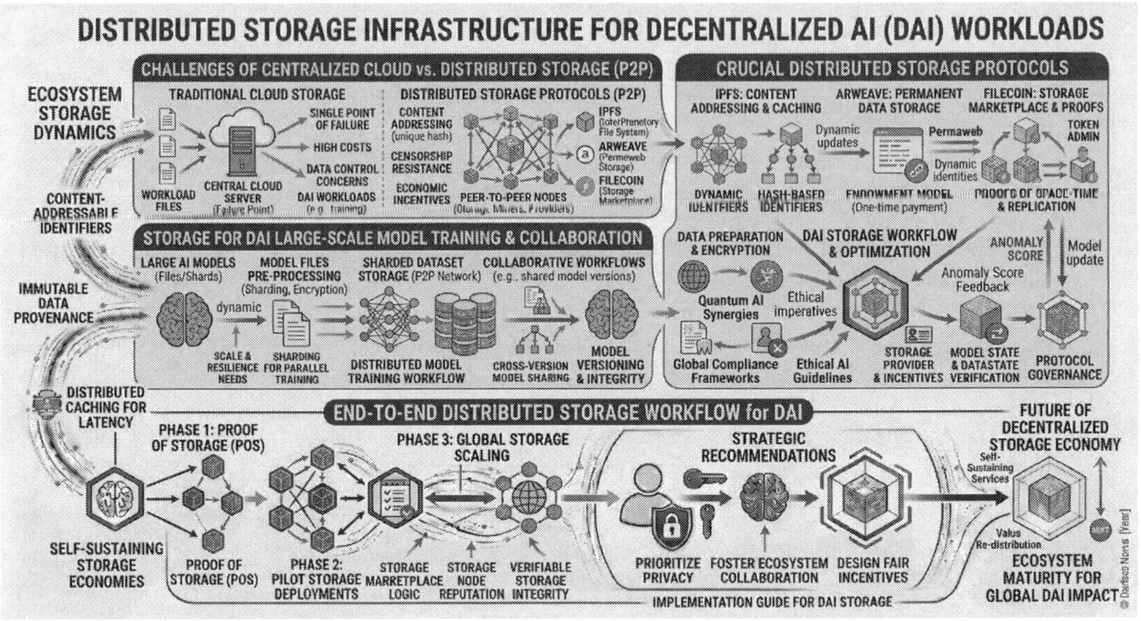

Figure 2.3: *Distributed storage infrastructure for decentralized AI workloads*

Decentralized storage matters for AI

Decentralized storage is essential for building scalable, secure, and compliant AI systems. It distributes massive AI datasets and model weights across numerous nodes, eliminating bottlenecks and enabling parallel, efficient data retrieval critical for federated learning. Protocols such as IPFS and Arweave give data owners full sovereignty over sensitive datasets (such as medical records) by enabling cryptographic proofs of data integrity, ensuring compliance with strict privacy regulations without exposing raw data. Additionally, decentralized storage leverages peer-to-peer economies to reduce costs compared to centralized cloud providers, using market-driven pricing models like Filecoin and one-time archival fees like Arweave to optimize expenditures across diverse AI data lifecycles. This combination of scalability, sovereignty, and cost efficiency makes decentralized storage indispensable for AI infrastructure in Web3 ecosystems.

Comparative analysis of IPFS vs. Arweave vs. Filecoin

Decentralized storage solutions vary significantly in their architecture, pricing models, and suitability for AI workloads. IPFS focuses on content-addressed storage and efficient data retrieval; Arweave emphasizes permanent data archiving with one-time fees, while Filecoin introduces a market-driven approach for scalable storage.

The following table offers a side-by-side comparison of these protocols to highlight their unique characteristics and approaches:

Feature	IPFS	Arweave	Filecoin
Storage model	Content-addressed, mutable	Permanent, immutable blockweave	Marketplace-based, renewable
Data permanence	Dependent on pinning	Guaranteed permanent	Contract-based renewal
Cost structure	Free protocol; hosting varies	One-time fee	Market-driven pricing
AI model storage	Ideal for versioned and evolving models	Best for archival snapshots	Flexible terms for large datasets
Training data storage	Good for dynamic datasets	Suited for historical datasets	Cost-effective bulk storage
Retrieval speed	Fast on local/federated networks	Moderate across global nodes	Varies by miner performance
Versioning	Native **directed acyclic graph** (**DAG**) versioning	Immutable version history	Manual version control
Consensus	None at the protocol layer	**Proof of access** (**PoA**)	Proof of Replication/ Spacetime
Scalability	High horizontal scaling	Limited by block size	Very high via market expansion
Privacy	Content addressing + encryption	Public by default	Encryption optional
Integration complexity	Low API complexity	Moderate blockchain integration	High marketplace management
Maturity	Mature (since 2015)	Growing (since 2018)	Mature (since 2020)
Recommended AI use cases	Federated learning datasets, active model versioning, and collaborative training shares	Immutable model provenance, regulatory audit trails, and historical dataset archiving	Large-scale training corpora, cost-optimized model backups, and enterprise data lakes
AI suitability	Dynamic datasets, model serving	Provenance, audit logs	Training data, cold storage

Table 2.1: *Comparative analysis of IPFS, Arweave, and Filecoin*

Each solution addresses distinct phases of AI development: IPFS for active model training and federated learning, Arweave for permanent audit trails and provenance, and Filecoin for cost-optimized archival and large-scale dataset hosting.

Integration patterns with AI pipelines

This explores strategic integration approaches that optimize AI workflows through blockchain. Hybrid tiering architectures combine IPFS for active data, Filecoin for warm storage, and Arweave for archival, enabling automated tier management. Content-addressed model management uses IPFS hashes to ensure immutable provenance and prevent configuration drift, simplifying model versioning in decentralized marketplaces. Federated learning coordination employs IPFS for aggregating models and IPFS objects for gradient contributions, with smart contracts verifying integrity and orchestrating collaborative training, all guaranteeing transparency, security, and verifiability in DAI ecosystems.

Hybrid tiering architectures

Deploy multi-layered storage strategies combining IPFS for hot data (frequently accessed model updates and small datasets), Filecoin for warm bulk storage, and Arweave for cold archival data such as finalized AI models and compliance logs. AI orchestration frameworks like MLflow automate data tiering based on usage intensity and cost efficiency, optimizing storage economics without compromising accessibility.

Content-addressed model management

AI model packages, including weights, metadata, and performance metrics, are stored as immutable **JavaScript Object Notation** (**JSON**) objects on IPFS. Smart contracts reference these content hashes to enforce model provenance and integrity within decentralized AI marketplaces, effectively eliminating configuration drift by linking deployed models directly to their verifiable content.

Federated learning coordination

Global model aggregations are published on IPFS, with participants retrieving the latest model by its content hash. Gradient contributions are submitted as new IPFS objects, while blockchain-based smart contracts validate updates and trigger subsequent aggregation rounds. This ensures a tamper-evident, transparent, and verifiable federated training process, cohesive with decentralized principles.

A sample pseudocode for the IPFS model storage is as follows:

```
// SPDX-License-Identifier: MIT
pragma solidity ^0.8.0;
// Simplified IPFS model storage
const ipfs = require('ipfs-http-client').create();
async function storeModel(buffer, metadata) {
  const pkg = { weights: buffer.toString('base64'), metadata };
  const { path } = await ipfs.add(JSON.stringify(pkg));
```

```
    return path; // content hash
  }
```

Privacy-preserving storage

Layering advanced cryptographic techniques such as homomorphic encryption or secure multi-party computation atop decentralized storage protocols like IPFS and Filecoin facilitates secure storage of encrypted data shards. **Zero-knowledge** (**ZK**) proofs verify model training on these encrypted datasets without revealing sensitive raw data, with proof artifacts immutably stored on Arweave to ensure permanent auditability.

Optimize efficiently by following these best practices:

- Implement smart contracts for automated tier management that migrate data across storage layers based on on-chain usage analytics.
- Employ redundancy strategies using pinning services and Filecoin contracts to maintain adequate replication of critical AI assets.
- Utilize geographic caching of IPFS gateway nodes close to AI compute clusters, minimizing latency for model updates and inferences.
- Align storage selection with AI workflow demands, using IPFS for low-latency access, Filecoin for economical bulk archival, and Arweave for immutable compliance and long-term archival.

When orchestrated strategically, decentralized storage systems mitigate centralization risks, uphold data integrity, and optimize performance and costs, offering resilient, transparent, and scalable storage infrastructures tailored for comprehensive AI workloads in Web3 environments.

Interoperability and cross-chain protocols

As DAI networks mature, they increasingly span multiple blockchain ecosystems, each optimized for distinct functions such as high-performance computation, low□cost transactions, or specialized storage. Achieving seamless interoperability is essential to unlock the full potential of composable AI services, enabling models, data, and economic flows to traverse blockchain boundaries without sacrificing security or decentralization.

Cross-chain communication protocols

Inter Blockchain Communication (**IBC**) was pioneered by the *Cosmos* ecosystem to facilitate trustless message and token transfers between sovereign blockchains while preserving each chain's security model. In AI contexts, IBC enables model sharing and federated dataset distribution across specialized compute chains. For example, a model trained on a high-throughput chain can be deployed on a low-cost settlement chain for inference, with IBC ensuring atomic, verifiable transfers of model hashes, parameters, and governance votes.

Chainlink's **Cross Chain Interoperability Protocol** (**CCIP**) extends beyond token movements to support arbitrary smart contract calls across chains. CCIP leverages multiple independent oracle networks and on-chain risk controls to deliver high-assurance cross-chain message delivery. AI applications use CCIP to implement automated license management, issuing access tokens on one chain while triggering usage-based payments on another, and to coordinate multi-chain inference workflows where data or model inputs reside on disparate platforms.

Bridge technologies for AI assets

Token bridges enable AI assets, including model NFTs, dataset fractions, and service tokens, to move between networks. Architecturally, bridges range from validator-based designs requiring federated signatures to fully trustless constructions using zero-knowledge proofs. Validator-based bridges offer high throughput but require careful validator decentralization, while ZK-bridges provide cryptographic guarantees of transfer correctness without revealing proprietary AI model details.

For instance, an AI model represented as an ERC-721 NFT on Ethereum can be ported to a specialized AI compute chain via an optimistic bridge. The bridge locks the original NFT, issues a wrapped representation on the target chain, and releases the original upon burning of the wrap. Fraud-proof safeguards safeguard against malicious behavior during the challenge period, balancing performance with security. Alternatively, privacy-sensitive models such as those processing medical data can use ZK-bridges that verify model integrity through succinct proofs, preserving data confidentiality while enabling cross-chain utility.

Multi-chain AI ecosystem standards

True interoperability demands standardized formats and governance mechanisms. AI model serialization standards such as **Open Neural Network Exchange** (**ONNX**) or TensorFlow SavedModel. It is combined with metadata schemas describing performance metrics, input/output interfaces, and licensing terms, allowing models to be plugged into any blockchain-based runtime without bespoke adapters.

Governance coordination across chains is equally critical. Multi-chain DAOs implement cross-chain voting frameworks where stakeholders on different networks vote on protocol upgrades, resource allocations, or dispute resolutions. Weighted voting combining token holdings on multiple chains ensures fair representation, while on-chain referenda enforce coherent decision execution across all connected networks.

Through the adoption of robust cross-chain communication protocols, secure bridge architectures, and standardized interoperability frameworks, DAI networks can harness the specialized strengths of diverse blockchains. This composable infrastructure unleashes new possibilities for collaborative model development, international data sharing, and frictionless monetization of AI services across the Web3 landscape.

Scalability solutions for DAI

DAI networks demand throughput, low-latency, and cost efficiency far beyond traditional blockchains. Scalability solutions, including **Layer 2 (L2)** technologies, rollups, sharding, and hybrid approaches, enable large-scale AI training, real-time inference, and autonomous agent coordination while preserving security and decentralization.

L2 scaling solutions

L2 solutions enhance blockchain scalability by offloading computation and transaction processing from the base **Layer 1 (L1)** chain to secondary frameworks, enabling substantial throughput improvements while preserving L1 security guarantees. Key approaches include:

- **Optimistic rollups**: Batch federated learning updates and microtransactions into L2 blocks, reducing gas costs by up to 90%, and use fraud proofs to challenge malicious activities within defined periods. Platforms like Optimism and Arbitrum accelerate AI model version settlement and automate incentive distributions with minimal L1 interaction.
- **State channels**: Establish off-chain pathways between AI service providers and consumers, ideal for high-frequency, low-latency operations such as chatbots and recommendation engines, where rapid signed state exchanges culminate in succinct final state commits on chain, eliminating per-interaction gas fees and ensuring near instant finality. These mechanisms collectively empower DAI ecosystems to scale efficiently without compromising security or decentralization.

Rollup technologies for AI

ZK-Rollups enable privacy-preserving, scalable batching of AI-related computations by generating succinct cryptographic proofs that validate off-chain AI processes without exposing underlying data.

For example, in sensitive healthcare collaborations, ZK-Rollups verify encrypted medical data training across multiple institutions while preserving patient confidentiality. These proofs are anchored on L1 blockchains, ensuring trust and immutability. Advanced projects like zkSync and StarkNet are pioneering optimized proof generation tailored specifically for efficient verification of AI model updates, bridging privacy, scalability, and decentralized AI integrity.

The following is a simplified pseudocode:

```
contract ZKAIValidator {
    function verifyModel(bytes32 modelHash, uint256[2] proof, uint256[] in-
puts) external {
        require(zkVerify(proof, inputs), "Invalid proof");
        validated[modelHash] = true;
    }
}
```

Recursive proofs

Recursive proofs chain together verifiable proofs of sequential AI training steps into a single, succinct proof that encapsulates the entire model evolution process. This methodology ensures an auditable, tamper-proof lineage for AI models while safeguarding proprietary training data privacy by avoiding exposure of intermediate datasets or parameter updates. Recursive proof frameworks enable scalable verification of complex, multi-stage AI workflows on blockchain infrastructures without compromising confidentiality or computational efficiency.

Sharding for AI workloads

Sharding is a critical scalability strategy for decentralized AI systems. It partitions blockchain state and execution across parallel subnetworks, enabling significant throughput improvements essential for distributed AI training and inference.

Sharding divides the blockchain into multiple parallel subnetworks, or shards, each independently executing a subset of AI tasks to enhance performance and scalability, illustrated as follows:

- **Compute optimized**: Shards allocate GPU-powered nodes specifically for training shards, handling intense gradient computations, while lighter nodes manage coordination shards, orchestrating model validation and consensus.
- **Dynamic shard**: Allocation mechanisms spawn additional shards during peak AI training activity and merge idle shards when demand subsides, leveraging predictive analytics on historical workloads to optimize resource and cost efficiency. Secure cross-shard protocols enable seamless routing of model updates and aggregation of results across shards without centralized control, preserving decentralized integrity while scaling AI compute and storage workloads efficiently.

Alternative scaling approaches

Alternative scaling approaches extend beyond traditional L2 solutions by introducing specialized architectures tailored to AI's unique computational and economic demands.

Collectively, the following alternative scaling patterns offer adaptable, efficient, and economically sustainable strategies for extending decentralized AI systems beyond the inherent constraints of conventional blockchain architectures:

- **Appchains (AI-specific rollups)**: Dedicated rollup chains like Swanchain deploy custom-built virtual machines optimized specifically for gradient computations, achieving cost savings of approximately 70% compared to general-purpose blockchain environments. These specialized chains streamline AI training operations by tailoring the execution layer around machine learning workloads.
- **Hybrid on-chain/off-chain architectures**: This approach partitions critical coordination tasks such as incentive mechanisms and governance onto the secure base layer while offloading computationally intensive AI model training to off-chain clusters. Periodic commitments of cryptographic proofs on-chain ensure trustworthiness and auditability, balancing between performance and decentralized security guarantees.
- **Economic scaling mechanisms**: Dynamic resource allocation emerges through prediction markets for compute power combined with staking-based incentives to regulate bandwidth and storage distribution. Automated market makers continuously discover equilibrium pricing for AI-related services, effectively harmonizing supply and demand across decentralized AI networks.

The following is an integration pseudocode:

```
javascript
class ScalableAI {
  constructor(l1, l2, zk) {
    this.l1 = l1;   // Ethereum mainnet
    this.l2 = l2;   // Optimistic rollup
    this.zk = zk;   // ZK-rollup
  }
  async updateModel(data, private=false) {
    return private
      ? this.zk.submitProof(data)
      : this.l2.batchUpdate(data);
  }
  async coordinateFL(nodes) {
    const session = await this.l2.startFL(nodes);
    const results = await this.l2.aggregate(session);
    return this.l1.finalize(results);
  }
}
```

The following table is an overview of the optimistic vs. ZK-Rollups decision matrix for AI workloads:

Workload type	Optimistic Rollups	ZK-Rollups
High-frequency inference (e.g., real-time APIs)	Fast, cheap, suits public data	Slower proofs; overkill
Privacy-sensitive training (e.g., federated healthcare)	Data exposure risk	Privacy-preserving proofs
High-value settlements (e.g., model licensing)	Cost-effective for most cases	Instant finality, max security
Latency tolerance	High (7-day challenge period)	Low (immediate validity)

***Table 2.2**: Optimistic vs. ZK-Rollups decision matrix*

Note: **Scalability solutions: L2 rollups, ZK proofs, sharding, and hybrid architectures provide the performance and economic efficiency required for decentralized AI systems. Networks achieve secure, high-throughput training and inference at scale while preserving the trust and transparency of blockchain infrastructure by tailoring these technologies to AI workloads.**

Gas optimization and cost management

Optimizing gas consumption is crucial for deploying AI workloads on blockchain to minimize costs while maintaining transparency and security. Major cost drivers include frequent model updates, extensive metadata storage (hashes, Merkle roots, provenance data), and complex logic such as reward calculations and contribution validations.

Effective strategies involve:

- **Batching**: Consolidate multiple model updates or data submissions into a single transaction to reduce overhead.
- **Off-chain computation**: Perform heavy processing like gradient aggregation or validation off-chain, submitting only cryptographic proofs such as zk-SNARKs.
- **Data compression**: Minimize calldata size by packing small values into compact byte arrays.
- **Proxy contracts**: Use lightweight proxy patterns for contract upgrades, reducing deployment and upgrade costs.

Tools like Hardhat Gas Reporter and Slither analyze and detect expensive functions or inefficiencies, while Chainlink oracles schedule transactions during low-fee periods. L2 solutions, such as rollups, further alleviate on-chain costs by batching numerous transactions off-chain, ensuring high-frequency AI activities remain economically feasible.

Practical implementation examples include batched gradient updates and optimized smart contracts that significantly lower gas consumption, enabling scalable AI operations on decentralized networks.

Development tools and frameworks

DAI systems blend complex smart contract logic, off-chain AI computation, and distributed governance. Effective development demands specialized toolchains and frameworks that accelerate contract authoring, testing, deployment, and continuous integration, while integrating AI-oriented protocols such as Ocean Protocol, Fetch.ai, and SingularityNET.

Smart contract frameworks

In DAI development, choosing the right smart contract framework is critical for efficiency, flexibility, and scalability. The following frameworks provide distinct advantages for compiling, testing, and deploying the sophisticated smart contracts required for DAI applications:

- **Hardhat**: A modern JavaScript-based environment that excels in compiling, testing, and debugging Solidity contracts. Its ability to fork mainnet state enables realistic simulation for AI marketplace contracts, such as those managing model licensing on Ocean Protocol. Hardhat's rich plugin ecosystem, including tools like hardhat deploy and gas reporters, facilitates precise cost analysis for complex AI workflows such as batched federated learning updates.
- **Truffle**: A mature Ethereum development suite offering a comprehensive toolkit for contract compilation, migration, and deployment, complemented by Ganache for local blockchain simulation. Truffle simplifies multi-network deployments of AI infrastructure, like token-curated registries, and integrates with front-end tools like Drizzle for real-time **user interface** (**UI**) updates tied to smart contract events.
- **Brownie**: Python-centric and ideal for AI practitioners already familiar with Python, Brownie tightly integrates smart contract testing with machine learning scripts. It allows seamless invocation of training pipelines within test suites, enabling validation that on-chain reward mechanisms accurately reflect AI model performance indicators.
- **Foundry**: A high-performance, Rust-based framework designed for rapid smart contract compilation and execution. Foundry's forge compiler and cast tool optimize continuous integration pipelines by supporting thousands of automated AI model update validations. Its advanced fuzz testing capabilities uncover edge case vulnerabilities essential for gas optimization and secure contract behavior in AI workflows.

Comparative takeaway: Hardhat and Foundry prioritize economic simulation and security auditing for high-stakes DAI economics. Truffle and Brownie excel in deployment pipelines and AI-native integration. Practitioners should match frameworks to their workflow's primary bottleneck, whether simulation fidelity, testing speed, or ML interoperability.

These frameworks together provide diverse developer experiences and capabilities, empowering decentralized AI projects to build robust, scalable, and secure smart contracts tailored to complex AI applications.

AI-specific integrations

These platforms illustrate how blockchain frameworks uniquely integrate with AI ecosystems to provide secure, scalable, and privacy-respecting infrastructures for decentralized intelligence. These protocols demonstrate distinct approaches to bridging on-chain consensus with off-chain intelligence.

Ocean Protocol

Ocean Protocol empowers DAI by providing **software development kits (SDKs)** and smart contracts that enable tokenized marketplaces for AI datasets. Its JavaScript library, `@oceanprotocol/lib`, facilitates seamless creation and management of data tokens and liquidity pools, allowing federated learning participants to access and monetize datasets securely. The protocol's compute-to-data feature ensures sensitive data remains private while enabling algorithmic processing, ideal for privacy-critical AI applications.

Fetch.ai

It introduces autonomous economic agents on a distributed ledger that negotiate resources and data access dynamically. Using the Python SDK, developers instantiate intelligent agents capable of bidding for compute time or datasets on decentralized pools, enabling scalable on-chain AI training and inference. This agent-driven model supports adaptive resource management and market-driven AI workflows.

SingularityNET

SingularityNET exposes AI capabilities as on-chain callable services managed by registry smart contracts. Developers deploy AI models as services discoverable and monetized through AGIX tokens. Its Python client enables orchestration of complex AI workflows by chaining services, such as combining computer vision with natural language processing, ensuring fully decentralized, broker-less, AI pipelines that operate autonomously.

DevOps for DAI

Operational excellence in DAI requires merging traditional software delivery pipelines with the unique constraints of immutable ledgers and probabilistic machine learning models. Developing production-grade DAI systems demands integrated DevOps practices covering both blockchain and AI stages.

Teams can ensure reliability and agility across the full stack by unifying these workflows as follows:

- **Continuous integration/continuous deployment (CI/CD)**: Automate Solidity contract compilation and testing using Hardhat or Foundry while retraining AI models on fresh data snapshots per release. Deploy contracts cross-chain with tools like Truffle migrations or Hardhat scripting to support Ethereum and sidechains.

- **Monitoring and alerting**: Track on-chain AI activities via event streams such as model updates and dataset usage. Leverage off-chain indexers like the graph to aggregate metrics on model accuracy and gas consumption. Incorporate AI-specific health checks, including drift detection alarms to signal performance degradation.
- **Infrastructure as code (IaC)**: Provision blockchain nodes (Ethereum, Ocean Protocol) and AI compute clusters (Kubernetes managed GPUs) via Terraform or CloudFormation. Co-deploy decentralized storage nodes (IPFS, Filecoin) to keep data proximate for quicker federated learning cycles.
- **Security and auditing**: Embed automated smart contract auditing in CI pipelines using Slither, Echidna, and AI-powered security scanners that identify anomalous transactions, guarding against adversarial AI model manipulations.
- **Versioning and rollback**: Manage on-chain smart contract versions with proxy patterns enabling seamless AI workflow upgrades without data loss. Utilize content-addressed storage for AI models to enable safe rollback to prior states during failures.

This holistic DevOps approach ensures a robust, scalable, secure, and maintainable decentralized AI infrastructure that bridges blockchain immutability with adaptive machine learning workflows.

AI-specific case studies

These case studies vividly demonstrate blockchain's role in powering practical decentralized AI by fostering token economies that incentivize data and compute contributions, enabling privacy-preserving collaboration, automating multi-agent coordination via smart contracts, and supporting substantial real-world economic activities across AI ecosystems.

Ocean Protocol and tokenized AI data markets

Ocean Protocol runs active marketplaces on Ethereum, Polygon, and BSC, facilitating over $2 million in data transactions. Leading enterprises like Mercedes-Benz and Deutsche Telekom utilize Ocean to monetize datasets securely while preserving privacy. Key features include data NFTs representing dataset ownership, Datatokens for access permissions, and compute-to-data enabling AI training on encrypted data through smart contracts. These mechanisms allow researchers to train AI models on sensitive information without exposing raw data while enabling automated revenue distribution to data owners.

SingularityNET as an AI service marketplace

SingularityNET hosts over 100 AI services across domains like computer vision, **natural language processing** (**NLP**), and robotics, processing thousands of monthly requests. Services are discoverable on-chain via a blockchain-based registry and orchestrated with smart contracts that enable multi-service AI workflows. Stakeholders use AGIX tokens for payments, with staking mechanisms ensuring service quality. This framework enables developers to compose complex AI pipelines without managing infrastructure, as exemplified by interactions with the Sophia robot autonomous agent.

Fetch.ai and autonomous economic agents

On Fetch.ai's network, 23,000-plus autonomous agents actively transact, including pilots in Cambridge, where agents autonomously book parking and coordinate mobility services. These agents autonomously own wallets and execute complex negotiations using blockchain protocols. Cross-chain interoperability through Cosmos SDK and IBC expands agent capabilities. Practical applications include agents managing peer-to-peer energy trading, improving grid efficiency with real-time micropayments, and eliminating human intervention.

Conclusion

The chapter has laid out the blockchain building blocks, such as consensus, smart contracts, tokenization, and decentralized storage, demonstrating how they enable secure, transparent, and scalable AI networks. We explored cost optimizations, L2 scaling, rollups, sharding, and privacy techniques, illustrating practical patterns for deploying production-grade DAI. These foundations empower trustless collaboration, privacy-preserving data exchange, and incentive-driven automation, crucial for democratizing AI.

The next chapter will focus on network architectures for decentralized AI, covering peer-to-peer topologies, node coordination, data and model distribution, resource management, fault tolerance, and secure authentication. We will learn design patterns for resilient, high-performance AI networks that support frictionless collaboration and scalable model sharing.

CHAPTER 3
Decentralized AI Network Architecture

Introduction

A **decentralized artificial intelligence** (**DAI**) network is a distributed system in which responsibility for computation, data storage, and decision□making is shared among multiple independent participants rather than centralized in a single organization or cluster. The architectural choices made at the outset profoundly shape the system's resilience, performance, and security posture. In this chapter, you will learn how to craft network topologies that balance latency and throughput, define clear roles for heterogeneous node types, select peer-to-peer protocols that guarantee consistency, and orchestrate data distribution strategies that preserve privacy while maximizing availability. We then examine how to ensure robust fault tolerance, enforce strong security and authentication, and continuously monitor performance metrics to maintain optimal operation. By the end of this chapter, you will possess a blueprint for designing DAI networks capable of scaling from a handful of nodes to thousands, supporting both collaborative model training and distributed inference across global participants.

Structure

The chapter covers the following topics:

- Network topology and design patterns
- Node types and responsibilities
- Peer-to-peer communication protocols
- Data distribution and replication
- Load balancing and resource management
- Fault tolerance and recovery
- Network security and authentication
- Performance optimization

- Monitoring and analytics
- Case studies
- DAI architecture and enabled capabilities

Objectives

The chapter equips readers with an actionable blueprint for constructing DAI infrastructures through ten cohesive sections covering network topology, node specialization, peer-to-peer protocols, data distribution, load balancing, fault tolerance, security, performance optimization, and monitoring systems. Readers will learn how topology design affects data flow and resilience, how specialized roles such as workers, coordinators, validators, storage, and incentive nodes, collectively power distributed learning, how gossip and **remote procedure call** (**RPC**) protocols enable efficient model synchronization, how sharding and erasure coding balance availability with privacy, and how Byzantine fault tolerance, cryptographic identity, and economic incentives create trustless **artificial intelligence** (**AI**) networks. Each section combines rigorous technical exposition with architectural workflow, protocol state machines, and real-world case studies from federated healthcare consortia and DAI marketplaces, enabling practitioners to design resilient, scalable systems supporting global collaborative intelligence.

Network topology and design patterns

The foundation of any DAI network lies in its topology, the structural arrangement of nodes and their interconnections that determines how computational resources, data, and intelligence flow throughout the system. DAI networks must carefully balance autonomy with coordination, efficiency with resilience, and scalability with governance, unlike traditional AI deployments, where a centralized server orchestrates all operations. As detailed in *Figure 3.1*, which outlines the primary decentralized AI network topologies and their corresponding design patterns, choosing the right structural layout is critical for minimizing latency and ensuring Byzantine fault tolerance:

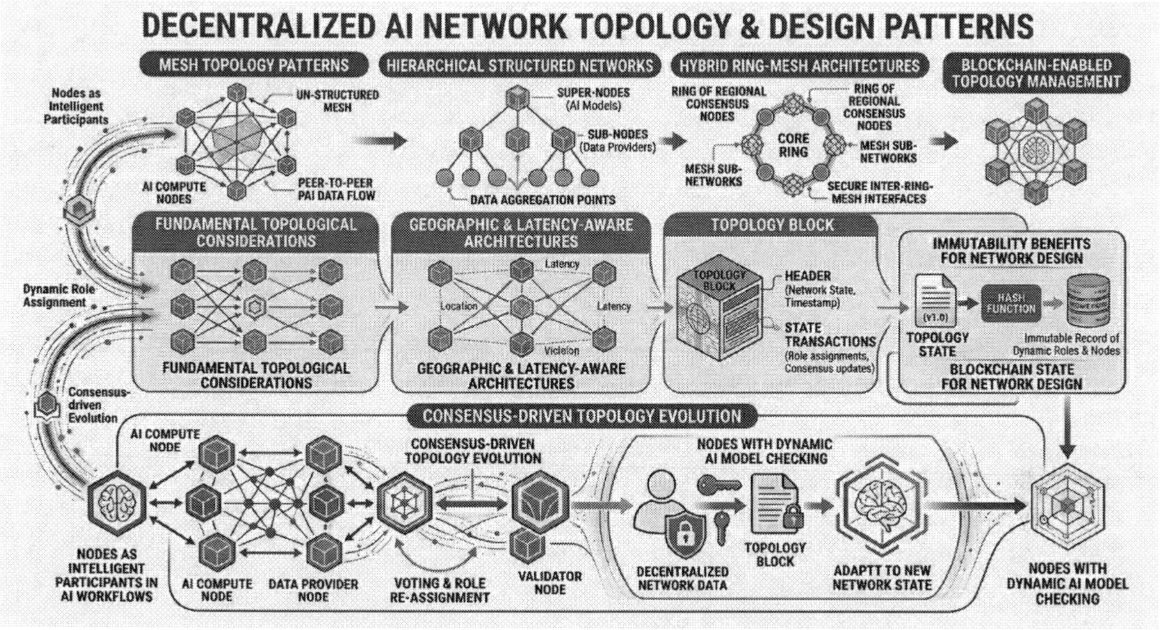

Figure 3.1: *Decentralized AI network topology and design patterns*

Fundamental topological considerations

The topology of a DAI network directly impacts its performance characteristics, fault tolerance, and ability to scale. Traditional peer-to-peer networks often employ flat topologies where all nodes have equal status and capabilities, which typically incur message complexity for global broadcasts, as every node must communicate with many peers. However, DAI networks require more sophisticated architectural patterns, such as hierarchical, expander, or tree-like overlays, that can reduce broadcast and coordination costs toward, while still maintaining decentralization, enabling large-scale training and inference without overwhelming the network.

Mesh topology patterns

In a pure mesh topology, every node maintains direct connections to multiple other nodes, creating redundant pathways for communication and computation. For DAI networks, mesh topologies offer exceptional fault tolerance since the failure of any single node or connection does not partition the network. However, in a fully connected or dense mesh, the number of links and thus the potential communication overhead grows quadratically with the number of nodes, making pure mesh designs impractical for large-scale AI workloads that require frequent model synchronization and data exchange.

Hierarchical structured networks

Hierarchical topologies introduce specialization layers within the decentralized architecture. At the base layer, worker nodes perform local training and inference tasks. Intermediate layers consist of aggregation nodes that combine and validate model updates from multiple workers. The top layer includes coordination nodes that manage global consensus and network governance. This structure reduces communication complexity while maintaining decentralization principles through blockchain-based coordination of the hierarchical roles.

To ensure decentralization guarantees persist under failure conditions, hierarchical DAI networks incorporate robust failure models. If an aggregation node fails, worker nodes automatically route updates through redundant paths or fallback to alternative aggregators elected via blockchain consensus, preventing bottlenecks while maintaining aggregation depth. Collusion among aggregation nodes is mitigated through Byzantine fault-tolerant protocols like proof of verifying, which tolerate up to 1/3 malicious actors by cross-validating updates cryptographically before propagating to coordination layers. Coordination node failures trigger on-chain role reassignment among staked participants, ensuring no single point of failure disrupts global consensus or governance.

Hybrid ring-mesh architectures

Advanced DAI networks often employ hybrid topologies that combine the efficiency of ring structures for routine operations with mesh connectivity for fault tolerance. In these architectures, nodes are organized into rings for efficient model parameter passing and gradient aggregation, while maintaining mesh connections for backup communication paths and consensus operations.

Blockchain-enabled topology management

The integration of blockchain technology introduces novel approaches to topology management that were not possible in traditional distributed systems. Smart contracts can dynamically manage network topology based on node performance, reputation scores, and computational contributions. This creates self-organizing networks that can adapt their structure to optimize for current workloads and network conditions.

Example smart contract workflow:

Consider a `TopologyManager` smart contract that receives oracle-reported node metrics (latency, uptime >95%, stake weight) as inputs every epoch. The contract computes a reputation score, then selects the top- scoring nodes as aggregation layer coordinators via on-chain sortition. Updated topology mappings (node IDs | layer assignments) are emitted as events, triggering off-chain P2P overlay reconfiguration while bonding selected nodes' stakes as slashable collateral.

Dynamic role assignment

Blockchain-based governance allows networks to dynamically assign roles to nodes based on their capabilities, reliability, and stake in the network. A node might serve as a worker node during normal operations but be promoted to an aggregation role when other aggregation nodes become unavailable. These role transitions are recorded on the blockchain, ensuring transparency and preventing malicious actors from assuming critical roles without proper authorization. To prevent role-flapping and Sybil-style escalation attacks, smart contracts enforce minimum stake thresholds (e.g., 1000 tokens for aggregators), 24-hour cooldown periods between role changes, and performance probation windows requiring sustained reliability before promotion eligibility.

Consensus-driven topology evolution

As the network grows and computational requirements change, the topology itself can evolve through consensus mechanisms. Nodes can propose topology modifications, such as creating new hierarchical layers or establishing direct connections to improve efficiency. These proposals are evaluated through blockchain-based voting mechanisms, ensuring that topology changes serve the collective benefit of the network.

Geographic and latency-aware architectures

DAI networks must explicitly navigate **consistency, availability, and partition tolerance** (**CAP**) theorem trade-offs when designing geographic architectures, as physical node distribution forces explicit choices between latency (favoring regional AP systems), consistency (favoring global CP), and partition tolerance.

In regional clustering strategies, nodes within the same geographic region form tight AP clusters for latency-sensitive training where eventual consistency suffices, achieving sub-50ms roundtrips for gradient exchanges. Global coordination layers operate as CP systems with quorum-based consensus (e.g., 2f+1 reads/writes), accepting higher latency (200-500ms) to guarantee strong model synchronization across continents while tolerating inter-region partitions. This hybrid PACELC approach, prioritizing latency within regions (EL) but consistency globally (PC), optimizes both local throughput and network-wide correctness.

Adaptive routing protocols

Advanced DAI networks implement adaptive routing protocols that can dynamically select communication paths based on current network conditions, node performance, and the type of AI workload being processed. These protocols leverage blockchain-recorded node performance metrics to make intelligent routing decisions that optimize both individual node performance and overall network efficiency.

Node types and responsibilities

The complexity of DAI operations necessitates specialized node types, each designed to fulfill specific roles within the network architecture. DAI networks benefit from heterogeneous node ecosystems where specialization drives efficiency and enables sophisticated AI workflows, unlike homogeneous peer-to-peer networks, where all nodes provide identical services.

Worker nodes as the computational foundation

Worker nodes in DAI networks execute federated learning algorithms like **federated averaging (FedAvg)** (simple weighted averaging of local models), **federated proximal (FedProx)** (FedAvg plus proximal term for system heterogeneity), and **Stochastic Controlled Averaging for Federated Learning (SCAFFOLD)** (control variates to correct client drift), enabling privacy-preserving collective intelligence from edge data.

These nodes perform local training on proprietary datasets, never sharing raw data, and then upload model updates (gradients or parameters) for global aggregation, directly interfacing with sensors, user devices, or enterprise silos. FedAvg suits IID data with fast convergence via multiple local epochs; FedProx handles nonIID/heterogeneous clients (e.g., varying compute) through L2 regularization ($\mu||w - w\_prev||^2$); SCAFFOLD excels in highly skewed distributions by maintaining per-client control vectors that reduce client drift during multi-step local optimization.

This triad covers core DAI use cases: FedAvg for baseline scalability, FedProx for robust edge deployment, SCAFFOLD for academic-grade convergence under real-world data skew.

Local training capabilities

Worker nodes perform federated learning operations on their local data, executing gradient computations, parameter updates, and model validation without ever exposing raw data to the network. This capability is fundamental to privacy-preserving AI, where data sovereignty must be maintained while still enabling collaborative learning. Worker nodes implement sophisticated cryptographic protocols to ensure that only encrypted or differentially private model updates are shared with the broader network.

Inference service provision

Worker nodes serve as distributed inference engines beyond training responsibilities, providing AI predictions and analysis services to end users and applications. The decentralized nature of these services ensures high availability and geographic distribution, reducing latency and eliminating single points of failure that plague centralized AI services.

Resource contribution and verification

Worker nodes contribute computational resources like **central processing unit** (**CPU**), **graphics processing unit** (**GPU**), memory, and storage to the network in exchange for token rewards. Blockchain-based mechanisms verify and record these contributions, creating a transparent accounting of each node's participation and ensuring fair compensation for resource provision.

Coordination nodes orchestrating distributed intelligence

Coordination nodes serve as the nervous system of DAI networks, managing the complex orchestration required to coordinate learning processes across thousands of autonomous participants. These nodes do not centralize control but rather facilitate consensus-driven coordination through blockchain-enabled governance mechanisms.

Model aggregation and consensus

Aggregation consensus focuses on combining model updates from worker nodes into a reliable global AI model using algorithms like weighted averaging (e.g., FedAvg) enhanced by **Byzantine fault tolerance** (**BFT**) to filter malicious or faulty contributions, while blockchain consensus ensures agreement on the immutable ledger of transactions, blocks, and network state via mechanisms like PoW or PoS.

Coordination nodes handle model aggregation at the application layer with sophisticated checks for update validity before incorporation, preventing poisoning attacks without needing full network-wide ledger finality, whereas blockchain consensus operates at the infrastructure layer, securing the shared state (e.g., model versions, rewards) across all nodes via cryptographic agreement on blocks.

This layered approach maintains efficiency, as aggregation tolerates up to 1/3 faulty nodes via BFT-inspired filtering while blockchain provides tamper-proof auditability and incentives without slowing iterative AI training, and conflating them risks scalability issues since full blockchain finality per update would bottleneck high-frequency model rounds in DAI systems.

Training round management

The coordination of distributed training requires precise timing and sequencing of operations across the network. Coordination nodes manage training epochs, coordinate parameter broadcasts, and ensure that all participants remain synchronized throughout complex multi-stage learning processes.

Network governance facilitation

Beyond technical coordination, these nodes facilitate democratic governance processes within the network. They manage proposal voting, implement governance decisions, and ensure that network evolution occurs through transparent, consensus-driven processes recorded on the blockchain.

Storage nodes preserving network memory

Storage nodes provide the persistent memory layer of DAI networks, maintaining critical data structures, model checkpoints, and historical records that enable continuous learning and network evolution. These nodes implement advanced distributed storage strategies that ensure data availability while maintaining privacy and security requirements.

Distributed model repository

Storage nodes collectively maintain a distributed repository of model states, training checkpoints, and versioning information. This distributed approach ensures that no single entity controls access to the network's accumulated intelligence while providing reliable access to model assets for authorized participants.

Blockchain integration

The integration with blockchain technology allows storage nodes to maintain cryptographically verifiable records of data operations, ensuring the integrity and authenticity of stored information. Smart contracts govern access permissions and automate data lifecycle management processes.

Privacy-preserving storage

Advanced storage nodes implement homomorphic encryption and other cryptographic techniques that allow them to store and serve encrypted data without ever accessing plaintext information. This capability is essential for maintaining data privacy while enabling network-wide data sharing and collaboration.

Validation nodes ensuring network integrity

Validation nodes serve as the quality assurance layer of DAI networks, implementing sophisticated verification mechanisms that ensure the integrity, security, and quality of all network operations. The following nodes prevent malicious attacks, detect corrupted data or models, and maintain the overall health of the DAI ecosystem:

- **Model quality assessment**: Validation nodes implement advanced testing and verification protocols that assess the quality, accuracy, and safety of AI models before network deployment, including adversarial testing, bias detection, and performance validation across diverse datasets and scenarios, with acceptance thresholds defined through decentralized governance votes or protocol constants set by token holder consensus to ensure adaptability and community accountability.

- **Consensus participation**: As key participants in blockchain consensus mechanisms, validation nodes help secure the network's transaction history and ensure that governance decisions are properly implemented. Their role in consensus extends beyond simple transaction validation to include verification of AI-specific operations like model updates and training round completions.
- **Security monitoring**: Validation nodes continuously monitor network operations for signs of malicious activity, coordinated attacks, or system anomalies. They implement sophisticated anomaly detection algorithms that can identify unusual patterns in model behavior, training performance, or network communication that might indicate security threats.

Incentive nodes managing economic coordination

Incentive nodes manage the economic mechanisms that drive participation and ensure the long-term sustainability of DAI networks. The following nodes implement token economics, manage reward distribution, and facilitate the market mechanisms that align individual incentives with collective network benefits:

- **Token distribution management**: Incentive nodes execute smart contracts that calculate and distribute token rewards based on node contributions, performance metrics, and network governance parameters. This process requires sophisticated accounting of computational contributions, data quality provisions, and consensus participation.
- **Market mechanism implementation**: Advanced DAI networks implement sophisticated market mechanisms for trading AI services, data access rights, and computational resources. Incentive nodes facilitate these markets by managing pricing mechanisms, matching buyers and sellers, and ensuring fair and transparent transactions.
- **Reputation system maintenance**: Long-term network health depends on accurate reputation systems that track node behavior over time. Incentive nodes maintain these reputation ledgers, implementing algorithms that reward consistent positive contributions while identifying and penalizing malicious or unreliable participants.

Peer-to-peer communication protocols

The communication infrastructure of DAI networks must support diverse types of data exchange, from high-frequency gradient updates during distributed training to low-latency inference requests and consensus messages. Traditional peer-to-peer protocols, designed for file sharing or general-purpose networking, are insufficient for the specialized requirements of AI workloads that demand high throughput, low latency, and sophisticated failure handling.

AI-optimized message passing

AI-optimized message passing ensures efficient data exchange tailored to machine learning requirements. DAI networks require specialized message passing protocols that can efficiently handle the unique characteristics of machine learning data structures. Model parameters, gradients, and activation patterns have distinct statistical properties that can be leveraged for more efficient compression and transmission protocols, with established theoretical convergence guarantees (e.g., $O(1/T)$ rates for error-feedback schemes like EF21 under contractive compression) addressing practitioner concerns about training stability. The following three core optimization techniques address these challenges:

- **Gradient compression and aggregation**: During distributed training, nodes must exchange gradient information that often contains significant redundancy. Advanced communication protocols implement sophisticated compression techniques designed explicitly for gradient data, including top-k sparsification, quantization, and error feedback mechanisms. These techniques can reduce communication overhead by orders of magnitude while preserving training convergence properties.
- **Adaptive batching strategies**: Communication protocols adapt their batching strategies based on current network conditions and the specific requirements of ongoing AI workloads. During periods of high network congestion, protocols might batch multiple minor updates into a single message, while during low-latency inference operations, they prioritize immediate message delivery.
- **Content-aware routing**: Unlike traditional networking protocols that treat all data equally, AI-optimized protocols implement content-aware routing that prioritizes different types of AI data based on their importance to ongoing operations. Critical model updates during the final stages of training might receive priority routing, while routine maintenance messages can tolerate longer delays.

Blockchain-integrated communication

Blockchain-integrated communication enables trustless, verifiable data exchange with economic incentives. The integration of blockchain technology into peer-to-peer communication protocols creates new possibilities for secure, verifiable, and incentivized data exchange. Traditional networking protocols lack built-in mechanisms for ensuring data integrity or compensating participants for communication services. The following three mechanisms leverage blockchain to enhance communication reliability:

- **Cryptographically verified messages**: All communication within blockchain-integrated networks can be cryptographically signed and verified, ensuring that messages originate from authorized nodes and have not been tampered with during transmission. This capability is crucial for maintaining the integrity of model updates and preventing malicious actors from injecting corrupted data into training processes.
- **Incentivized relay networks**: Blockchain technology enables the creation of incentivized relay networks where nodes are compensated for forwarding messages on behalf of other participants. This creates a robust communication infrastructure that does not rely on altruistic behavior, ensuring reliable message delivery even in adversarial environments.
- **Smart contract-mediated protocols**: Advanced communication protocols can be governed by smart contracts that automatically adapt protocol parameters based on network conditions, node performance, and economic incentives. These self-modifying protocols can optimize themselves for changing conditions without requiring manual intervention or centralized control.

Gossip protocols for AI networks

Gossip protocols for AI networks enable scalable, fault-tolerant information dissemination across decentralized systems. Gossip protocols provide an elegant solution for disseminating information throughout decentralized networks in a scalable and fault-tolerant manner. However, traditional gossip protocols must be adapted to handle the specific requirements of AI workloads and the integration with blockchain systems. The following three adaptations optimize gossip for DAI:

- **Model state synchronization**: Gossip protocols can efficiently synchronize model states across large networks by probabilistically selecting communication partners and gradually propagating updates throughout the system. This approach provides eventual consistency while maintaining scalability as the network grows.
- **Epidemic learning algorithms**: Advanced implementations combine gossip protocols with epidemic learning algorithms that allow knowledge to spread throughout the network in a manner analogous to biological disease transmission. These algorithms can adapt their propagation strategies based on the importance and urgency of different types of information.
- **Blockchain-anchored gossip**: Networks achieve eventual consistency for gossip messages by anchoring gossip protocols to periodic blockchain checkpoints, ensuring messages align with the authoritative blockchain state at checkpoint times while leveraging epidemic propagation's speed and scalability for off-chain dissemination. Between checkpoints, nodes may hold divergent views, but convergence occurs upon the next anchor. Eventual consistency is achieved as gossip propagates rapidly via flooding, with final settlement deferring to blockchain consensus at checkpoints

every N blocks or epochs, where nodes reconcile via proofs of inclusion or exclusion against the checkpoint. Benefits retained include low-latency local coordination, with blockchain handling global ordering only as needed to avoid full-on chain gossip overhead. Trade-offs involve temporary forks, possible pre-checkpoints, mitigated by short intervals and cryptographic commitments such as Merkle proofs. In Hedera-like systems, gossip about gossip disseminates events with hashgraph virtual voting, ensuring asynchronous Byzantine fault tolerance, while anchoring to a blockchain such as Ethereum provides durable finality, blending gossip efficiency with checkpoint durability.

Quality of service management

Quality of service management guarantees predictable performance for diverse AI operations. DAI networks must provide quality of service guarantees for different types of operations, from real-time inference services to long-running training jobs. Traditional best-effort networking is insufficient for mission-critical AI applications that require predictable performance characteristics. The following three mechanisms ensure reliable service delivery:

- **Traffic classification and prioritization**: Communication protocols implement sophisticated traffic classification mechanisms that can identify different types of AI workloads and apply appropriate quality of service policies. Real-time inference requests might receive guaranteed low-latency delivery, while batch training updates can tolerate higher delays in exchange for improved throughput.
- **Congestion control for AI workloads**: Traditional congestion control algorithms are designed for general-purpose network traffic and do not account for the bursty, synchronized nature of AI communication patterns. Specialized congestion control mechanisms adapt to the periodic synchronization points in distributed training and the sudden traffic spikes associated with model deployment and inference scaling.
- **Fault-tolerant multicast**: Many AI operations require synchronized communication among multiple nodes, such as parameter broadcasting during training or coordinated inference serving. Fault-tolerant multicast protocols ensure that these operations can complete successfully even when individual nodes fail or network partitions occur.

Data distribution and replication

The management of data within DAI networks presents unique challenges that extend far beyond traditional distributed systems. AI workloads generate, consume, and transform vast amounts of heterogeneous data, from raw training datasets to model parameters, gradients, activations, and inference results. This data must be distributed across the network in ways that optimize performance, ensure privacy, maintain consistency, and provide fault tolerance.

Intelligent data partitioning strategies

Intelligent data partitioning strategies optimize performance while preserving data integrity and privacy. Effective data partitioning is crucial for achieving optimal performance in DAI networks. AI data requires more sophisticated partitioning strategies that consider the mathematical properties of machine learning algorithms and the interdependencies between different data elements, unlike traditional distributed databases that can partition data based on simple key-value relationships. The following three strategies address AI-specific partitioning challenges:

- **Feature-aware partitioning**: Advanced partitioning strategies consider the feature relationships within training datasets, ensuring that related features are co-located to minimize communication overhead during distributed training operations. This approach requires a deep understanding of the underlying AI models and their computational patterns to make optimal partitioning decisions.

- **Temporal partitioning for sequential data**: Many AI applications involve sequential or temporal data that must be partitioned while preserving temporal relationships. Specialized partitioning algorithms ensure that sequential dependencies are maintained across partition boundaries, enabling efficient distributed processing of time-series data, natural language sequences, and video streams.

- **Privacy-preserving partitioning**: Data partitioning strategies must also consider privacy requirements, ensuring that sensitive information is distributed in ways that prevent unauthorized inference or reconstruction of private data. This involves sophisticated techniques like differential privacy-aware partitioning and secure multi-party computation protocols that can operate on distributed encrypted data.

Blockchain-enabled data provenance

Blockchain-enabled data provenance creates immutable records of data lifecycles and usage. The integration of blockchain technology provides unprecedented capabilities for tracking data provenance and ensuring data integrity throughout its lifecycle within the decentralized network. This capability is essential for maintaining trust in collaborative AI systems where data from multiple sources must be combined and processed. The following three mechanisms utilize blockchain to enable data governance:

- **Immutable data lineage**: Blockchain technology enables the creation of immutable records that track the complete lineage of data as it flows through the network, including transformations, aggregations, and derivative datasets. This capability is crucial for regulatory compliance, scientific reproducibility, and debugging complex AI systems.

- **Cryptographic data integrity**: Every data operation within the network can be cryptographically verified and recorded on the blockchain, ensuring that data has not been corrupted or maliciously modified during storage or transmission. This provides strong guarantees about data integrity that are essential for maintaining the quality of AI training processes.

- **Automated data governance**: Smart contracts can implement sophisticated data governance policies that automatically enforce data usage restrictions, access controls, and retention policies. These automated governance mechanisms ensure that data is used in compliance with privacy regulations and organizational policies without requiring manual oversight.

Adaptive replication mechanisms

Data replication within DAI networks must balance availability, performance, and resource efficiency while adapting to the dynamic nature of AI workloads. Traditional replication strategies that maintain fixed numbers of replicas are insufficient for AI applications where data access patterns can vary dramatically based on training schedules, model deployment patterns, and inference demand. The following three mechanisms optimize replication in DAI:

- **Demand-driven replication**: Advanced replication mechanisms monitor data access patterns and automatically adjust replication levels based on demand. Frequently accessed model parameters might be replicated across many nodes to improve access latency, while rarely used historical data might be maintained with minimal replication to conserve storage resources.
- **Geographic replication for global networks**: Global DAI networks must consider the geographic distribution of replicas to minimize latency and ensure compliance with data sovereignty requirements. Intelligent replication strategies place data copies in optimal geographic locations based on usage patterns, regulatory requirements, and network topology.
- **Consensus-based replication management**: The number and placement of replicas can be managed through blockchain-based consensus mechanisms, ensuring that replication decisions are made democratically and transparently. This prevents any single entity from controlling data availability and ensures that replication strategies serve the collective interests of the network.

Privacy-preserving data sharing

Privacy-preserving data sharing enables collaborative learning without exposing sensitive information. One of the most significant advantages of DAI networks is their ability to enable collaborative learning while preserving data privacy. This requires sophisticated approaches to data sharing that allow nodes to contribute their data to collective learning processes without revealing sensitive information. Data distribution strategies must seamlessly integrate with federated learning protocols that allow models to be trained on distributed data without ever centralizing the raw datasets. This requires careful coordination of data access patterns with training schedules and gradient aggregation processes. The following three cryptographic techniques ensure data privacy during collaboration:

- **Homomorphic encryption support**: Advanced data distribution systems can store and process encrypted data homomorphically, allowing computations to be performed on encrypted datasets without ever decrypting them. This capability enables true privacy-preserving collaborative AI where sensitive data never leaves its encrypted state.
- **Secure multi-party computation**: Data sharing protocols can implement secure multi-party computation techniques that allow multiple nodes to jointly compute functions over their combined datasets without revealing their individual data contributions. These protocols enable sophisticated collaborative analytics while maintaining strict privacy guarantees.

Load balancing and resource management

The dynamic and heterogeneous nature of DAI networks creates complex challenges for load balancing and resource management. Unlike traditional distributed systems that deal with relatively uniform computational tasks, AI workloads exhibit extreme variability in resource requirements, execution times, and interdependencies. Training a large language model might require sustained GPU computation for hours or days, while inference requests demand low-latency responses with unpredictable arrival patterns.

Dynamic resource allocation algorithms

Dynamic resource allocation algorithms enable DAI networks to match computational demand with heterogeneous node capabilities in real time. Effective resource management in DAI networks requires algorithms that can dynamically allocate computational resources based on real-time demand, node capabilities, and economic incentives. These algorithms must operate without centralized control while ensuring fair and efficient resource utilization across the network. Key strategies include:

- **Capability-aware task assignment**: Resource allocation algorithms must consider the specific capabilities of different nodes when assigning AI tasks. GPU-accelerated training tasks should be preferentially assigned to nodes with appropriate hardware, while CPU-intensive inference tasks can be distributed across a broader range of nodes. This capability matching ensures optimal resource utilization and task performance.
- **Multi-objective optimization**: Resource allocation decisions must balance multiple competing objectives, including minimizing task completion time, maximizing network throughput, ensuring fair resource distribution, and optimizing economic efficiency. Advanced algorithms implement multi-objective optimization techniques that can find Pareto-optimal solutions that balance these competing requirements.

- **Predictive resource scheduling**: Machine learning techniques can be applied to predict future resource demands based on historical usage patterns, enabling proactive resource allocation that prevents bottlenecks before they occur. These predictive models consider factors such as training schedules, inference demand patterns, and node availability patterns to optimize resource allocation decisions.

Blockchain-based resource markets

Blockchain-based resource markets transform compute, storage, and bandwidth into tradable digital commodities within DAI networks. The integration of blockchain technology enables the creation of sophisticated resource markets where computational resources can be traded dynamically based on supply and demand. These markets provide economic incentives for resource contribution while ensuring efficient allocation of scarce resources. Three core mechanisms structure these markets:

- **Dynamic pricing mechanisms**: Resource markets implement dynamic pricing algorithms that adjust resource prices based on current supply and demand conditions. During periods of high demand, prices increase to encourage additional resource contribution and discourage non-essential usage. These pricing mechanisms help balance supply and demand while providing fair compensation for resource providers.
- **Reputation-based resource allocation**: Long-term resource allocation decisions can consider node reputation scores that reflect historical performance, reliability, and contribution to the network. Nodes with higher reputation scores might receive preferential access to scarce resources or better compensation for their resource contributions.
- **Automated resource contracts**: Smart contracts can automate the process of resource allocation and payment, eliminating the need for manual intervention in resource trading. These contracts can implement complex service level agreements that specify performance requirements, failure handling procedures, and compensation mechanisms.

Fault-tolerant load distribution

Fault-tolerant load distribution ensures that DAI networks maintain reliable operation despite node failures, churn, or adverse network conditions. DAI networks must continue operating effectively even when individual nodes fail or become unavailable. This requires sophisticated load-balancing mechanisms that can detect failures, redistribute workloads, and maintain service quality despite node churn. The following three strategies are particularly important:

- **Redundant task execution**: Critical AI tasks can be executed redundantly across multiple nodes to ensure completion even if some nodes fail. The level of redundancy can be adjusted based on task importance, deadline constraints, and resource availability. Byzantine fault tolerance techniques ensure that correct results can be obtained even when some nodes produce incorrect outputs.

- **Graceful degradation strategies**: When network resources become constrained due to node failures or high demand, load balancing algorithms implement graceful degradation strategies that maintain core functionality while temporarily reducing non-essential services. These strategies ensure that the most important AI operations continue functioning even under adverse conditions.
- **Adaptive checkpointing**: Long-running AI tasks implement adaptive checkpointing mechanisms that save intermediate results at strategic points during computation. This allows failed tasks to be resumed from recent checkpoints rather than restarting from the beginning, significantly improving fault tolerance and resource efficiency.

Performance optimization through learning

Performance optimization through learning allows DAI infrastructure itself to behave like an adaptive AI system, continually refining how it uses resources. Advanced resource management systems can apply machine learning techniques to continuously improve their own performance by learning from historical allocation decisions and their outcomes. This creates self-optimizing systems that become more efficient over time. This creates self-optimizing systems that become more efficient over time. Key approaches include:

- **Reinforcement learning for resource allocation**: Reinforcement learning algorithms can learn optimal resource allocation policies by exploring different allocation strategies and learning from their success or failure. These algorithms can adapt to changing network conditions and workload patterns without requiring manual tuning of allocation parameters.
- **Transfer learning for new workloads**: When new types of AI workloads are introduced to the network, transfer learning techniques can apply knowledge gained from managing similar workloads to quickly develop effective resource allocation strategies for the new tasks.
- **Collaborative learning among networks**: Multiple DAI networks can share anonymized performance data and resource allocation strategies, enabling collaborative learning that benefits all participating networks. This approach accelerates the development of effective resource management techniques across the entire ecosystem of DAI systems.

Fault tolerance and recovery

The distributed and autonomous nature of DAI networks introduces numerous potential failure modes that must be anticipated and handled gracefully. Unlike centralized systems, where failures can be addressed through redundant infrastructure and manual intervention, decentralized networks must implement autonomous fault tolerance mechanisms that can detect, isolate, and recover from failures without central coordination.

Byzantine fault tolerance for AI workloads

Byzantine fault tolerance for AI workloads ensures that decentralized learning remains reliable even in adversarial environments. The adversarial environment of decentralized networks, where malicious actors might attempt to disrupt operations or corrupt results, requires robust Byzantine fault tolerance mechanisms specifically designed for AI applications. Traditional Byzantine fault tolerance algorithms must be extended to handle the unique characteristics of machine learning computations. Key enhancements include:

- **Model poisoning prevention**: Malicious nodes might attempt to corrupt AI models by contributing poisoned training data or malicious gradient updates. Advanced fault tolerance mechanisms implement statistical analysis techniques that can detect and filter out suspicious contributions before they affect the global model state. These techniques consider the statistical properties of legitimate model updates to identify anomalous contributions.
- **Consensus on continuous values**: Traditional Byzantine consensus algorithms are designed for discrete decisions, while AI applications often require consensus on continuous values such as model parameters and gradient updates. Specialized consensus algorithms have been developed that can achieve agreement on continuous values while tolerating Byzantine failures.
- **Incentive-compatible fault tolerance**: Economic incentives within blockchain-based networks can be designed to discourage malicious behavior and encourage honest participation in fault tolerance mechanisms. Nodes that consistently contribute to network security through reliable failure detection and recovery operations can receive additional token rewards.

Automated recovery mechanisms

Automated recovery mechanisms enable DAI networks to restore normal operations quickly and autonomously after failures. DAI networks must implement sophisticated automated recovery mechanisms that can restore normal operations after failures without requiring manual intervention. These mechanisms must be able to handle both individual node failures and more systemic network-wide issues. Core capabilities include:

- **Distributed checkpointing systems**: Training processes in decentralized networks implement distributed checkpointing systems that regularly save the global state across multiple nodes. When failures occur, these checkpoints enable rapid recovery of training processes without losing significant progress. The checkpointing systems use blockchain technology to ensure the integrity and consistency of saved states.
- **Self-healing network topology**: Network topology can automatically adapt to node failures by establishing new connections and redistributing responsibilities among

remaining nodes. These self-healing mechanisms ensure that network connectivity and functionality are maintained even as nodes join and leave the network unpredictably.

- **Predictive failure detection**: Machine learning techniques are applied to monitor node behavior and network performance metrics to predict potential failures before they occur. Early detection enables proactive migration of critical tasks and data to healthy nodes, minimizing the impact of failures on ongoing operations.

Data recovery and consistency

Data recovery and consistency mechanisms ensure that DAI networks can withstand data loss, corruption, and partitioning while preserving a coherent global state. Maintaining data consistency and enabling recovery from data loss or corruption is particularly challenging in DAI networks where data is distributed across many autonomous nodes. Advanced recovery mechanisms must ensure that data remains consistent and available despite node failures and network partitions. Key techniques include:

- **Erasure coding for model data**: Critical model data and training checkpoints are protected using erasure coding techniques that allow data recovery even when multiple storage nodes fail simultaneously. These techniques provide strong fault tolerance guarantees while minimizing storage overhead compared to simple replication strategies.
- **Blockchain-anchored consistency**: Data consistency is maintained through blockchain-anchored Merkle trees that provide cryptographic proof of data integrity. When inconsistencies are detected, the blockchain record serves as the authoritative source for resolving conflicts and restoring a consistent state.
- **Consensus-based recovery decisions**: When multiple nodes hold conflicting versions of critical data, consensus mechanisms determine which version is authoritative and should be used for recovery purposes. These decisions are made democratically through voting mechanisms that prevent any single node from unilaterally determining recovery outcomes.

Network partition handling

Network partition handling allows DAI networks to remain useful even when connectivity is fragmented and to safely reconcile once the network heals. Network partitions, where the decentralized network becomes split into isolated segments, present particularly challenging fault tolerance problems. AI operations must be designed to continue functioning within partitioned segments while ensuring that proper reconciliation occurs when connectivity is restored. The following three techniques address this challenge:

- **Partition-tolerant training algorithms**: Distributed training algorithms are designed to continue making progress even when the network becomes partitioned. Different partitions can continue training on their available data and then reconcile their model updates when connectivity is restored through sophisticated merging algorithms.

- **Conflict resolution mechanisms**: When network partitions are healed, conflicts may arise between the different states that evolved independently in each partition. Automated conflict resolution mechanisms use timestamps, version vectors, and consensus algorithms to determine how to merge conflicting states in ways that preserve the most valuable progress from each partition.
- **Economic incentives for partition healing**: Economic incentives encourage nodes to actively work toward healing network partitions by establishing connections across partition boundaries. Nodes that successfully bridge partitions and enable network healing receive additional token rewards for their contribution to network resilience.

Network security and authentication

Security in DAI networks encompasses multiple layers of protection, from individual node authentication and communication encryption to network-wide consensus mechanisms and economic security through tokenomics. The absence of centralized control requires distributed security mechanisms that can protect against both external attackers and malicious network participants. *Figure 3.2* details the multi-layered security and authentication framework required to protect the network from both external and internal threats. This defense-in-depth strategy ensures that compromised nodes cannot easily disrupt the global consensus state.

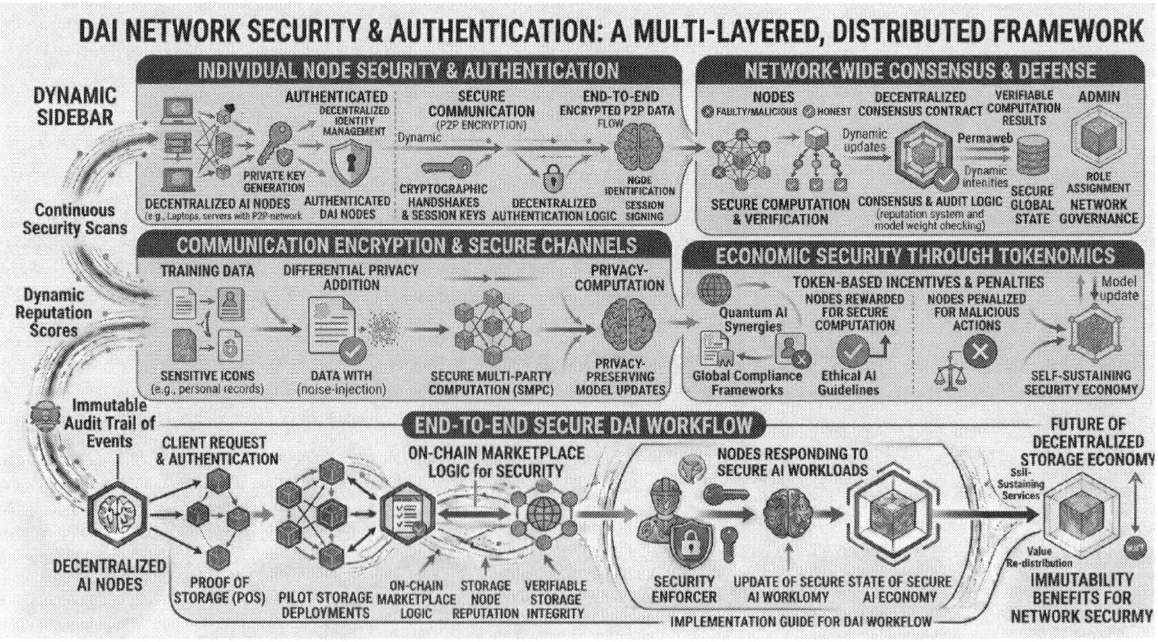

***Figure 3.2**: DAI network security and authentication*

Cryptographic identity and authentication

Cryptographic identity and authentication establish trusted participation in DAI networks without relying on centralized identity providers. Every participant in a DAI network must have a verifiable cryptographic identity that enables secure authentication and authorization. Decentralized networks use cryptographic key pairs and blockchain-based identity systems, unlike traditional systems that rely on username and password authentication backed by centralized identity providers. Core mechanisms include:

- **Self-sovereign identity systems**: Nodes maintain their own cryptographic identities without relying on external authorities for identity verification. These self-sovereign identity systems use digital signatures to prove identity and authenticate communications, while blockchain technology provides a decentralized infrastructure for identity verification and reputation tracking.
- **Multi-signature authentication**: Critical operations within the network require multi-signature authentication, where multiple authorized parties must approve transactions before they can be executed. This prevents single points of failure and ensures that important decisions reflect genuine consensus among network participants.
- **Zero-knowledge identity proofs**: Advanced authentication systems allow nodes to prove their identity and authorization without revealing sensitive information about their identity or capabilities. These **zero-knowledge** (**ZK**) proof systems enable privacy-preserving authentication that protects node operators while maintaining network security.

Secure communication protocols

Secure communication protocols ensure that high-volume, latency-sensitive DAI traffic remains confidential and tamper-proof. All communication within DAI networks must be encrypted and authenticated to prevent eavesdropping, man-in-the-middle attacks, and message tampering. The high-volume, latency-sensitive nature of AI workloads requires efficient encryption protocols that provide strong security without significantly impacting performance. Key capabilities include:

- **End-to-end encryption**: All data and model information exchanged between nodes is protected using end-to-end encryption that ensures only authorized recipients can access transmitted information. These encryption protocols use forward secrecy techniques that prevent historical data compromise even if current encryption keys are compromised.
- **Authenticated channels**: Communication channels between nodes implement authentication mechanisms that verify the identity of communication partners and detect any attempts to inject malicious messages into the network. These authenticated channels prevent impersonation attacks and ensure message integrity.

- **Traffic analysis resistance**: Advanced communication protocols implement techniques to resist traffic analysis attacks that might allow adversaries to infer information about network operations by observing communication patterns. These techniques include message padding, timing obfuscation, and decoy traffic generation.

Consensus security mechanisms

Consensus security mechanisms protect coordinated decision-making in DAI networks against economic and protocol-level attacks. The consensus mechanisms that coordinate DAI operations must be designed to resist various forms of attack while maintaining the democratic principles of decentralized governance. Economic incentives and cryptographic techniques work together to ensure the security and integrity of consensus processes. Key mechanisms include:

- **Stake-based security**: Security in blockchain-based consensus mechanisms is often based on economic stakes, where participants must commit valuable tokens to participate in consensus processes. Malicious behavior results in the loss of staked tokens, creating strong economic disincentives for attacks against the network.

- **Slashing conditions**: Automated mechanisms detect and punish malicious behavior through slashing conditions that automatically confiscate staked tokens when nodes violate consensus rules. These mechanisms ensure that malicious behavior is quickly detected and punished without requiring manual intervention.

- **Randomized committee selection**: Consensus processes use cryptographically secure randomness to select committees of nodes responsible for validating transactions and model updates. This randomization prevents adversaries from predicting which nodes will be responsible for validation, making targeted attacks more difficult.

Privacy-preserving security

Privacy-preserving security ensures that DAI networks remain both accountable and confidential. DAI networks must balance transparency requirements for security and accountability with privacy requirements for protecting sensitive data and preserving node anonymity. Advanced security mechanisms enable strong protection while maintaining necessary privacy guarantees. The following three key techniques support this balance:

- **Homomorphic encryption**: Security monitoring and anomaly detection can operate on homomorphically encrypted data, allowing network-wide security analysis without compromising the privacy of individual nodes or their data. These techniques enable comprehensive security monitoring while preserving data confidentiality.

- **Private information retrieval**: Nodes can query network databases and model repositories without revealing which specific information they are accessing. These private information retrieval techniques prevent adversaries from learning about node interests and capabilities based on their data access patterns.

- **Anonymous reputation systems**: Reputation and performance metrics can be tracked and maintained while preserving node anonymity through advanced cryptographic techniques. These systems enable merit-based resource allocation and decision-making while protecting node operator privacy.

Performance optimization

Achieving optimal performance in DAI networks requires sophisticated optimization techniques that operate across multiple layers of the system architecture. AI networks must also consider model quality, convergence speed, and resource efficiency while maintaining decentralization principles, unlike traditional distributed systems that primarily optimize for throughput and latency.

Computational optimization strategies

The heterogeneous nature of DAI networks, where nodes have varying computational capabilities and network connections, requires adaptive optimization strategies that can maximize overall system performance while accommodating diverse node characteristics. These strategies are:

- **Heterogeneity-aware algorithms**: Optimization algorithms must account for the significant differences in computational capabilities, network bandwidth, and energy constraints across network nodes. Advanced scheduling algorithms assign computational tasks based on node capabilities, ensuring that GPU-intensive operations are allocated to appropriate hardware while CPU-bound tasks can utilize a broader range of nodes.

- **Dynamic model compression**: Large AI models must be compressed for efficient transmission and storage across the network. Dynamic compression algorithms adapt compression ratios based on current network conditions, node capabilities, and model performance requirements. These algorithms can trade off model accuracy for improved communication efficiency when network resources are constrained.

- **Asynchronous optimization**: Traditional synchronous training requires all nodes to complete their computations before proceeding to the next training step, leading to performance bottlenecks when slower nodes hold up the entire network. Asynchronous optimization algorithms allow faster nodes to proceed without waiting for slower nodes, improving overall training throughput while maintaining convergence guarantees.

- **Network-level optimization**: Performance optimization must consider the network as a whole system, implementing techniques that improve global performance even when individual node performance varies significantly.

- **Intelligent caching systems**: Frequently accessed model parameters, datasets, and intermediate results are cached strategically throughout the network to minimize redundant computations and reduce communication overhead. Machine learning algorithms predict which data should be cached based on usage patterns and optimize cache placement to minimize access latency.
- **Adaptive routing optimization**: Network traffic is routed dynamically based on current congestion levels, node performance, and data priority. These adaptive routing systems use real-time network monitoring to select optimal paths for different types of AI traffic, ensuring that latency-sensitive operations receive priority while bulk data transfers utilize available bandwidth efficiently.
- **Load prediction and balancing**: Machine learning models predict future computational load based on historical patterns, planned training schedules, and inference demand forecasts. These predictions enable proactive load balancing that prevents bottlenecks before they occur and ensures optimal resource utilization across the network.
- **Economic optimization mechanisms**: The blockchain-based economic systems within DAI networks provide additional levers for performance optimization through market mechanisms and incentive alignment.
- **Performance-based incentives**: Token reward mechanisms can be designed to incentivize performance improvements by providing higher rewards for nodes that contribute superior computational performance, maintain high availability, or provide valuable specialized services to the network.
- **Dynamic pricing for resource optimization**: Market-based pricing mechanisms adjust resource costs based on supply and demand, encouraging efficient resource utilization. During peak demand periods, higher prices encourage additional resource contribution while discouraging non-essential resource consumption.
- **Reputation-based optimization**: Node reputation systems track long-term performance metrics and use this information to make optimization decisions. High-reputation nodes might receive preferential treatment in task assignment or access to premium network services, creating incentives for consistent high performance.
- **Quality of service management**: DAI networks must provide differentiated service levels for different types of applications and users while maintaining fairness and preventing resource monopolization by high-paying users.
- **Service level agreements**: Smart contracts implement automated service level agreements that guarantee specific performance characteristics for different classes of AI services. These agreements automatically monitor performance metrics and provide compensation when service levels are not met.
- **Priority queuing systems**: Network traffic and computational tasks are prioritized based on urgency, economic value, and service level requirements. Real-time inference

requests receive higher priority than batch training jobs, while critical system operations take precedence over user applications.

- **Congestion control**: Sophisticated congestion control mechanisms prevent network overload by implementing backpressure systems that slow down less critical operations when network resources become scarce. These mechanisms ensure that the network remains responsive even under high load conditions.

Monitoring and analytics

Comprehensive monitoring and analytics capabilities are essential for maintaining the health, performance, and security of DAI networks. Decentralized networks require distributed monitoring approaches that can provide network-wide visibility while respecting privacy and autonomy principles. This is unlike centralized systems, where monitoring can be implemented through centralized logging and analysis systems.

Distributed performance monitoring

Performance monitoring in DAI networks must capture metrics across multiple dimensions, including computational performance, network efficiency, model quality, and economic indicators. This monitoring must operate without centralized control while providing comprehensive visibility into network operations. The following are the monitoring methods:

- **Real-time metrics collection**: Nodes throughout the network collect and report performance metrics, including CPU and GPU utilization, memory usage, network bandwidth consumption, training convergence rates, and inference latency. These metrics are aggregated using privacy-preserving techniques that protect individual node information while providing network-wide visibility.
- **Model performance tracking**: Specialized monitoring systems track the quality and performance of AI models as they evolve through distributed training processes. These systems monitor metrics such as accuracy, loss functions, convergence rates, and generalization performance across different datasets and use cases.
- **Network health dashboards**: Blockchain-based systems maintain distributed dashboards that provide real-time visibility into network health, performance trends, and emerging issues. These dashboards are accessible to all network participants and provide transparency into network operations without compromising individual node privacy.

Anomaly detection systems

Automated anomaly detection is crucial for identifying security threats, performance problems, and system failures in large-scale decentralized networks where manual monitoring is impractical. The following are the detection systems:

- **Behavioral anomaly detection**: Machine learning algorithms analyze normal patterns of node behavior, network traffic, and system performance to identify anomalies that might indicate security threats, hardware failures, or malicious activity. These systems adapt to changing normal behavior patterns and can detect subtle anomalies that might escape rule-based detection systems.
- **Distributed attack detection**: Coordinated attacks against decentralized networks might involve multiple compromised nodes working together to disrupt operations or corrupt results. Advanced detection systems correlate activities across multiple nodes to identify coordinated attack patterns that might not be apparent when examining individual nodes in isolation.
- **Economic anomaly monitoring**: Unusual patterns in token transactions, resource utilization, or market behavior can indicate attempts to manipulate network economics or exploit system vulnerabilities. Specialized monitoring systems track economic metrics and alert network participants to suspicious patterns.

Privacy-preserving analytics

Analytics systems must be able to provide valuable insights about network operations while protecting the privacy of individual participants and their data. The following are the types of privacy-preserving analytics:

- **Federated analytics**: Analytics computations are performed in a federated manner where individual nodes contribute to aggregate statistics without revealing their individual data. These federated analytics systems can compute network-wide metrics while preserving node privacy through techniques such as differential privacy and secure aggregation.
- **ZK performance proofs**: Nodes can provide cryptographic proofs of their performance characteristics without revealing sensitive information about their operations or capabilities. These ZK proofs enable performance-based incentives and quality assurance without compromising operational privacy.
- **Homomorphic analysis**: Advanced analytics systems can perform computations on encrypted monitoring data, enabling comprehensive network analysis while maintaining data confidentiality. These systems provide network operators with valuable insights while ensuring that sensitive operational data remains protected.

Predictive analytics and optimization

Historical monitoring data can be analyzed to predict future network behavior and optimize system operations proactively. These predictions are:

- **Capacity planning**: Predictive models analyze historical usage patterns, growth trends, and seasonal variations to forecast future resource requirements and guide network expansion decisions. These models help ensure that network capacity remains adequate to meet growing demand.

- **Failure prediction**: Machine learning algorithms analyze patterns in performance metrics, error rates, and node behavior to predict potential failures before they occur. Early warning systems enable proactive maintenance and resource reallocation to prevent service disruptions.
- **Performance optimization recommendations**: Analytics systems can identify opportunities for performance improvements by analyzing patterns in resource utilization, communication flows, and computational efficiency. These recommendations can be implemented automatically or presented to network participants for democratic decision-making.

Case studies

These production deployments demonstrate how DAI architectures translate theory into measurable impact across healthcare, manufacturing, and large-scale research networks. Each case study validates architectural principles through quantified performance improvements, privacy guarantees, and economic sustainability metrics.

Flower labs implementation

The Flower framework demonstrates a practical implementation of the DAI topology for privacy-preserving federated learning. In healthcare applications, multiple hospitals maintain worker nodes that:

- Train models locally on sensitive patient data.
- Share only encrypted gradient updates through the coordination layer.
- Participate in global model aggregation without data exposure.
- Maintain compliance with HIPAA and GDPR regulations.

Unlike traditional federated learning, blockchain integration enables trustless coordination without central aggregation servers, eliminating single points of failure while maintaining medical data privacy.

Macrocosmos on Bittensor implementations

Macrocosmos on Bittensor demonstrates how a coordinated suite of specialized subnets can deliver an end-to-end DAI pipeline, from data ingestion through training to incentive alignment. The Macrocosmos implementation showcases advanced node specialization across five specialized subnets:

- **Pretraining subnet**: Handles large-scale model pretraining using the IOTA framework. IOTA enables permissionless, pipeline-parallel training of large language models on heterogeneous devices.
- **Fine-tuning subnet**: Manages task-specific model adaptation, allowing models pretrained on generic data to be specialized for downstream applications.
- **Data collection subnet**: Coordinates distributed data gathering to feed training and fine-tuning workflows with diverse, high-quality datasets.
- **Validation subnet**: Ensures model quality and prevents poisoning attacks by continuously evaluating miners' outputs and filtering low-quality or adversarial contributions.
- **Incentive subnet**: Manages token distribution based on contribution metrics, using Bittensor's incentive mechanisms and validator weights to reward useful work.

Performance metrics show that 1B+ parameter model training with plans to scale to larger parameter models has been successfully demonstrated, showing the practical viability of specialized node architectures.

FLChain implementation performance

FLChain implementation performance highlights how integrating blockchain with federated learning can improve scalability, auditability, and trust while keeping overheads manageable in edge and IoT environments. In particular, *Ren et al.* (2024) evaluate an FLChain-style architecture called FLCoin and demonstrate practical performance improvements over baseline **practical Byzantine fault tolerance** (**PBFT**)-based blockchain FL systems. Research by *Ren et al.* (2024) demonstrates practical performance improvements, such as:

- 90% reduction in communication overhead compared to traditional PBFT-based systems. This is achieved through a committee-based BFT protocol with linear instead of all-to-all communication patterns.
- 35% reduction in training time through optimized committee-based consensus, which keeps consensus latency low even as more nodes join training.
- Sub-3-second consensus latency even with increasing network participation, enabling timely global model aggregation in large federated deployments.

A key innovation of the system is the committee-based approach, which limits consensus operations to a subset of high-performing nodes. This has dramatically improved scalability while maintaining security through economic incentives.

Prime Intellect distributed training

Prime Intellect distributed training illustrates how a globally decentralized network can efficiently coordinate unreliable, heterogeneous compute into a single high-performance training system. Prime Intellect's decentralized training implementation demonstrates practical load balancing.

Architecture highlights include:

- **Heterogeneous hardware support**: GPU clusters, edge devices, and mobile phones can all participate as training workers under a unified orchestration layer.
- **Adaptive task splitting**: Large models are divided based on available resources, leveraging techniques like DiLoCo-style low-communication data parallelism and quantized gradient exchange.
- **Fault-tolerant scheduling**: Training jobs are automatically reallocated when nodes disconnect, using elastic process groups, live checkpoint recovery, and asynchronous synchronization to preserve progress.
- **Economic sustainability**: Token rewards align individual incentives with network performance, rewarding high-uptime, high-quality compute participation.

Performance results are as follows:

- Successfully trained 7B parameter models across 1000+ heterogeneous nodes.
- 23% improvement in training efficiency through optimal resource matching.
- 99.7% uptime despite 15% average node churn rate.

Healthcare AI security implementation

Healthcare AI security implementations for multi-hospital federated learning must satisfy strict privacy, safety, and compliance requirements while still enabling high-utility collaborative models across jurisdictions. A robust design combines regulatory controls, cryptographic protections, and Byzantine-resilient coordination so that hospitals can jointly train AI systems without exposing raw patient data or weakening institutional security postures.

Security requirements include:

- **Health Insurance Portability and Accountability Act** (**HIPAA**) compliance for patient data protection. This typically requires strong access controls, de-identification safeguards, and demonstrably low re-identification risk for any shared outputs.
- ZK verification of model quality, enabling verifiable proofs that updates or global models satisfy specified accuracy or performance thresholds without revealing underlying patient data.

- Resistance to model poisoning attacks through robust aggregation, anomaly detection on updates, and Byzantine-tolerant learning protocols.
- Regulatory audit trail maintenance, including tamper-evident logs of training rounds, participating institutions, privacy budgets, and model deployment changes.

Technical implementation includes:

- **Identity**: Self-sovereign **Decentralized Identifiers** (**DIDs**) for each hospital.
- **Communication**: **Transport Layer Security** (**TLS**) 1.3 with perfect forward secrecy to protect model updates in transit and limit the impact of key compromise.
- **Model updates**: Homomorphically encrypted gradients so the coordinator can aggregate updates without decrypting them, preserving confidentiality of local learning signals.
- **Validation**: Committee-based Byzantine fault tolerance to cross-check updates, filter anomalous contributions, and maintain a reliable global model despite faulty or adversarial clients.
- **Monitoring**: Encrypted anomaly detection with 96.2% accuracy, targeting high detection accuracy for abnormal or malicious behavior while keeping signals privacy-preserving.
- **Privacy**: Differential privacy with $\varepsilon=0.1$ for regulatory compliance.

The results are as follows:

- Zero security incidents over 18-month deployment.
- 7.4% privacy leakage under membership inference attacks (industry-leading).
- 91.8% attack detection rate for novel threats.
- Full regulatory compliance across all participating jurisdictions, aligning technical controls with HIPAA, GDPR, and sector-specific AI guidance for clinical deployments.

Production-ready frameworks

Production-ready frameworks show that decentralized and federated AI can already be deployed in real-world settings with open-source tooling, strong security, and integration into existing infrastructure. Production-ready DAI platforms have matured with robust, open-source implementations, such as:

- **Aether framework**: Complete DAI platform with modular agents, blockchain integration, and swarm intelligence capabilities.
- **Flower framework**: Production federated learning framework used in healthcare and finance for privacy-preserving collaborative AI.

- **FLCoin implementation**: Open-source blockchain-enabled federated learning with committee-based consensus and **InterPlanetary File System** (**IPFS**) integration.

Future research directions

Future research will extend DAI's security and interoperability frontier with emerging areas:

- **Quantum-resistant security**: Integration of post-quantum cryptographic methods to harden long-lived DAI networks against future quantum adversaries.
- **Cross-chain AI coordination**: Multi-blockchain federated learning protocols and interchain messaging for model updates, incentives, and proofs across heterogeneous ledgers.
- **Neuromorphic edge integration**: Hardware-optimized DAI architectures that leverage neuromorphic and ultra-low-power edge chips for real-time, on-device intelligence.
- **Regulatory-compliant privacy**: ZK proofs for AI model verification so that performance, fairness, and compliance properties can be attested on-chain without revealing sensitive data or model internals.

DAI architecture and enabled capabilities

The architecture of DAI networks represents a fundamental reimagining of how artificial intelligence systems can be designed, deployed, and operated. These networks create new possibilities for collaborative AI development that preserve privacy, ensure transparency, and democratize access to advanced AI capabilities by leveraging blockchain technology and distributed systems principles.

Architectural building blocks synthesis

Architectural building blocks synthesis describes how the major technical layers of a DAI network fit together into an integrated whole. The ten key architectural components explored in this chapter interlock to form a cohesive DAI system that is greater than the sum of its parts. Together, they define how intelligence, data, and incentives flow through the network to deliver scalable, trustworthy AI.

- **Network topology and node specialization**: Provide the structural foundation, with intelligent topology designs enabling efficient communication while specialized node types optimize resource utilization and ensure comprehensive functionality across training, inference, storage, validation, and economic coordination.
- **Communication and data management**: Layers ensure that information flows efficiently throughout the network while maintaining privacy and security. Advanced peer-to-peer protocols handle the unique requirements of AI workloads, while

sophisticated data distribution strategies balance performance, availability, and privacy requirements.

- **Operational excellence through automation**: It is achieved through advanced load balancing, fault tolerance, and performance optimization mechanisms that ensure the network operates efficiently and reliably without centralized control. These systems adapt dynamically to changing conditions and self-optimize based on historical performance data.
- **Security and monitoring infrastructure**: Provides comprehensive protection against attacks while maintaining transparency and accountability. Multi-layered security mechanisms protect against both external threats and malicious participants, while distributed monitoring systems provide visibility into network operations without compromising privacy.

Synergistic effects and emergent properties

The integration of these architectural components creates emergent properties that would not be possible in traditional centralized AI systems. These emergent properties include:

- **Collective intelligence**: The network as a whole becomes more intelligent than any individual node, with distributed learning processes enabling the development of AI capabilities that no single participant could achieve independently.
- **Adaptive resilience**: The combination of fault tolerance mechanisms, self-healing topologies, and economic incentives creates networks that become more robust and efficient over time, adapting to new challenges and optimizing themselves continuously.
- **Democratic innovation**: Blockchain-based governance mechanisms ensure that network evolution is driven by community consensus rather than centralized control, enabling innovation that serves the collective interests of all participants.

Design principles for practitioners

The architectural patterns and techniques presented in this chapter are guided by several key design principles that practitioners should consider when building DAI systems. These principles are:

- **Autonomy with coordination**: Individual nodes must be able to operate autonomously while contributing to collective objectives through sophisticated coordination mechanisms that do not require centralized control.
- **Privacy by design**: Privacy protection must be built into the fundamental architecture rather than added as an afterthought, with techniques such as federated learning, homomorphic encryption, and zero-knowledge proofs integrated throughout the system.

- **Economic sustainability**: Long-term network health requires carefully designed economic incentives that align individual node interests with collective network benefits, creating sustainable ecosystems that can grow and evolve over time.
- **Scalability through distribution**: System architecture must be designed to scale horizontally by adding more nodes rather than relying on increasingly powerful centralized infrastructure, enabling networks to grow organically as demand increases.

Conclusion

Through careful attention to these architectural principles and systematic implementation of the techniques and patterns presented in this chapter, practitioners can build DAI networks that provide superior capabilities while maintaining the transparency, privacy, and democratic governance that make these systems truly revolutionary. The future of artificial intelligence lies not in centralized control but in distributed intelligence systems that empower individuals and communities while creating collective capabilities that benefit all of humanity.

The next chapter translates these principles into smart contract patterns for real-world DAI deployments.

Chapter 4
Smart Contracts for AI Applications

Introduction

Smart contracts represent a revolutionary approach to automating complex agreements and processes on blockchain networks. When specifically designed for AI applications, these self-executing contracts unlock unprecedented possibilities for DAI systems. This chapter explores the critical intersection of smart contract technology and AI applications, providing comprehensive guidance on designing, implementing, and deploying contracts that can effectively manage AI models, coordinate distributed computation, and facilitate secure AI collaboration.

Traditional AI systems often suffer from centralization, opacity, and limited interoperability. In DAI architectures, heavy AI computation, such as model training and large-scale inference, remains off-chain on specialized compute infrastructure, while smart contracts run on-chain to orchestrate these processes, enforce rules, verify submitted results, and settle payments. By separating off-chain computation from on-chain coordination in this way, smart contracts address fundamental challenges by providing transparent, trustless mechanisms for AI model registration, automated payment systems, and secure data access controls. Through careful contract design, developers can create robust AI ecosystems that operate autonomously while maintaining security, efficiency, and fairness.

This chapter covers ten essential topics that form the foundation of smart contract development for AI applications. Readers will learn industry-standard design patterns, master Solidity programming techniques specific to AI use cases, understand model management strategies, implement automated payment systems, establish comprehensive security frameworks, and optimize contracts for production deployment. Each section builds upon previous concepts while providing practical examples and real-world applications.

Structure

The chapter covers the following topics:

- Smart contract design patterns for AI
- Solidity programming for AI applications
- Code organization and modularity
- AI model registration and management
- Automated payment and reward systems
- Data access control and permissions
- Oracle integration for external data
- Contract testing and validation
- Gas optimization techniques
- Security best practices
- Implementation roadmap and future directions

Objectives

Smart contracts represent the programmable foundation of DAI systems, serving as autonomous digital agents that execute predetermined logic without intermediaries. This chapter equips you to design, develop, and deploy smart contracts engineered for AI applications within blockchain networks. As the critical middleware between AI models and blockchain infrastructure, smart contracts enable trustless, transparent, and economically sustainable AI ecosystems. You will master sophisticated contract architectures using factory, registry, proxy, and DAO patterns optimized for AI workloads; write gas-optimized Solidity code with complex data structures for AI metadata and real-time event coordination.

The chapter will also enable the implementation of comprehensive model lifecycle management, including registration, version control, performance tracking, and community-driven validation. Engineering sustainable tokenomic models with automated payment distribution and dynamic pricing mechanisms, implementing multi-layered access control combining **role-based access control** (**RBAC**)/**attribute-based access control** (**ABAC**) approaches with zero-knowledge proofs, are areas this chapter touches, along with secure multi-party computation and decentralized identity systems. You will design oracle architectures with AI-enhanced validation and cross-chain capabilities for tamper-proof external data access and achieve testing expertise through advanced security audits, gas optimization, and comprehensive testing strategies specific to AI-blockchain integrations.

By the chapter's end, you will possess the architectural vision and hands-on expertise to build the programmable infrastructure powering next-generation decentralized AI networks.

Smart contract design patterns for AI

This section unveils a tailored set of smart contract design patterns that address the unique demands of DAI systems. Moving beyond traditional factory and registry models, it introduces the model-factory pattern for standardized AI model deployment, the proxy-upgrade pattern enabling seamless model logic evolution without changing contract addresses, and the task-registry pattern for decoupling training jobs from model definitions. Building on these, the access-oriented pattern weaves role- and attribute-based permission layers directly into contract logic. At the same time, the economic incentive pattern embeds on-chain token flows and micropayment streams to reward data providers, trainers, and validators. Together, these patterns form a modular blueprint that empowers developers to architect robust, extensible, and future-proof smart contracts at the heart of DAI networks. How these established smart contract design patterns unlock automation and immutability for decentralized AI services is structurally diagrammed in *Figure 4.1*. It provides a blueprint for autonomous execution without human intervention and to ensure long-term resilience, how these established smart contract design patterns unlock automation and immutability for decentralized AI services.

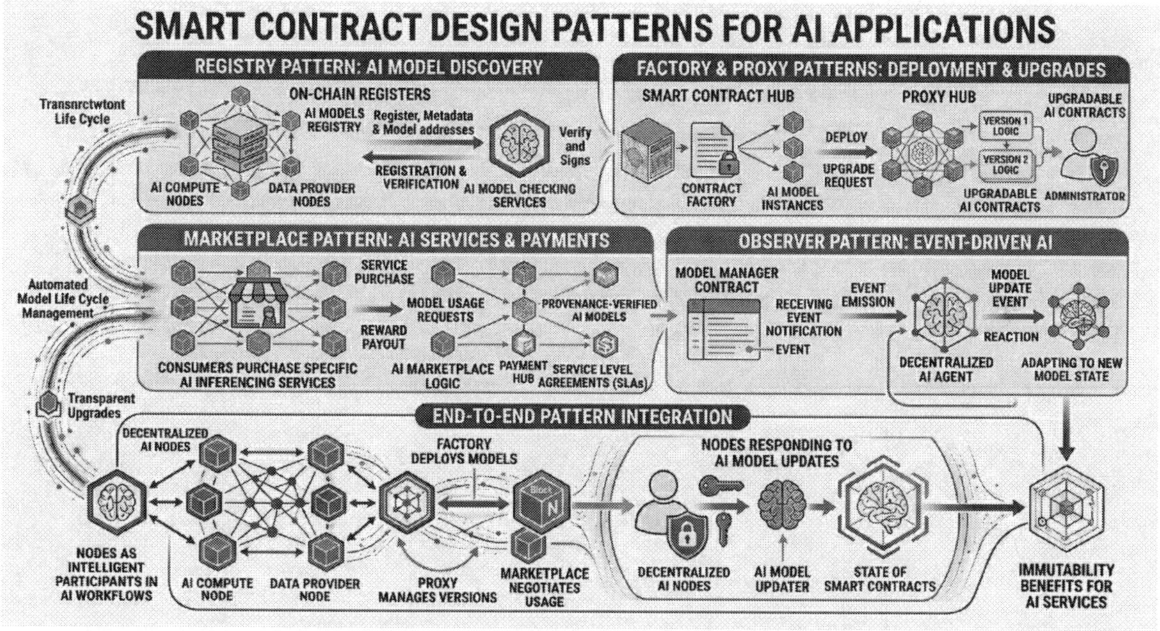

***Figure 4.1**: Smart contract design patterns for AI applications*

Factory pattern for AI model creation

The factory pattern serves as a cornerstone design pattern for creating and managing multiple instances of AI model contracts. This pattern enables efficient deployment of standardized AI model contracts while maintaining consistency across the ecosystem. In DAI networks, the factory pattern facilitates the creation of model-specific contracts that inherit common functionality while allowing for customization. The fundamental concept behind the factory pattern in AI applications lies in separating the creation logic from the actual implementation. This separation allows for standardized deployment processes while maintaining flexibility for different AI model types.

Code example for the high-level factory pattern for model deployment is as follows:

```
// SPDX-License-Identifier: MIT
pragma solidity ^0.8.19;
contract AIModelFactory {
    address[] public deployedModels;
    mapping(address => bool) public isValidModel;

    // Include modelHash for traceability; you could also add a version or
metadataHash here.
    event ModelDeployed(
        address indexed modelAddress,
        address indexed creator,
        string modelType,
        bytes32 modelHash,
        uint256 initialPrice
    );

    function createAIModel(
        string memory _modelName,
        string memory _modelType,
        bytes32 _modelHash,
        uint256 _initialPrice
    ) public returns (address) {
        // Basic input validation
        require(_modelHash != bytes32(0), "Invalid model hash");
        require(_initialPrice > 0, "Initial price must be > 0");
        AIModel newModel = new AIModel(
            _modelName,
            _modelType,
            _modelHash,
            _initialPrice,
            msg.sender
        );
        address modelAddr = address(newModel);
        deployedModels.push(modelAddr);
        isValidModel[modelAddr] = true;
```

```
        emit ModelDeployed(modelAddr, msg.sender, _modelType, _modelHash,
_initialPrice);
        return modelAddr;
    }
}
```

For the text around this example, direct deployment with **`new AIModel()`** is simple but can become expensive at scale.

For large DAI ecosystems, consider:

- CREATE2 for deterministic addresses, or
- The minimal proxy (EIP-1167) pattern to deploy many lightweight instances cheaply.

Note:

- **`_modelHash` is validated to avoid registering empty/placeholder models.**
- **`initialPrice` > 0 prevents nonsensical pricing.**
- **Emitting `modelHash` (or a separate `metadataHash`/version field if you add one) improves auditability and traceability.**
- **For production-scale deployments, CREATE2 and EIP1167 are preferred patterns for gas efficiency and deterministic addressing.**

The factory pattern provides several advantages for AI applications. It ensures consistent contract interfaces across all deployed models, facilitates model discovery through centralized registration, enables bulk operations across multiple models, and maintains upgrade paths for contract logic. This pattern is particularly valuable in federated learning scenarios where multiple participants need to deploy compatible model contracts.

Registry pattern for model discovery

The registry pattern complements the factory pattern by providing a centralized directory for AI model discovery and verification. This pattern enables efficient searching, filtering, and validation of AI models within the decentralized network. The registry maintains metadata about models, their capabilities, and their current status.

Code example for the high-level registry pattern for model discovery is as follows:

```
// SPDX-License-Identifier: MIT
pragma solidity ^0.8.19;
contract AIModelRegistry {
    struct ModelInfo {
        address modelContract;
        string name;
        string category;
```

```
        bytes32 metadataHash;
        uint256 reputation;
        bool isActive;
        address owner;
    }
    mapping(bytes32 => ModelInfo) public models;
    mapping(address => bool) public approvedPublishers; // or use
AccessControl
    uint256 public minRegistrationStake;                // optional anti-spam
stake
    mapping(bytes32 => uint256) public modelStake;      // stake per model
    address public admin;
    modifier onlyAdmin() {
        require(msg.sender == admin, "Not admin");
        _;
    }
    modifier onlyPublisher() {
        require(approvedPublishers[msg.sender], "Not approved publisher");
        _;
    }

    constructor(uint256 _minRegistrationStake) {
        admin = msg.sender;
        minRegistrationStake = _minRegistrationStake;
        approvedPublishers[msg.sender] = true; // bootstrap
    }

    function approvePublisher(address _publisher) external onlyAdmin {
        approvedPublishers[_publisher] = true;
    }

    function setMinRegistrationStake(uint256 _amount) external onlyAdmin {
        minRegistrationStake = _amount;
    }

    // If you want a stake requirement, make this function payable
    function registerModel(
        bytes32 _modelId,
        address _modelContract,
        string memory _name,
        string memory _category,
        bytes32 _metadataHash
```

```
    ) external payable onlyPublisher {
        require(models[_modelId].modelContract == address(0), "Model already
registered");
        require(_modelContract != address(0), "Invalid model contract");
        require(_metadataHash != bytes32(0), "Invalid metadata hash");
        if (minRegistrationStake > 0) {
            require(msg.value >= minRegistrationStake, "Insufficient stake");
            modelStake[_modelId] = msg.value;
        }
        models[_modelId] = ModelInfo({
            modelContract: _modelContract,
            name: _name,
            category: _category,
            metadataHash: _metadataHash,
            reputation: 0,
            isActive: true,
            owner: msg.sender
        });
    }
}
```

In open DAI marketplaces, **`registerModel()`** should rarely be fully permissionless. A common pattern is to gate registration by an approved publisher role or require a minimum stake / fee per model, which can later be slashed or forfeited for malicious behavior.

The registry pattern enables sophisticated model discovery mechanisms that are essential for large-scale AI networks. Users can search for models by category, performance metrics, or specific capabilities. The pattern supports reputation systems that track model performance over time, helping users make informed decisions about which models to use. Additionally, the registry can implement quality gates and validation mechanisms to ensure only verified models are available for public use.

Proxy pattern for upgradeable AI contracts

The proxy pattern enables contract upgradeability while preserving state and maintaining consistent addresses. This pattern is crucial for AI applications where models and algorithms evolve over time. A proxy contract holds the state and delegates calls to an implementation contract, allowing logic updates without disrupting existing integrations.

In AI applications, the proxy pattern addresses the challenge of immutable smart contracts in an environment where AI models require continuous improvement. Machine learning models are iteratively refined through training, and their implementation logic may need updates to incorporate new algorithms, security patches, or performance optimizations. The proxy pattern provides a structured approach to handle these requirements while maintaining backward compatibility, supporting gradual rollouts of new features (for example, testing a new inference pipeline with a subset of users), and enabling emergency upgrades for critical fixes.

Two widely used variants are the transparent proxy pattern (where only an admin can upgrade and regular users interact as if with a normal contract) and the **Universal Upgradeable Proxy Standard** (**UUPS**) pattern, where the upgrade logic resides in the implementation contract itself. Both approaches must carefully manage storage layout: storage variables in the proxy and implementation must remain aligned across versions to avoid storage collisions and catastrophic state corruption. When upgrading, developers must never reorder, remove, or change the type of existing storage variables; instead, they should only append new variables in reserved gap slots and thoroughly test migration paths before mainnet deployment.

Observer pattern for event-driven AI

The observer pattern facilitates event-driven architectures in AI systems, enabling different components to react to model updates, training completions, or inference requests without tight coupling. On-chain, this is typically expressed through events that smart contracts emit; however, contracts themselves cannot **subscribe** to events or receive callbacks. Instead, off-chain indexers and services (such as the graph, custom indexers, or backend services) listen to these events, react to them, and then optionally trigger new on-chain transactions in response. This makes event-driven AI coordination off-chain reactive rather than on-chain callback-based, allowing scalable orchestration of distributed AI workflows while keeping on-chain logic simple and deterministic.

The observer pattern is particularly valuable in federated learning scenarios where multiple participants need to coordinate their activities based on network events. Event-driven architectures are essential for scalable AI systems because they enable asynchronous processing and reduce the need for continuous polling. The observer pattern implements a publish-subscribe mechanism where contracts can register interest in specific events and receive notifications when those events occur. This approach is more gas-efficient than polling-based systems and provides better scalability for large networks.

The observer pattern enables sophisticated coordination mechanisms in DAI networks. It allows for real-time responses to network events, efficient resource allocation based on demand patterns, and automated quality assurance processes. The pattern supports complex workflows where multiple AI models collaborate, compete, or contribute to collective intelligence systems.

Marketplace pattern for AI services

The marketplace pattern creates standardized interfaces for AI service trading, including model licensing, inference services, and training data access. This pattern incorporates pricing mechanisms, quality assurance, and dispute resolution systems essential for AI commerce.

The foundation of any DAI network lies in its topology, the structural arrangement of nodes and their interconnections that determines how computational resources, data, and intelligence flow throughout the system. Unlike traditional AI deployments, where a centralized server orchestrates all operations, DAI networks must carefully balance autonomy with coordination, efficiency with resilience, and scalability with governance.

AI marketplaces require sophisticated mechanisms to handle diverse service types, pricing models, and quality guarantees. The marketplace pattern provides a framework for standardizing these interactions while allowing for innovation in service delivery and business models. It includes mechanisms for service discovery, reputation management, automated payments, and dispute resolution.

Solidity programming for AI applications

Solidity programming for AI applications requires understanding both blockchain fundamentals and AI-specific requirements. AI contracts must handle complex data structures, manage computational resources efficiently, and provide secure interfaces for model interaction. Critically, large binary artifacts such as model weights or training datasets should not be stored directly on-chain, as this is prohibitively expensive and unnecessary; instead, they should be kept off-chain in content-addressable storage systems like IPFS or Arweave, with only their cryptographic hashes (or metadata hashes) anchored in the contract for integrity verification. Key Solidity concepts essential for AI development include advanced data types, event systems, modifier patterns, and library usage, all applied in a way that keeps on-chain state minimal while referencing rich off-chain AI assets securely.

AI applications on blockchain face unique challenges compared to traditional smart contracts. They must process large amounts of data, coordinate complex workflows, and maintain high availability for real-time inference requests. Understanding these requirements is crucial for developing effective AI smart contracts that can operate efficiently within the constraints of blockchain networks.

Code example for the **`AIModelLibrary`** of the smart contract library for DAI model management and training configuration is as follows:

```
pragma solidity ^0.8.19;
library AIModelLibrary {
    struct ModelMetadata {
        string name;
        string version;
        bytes32 algorithmHash;
        uint256 inputDimensions;
        uint256 outputDimensions;
        string[] requiredDataTypes;
        uint256 computationalComplexity;
```

```
    }

    struct TrainingParameters {
        uint256 learningRate;
        uint256 batchSize;
        uint256 epochs;
        bytes32 optimizerType;
    }

    function validateModelMetadata(ModelMetadata memory _metadata)
        internal
        pure
        returns (bool) {
        return bytes(_metadata.name).length > 0 &&
               bytes(_metadata.version).length > 0 &&
               _metadata.inputDimensions > 0 &&
               _metadata.outputDimensions > 0;
    }
}
```

Data structures for AI models

Effective data structure design is critical for AI smart contracts. Models require complex metadata storage, version tracking, and parameter management. Solidity provides several data structure options, each with specific gas cost implications and use case optimizations.

Structs enable complex data modeling for AI applications and should be designed to minimize storage costs while providing necessary functionality. The packed struct example demonstrates how to optimize storage layout by arranging fields to minimize the number of storage slots used. Mappings offer efficient key-value storage for model registries and user permissions, with lookup times regardless of dataset size. Arrays support sequential data but require careful gas management for large datasets, particularly when performing iterations or modifications.

AI models generate and consume large amounts of structured data, including training parameters, performance metrics, and inference results. Smart contracts must efficiently store and manage this data while minimizing gas costs and maintaining query performance. The choice of data structures significantly impacts both the functionality and economic viability of AI contracts.

Code example for smart contract data architecture for AI model inference, i.e., request tracking and reputation management:

```
// SPDX-License-Identifier: MIT
pragma solidity ^0.8.19;
library AIModelLibrary {
    struct ModelMetadata {
        string name;
        string category;
        bytes32 algorithmHash;   // hash of model/algorithm definition
        uint256 inputDim;
        uint256 outputDim;
        bytes32 metadataHash;    // off-chain metadata (e.g., IPFS)
    }
}
contract AIModelContract {
    using AIModelLibrary for AIModelLibrary.ModelMetadata;
    struct InferenceRequest {
        bytes32 requestId;
        address requester;
        bytes  inputData;
        uint256 timestamp;
        bool   completed;
        bytes  result;
    }

    AIModelLibrary.ModelMetadata public modelMetadata;
    mapping(bytes32 => InferenceRequest) public inferenceRequests;
    mapping(address => uint256) public userReputation;
    event InferenceRequested(bytes32 indexed requestId, address indexed
requester);
    event InferenceCompleted(bytes32 indexed requestId, bytes32 resultHash);
    uint256 public constant MAX_DIMENSION = 10_000; // example upper bound

    constructor(
        string memory _name,
        string memory _category,
        bytes32 _algorithmHash,
        uint256 _inputDim,
        uint256 _outputDim,
        bytes32 _metadataHash
    ) {
        // Basic sanity checks for model registration
        require(_algorithmHash != bytes32(0), "Invalid algorithm hash");
        require(_metadataHash != bytes32(0), "Invalid metadata hash");
```

```
        require(_inputDim > 0 && _inputDim <= MAX_DIMENSION, "Invalid input
dimension");
        require(_outputDim > 0 && _outputDim <= MAX_DIMENSION, "Invalid
output dimension");

        modelMetadata = AIModelLibrary.ModelMetadata({
            name: _name,
            category: _category,
            algorithmHash: _algorithmHash,
            inputDim: _inputDim,
            outputDim: _outputDim,
            metadataHash: _metadataHash
        });
    }
    // ... existing inference logic using inferenceRequests / userReputation
...
}
```

In production DAI systems, model metadata validation should go beyond checking for duplicate IDs. At a minimum, contracts should enforce **`algorithmHash != bytes32(0)`** and require input/output dimensions to fall within reasonable bounds. This prevents malformed or intentionally broken model registrations that could later disrupt inference or reputation logic.

Event handling and logging

Events provide crucial functionality for AI applications, enabling off-chain systems to monitor model updates, training progress, and inference completions. Proper event design facilitates integration with AI frameworks and enables comprehensive audit trails. Events are also more gas-efficient than storage for historical data that does not need to be accessed by smart contracts.

AI systems generate significant amounts of operational data that need to be tracked and analyzed. Events enable this data collection without the high gas costs of on-chain storage. Well-designed events support real-time monitoring, analytics, and integration with external AI tools and frameworks.

Events should be designed with careful consideration of indexed parameters, which enable efficient filtering by off-chain applications. The Ethereum Virtual Machine allows up to three indexed parameters per event, and these should be chosen based on the most common query patterns. Non-indexed parameters can store additional data, but are not efficiently searchable.

Error handling and validation

Robust error handling ensures AI contracts fail gracefully and provide meaningful feedback. Custom errors reduce gas costs compared to traditional require statements while providing detailed error information for debugging and user interfaces. Proper validation prevents invalid states and protects against malicious inputs.

AI applications require comprehensive validation due to the complexity of data and operations involved. Input validation, state checks, and access control must be implemented systematically to prevent errors and security vulnerabilities. Custom errors introduced in Solidity 0.8.4 provide a more gas-efficient way to handle error conditions while maintaining code readability.

Comprehensive error handling includes input validation, state verification, resource checks, and graceful degradation patterns. The code demonstrates best practices for handling various error conditions while maintaining gas efficiency and providing meaningful feedback to users and off-chain systems.

Code example for **`AIEventValidation`** of smart contract error handling, event logging, and input validation for AI training and inference is as follows:

````
```solidity
// SPDX-License-Identifier: MIT
pragma solidity ^0.8.19;
/**
 * @title AIEventValidation
 * @dev Basic event handling, logging, error handling, and validation for AI
training & inference
 */
contract AIEventValidation {
    // Custom errors
    error InvalidModel(bytes32 modelId);
    error Unauthorized(address user);
    error InvalidAccuracy(uint256 accuracy);
    error NoPayment();
    // Events
    event ModelTrainingStarted(
        bytes32 indexed modelId,
        address indexed trainer,
        uint256 indexed round,
        uint256 timestamp
    );
    event TrainingRoundCompleted(
        bytes32 indexed modelId,
````
````

```
        uint256 indexed round,
        address indexed participant,
        uint256 accuracy,   // Scaled by 1e4
        uint256 timestamp
    );
    event InferenceRequested(
        bytes32 indexed modelId,
        address indexed user,
        uint256 payment,
        uint256 timestamp
    );

    // State
    mapping(bytes32 => bool) public activeModel;
    mapping(bytes32 => uint256) public roundOf;
    mapping(address => bool) public authorized;
    uint256 public constant MIN_ACCURACY = 5000; // 50%

    address public admin;
    // Modifiers
    modifier onlyActiveModel(bytes32 modelId) {
        if (!activeModel[modelId]) revert InvalidModel(modelId);
        _;
    }
    modifier onlyAuthorized() {
        if (!authorized[msg.sender]) revert Unauthorized(msg.sender);
        _;
    }
    modifier onlyAdmin() {
        if (msg.sender != admin) revert Unauthorized(msg.sender);
        _;
    }
    constructor() {
        admin = msg.sender;
        authorized[msg.sender] = true; // bootstrap admin as authorized
trainer
    }
    // Register model (admin-only to avoid spam/abuse)
    function registerModel(bytes32 modelId) external onlyAdmin {
        activeModel[modelId] = true;
    }
    // Authorize user (admin-only in this simple example)
```

```
    function authorizeUser(address user) external onlyAdmin {
        authorized[user] = true;
    }

    // Start training
    function startTraining(bytes32 modelId)
        external
        onlyActiveModel(modelId)
        onlyAuthorized
    {
        uint256 r = ++roundOf[modelId];
        emit ModelTrainingStarted(modelId, msg.sender, r, block.timestamp);
    }

    // Complete round
    function completeRound(bytes32 modelId, uint256 accuracy)
        external
        onlyActiveModel(modelId)
        onlyAuthorized
    {
        if (accuracy < MIN_ACCURACY) revert InvalidAccuracy(accuracy);
        uint256 r = roundOf[modelId];
        emit TrainingRoundCompleted(modelId, r, msg.sender, accuracy, block.
timestamp);
    }

    // Request inference
    function requestInference(bytes32 modelId)
        external
        payable
        onlyActiveModel(modelId)
    {
        if (msg.value == 0) revert NoPayment();
        emit InferenceRequested(modelId, msg.sender, msg.value, block.
timestamp);
    }
}
```
```

In this example, **registerModel()** and **authorizeUser()** are restricted to an admin address to prevent arbitrary accounts from activating models or granting training permissions. In production DAI systems, you would typically replace this simple admin with a more robust
```

mechanism such as a multi-sig or DAO-governed access control contract; in either case, model registration and user authorization should never be fully permissionless to avoid spam, malicious models, and privilege escalation.

Code organization and modularity

Modular contract design enables reusability and maintainability in AI applications. Libraries, interfaces, and inheritance patterns help create clean, efficient contract architectures that can evolve with advancing AI technologies. Proper code organization also facilitates testing, auditing, and upgrading of AI systems.

Modular design is particularly important for AI applications due to their complexity and the rapid pace of technological advancement. Well-structured code enables teams to work on different components independently, facilitates code reuse across projects, and makes it easier to integrate new AI techniques or algorithms as they become available.

Code example of **`AITraining`** for modular smart contract architecture with separated concerns like libraries, interfaces, and access control is as follows:

````
```solidity
// SPDX-License-Identifier: MIT
pragma solidity ^0.8.19;
/* ========== LIBRARY: MathUtils.sol ========== */
library MathUtils {
    function average(uint256 a, uint256 b) internal pure returns (uint256) {
        return (a + b) / 2;
    }

    function max(uint256 a, uint256 b) internal pure returns (uint256) {
        return a >= b ? a : b;
    }
}
/* ========== INTERFACE: ITraining.sol ========== */
interface ITraining {
    function startTraining(bytes32 modelId) external;
    function completeRound(bytes32 modelId, uint256 accuracy) external;
}
/* ========== CONTRACT: AccessControl.sol ========== */
contract AccessControl {
    mapping(address => bool) public admins;
    modifier onlyAdmin() {
        require(admins[msg.sender], "Not admin");
        _;
````
````

```
    }
    constructor() { admins[msg.sender] = true; }
    function addAdmin(address user) external onlyAdmin {
        admins[user] = true;
  }
}
/* ========== CONTRACT: AITraining.sol ========== */
import «./MathUtils.sol»;
import "./ITraining.sol";
import "./AccessControl.sol";
contract AITraining is ITraining, AccessControl {
    using MathUtils for uint256;

    mapping(bytes32 => bool) public validModel;
    mapping(bytes32 => uint256) public roundOf;
    mapping(address => bool) public trainers;
    event TrainingStarted(bytes32 modelId, uint256 round);
    event RoundCompleted(bytes32 modelId, uint256 round, uint256 accuracy);

    modifier onlyTrainer() {
        require(trainers[msg.sender], "Not trainer");
        _;
    }

    function registerModel(bytes32 modelId) external onlyAdmin {
        validModel[modelId] = true;
    }

    function authorizeTrainer(address user) external onlyAdmin {
        trainers[user] = true;
    }

    function startTraining(bytes32 modelId) external override onlyTrainer {
        require(validModel[modelId], "Invalid model");
        uint256 r = ++roundOf[modelId];
        emit TrainingStarted(modelId, r);
    }

    function completeRound(bytes32 modelId, uint256 accuracy)
        external
        override
```

```
        onlyTrainer
    {
        require(validModel[modelId], "Invalid model");
        require(accuracy <= 10000, "Accuracy >100%");
        uint256 r = roundOf[modelId];
        emit RoundCompleted(modelId, r, accuracy);
    }
        // Example use of library
    function compareAccuracies(uint256 a, uint256 b) external pure re-
turns (uint256) {
        return MathUtils.max(a, b);
    }
}
```

This modular architecture demonstrates several key principles: interfaces define contracts between components, enabling loose coupling and easier testing; abstract base contracts provide common functionality that can be inherited by specific implementations; libraries contain reusable utility functions that can be shared across multiple contracts; and factory patterns enable standardized deployment and management of contract instances. This approach facilitates maintenance, testing, and future upgrades while keeping gas costs manageable.

AI model registration and management

This section defines a decentralized registry for AI models that ensures transparent provenance, rigorous version control, and community-driven quality curation. Core components include unique on-chain identifiers linked to off-chain model artifacts, immutable metadata anchors for auditing, and upgradeable proxies for seamless model evolution. Reputation-based governance mechanisms allow validator attestations and user ratings to dynamically adjust model trust scores. Together, these elements create a self-sovereign model marketplace where deployments, updates, and retirements occur under transparent, tamper-resistant protocols.

Model metadata and schema design

Effective AI model registration requires comprehensive metadata schemas that capture essential model characteristics while remaining gas efficient. The metadata schema must balance completeness with storage costs, ensuring all necessary information is available for model discovery and validation, while minimizing transaction fees. A well-designed schema serves as the foundation for interoperability, enabling different AI systems to understand and interact with models across the decentralized network.

The complexity of AI models demands sophisticated metadata structures that go beyond simple name-value pairs. Models have intricate dependencies, versioning requirements, performance characteristics, and operational constraints that must be captured accurately. The schema design must accommodate various AI model types, from simple linear regression models to complex deep neural networks, while providing standardized interfaces for common operations.

Code example of **`AIModelManager`** for a comprehensive model registration system with rich metadata schema and capability tracking is as follows:

```
pragma solidity ^0.8.19;
contract AIModelManager {
    struct ModelRegistration {
        bytes32 modelId;
        string name;
        string description;
        bytes32 modelHash;
        string modelType;
        uint256 version;
        address owner;
        uint256 registrationTime;
        bool isActive;
        ModelCapabilities capabilities;
        ModelRequirements requirements;
    }

    struct ModelCapabilities {
        string[] supportedTasks;
        uint256 maxInputSize;
        uint256 averageProcessingTime;
        uint256 accuracyMetric;
    }

    struct ModelRequirements {
        uint256 minComputeUnits;
        uint256 minMemory;
        string[] requiredLibraries;
    }
    mapping(bytes32 => ModelRegistration) public registeredModels;
    mapping(address => bytes32[]) public ownerModels;
}
```

The separation of concerns into different structs (metadata, capabilities, metrics, training info) allows for targeted updates and reduces gas costs when only specific information needs modification. The indexing structure enables complex queries while maintaining reasonable gas consumption for registration and updates.

Version control for AI models

AI models evolve through training iterations, algorithm improvements, and performance optimizations. Smart contracts must provide robust version control mechanisms that track model evolution while maintaining backward compatibility for existing integrations.

Version control systems should support semantic versioning, dependency tracking, and rollback capabilities. Each model version maintains its own metadata while linking to previous versions for audit trails and comparison purposes. The version control system must also support branching and merging workflows common in collaborative AI development.

Version control systems must handle various types of model updates: parameter updates from continued training, architectural changes, bug fixes, and performance optimizations. Each type of update has different implications for compatibility and requires different validation procedures. The version control system must also support branching and merging workflows common in collaborative AI development.

Model lifecycle management

Comprehensive lifecycle management encompasses model registration, activation, updates, deprecation, and removal. Each lifecycle stage requires specific permissions, validation checks, and state transitions that maintain system integrity. The lifecycle management system must handle the complex interdependencies between models, their versions, and their deployments across the network.

The lifecycle of an AI model in a decentralized network involves multiple phases, each with distinct requirements and constraints. The system must track not only the technical aspects of model evolution but also the governance decisions, usage patterns, and community feedback that influence model progression through its lifecycle.

Access control and permissions

Sophisticated permission systems ensure only authorized parties can modify model registrations, access sensitive model data, or perform administrative functions. RBAC provides flexible permission management while maintaining security.

The access control system must handle complex scenarios, including multi-party model ownership, delegated permissions, and time-based access restrictions.

Access control in AI model management involves multiple dimensions, such as functional permissions (what actions can be performed), data permissions (what information can be accessed), and temporal permissions (when access is allowed). The system must also support hierarchical permissions and delegation patterns common in collaborative AI development.

Model discovery and search

Efficient search functionality enables users to discover relevant AI models based on capabilities, performance metrics, and compatibility requirements. Search systems should support filtering, ranking, and recommendation algorithms to improve user experience.

The discovery system must handle large-scale model catalogs while providing fast, relevant results and supporting complex query patterns.

Model discovery in DAI networks faces unique challenges due to the distributed nature of the data and the need for trustless operation. The search system must aggregate information from multiple sources, validate model claims, and provide reliable recommendations without centralized authority.

Automated payment and reward systems

This section codifies on-chain economics for AI networks, from per-inference micropayments to dynamic subscription models. Smart contracts autonomously split revenue among model creators, data providers, and validators according to predefined tokenomic rules, enabling real-time settlement without intermediaries. Advanced mechanisms include demand-driven pricing curves, stake-weighted reward pools for federated contributions, and time-locked escrow for dispute-free transactions. This automated framework aligns incentives, scales seamlessly, and ensures transparent, trustless compensation across the DAI ecosystem.

Payment flow design

Automated payment systems for AI applications must handle diverse pricing models, from one-time inference fees to subscription-based model access. The payment flow design should accommodate micro-payments for individual predictions, bulk pricing for batch processing, and complex revenue-sharing arrangements.

Code example of **`AIPaymentProcessor`** for an automated payment flow system for AI inference services with balance tracking and a refund mechanism is as follows:

```
contract AIPaymentProcessor {
    struct PaymentRequest {
        bytes32 requestId;
        address payer;
        address recipient;
```

```
        uint256 amount;
        bytes32 serviceType;
        uint256 timestamp;
        PaymentStatus status;
    }
    enum PaymentStatus { PENDING, COMPLETED, FAILED, REFUNDED }
    mapping(bytes32 => PaymentRequest) public payments;
    mapping(address => uint256) public balances;
    event PaymentProcessed(bytes32 indexed requestId, address indexed pay-
er, uint256 amount);
     function processInferencePayment(
        bytes32 _requestId,
        address _modelOwner,
        uint256 _inferencePrice
    ) external payable {
        require(msg.value >= _inferencePrice, "Insufficient payment");

        payments[_requestId] = PaymentRequest({
            requestId: _requestId,
            payer: msg.sender,
            recipient: _modelOwner,
            amount: _inferencePrice,
            serviceType: "INFERENCE",
            timestamp: block.timestamp,
            status: PaymentStatus.PENDING
        });

        balances[_modelOwner] += _inferencePrice;
           if (msg.value > _inferencePrice) {
            payable(msg.sender).transfer(msg.value - _inferencePrice);
        }
    }
}
```

Escrow and multi-signature contracts

Escrow mechanisms protect both service providers and consumers in AI transactions. Multi-signature contracts enable shared control over high-value transactions, requiring multiple parties to approve fund releases. These mechanisms are essential for complex AI collaborations involving multiple stakeholders:

- **Dynamic pricing models**: AI services often require dynamic pricing based on computational complexity, market demand, or quality metrics. Smart contracts can implement algorithmic pricing that adjusts rates in real-time based on network conditions and service demand.
- **Reward distribution algorithms**: DAI networks require fair reward distribution among contributors, including model developers, data providers, and computational resource providers. Reward algorithms must account for contribution quality, network participation, and performance metrics.
- **Fee structure and economics**: Sustainable AI networks require carefully designed fee structures that incentivize participation while maintaining affordability. Fee mechanisms should consider gas costs, network fees, and value distribution among ecosystem participants.

Data access control and permissions

This section establishes multi-layered access control that combines role-based permissions with **zero-knowledge (ZK)** proofs for privacy-preserving AI operations. Advanced mechanisms include attribute-based policies that evaluate reputation scores and staking amounts, secure multi-party computation frameworks enabling collaborative training without data exposure, and decentralized identity integration for self-sovereign credential management. Dynamic permission systems adapt access rights based on real-time behavior and contribution quality, creating a trustless security model that protects sensitive data while enabling permissionless innovation in DAI networks. These permission systems are:

- **RBAC**: RBAC systems provide structured permission management for AI applications, defining roles such as model owners, data scientists, validators, and consumers. Each role receives specific permissions that align with its responsibilities and trust levels within the system.

  Code example of AI access control for a role-based access control system with hierarchical permissions for AI model governance is as follows:

```
contract AIAccessControl {
    bytes32 public constant MODEL_OWNER_ROLE = keccak256("MODEL_OWNER");
    bytes32 public constant DATA_SCIENTIST_ROLE = keccak256("DATA_
SCIENTIST");
    bytes32 public constant VALIDATOR_ROLE = keccak256("VALIDATOR");
    bytes32 public constant CONSUMER_ROLE = keccak256("CONSUMER");
    mapping(bytes32 => mapping(address => bool)) public hasRole;
    mapping(bytes32 => bytes32) public roleAdmin;

    modifier onlyRole(bytes32 role) {
        require(hasRole[role][msg.
```

```
sender], "AccessControl: insufficient permissions");
        _;
    }

    function grantRole(bytes32 role, address account) public onlyRo-
le(roleAdmin[role]) {
        hasRole[role][account] = true;
        emit RoleGranted(role, account, msg.sender);
    }
    event RoleGranted(bytes32 indexed role, address indexed account, ad-
dress indexed sender);
}
```

- **Attribute-based access control (ABAC)**: ABAC provides more granular permission control based on user attributes, resource characteristics, and environmental conditions. This approach enables context-aware access decisions that consider factors like time, location, and data sensitivity.
- **Time-based access restrictions**: Temporal access controls limit data availability to specific time windows, supporting use cases like limited-time model access, scheduled training sessions, or time-expired permissions. These mechanisms help manage resource utilization and enforce business rules.
- **Data usage tracking**: Comprehensive usage tracking monitors how AI models and datasets are accessed and utilized. This information supports billing, compliance reporting, and abuse detection while maintaining user privacy through appropriate anonymization techniques.
- **Privacy-preserving access logs**: Access logging systems must balance transparency with privacy protection. Privacy-preserving techniques like ZK proofs enable audit trails without exposing sensitive user information or proprietary model details.

Oracle integration for external data

This section architects a trust-minimized bridge between on-chain AI systems and dynamic real-world information. It covers decentralized oracle networks with AI-driven data validation, real-time streaming feeds, and cross-chain interoperability layers. Techniques include reputation- and stake-weighted oracle selection, machine learning-powered anomaly detection for feed integrity, and privacy-preserving proofs to protect sensitive data. Together, these foundations enable DAI to operate on up-to-the-minute, verifiable external data without sacrificing security or decentralization. This ingest and verification pipeline, encompassing decentralized oracle networks, machine learning-powered anomaly detection, and privacy-preserving proofs, is systematically mapped out in *Figure 4.2*. To ensure trust-minimized data delivery, this ingest and verification pipeline encompasses decentralized oracle networks, machine learning-powered anomaly detection, and privacy-preserving proofs.

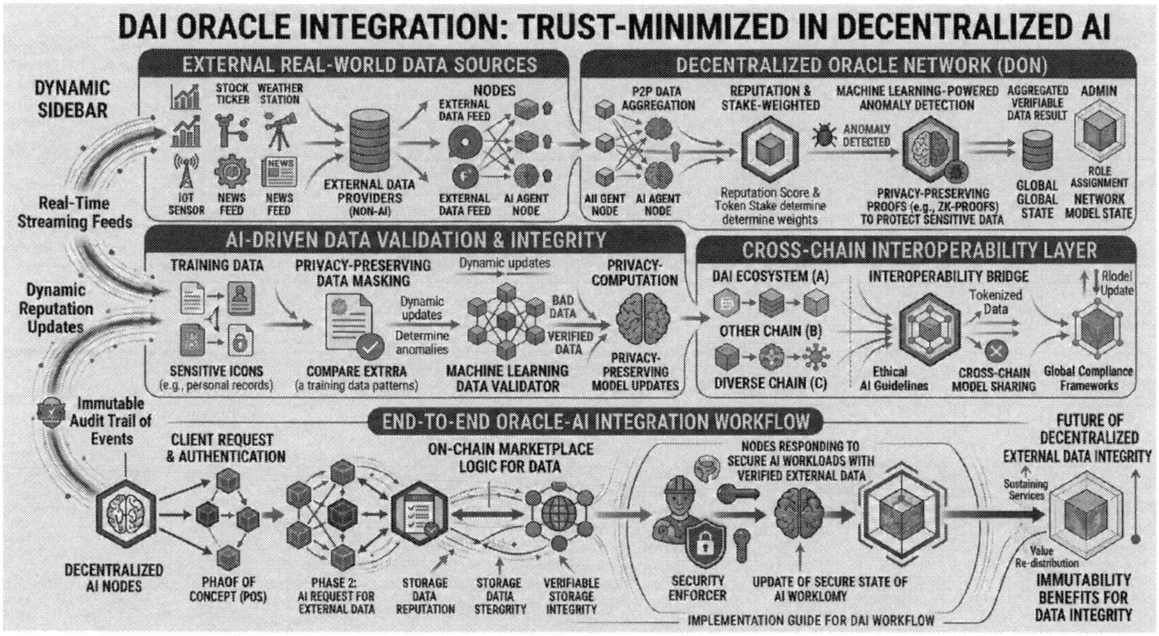

***Figure 4.2**: DAI oracle integration*

These oracle networks are as follows:

- **Oracle design patterns**: Oracle bridges the gap between blockchain smart contracts and external data sources, essential for AI applications. Oracle design patterns must address data reliability, update frequency, and cost optimization while maintaining security against manipulation attacks.

  Code example of AI data oracle for decentralized oracle design pattern with confidence-weighted data feeds and provider authorization is as follows:

```
// SPDX-License-Identifier: MIT
pragma solidity ^0.8.19;
contract AIDataOracle {
    struct DataFeed {
        bytes32 feedId;
        string description;
        address dataProvider;
        uint256 lastUpdate;
        bytes data;
        uint256 confidence;
    }
    mapping(bytes32 => DataFeed) public dataFeeds;
    mapping(address => bool) public authorizedProviders;
```

```
    event DataFeedUpdated(bytes32 indexed feedId, address indexed
provider, uint256 confidence, uint256 timestamp);

    // Example separate registration to set description & initial
provider
    function registerDataFeed(
        bytes32 _feedId,
        string calldata _description
    ) external {
        require(dataFeeds[_feedId].feedId == bytes32(0), "Feed already
exists");
        dataFeeds[_feedId].feedId = _feedId;
        dataFeeds[_feedId].description = _description;
        dataFeeds[_feedId].dataProvider = msg.sender;
        dataFeeds[_feedId].lastUpdate = block.timestamp;
    }

    function updateDataFeed(
        bytes32 _feedId,
        bytes calldata _data,
        uint256 _confidence
    ) external {
        require(authorizedProviders[msg.sender], "Unauthorized data
provider");
        DataFeed storage feed = dataFeeds[_feedId];

        // Ensure feed exists before updating
        require(feed.feedId != bytes32(0), "Unknown data feed");
        // Optional: enforce same provider or allow multiple providers
        // require(feed.dataProvider == msg.sender, "Not feed owner");
        feed.dataProvider = msg.sender;
        feed.lastUpdate = block.timestamp;
        feed.data = _data;
        feed.confidence = _confidence;
        emit DataFeedUpdated(_feedId, msg.sender, _confidence, block.
timestamp);
    }
}
```

- **Chainlink integration for AI**: Chainlink provides a robust oracle infrastructure for AI applications, offering price feeds, random number generation, and custom data integration. Chainlink's decentralized oracle networks provide reliable external data access with built-in security mechanisms.
- **Custom oracle development**: Custom oracles enable integration with specialized AI data sources, proprietary APIs, and complex data processing pipelines. Custom Oracle development requires careful consideration of security, reliability, and gas optimization.
- **Data quality and validation**: Oracle systems must implement comprehensive data validation to ensure accuracy and reliability. Validation mechanisms include multi-source verification, statistical analysis, and reputation-based filtering.
- **Oracle security considerations**: Oracle security addresses manipulation attacks, data source reliability, and economic incentives. Security measures include decentralized data aggregation, cryptographic verification, and economic penalties for malicious behavior.

Contract testing and validation

This section establishes a comprehensive testing framework for AI smart contracts that goes beyond traditional unit testing to address the unique challenges of probabilistic AI systems. It covers multi-scenario testing for federated learning workflows, property-based testing for economic invariants, and AI-assisted fuzzing to uncover edge cases in complex state transitions. Advanced validation techniques include formal verification of tokenomic properties, simulation-based testing of oracle dependencies, and continuous monitoring systems that detect anomalous behavior in production. This robust methodology ensures AI contracts remain secure, reliable, and economically sound under real-world conditions. The contract testing and validation methodologies are as follows:

- **Unit testing with hardhat**: Comprehensive testing ensures AI smart contracts function correctly under various conditions. Hardhat provides a robust testing framework that supports complex test scenarios, gas analysis, and integration testing.

  Code example of AI model contract unit test suite for comprehensive test coverage with **`hardhat`** and **`chai`** for model registration and inference operations is as follows:

```
const { expect } = require("chai");
const { ethers } = require("hardhat");
describe("AIModelContract", function () {
    let aiModel, owner, user1, user2;

    beforeEach(async function () {
        [owner, user1, user2] = await ethers.getSigners();
```

```
        const AIModel = await ethers.
getContractFactory("AIModelContract");
        aiModel = await AIModel.
deploy("TestModel", "Classification", owner.address);
    });

    it("Should register a new model", async function () {
        await expect(aiModel.connect(owner).
updateModel("v1.0", "0x123..."))
            .to.emit(aiModel, "ModelUpdated");
    });

    it("Should handle inference requests", async function () {
        const inputData = ethers.utils.toUtf8Bytes("test input");
        await expect(aiModel.connect(user1).
requestInference(inputData, { value: ethers.utils.parseEther("0.1") }))
            .to.emit(aiModel, "InferenceRequested");
    });
});
```

- **Integration testing strategies**: Integration testing validates interactions between multiple contracts and external systems. These tests ensure AI workflows function correctly across contract boundaries and with oracle integrations.
- **Formal verification methods**: Formal verification provides mathematical proof of contract correctness for critical AI applications. Tools like Certora and Slither enable verification of security properties and business logic correctness.
- **Security testing and audits**: Security testing identifies vulnerabilities specific to AI applications, including oracle manipulation, access control bypasses, and economic attacks. Regular security audits by specialized firms ensure production readiness.
- **Performance testing**: Performance testing evaluates gas consumption, transaction throughput, and scalability limitations. This testing identifies optimization opportunities and capacity planning requirements for production deployment.

Gas optimization techniques

This section reveals targeted strategies to slash gas costs in AI smart contracts without sacrificing functionality. It covers storage packing for model metadata, calldata minimization for inference requests, and event-driven logging to reduce on-chain writes. Advanced tactics include looping with unchecked increments, use of constants and immutables, assembly-based keccak optimizations, and offloading heavy computation to Layer 2 networks. Together, these techniques deliver high-throughput AI workflows at a fraction of the typical gas footprint. These optimization techniques are as follows:

- **Gas cost analysis**: Understanding gas consumption patterns in AI contracts enables targeted optimization efforts. Gas analysis tools help identify expensive operations and guide optimization strategies for production deployment.

  Code example of optimized AI model for gas-efficient smart contract design with storage packing, event logging, and unchecked arithmetic is as follows:

```
// Optimized storage layout
contract OptimizedAIModel {
    struct PackedModelData {
        uint128 version;          // Packed into single slot
        uint128 timestamp;        // with timestamp
        address owner;            // 20 bytes
        uint96 price;            // 12 bytes - packed with address
    }

    // Use events for cheaper data storage
    event ModelUpdate(bytes32 indexed modelHash, string ipfsHash);

    // Optimize array operations
    function batchProcessInferences(bytes32[] calldata requestIds) ex-
ternal {
        uint256 length = requestIds.length;
        for (uint256 i; i < length; ) {
            // Process inference
            unchecked { ++i; }
        }
    }
}
```

- **Storage optimization**: Storage operations consume significant gas in smart contracts. Optimization techniques include data packing, event usage for historical data, and efficient mapping structures that minimize storage reads and writes.
- **Function call optimization**: Function optimization reduces gas consumption through efficient parameter handling, modifier design, and call patterns. Techniques include parameter packing, external vs public function selection, and batch operation design.
- **Batch processing techniques**: Batch processing enables efficient handling of multiple AI operations in a single transaction. This approach reduces per-operation overhead and improves overall system throughput.

- **Layer 2 solutions for AI**: Layer 2 scaling solutions provide cost-effective environments for AI applications requiring frequent interactions. Solutions like Polygon, Arbitrum, and Optimism enable sophisticated AI workflows at reduced costs while maintaining security through the main chain.

  Layer 2 solutions are particularly beneficial for AI applications due to their high transaction frequency and data intensity. These solutions enable complex AI workflows that would be prohibitively expensive on the main chain.

Security best practices

This section outlines proactive defenses for AI smart contracts, combining traditional and AI-specific safeguards. It covers reentrancy guards, time-lock emergency stops, and robust input validation to prevent common exploits. Specialized measures include on-chain anomaly detection for malicious model updates, ZKP attestation for data integrity, and continuous AI-driven security audits. Defense-in-depth patterns like immutable governance modules, multi-sig role control, and automated slashing for misbehavior ensure resilient, tamper-proof AI ecosystems.

Common vulnerabilities in AI contracts

AI smart contracts face unique security challenges beyond traditional contract vulnerabilities. Understanding these risks enables developers to implement appropriate protective measures and design secure AI systems. The OWASP Smart Contract Top 10 provides a framework for understanding these vulnerabilities, with AI-specific considerations requiring additional attention.

AI contracts introduce new attack vectors, including model poisoning attacks, oracle manipulation for AI data feeds, inference result manipulation, economic attacks on AI marketplaces, and privacy attacks on federated learning systems. These vulnerabilities require specialized defensive strategies.

Code example of a secure AI model for a security-hardened smart contract with reentrancy protection, oracle data validation, and access control is as follows:

```
// Security-hardened AI contract demonstrating best practices
// SPDX-License-Identifier: MIT
pragma solidity ^0.8.19;
// Security-hardened AI contract demonstrating best practices
contract SecureAIModel {
    // Prevent reentrancy attacks
    bool private locked;
    modifier nonReentrant() {
        require(!locked, "ReentrancyGuard: reentrant call");
```

```
        locked = true;
        _;
        locked = false;
    }

    // Example oracle data structure
    struct OracleData {
        uint256 lastUpdate;
        uint256 confidence;
    }
    mapping(bytes32 => OracleData) public oracles;
    uint256 public constant MAX_DATA_AGE = 10 minutes;
    uint256 public constant MIN_CONFIDENCE = 8_000; // e.g., 80%

    // Secure oracle integration
    modifier validOracleData(bytes32 feedId) {
        OracleData storage od = oracles[feedId];
        require(block.timestamp - od.lastUpdate <= MAX_DATA_AGE, "Stale
oracle data");
        require(od.confidence >= MIN_CONFIDENCE, "Low confidence data");
        _;
    }

    // Access control validation
    modifier onlyAuthorized(bytes32 action) {
        require(hasPermission(msg.sender, action), "Unauthorized access");
        _;
    }

    function hasPermission(address user, bytes32 action) internal view
returns (bool) {
        // Implement your permission logic here
        return true;
    }
}
```

The best security practices are as follows:

- **Secure coding practices**: Secure coding practices for AI contracts include input validation, overflow protection, and proper error handling. These practices prevent common attack vectors and ensure robust contract behavior under adversarial conditions.

- **Access control security**: Access control systems must resist privilege escalation, unauthorized access, and social engineering attacks. Multi-layered security approaches provide defense in depth for critical AI operations.
- **Cryptographic security**: Cryptographic security protects sensitive AI data, model parameters, and user information. Proper implementation of hashing, encryption, and digital signatures ensures data integrity and privacy.
- **Incident response planning**: Comprehensive incident response plans prepare teams for security breaches, contract vulnerabilities, and operational failures. Response plans should include detection mechanisms, containment procedures, and recovery protocols.

Implementation roadmap and future directions

Smart contract deployment for AI systems demands disciplined, phased execution beginning with foundational model registration and access control, then progressively layering advanced economic, privacy, and oracle mechanisms as systems mature and security hardens. As blockchain-AI convergence accelerates, emerging techniques like privacy-preserving computation, cross-chain orchestration, and autonomous AI agents will reshape the landscape. By systematically building robust smart contract infrastructure today, developers unlock the potential to democratize AI development, align ecosystem incentives, and establish transparent governance, transforming AI from a centralized capability into a genuinely collaborative, trustworthy global platform.

Phased deployment strategy

Successful AI smart contract deployment requires careful planning and phased implementation. Begin with core model registration and access control functionality, establishing a stable foundation for trustless model governance. This initial phase should include basic inference request handling and simple payment mechanisms. Once core systems are validated through extensive testing, gradually add advanced features such as automated payment distribution, reputation systems, and sophisticated access control layers. Subsequently, introduce oracle integration for external data feeds, federated learning coordination mechanisms, and cross-chain interoperability. Thorough testing and security auditing are essential at each phase before advancing to production deployment, ensuring system reliability and participant confidence.

Emerging trends and future evolution

The convergence of AI and blockchain technology continues to evolve rapidly. Emerging trends include privacy-preserving AI techniques leveraging homomorphic encryption and zero-knowledge proofs, cross-chain AI collaboration enabling resource coordination across heterogeneous blockchains, and autonomous AI agents operating through smart contracts with minimal human oversight. Developers should remain informed about these developments while focusing on building robust, secure foundations that can accommodate future innovations. Advanced cryptographic protocols, Layer 2 scaling solutions, and decentralized governance mechanisms will increasingly shape the landscape of AI smart contract architecture.

Building the DAI infrastructure

Smart contracts for AI applications represent a critical enabling technology for the decentralized AI future. By mastering the concepts and techniques presented in this chapter, developers can build the infrastructure necessary to democratize AI development, ensure fair compensation for contributors, and create transparent, trustworthy AI systems that benefit all participants in the ecosystem. The programmable, trustless nature of smart contracts transforms AI from a centralized capability into a genuinely collaborative global enterprise, where innovation, incentives, and governance operate through transparent, immutable protocols.

Conclusion

This chapter has provided comprehensive coverage of smart contract development for AI applications, spanning design patterns, implementation techniques, security considerations, and optimization strategies. The integration of AI with blockchain technology through smart contracts represents a paradigm shift toward decentralized, transparent, and autonomous AI systems that can operate without traditional centralized control while maintaining security and efficiency.

The frameworks and principles presented in this chapter form the architectural foundation upon which the next generation of DAI applications will be built, systems that are secure by design, economically sustainable, and genuinely owned and governed by their communities.

The next chapter will explore federated learning with blockchain, building upon the smart contract foundations established here to enable collaborative AI training across distributed networks, and explore how smart contracts coordinate multi-party model training across geographically dispersed participants without requiring central aggregation servers. You will discover how blockchain-enforced incentives align trainer behavior, cryptographic verification ensures training integrity, and reputation systems build trust among autonomous nodes.

CHAPTER 5
Federated Learning with Blockchain

Introduction

AI development remains trapped within centralized paradigms that concentrate power, limit collaboration, and compromise privacy. While **federated learning** (**FL**) promised collaborative model training without centralizing raw data by enabling hospitals to improve diagnostics, banks to detect fraud, and **Internet of Things** (**IoT**) networks to share insights, FL's reliance on trusted central coordinators introduced new vulnerabilities such as single points of failure, opaque aggregation, and misaligned incentives. Blockchain technology transforms this landscape by embedding cryptographic consensus, immutable audit trails, and programmable incentives directly into FL, creating **blockchain-enabled federated learning** (**BCFL**) systems that significantly reduce reliance on institutional intermediaries by shifting trust to cryptographic protocols, smart contracts, and distributed consensus among independent validators. These systems still operate under explicit assumptions such as an honest-majority or Byzantine-resilient consensus, secure key management, and correctly implemented smart contracts, but they remove the need for a single central coordinator.

This chapter equips readers with theoretical foundations and practical skills to architect, implement, and govern such collaborative AI systems. Through BCFL, smart contracts automate training coordination while homomorphic encryption, secure multi-party computation, and differential privacy provide mathematical privacy guarantees. Token-based incentive mechanisms reward genuine contributions and prevent free-riding, and zero-knowledge proofs enable model verification without exposing proprietary data. By the chapter's end, readers will understand how to integrate federated learning with blockchain, deploy cryptographic aggregation protocols, design sustainable economic models, and ensure regulatory compliance, positioning them to lead the transformation toward democratic, transparent, and privacy-preserving artificial intelligence development.

Structure

The chapter covers the following topics:

- Federated learning fundamentals
- Blockchain-based coordination
- Privacy-preserving aggregation
- Incentive mechanisms for participation
- Model verification and validation
- Differential privacy techniques
- Secure multi-party computation
- Implementation with TFF
- Performance optimization
- Real-world case studies

Objectives

By the end of this chapter, readers will understand how to integrate federated learning with blockchain technology, gaining both the theoretical foundations and practical skills needed to build secure, decentralized AI systems. They will learn to design blockchain-coordinated federated learning architectures that replace centralized coordinators with smart contracts and consensus mechanisms, and to implement privacy-preserving distributed training using homomorphic encryption, secure multi-party computation, and differential privacy to achieve formal privacy guarantees. Readers will also learn how to design token-based incentive mechanisms that reward high-quality contributions while discouraging malicious behavior, and how to work with TensorFlow Federated in blockchain-enabled environments to support scalable, real-world deployments.

Along the way, they will develop expertise in cryptographic protocol implementation, blockchain-native architecture design, performance optimization, and security engineering against threats such as gradient leakage and model poisoning. Finally, readers will gain a strategic understanding of how to assess BCFL applicability across healthcare, finance, and IoT domains, navigate regulatory and compliance requirements, and shape organizational adoption of decentralized AI through well-governed, end-to-end BCFL workflows that include participant registration, secure training, cryptographic aggregation, and automated reward distribution.

Federated learning fundamentals

FL represents a revolutionary approach to machine learning that fundamentally transforms how distributed systems learn from data while preserving privacy. FL enables collaborative model training across multiple participants without requiring raw data sharing, unlike traditional centralized **machine learning** (**ML**), where data is collected into a single repository.

The core principle of FL lies in bringing the computation to the data rather than bringing data to the computation. This paradigm shift addresses critical challenges in data privacy, regulatory compliance, and bandwidth limitations that plague traditional centralized approaches. Each participant trains a model locally using their private dataset, then shares only model updates with a coordinating entity, preserving data locality and privacy. As illustrated in *Figure 5.1*, which outlines the foundational mechanics of blockchain-coordinated federated learning and its collaborative global model evolution lifecycle:

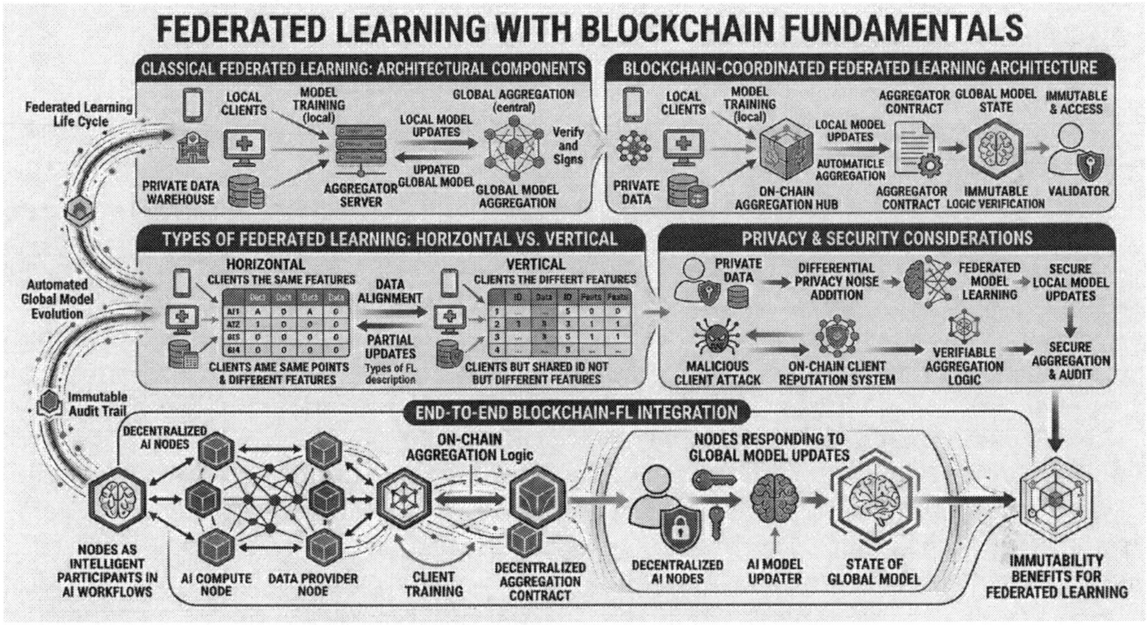

Figure 5.1: *Federated learning with blockchain fundamentals*

Architectural components and design patterns

FL can be realized in two distinct architectural styles: the classical, servercentric architecture and a blockchaincoordinated architecture, where coordination is distributed across validator nodes and smart contracts. Understanding this distinction is essential before introducing decentralized designs.

In its traditional form, the FL architecture consists of three essential components: local training on distributed devices, a central server for coordination, and secure aggregation mechanisms. Participants maintain complete control over their local data while contributing to collaborative model development through encrypted or masked parameter sharing, but they still depend on a single coordinating server to schedule rounds, collect updates, and produce the global model.

Core components of classical federated learning

The coordination process follows a structured pattern where participants receive the global model, train locally on private datasets, and submit encrypted model updates. The central aggregator performs model aggregation while maintaining cryptographic security, ensuring that raw data never leaves local devices.

These components define the baseline FL pattern that blockchaincoordinated designs later decentralized:

- Client devices that hold local data and perform model training.
- Central server that orchestrates the process and aggregates model updates.
- Global model that improves through collaborative learning.
- Aggregation algorithms like **federated averaging** (**FedAvg**).

Blockchain-coordinated federated learning architecture

In BCFL, the logical roles remain (clients, aggregation, and a global model), but the coordination function is implemented by a distributed set of blockchain nodes running a consensus protocol and smart contracts, rather than a single central server. Scheduling of training rounds, aggregation commitments, incentive distribution, and model versioning are all moved on-chain, reducing reliance on any single institution and providing an immutable audit trail of model evolution and participation. In this architecture, client devices train locally and interact with the blockchain via transactions; validator or consensus nodes replace the central server by coordinating rounds and recording commitments; smart contracts encode participation rules, aggregation workflows, and incentive logic; and off-chain storage systems such as IPFS hold large model artifacts while on-chain hashes anchor their integrity and provenance.

Table 5.1 presents a comparison between classical FL and BCFL:

Aspect	Classical FL	BCFL
Coordinator	Single central server	Distributed validator set under consensus
Trust model	Trust in server operator	Trust in cryptography, consensus, and smart contract correctness
Aggregation logging	Typically offchain, limited transparency	Onchain commitments and immutable audit trails
Incentive mechanisms	Often ad hoc or absent	Tokenbased, contractenforced incentives and penalties
Single point of failure	Yes (central server)	Mitigated via decentralized coordination
Governance and updates	Centralized application logic	Onchain governance and protocollevel upgrades

***Table 5.1**: Classical FL vs. BCFL*

Types of federated learning

FL can be organized into distinct types depending on how data is distributed across participating organizations and systems. Understanding these paradigms helps practitioners select suitable architectures, privacy strategies, and aggregation methods for real-world deployments.

FL encompasses several paradigms based on data distribution characteristics:

- **Horizontal FL**: It applies when datasets share the same feature space but different samples. This is common in scenarios where similar organizations (e.g., hospitals, banks) have datasets with identical structure but different users.
- **Vertical FL**: Addresses scenarios where datasets contain the same samples but different features. For example, a bank and an e-commerce platform might have data about the same customers but with different feature sets. In practice, vertical FL typically requires privacypreserving entity alignment (for example, private set intersection-based secure ID matching) to reliably identify common users across parties before joint training.
- **Federated transfer learning**: Bridges gaps when datasets have limited overlap in both users and features, transferring knowledge from feature-rich parties to those with insufficient data for effective model training.

Privacy and security considerations

Traditional FL faces several privacy and security challenges despite not sharing raw data directly. Model updates can leak sensitive information about training data through gradient inversion attacks (such as **Deep Leakage from Gradients** (**DLG**) and gradient-based membership inference attacks that infer whether a specific record participated in training. Critically, raw gradients or model updates, even if encrypted in transit, may still reveal private information to an honest-but-curious or malicious aggregator unless they are properly protected (for example, via secure aggregation, differential privacy, or trusted execution) before or during aggregation. Additionally, malicious participants can submit poisoned or backdoored model updates to compromise global model integrity.

These vulnerabilities necessitate advanced privacy-preserving techniques and secure aggregation protocols. The integration with blockchain technology addresses many of these concerns by providing immutable audit trails, cryptographic verification, and decentralized coordination mechanisms that complement cryptographic and statistical privacy defenses at the federated learning layer.

Blockchain-based coordination

Blockchain transforms FL's centralized orchestration into a decentralized coordination fabric that enforces protocol rules, records contributions immutably, and automates governance through smart contracts. In **decentralized artificial intelligence** (**DAI**) systems, blockchain serves three core roles: consensus-driven scheduling of training rounds, transparent audit trails of model updates, and programmable economic incentives. This section dissects these roles, explores suitable consensus mechanisms, and presents smart-contract workflows and hybrid architectures that empower trustless collaboration.

Decentralized coordination architecture

Blockchain-based coordination fundamentally transforms federated learning from centralized orchestration to decentralized consensus-driven collaboration. Traditional federated learning relies on a central server that represents a single point of failure and trust bottleneck. Blockchain technology eliminates this limitation by distributing coordination responsibilities across a network of nodes that maintain consensus through cryptographic protocols.

Coordination structures in blockchain-enabled federated learning

The architectural topology of a DAI system determines latency, privacy boundaries, governance authority, and resilience to failures or adversaries. Organizations deploying BCFL must choose from among three primary coordination models:

- **Centralized coordination with blockchain verification**: It preserves traditional federated learning's star topology while incorporating blockchain for verification and audit trails. This approach allows organizations to leverage existing infrastructure while gaining transparency benefits. The central aggregator manages training rounds while blockchain nodes provide immutable verification of participant authenticity and contribution tracking.
- **Hierarchical multi-layer architectures**: They organize participants into multiple coordination layers that mirror organizational and geographical boundaries. Local clusters coordinate within regions, intermediate layers manage cross-regional aggregation, and blockchain networks operate at different hierarchical levels with specialized consensus mechanisms optimized for each tier's requirements.
- **Decentralized peer-to-peer networks**: They eliminate all coordination hierarchies, with participants communicating directly through blockchain-mediated distributed protocols. Every participant functions as both learner and coordinator while the blockchain network serves as the primary coordination infrastructure, achieving maximum censorship resistance and privacy preservation.

Consensus mechanisms for federated learning

Traditional blockchain consensus mechanisms like PoW cause extreme resource consumption that reduces federated learning efficiency, particularly for wireless and resource-limited devices. Novel consensus mechanisms have been developed specifically for FL contexts to address these limitations.

Proof of quality

Proof of quality (PoQ) mechanisms repurpose computational work from arbitrary cryptographic puzzles to productive machine learning tasks. Participants demonstrate computational effort through model training quality rather than solving meaningless hash puzzles, creating a productive consensus that benefits the learning objective. To make model quality verifiable without trusting any single party, PoQ evaluates submitted models against a shared, predefined validation task (for example, a public benchmark dataset or an onchain evaluation model) executed by validator nodes, and can optionally embed cryptographic proofs (such as zero-knowledge proofs of evaluation) so that anyone can verify that the claimed accuracy was obtained on the agreed validation data and scoring function. This separation between fixed validation logic and minerchosen training strategies is essential; without it, miners could game PoQ by cherrypicking private validation data or fabricating scores.

Proof of federated learning

Consensus algorithms specifically designed for federated environments evaluate participant contributions based on model accuracy improvements and training effort. **Proof of federated learning (PoFL)** mechanisms incentivize high-quality contributions while maintaining network security through cryptographic verification.

Byzantine fault tolerance

Adaptations provide robustness against malicious participants who might submit poisoned model updates. Modified **Byzantine fault tolerance (BFT)** protocols incorporate model validation and quality assessment into consensus decisions, ensuring that only verified, high-quality updates influence global model evolution.

Smart contracts for automated governance

Smart contracts automate critical federated learning processes, including participant registration, model validation, and reward distribution, without requiring trusted intermediaries. These self-executing contracts enforce privacy policies and learning protocols through immutable code deployed on the blockchain network.

Automated FL workflows

DAI systems achieve transparency (all rules are auditable), consistency (rules apply uniformly to all participants), and trustlessness (no single operator can deviate from agreed protocols) by encoding FL workflows as deterministic on-chain logic. The following core workflow modules power blockchain-coordinated BCFL:

- **Participant registration**: Smart contracts verify participant credentials and establish access permissions.
- **Training round coordination**: Automated initiation of learning rounds based on predefined triggers.
- **Model validation**: Cryptographic verification of submitted model updates.
- **Reward distribution**: Automatic token allocation based on contribution quality and consensus rules.

Smart contracts ensure transparency and fairness by codifying all governance rules in immutable, auditable code. Participants can verify system behavior and trust that rewards will be distributed according to predetermined algorithms rather than centralized decision-making.

Off-chain storage and metadata management

Blockchains are ill-suited for large model weight storage. DAI architectures, therefore, adopt hybrid on-chain/off-chain patterns as follows:

- **Off-chain model storage**: Model checkpoints and large encrypted updates reside in distributed storage systems (IPFS, Arweave, or cloud storage with content-addressable hashes).
- **On-chain hash commitments**: Smart contracts record Merkle root hashes of off-chain payloads, ensuring data integrity and tamper evidence.
- **Metadata schemas**: Each update references metadata like participant **identity document** (**ID**), round number, aggregation algorithm, encryption parameters, allowing clients and auditors to reconstruct the learning process.
- **Data availability guarantees**: Since Merkle roots alone only prove integrity when data is present, practical deployments pair them with explicit availability strategies such as IPFS pinning across multiple independent nodes or services, redundancy across storage backends (for example, IPFS plus Filecoin or cloud), and, in more advanced designs, data availability sampling or monitoring to detect and repair missing chunks.

This separation enables the blockchain to function as the trust anchor while off-chain storage handles data throughput, with explicit mechanisms to keep model artifacts durably retrievable.

Hybrid topologies and cross-chain coordination

Large-scale DAI networks benefit from hierarchical FL topologies aligned with organizational or geographic domains:

- **Regional sub-chains**: Local participants coordinate on lightweight sidechains optimized for low latency; periodic cross-chain commits synchronize global model states on a mainnet.
- **Cross-chain aggregators**: Smart contracts on different chains communicate through interoperability protocols (e.g., **Inter-Blockchain Communication** (**IBC**), cross-chain bridges) to aggregate model updates across domains. Given that traditional lock-and-mint bridges have been one of the most exploited components in the blockchain stack, practical DAI deployments should favor trust-minimized designs such as light client-based protocols (as in IBC) or zk-bridges that verify source-chain state with succinct proofs, and apply hardening measures like audited contracts, rate limits, and continuous monitoring to reduce the attack surface.
- **Shard-based delegation**: Model updates partitioned by feature subsets or data types are processed in parallel shards, each running independent FL rounds; a root chain aggregates shard-level models into a global consensus.

These hybrid designs balance throughput, privacy, and decentralization. Regional chains contain sensitive data closer to its source for compliance, while global aggregation on the mainnet unifies model evolution across the full network.

Communication protocols and efficiency

Blockchain-based coordination requires carefully designed communication protocols that balance decentralization benefits with performance requirements. Standard protocols include modifications of FedAvg adapted for blockchain environments and specialized secure aggregation techniques. To make these systems scalable and practical in real-world networks, two complementary design directions are particularly important:

- **DAG-based coordination**: Using **directed acyclic graph** (**DAG**) structures addresses scalability limitations of traditional blockchain architectures. DAG-FL frameworks enable asynchronous participation and reduce coordination overhead while maintaining security guarantees through cryptographic verification.
- **Compression and optimization techniques**: Reduce communication costs through quantization, sparse updates, and knowledge distillation. These optimizations are significant in blockchain environments where transaction costs and network latency can impact system performance.

Privacy-preserving aggregation

It is paramount for DAI systems to ensure that no participant's individual gradients or model parameters are exposed during aggregation. In centralized federated learning, a trusted server collects all gradients and computes their aggregate; trust is placed in that server's operational security and governance. In BCFL, no single trusted party exists. Thus, aggregation must be cryptographically blind; participants cannot see others' updates, aggregators cannot access raw gradients, and even a compromised blockchain network cannot leak individual contributions.

Cryptographic aggregation techniques

Privacy-preserving aggregation in BCFL requires sophisticated cryptographic techniques that protect individual contributions while enabling collective model improvement. Traditional aggregation methods that rely on trusted central servers are inadequate for decentralized blockchain environments where no single entity should access raw model parameters.

Homomorphic encryption for secure aggregation

This enables computations on encrypted data without revealing underlying model parameters. Participants encrypt their local model updates using homomorphic encryption schemes, allowing the blockchain network to perform aggregation operations on ciphertext while maintaining mathematical properties necessary for federated averaging.

The Paillier homomorphic encryption system provides additive homomorphism, which is well-suited to summing or computing weighted averages of model updates in secure aggregation, but it does not support arbitrary multiplications between encrypted values and therefore cannot directly express the nonlinear operations used inside neural networks. In practice, this means Paillier-based schemes are typically used only for the aggregation phase (for example, securely summing encrypted gradients or parameters), while the forward and backward passes of the model remain in the clear on each client or rely on additional cryptographic protocols if full encrypted computation is required. Moreover, Paillier and related homomorphic schemes introduce nontrivial computational and communication overhead, so system designers must balance security against latency, bandwidth, and device constraints when choosing parameter sizes and how much of the model to encrypt.

Threshold cryptography

Distributes decryption capabilities across multiple blockchain nodes, ensuring that no single entity can access individual model parameters. The system requires collaboration among multiple nodes to decrypt aggregated results, providing security against both external attacks and internal malicious behavior.

Secure multi-party computation integration

Secure multi-party computation (**SMPC**) protocols enable privacy-preserving aggregation through cryptographic techniques that allow multiple parties to jointly compute functions over their private inputs without revealing individual data. In BCFL systems, SMPC addresses scenarios where homomorphic encryption is too computationally expensive or secret sharing alone lacks functionality for complex aggregation. The following approaches integrate SMPC effectively with blockchain coordination:

- **Secret sharing-based aggregation**: Distributes model parameters across multiple blockchain nodes using Shamir's secret sharing scheme. Each participant splits their local model updates into shares distributed among network nodes. Aggregation occurs through secure computation on shared values, with final results reconstructed only after consensus is reached.
- **Garbled circuits for model aggregation**: Provides another SMPC approach where aggregation functions are compiled into obfuscated Boolean circuits. Participants provide encrypted inputs to circuit evaluation, enabling secure computation of federated averaging without revealing individual model parameters.
- **Multi-party computation with authentication**: Addresses the challenge of participant verification in decentralized environments. Novel authenticable multi-party computation algorithms combine secret sharing with Diffie-Hellman key agreement and functional encryption to provide both privacy preservation and participant authentication without trusted third parties.

Differential privacy in distributed settings

Differential privacy provides mathematical guarantees that individual contributions cannot be inferred from aggregated results, even under sophisticated attacks. In blockchain-federated learning, differential privacy techniques must be adapted for decentralized environments where no trusted aggregator exists. These are:

- **Distributed differential privacy**: Ensures that participation in the federated learning system reveals negligible information about individual datasets. Each participant adds calibrated noise to their model updates before encryption and submission to the blockchain network. The cumulative noise across all participants provides system-wide privacy guarantees while maintaining model utility.
- **Gaussian differential privacy (GDP)**: GDP mechanisms add noise sampled from Gaussian distributions to model gradients, providing stronger composition properties than traditional Laplacian noise. The blockchain network can verify noise addition through ZK proofs, ensuring compliance with privacy requirements without trusted verification. GDP is a private accounting framework that characterizes mechanisms by a single parameter μ, giving tight, closed-form composition rules for repeated applications of (typically) Gaussian mechanisms, rather than just adding Gaussian noise. In practice, DAI systems often use a Gaussian mechanism (for example, DP-SGD that injects Gaussian noise into clipped gradients) and then use GDP as the formalism to track the cumulative privacy loss across training rounds; the blockchain network can verify that noise sampling and clipping parameters are consistent with a target μ (for example, via ZK proofs of correctly parameterized Gaussian draws), without conflating the accounting framework itself with the underlying noise distribution.

- **Local differential privacy (LDP)**: LDP provides the strongest privacy guarantees by ensuring that individual model updates are differentially private before any aggregation occurs. This approach protects against both external attackers and malicious aggregation nodes, as even compromised blockchain infrastructure cannot access meaningful information about individual contributions.

Secure aggregation protocols

Specialized aggregation protocols designed for blockchain environments must balance privacy preservation, fault tolerance, and computational efficiency. These protocols enable secure computation of federated averaging while maintaining the blockchain's decentralization and immutability properties:

- **Boneh-Goh-Nissim (BGN) cryptosystem**: BGN supports an arbitrary number of homomorphic additions but only a single multiplication on ciphertexts, which means it can securely evaluate quadratic functions or aggregation rules with one multiplicative layer, but not deep neural networks with many nonlinear layers. In the context of DAI, this makes BGN suitable for richer encrypted aggregation logic than purely additive schemes (for example, computing weighted sums that depend on encrypted reputation scores or quality weights), while still facing scalability and performance constraints that limit its practicality for large models or high-frequency federated updates compared to more modern, leveled, and fully homomorphic encryption schemes.
- **Verifiable secret sharing**: Ensures that aggregation participants cannot submit invalid shares without detection. The blockchain network can cryptographically verify the correctness of secret shares before including them in aggregation computations, providing robustness against malicious participants who might attempt to poison the aggregation process.
- **Secure aggregation with dropout resilience**: Handles the practical challenge of participants going offline during aggregation rounds. These protocols use redundant secret sharing and recovery mechanisms to ensure that aggregation can proceed even when some participants disconnect unexpectedly.

Incentive mechanisms for participation

DAI networks thrive on active, high-quality contributions from diverse participants like hospitals sharing diagnostic data, banks trading fraud signals, and edge devices pooling sensor readings. However, absent economic incentives, participants face misaligned interests, contributing valuable data may benefit competitors, sharing compute cycles consumes resources, and free-riding (using the global model without training locally) offers a free advantage. BCFL solves this through token-based incentive mechanisms that reward genuine contributions, penalize malicious behavior, and align participant incentives with network objectives. This section examines reward systems, auction-based client selection, staking and reputation frameworks, and fairness measures that sustain equitable, sustainable DAI ecosystems.

Token-based reward systems

Blockchain technology enables sophisticated incentive mechanisms that motivate high-quality participation in FL through cryptographic tokens and automated reward distribution. Traditional FL lacks built-in mechanisms to reward participants for contributing valuable data and computational resources, limiting participation and potentially degrading model quality. These mechanisms are:

- **Contribution-based token allocation**: Rewards participants based on the quality and quantity of their contributions to global model improvement. Smart contracts automatically evaluate model accuracy improvements, training effort, and data quality metrics to determine appropriate token rewards. This creates direct financial incentives for participants to contribute high-quality training data and computational resources.
- **Reputation-weighted rewards**: Incorporate participant history and reliability into reward calculations. The blockchain maintains immutable records of participant contributions, enabling reputation scores that influence future reward allocation. Participants with consistent high-quality contributions receive higher rewards, creating long-term incentives for reliable participation.
- **Multi-objective incentive design**: Balances competing objectives, including model accuracy, privacy preservation, and computational efficiency. Hybrid incentive mechanisms combine alignment-based rewards for model quality, fairness checks for equitable participation, and consistency multipliers for reliable contributors.

Auction-based participant selection

Market-based mechanisms enable efficient allocation of federated learning tasks through competitive bidding processes managed by smart contracts. Participants bid for inclusion in training rounds based on their computational capabilities, data quality, and desired compensation, as follows:

- **Reverse auctions for computing resources**: Allow the system to select optimal participants by minimizing costs while maximizing expected model improvement. Participants submit bids indicating their desired compensation for participation, and smart contracts automatically select the most cost-effective combination of contributors.
- **Quality-adjusted bidding**: Incorporates predicted contribution quality into auction mechanisms. Participants with higher reputation scores or superior computational resources can command premium pricing, creating incentives for infrastructure investment and data quality improvements.

- **Dynamic pricing models**: Adjust reward rates based on market conditions, data scarcity, and model performance requirements. Smart contracts can implement sophisticated pricing algorithms that respond to supply and demand dynamics in real-time.

Staking and reputation mechanisms

PoS adaptations for federated learning create security deposits that align participant incentives with system integrity. Participants must stake tokens to participate in training rounds, with stakes subject to slashing penalties for malicious behavior, as follows:

- **Reputation-based consensus**: Uses historical performance data to determine participant influence in consensus decisions. Participants with higher reputation scores receive greater weight in model aggregation and blockchain consensus, creating incentives for consistent high-quality contributions.

- **Slashing for malicious behavior**: Automatically penalizes participants who submit poisoned models or attempt to manipulate the learning process. Smart contracts can detect various forms of malicious behavior through statistical analysis and cryptographic verification, imposing financial penalties that deter attacks.

- **Long-term incentive alignment**: Rewards participants for sustained engagement through vesting schedules and loyalty bonuses. Token rewards may be locked for specified periods to encourage long-term participation and prevent short-term gaming of incentive systems.

Fairness and anti-gaming measures

Sophisticated incentive design must prevent gaming behaviors that could undermine system integrity while ensuring fair reward distribution across diverse participants. Anti-gaming measures protect against various manipulation strategies while maintaining incentives for genuine high-quality participation. These mechanisms leverage blockchain's transparency and cryptographic primitives to detect and deter abuse automatically:

- **Sybil attack prevention**: Uses identity verification and computational challenges to prevent participants from creating multiple fake identities to claim excessive rewards. Blockchain-based identity systems provide cryptographic proof of unique participation without compromising privacy.

- **Collusion detection**: Employs statistical analysis and pattern recognition to identify coordinated malicious behavior among groups of participants. Smart contracts can automatically detect suspicious correlations in submitted model updates and impose penalties on colluding parties.

- **Fairness auditing**: Ensures equitable reward distribution across participants with different computational capabilities and data characteristics. Periodic fairness checks via cumulative scoring prevent systematic bias against smaller contributors while maintaining incentives for high-quality participation.

Model verification and validation

Ensuring the integrity of global models and detecting malicious contributions are critical for trust in DAI systems. In centralized FL, a trusted aggregator validates updates before incorporation; in BCFL, no single trusted authority exists. Instead, cryptographic proofs, distributed validation protocols, and on-chain audit trails provide mathematical assurance that models are authentic, aggregation is correct, and malicious contributions are detected and excluded. This section covers Merkle-based audit trails, ZK proofs, Byzantine-resilient aggregation, and real-time anomaly detection mechanisms that collectively form a robust model verification framework for DAI.

Cryptographic model verification

Blockchain-enabled federated learning requires robust verification mechanisms to ensure model integrity and prevent poisoning attacks without compromising participant privacy. Traditional centralized verification approaches are inadequate for decentralized environments where no trusted authority exists to validate submitted model updates. Cryptographic verification techniques provide mathematical assurance that models are authentic and aggregation is correct. The following approaches integrate seamlessly with BCFL systems:

- **ZK proofs for model validation**: Zero-knowledge proofs can be used at different layers of the pipeline (for example, to prove that an aggregator correctly computed a weighted average of client updates, to prove that a given model inference was produced by a committed network on a specific input, or, more ambitiously, to prove full training correctness across many gradient steps). Because generating ZK proofs for full deep network training is still orders of magnitude more expensive than native execution, most practical DAI designs focus ZK usage on aggregation correctness and (in some cases) inference correctness, rather than per-step training proofs, balancing verifiability against prover overhead and latency.

- **Merkle tree-based model tracking**: Provides immutable audit trails of global model evolution through cryptographic hash trees. Each model version is represented by a Merkle root that cryptographically commits to all model parameters, enabling efficient verification of model integrity and change tracking.

- **Homomorphic verification schemes**: Allow validation of aggregated model updates without decrypting individual contributions. Validators can verify that aggregation was performed correctly on encrypted model parameters, ensuring mathematical correctness while preserving privacy.

Consensus-based validation

Distributed validation protocols leverage blockchain consensus mechanisms to verify model quality and detect malicious contributions through collective decision-making. Multiple validator nodes independently assess submitted model updates using cryptographic proofs and statistical analysis:

- **Byzantine fault tolerant validation**: Protects against coordinated attacks by malicious validators through robust consensus protocols that tolerate up to one-third malicious participants. Modified BFT algorithms incorporate model-specific validation criteria and quality metrics into consensus decisions.
- **PoQ consensus**: Repurposes blockchain mining to perform productive model validation work instead of solving meaningless cryptographic puzzles. Validator nodes demonstrate computational effort by evaluating model quality, creating a productive consensus that benefits the federated learning objective.
- **Multi-signature validation**: Requires multiple independent validators to approve model updates before inclusion in the blockchain ledger. This distributed validation approach prevents single points of failure while maintaining efficiency through threshold signature schemes.

Anomaly detection and quality assessment

Automated detection of low-quality or malicious model contributions is essential for maintaining federated learning system integrity. Statistical analysis and machine learning techniques can identify suspicious patterns in submitted model updates without accessing the underlying training data. These mechanisms operate alongside cryptographic verification to provide layered protection against model degradation, ensuring that only high-quality updates contribute to global model improvement:

- **Statistical outlier detection**: Identifies model updates that deviate significantly from expected patterns based on historical data and peer contributions. Blockchain nodes can perform statistical tests on encrypted model parameters to detect potential anomalies without compromising privacy.
- **Gradient analysis techniques**: Examine the mathematical properties of submitted model updates to identify potential poisoning attacks. Validators can analyze gradient norms, directions, and convergence properties to detect malicious contributions while maintaining differential privacy.
- **Peer review mechanisms**: Leverage multiple participants to cross-validate model contributions through distributed assessment protocols. Participants evaluate each other's contributions using cryptographic protocols that preserve privacy while enabling quality assessment.

Model integrity assurance

Comprehensive integrity assurance mechanisms protect against various forms of model manipulation while maintaining the collaborative benefits of federated learning. These systems provide mathematical guarantees about model authenticity and training correctness:

- **Digital signatures for model authentication**: Ensure that submitted model updates originate from authorized participants and have not been tampered with during transmission. Each participant cryptographically signs their model contributions, enabling verification of authenticity and integrity.
- **Trusted execution environment integration**: Provides hardware-level security guarantees for model training and validation processes. TEE-enabled participants can generate cryptographic attestations proving that training was performed correctly within secure enclaves.
- **Audit trail immutability**: Leverages blockchain's inherent immutability to create permanent records of all model updates and validation decisions. This enables post-hoc analysis of system behavior and provides accountability for participant actions.

Differential privacy techniques

Differential privacy (DP) offers rigorous, quantifiable guarantees that individual training records cannot be reverse-engineered from shared model updates, even in the presence of powerful attacks, auxiliary information, or compromised infrastructure. Cryptographic techniques like homomorphic encryption and secure multi-party computation protect gradients during transmission and aggregation, and differential privacy provides an additional, orthogonal defense. At the same time, mathematical techniques guarantee that participation in federated learning reveals negligible information about any individual's data. Integrating DP into DAI systems demands adaptations to FL's distributed architecture and blockchain's auditable environment. This section presents foundational DP concepts, noise-addition mechanisms, distributed privacy budgeting, and on-chain proofs to achieve end-to-end privacy guarantees that satisfy both regulatory mandates and theoretical standards.

Mathematical foundations of differential privacy

Differential privacy provides rigorous mathematical guarantees that individual participation in federated learning systems reveals negligible information about private data. The formal definition ensures that the statistical distribution of system outputs remains nearly identical whether any individual participant includes or excludes their data from the learning process. These privacy techniques are:

- **Epsilon-delta privacy parameters**: Quantify the privacy-utility tradeoff through two key parameters:

  - **Epsilon (ε)**: Controls the privacy budget with smaller values providing stronger privacy guarantees.
  - **Delta (δ)**: Accounts for cryptographic failure probabilities.

  The relationship between these parameters determines the noise magnitude required to achieve specified privacy levels.

- **Composition theorems**: Enable privacy analysis across multiple training rounds and aggregation operations. Sequential composition bounds accumulate privacy loss over time, while parallel composition allows simultaneous operations on disjoint datasets without additional privacy degradation. Advanced composition techniques like Rényi differential privacy provide tighter bounds for iterative machine learning processes.
- **Global vs. local privacy models**: Distinguish between centralized noise addition (global model) and individual participant noise injection (local model). Local differential privacy provides stronger guarantees by ensuring individual privacy before any aggregation, while global models can achieve better utility by coordinating noise addition across participants.

Noise addition mechanisms

Systematic noise injection techniques preserve differential privacy while maintaining model utility in federated learning environments. Different noise distributions provide varying privacy-utility tradeoffs suitable for various application requirements. These are:

- **Laplacian noise mechanisms**: Add noise sampled from Laplace distributions with a scale parameter calibrated to query sensitivity and desired privacy level. For federated learning, gradient sensitivity analysis determines appropriate noise scales for model parameter updates while preserving convergence properties.
- **Gaussian noise with advanced composition**: Provides superior privacy accounting through Rényi differential privacy analysis. Gaussian mechanisms offer tighter composition bounds for iterative algorithms, enabling extended training periods or stronger privacy guarantees compared to Laplacian approaches.
- **Exponential mechanism for discrete choices**: Handles non-numeric privacy-sensitive decisions like participant selection or hyperparameter choices. This mechanism samples from probability distributions proportional to exponential utility functions, providing differential privacy for categorical decisions in federated learning protocols.

Distributed privacy preservation

Decentralized federated learning environments require specialized differential privacy techniques that operate without trusted central authorities. Distributed privacy mechanisms must coordinate noise addition across participants while preventing privacy violations through collusion or system compromise:

- **Local differential privacy implementation**: Requires each participant to add sufficient noise to achieve individual privacy guarantees before sharing any information. Participants independently inject noise into model updates using predetermined privacy budgets, providing protection against both external attackers and compromised aggregation infrastructure.
- **Secure aggregation with differential privacy**: Combines cryptographic techniques with noise injection to provide both privacy and security guarantees. Participants add noise to model updates before encryption, then use secure multi-party computation protocols for privacy-preserving aggregation.
- **Distributed privacy budget management**: Coordinates privacy expenditure across multiple participants and training rounds through blockchain-based accounting systems. Smart contracts can track cumulative privacy loss and enforce budget constraints while enabling flexible privacy allocation strategies.

Privacy-utility optimization

Balancing privacy protection with model utility requires sophisticated optimization techniques that minimize accuracy degradation while maintaining differential privacy guarantees. Advanced mechanisms adaptively adjust noise parameters based on model convergence and privacy consumption patterns:

- **Adaptive privacy budgeting**: Dynamically allocates privacy resources based on model training progress and utility requirements. Early training phases may use smaller privacy budgets when gradients are large, while later phases require careful budget management as gradients become smaller and more sensitive.
- **Gradient clipping and sensitivity analysis**: Bounds the maximum influence of individual data points on model updates, enabling precise noise calibration. Proper gradient clipping ensures that sensitivity analysis accurately reflects worst-case privacy implications while minimizing necessary noise injection.
- **Personalized privacy preferences**: Accommodate varying privacy requirements across participants through flexible privacy parameter selection. Blockchain-based systems can implement personalized privacy budgets while maintaining global differential privacy guarantees through advanced composition analysis.

Secure multi-party computation

SMPC allows N participants to jointly compute an aggregate function on their private inputs without revealing those inputs to any other party or to any third party, even the aggregator. Homomorphic encryption protects gradients through mathematical operations on ciphertext, and secret sharing distributes trust among custodians. At the same time, SMPC protocols directly compute functions in the presence of adversaries, providing information-theoretic or computational security guarantees. In DAI networks, SMPC serves as a complementary privacy mechanism to cryptographic aggregation: participants can collaboratively train models while maintaining the strict confidentiality of local datasets, enabling trustless computation even when no cryptographic authority (like an HE key holder) can be relied upon. This section explores SMPC fundamentals, practical protocols, integration with blockchain coordination, and optimization techniques essential for production BCFL systems.

SMPC fundamentals for FL

Secure multi-party computation enables multiple parties to jointly compute functions over their private inputs without revealing individual data to any participant. In blockchain-federated learning contexts, SMPC protocols facilitate privacy-preserving model aggregation where participants can collaboratively train models while maintaining the strict confidentiality of local datasets.

Garbled circuits for neural network training

Compile model aggregation functions into obfuscated Boolean circuits that enable secure evaluation without revealing intermediate computations. Participants provide encrypted inputs to circuit evaluation, enabling secure computation of federated averaging operations while preserving the privacy of individual model parameters.

Secret sharing schemes

Distribute model parameters across multiple computation parties using mathematical techniques that require a threshold number of participants to reconstruct secret values. Shamir's secret sharing provides information-theoretic security by ensuring that any subset smaller than the threshold reveals no information about the original secret.

Homomorphic encryption integration

Enables computation directly on encrypted data without decryption, facilitating secure aggregation operations in distributed environments. Fully homomorphic encryption schemes theoretically support arbitrary computations on encrypted data, though practical implementations focus on specific operations required for federated learning aggregation.

Efficient SMPC protocols for model aggregation

Practical SMPC implementations for federated learning must balance security guarantees with computational and communication efficiency requirements. Standard SMPC protocols often impose significant overhead that can be prohibitive for real-world federated learning deployments. To achieve practical performance in BCFL systems, researchers, and practitioners have developed specialized optimizations that preserve security while reducing resource demands:

- **Ben-Or–Goldwasser–Wigderson (BGW) protocol adaptations**: Modify classical secure multiparty computation protocols for federated learning-specific operations. These adaptations focus on secure arithmetic operations required for weighted averaging while optimizing for the specific structure of neural network parameters.
- **Partially encrypted multi-party computation**: Reduces overhead by selectively encrypting only the most privacy-sensitive model components. Research demonstrates that encrypting only first-layer parameters while transmitting remaining layers in plaintext can maintain privacy against gradient inversion attacks while significantly reducing computational costs.
- **Threshold cryptosystems**: Distribute decryption capabilities across multiple parties, ensuring robust security even when some participants are compromised. These systems enable secure aggregation without single points of failure while maintaining efficiency through parallelizable operations.

Authentication and identity in SMPC

Decentralized SMPC environments require robust authentication mechanisms to prevent impersonation attacks and ensure that only authorized participants contribute to secure computations. Traditional SMPC assumes authenticated channels, but blockchain environments necessitate cryptographic identity verification without trusted authorities. The following approaches integrate identity management seamlessly with privacy-preserving computation:

- **Authenticable multi-party computation**: Integrates identity verification directly into SMPC protocols through combined secret sharing, Diffie-Hellman key agreement, and functional encryption techniques. These protocols provide both secure computation and participant authentication without requiring trusted third parties.
- **ZK identity proofs**: Enable participants to prove their authorization to participate in SMPC protocols without revealing identifying information. These techniques maintain privacy while preventing unauthorized access to sensitive computation processes.
- **Blockchain-based identity management**: Leverages distributed ledger technology to maintain participant registries and authorization credentials. Smart contracts can automate identity verification and access control for SMPC protocols while maintaining immutable audit trails.

Performance optimization and practical deployment

Real-world SMPC deployment requires careful optimization of computational and communication overhead to achieve practical performance for federated learning applications. Various optimization techniques can significantly improve SMPC efficiency while maintaining security guarantees, such as:

- **Communication complexity reduction**: Employs compression techniques and optimized protocols to minimize data transmission requirements. Techniques include gradient quantization, sparse communication protocols, and efficient encoding schemes for secret shares.
- **Parallel processing architectures**: Leverage modern computing infrastructure to distribute SMPC computations across multiple processors and machines. Parallelizable secret sharing schemes and concurrent circuit evaluation can significantly improve performance for large-scale federated learning applications.
- **Hybrid security models**: Combine SMPC with other privacy-preserving techniques to optimize the security-performance tradeoff. Approaches include using SMPC for critical operations while employing differential privacy or secure aggregation for less sensitive computations.
- **Hardware acceleration**: Utilizes specialized computing hardware to improve SMPC performance. **Graphics processing unit** (**GPU**) acceleration for cryptographic operations and dedicated secure computation hardware can significantly reduce execution time for privacy-preserving federated learning protocols.

Implementation with TFF

TFF provides a comprehensive, production-grade framework for implementing federated learning systems with explicit support for privacy-preserving techniques, secure aggregation, and decentralized coordination. Integrating TFF with blockchain mechanisms enables end-to-end DAI systems where model training, validation, and reward distribution are governed by transparent, immutable on-chain logic while heavy computation remains off-chain for efficiency. This section details **TensorFlow Federated** (**TFF**)'s architecture, integration patterns with blockchain networks, deployment strategies, and practical code examples enabling readers to prototype and deploy BCFL systems using industry-standard tooling.

TFF architecture overview

TFF provides a comprehensive open-source framework for implementing federated learning systems with support for blockchain integration and advanced privacy-preserving techniques. The platform consists of two primary layers: FL for high-level interfaces and FC for low-level distributed computation primitives.

Two-phase execution model

This model separates compilation from execution in federated computations. TFF first compiles federated learning algorithms into abstract serialized representations of distributed computations, including TensorFlow model serialization and communication protocols. The execution phase provides local simulation capabilities for development and testing, with provisions for deployment to distributed environments.

Federated computation abstraction

This represents distributed machine learning algorithms as platform-independent computational graphs. These representations include serialized model code, declarative communication specifications between clients and servers, and interleaved local and distributed computation patterns.

Building blocks for blockchain integration

This includes TensorFlow computations wrapped as reusable components and federated operators for distributed communication. Intrinsic functions like `tff.federated_sum` and `tff.federated_broadcast` provide the foundation for implementing blockchain-based coordination and secure aggregation protocols.

Blockchain-coordinated federated learning

Practical implementation of blockchain-coordinated federated learning requires integration of TFF with blockchain networks and smart contract systems. Open-source implementations demonstrate various approaches to combining federated learning frameworks with distributed ledger technology. The following patterns represent proven architectural building blocks for production BCFL systems:

- **Smart contract integration**: Automates federated learning workflows through blockchain-based coordination. Smart contracts handle participant registration, training round initiation, model validation, and reward distribution, while TFF manages the actual machine learning computations.
- **IPFS integration for model storage**: Addresses blockchain storage limitations by storing large model parameters off-chain while maintaining cryptographic integrity through blockchain-recorded hashes. This hybrid approach balances decentralization with practical storage requirements for neural network models.
- **Ganache development environment**: Provides local blockchain simulation for federated learning development and testing. Developers can prototype blockchain-federated learning systems using local networks before deploying to production blockchain infrastructure.

Privacy-preserving implementation patterns

TFF supports various privacy-preserving techniques essential for blockchain-federated learning through specialized APIs and integration patterns. Implementation requires careful coordination between TFF's federated learning capabilities and external cryptographic libraries. These implementation patterns are:

- **Differential privacy integration**: Incorporates noise addition mechanisms into TFF model training pipelines. Developers can implement custom differential privacy mechanisms using TFF's functional programming abstractions while maintaining compatibility with blockchain verification systems.
- **Secure aggregation protocols**: Utilize TFF's federated operators to implement cryptographic aggregation schemes. Custom aggregation functions can incorporate homomorphic encryption, secret sharing, or other cryptographic techniques while leveraging TFF's distributed computation framework.
- **Model serialization and verification**: Ensures compatibility between TFF model representations and blockchain verification requirements. Proper serialization enables cryptographic hashing and verification of model updates while maintaining TFF's execution efficiency.

Performance optimization and scalability

Practical deployment of TFF-based blockchain federated learning requires careful attention to performance optimization and scalability considerations. Various techniques can improve system efficiency while maintaining security and privacy guarantees, such as:

- **Client selection and scheduling**: Optimizes participant selection for both learning efficiency and blockchain consensus requirements. Adaptive selection algorithms can balance model improvement objectives with blockchain network constraints.
- **Communication optimization**: Reduces bandwidth requirements through gradient compression, quantization, and sparse update protocols. These optimizations are particularly important in blockchain environments where transaction costs and network latency impact system performance.
- **Asynchronous training support**: Enables flexible participation patterns that accommodate varying device capabilities and network conditions. Asynchronous protocols reduce synchronization overhead while maintaining convergence guarantees for federated learning algorithms.
- **Simulation and testing frameworks**: Provide comprehensive development environments for blockchain-federated learning systems. TFF's simulation capabilities enable thorough testing of privacy-preserving and blockchain-integrated systems before production deployment.

Performance optimization

Scalable, production-grade DAI systems must achieve practical throughput and latency while maintaining privacy, security, and decentralization. FL's communication costs (model updates across thousands of participants), blockchain's consensus overhead (validation and finality latency), and cryptographic operations (encryption, proofs, threshold decryption) collectively create resource bottlenecks that can render BCFL systems impractical without careful optimization.

Communication efficiency optimization

Communication overhead represents a critical bottleneck in blockchain-enabled federated learning systems, where both federated learning model updates and blockchain consensus messages compete for limited network resources. Optimizing communication efficiency requires coordinated approaches that consider both machine learning convergence requirements and blockchain network constraints.

Gradient compression techniques

They significantly reduce communication overhead by compressing model updates before transmission. Quantization reduces parameter precision, sparsification transmits only significant updates, and knowledge distillation creates smaller model representations while maintaining accuracy. In blockchain environments, compression must balance communication savings with cryptographic verification requirements.

Adaptive communication protocols

They dynamically adjust update frequency and size based on model convergence progress and network conditions. Early training phases with large gradient magnitudes can tolerate aggressive compression, while later phases require more precise updates to achieve convergence. Blockchain-based systems can use smart contracts to coordinate adaptive communication strategies across participants.

Hierarchical aggregation structures

They reduce communication complexity through multi-tier aggregation that aligns with blockchain network topology. Regional aggregators can perform preliminary model combination before submitting to global blockchain consensus, reducing both communication overhead and consensus latency.

Computational resource management

Blockchain-federated learning systems must efficiently allocate computational resources across machine learning training, cryptographic operations, and blockchain consensus participation. Resource optimization requires understanding the computational requirements of each system component and designing allocation strategies that maximize overall performance.

Joint optimization of training and consensus

It formulates resource allocation as a multi-objective optimization problems that simultaneously maximize federated learning performance and blockchain throughput. Advanced optimization techniques like penalty dual decomposition and block successive minimization can solve these complex non-convex problems.

Dynamic resource allocation

It adapts computational resource distribution based on real-time system conditions and performance metrics. Participants can dynamically adjust the allocation between local training, cryptographic operations, and consensus participation based on network conditions and learning objectives.

Energy-efficient protocol design

It minimizes power consumption through optimized consensus mechanisms and reduced cryptographic overhead. Proof of stake adaptations and lightweight cryptographic protocols can significantly reduce energy requirements compared to traditional blockchain systems.

Scalability enhancement strategies

Scalability challenges in blockchain-federated learning arise from both federated learning coordination complexity and blockchain consensus limitations. Addressing these challenges requires architectural innovations that maintain security guarantees while supporting large numbers of participants. The enhancement strategies are:

- **DAG-based blockchain architectures**: They replace traditional linear blockchain structures with DAGs that support higher transaction throughput and parallel processing. DAG-FL frameworks enable asynchronous federated learning participation while maintaining cryptographic security and decentralization.
- **Sharding and Layer 2 solutions**: They partition blockchain networks to improve scalability while maintaining global consensus properties. Federated learning tasks can be distributed across blockchain shards, with cross-shard communication coordinating global model aggregation.
- **Efficient consensus mechanisms**: They optimize blockchain consensus for federated learning workloads through specialized protocols that repurpose mining work for productive machine learning tasks. These approaches achieve consensus efficiency while generating value for federated learning objectives.

Performance monitoring and optimization

Comprehensive performance monitoring enables continuous optimization of blockchain-federated learning systems through real-time analysis of system metrics and bottleneck identification. Performance optimization requires monitoring both machine learning metrics and blockchain network performance indicators. These monitoring and optimization techniques form a feedback loop that maintains system performance as participant count, data complexity, and network conditions evolve:

- **Multi-dimensional performance metrics**: Track federated learning convergence, communication overhead, consensus latency, and energy consumption to provide comprehensive system visibility. Advanced monitoring systems can correlate metrics across different system components to identify optimization opportunities.
- **Adaptive optimization algorithms**: Automatically adjust system parameters based on performance monitoring data. Machine learning techniques can optimize resource allocation, participant selection, and protocol parameters to maximize system performance under varying conditions.
- **Predictive performance modeling**: Uses historical data and system modeling to anticipate performance bottlenecks and proactively optimize system configuration. Predictive models can guide resource provisioning and participant scheduling to maintain optimal performance.

Real-world case studies

This section presents domain-specific deployments of BCFL, illustrating DAI's transformative impact across healthcare, finance, IoT, and autonomous systems. Each case demonstrates the convergence of privacy-preserving ML, cryptographic coordination, economic incentives, and regulatory compliance that characterize production DAI systems.

Healthcare consortium applications

Healthcare represents one of the most promising application domains for blockchain-enabled federated learning, where strict privacy regulations and sensitive patient data create natural requirements for decentralized, privacy-preserving machine learning solutions.

Multi-hospital collaborative diagnosis

These systems enable medical institutions to collaboratively train diagnostic models without sharing patient records. Kakao Healthcare's implementation with Google Cloud demonstrates practical federated learning deployment across Korean hospitals, achieving a prediction performance of 0.8482 compared to individual hospital performances ranging from 0.6397 to 0.8362. The system standardizes medical data formats while maintaining strict privacy controls and regulatory compliance.

Cancer detection and treatment prediction

It leverages federated learning to improve rare disease diagnosis through multi-institutional collaboration. Owkin's federated learning platform enables hospitals to train models on histopathology and medical imaging data without violating the **Health Insurance Portability and Accountability Act** (**HIPAA**) or the **General Data Protection Regulation** (**GDPR**) regulations. Blockchain integration ensures transparent audit trails and secure model verification across participating institutions.

Drug discovery and clinical trials

They benefit from federated learning by enabling pharmaceutical companies to collaborate with hospitals and research institutions without exposing proprietary data. Blockchain-based systems can track patient consent, manage data access permissions, and distribute incentives for participation in collaborative research.

Hierarchical privacy protection

Implementations combine LDP, GDP, and SMPC to provide comprehensive privacy guarantees in healthcare FL. Novel aggregated gradient perturbation mechanisms reduce noise impact while maintaining privacy, achieving high accuracy on real healthcare datasets and **generative adversarial network** (**GAN**)- generated synthetic data.

Financial services and fraud detection

Financial institutions leverage blockchain-federated learning for collaborative fraud detection and risk assessment while maintaining the strict confidentiality of customer data and proprietary algorithms. Regulatory requirements and competitive concerns make traditional data sharing impractical, creating strong incentives for privacy-preserving collaborative learning.

Cross-bank fraud detection

These systems enable financial institutions to collaboratively train fraud detection models without sharing transaction data or customer information. Secure multi-party computation protocols facilitate privacy-preserving model aggregation while blockchain systems provide transparent audit trails and automated compliance reporting.

Credit scoring enhancement

FL allows banks and alternative data providers to improve credit risk models without exposing individual customer profiles. Blockchain-based incentive mechanisms can compensate data contributors while ensuring fair and transparent model improvement processes.

Real-world performance evaluation

Real-world evaluations of federated and blockchain-assisted fraud and intrusion detection report substantial but context-dependent gains. For instance, a federated meta-learning framework for credit card fraud achieved between roughly 97% and 99.9% accuracy across four open-source datasets with severe class imbalance, including a 99.01% accuracy result on one benchmark when compared against state-of-the-art centralized baselines. Separately, an AI-driven intrusion detection deployment on a government network reported reducing incident response times from about 24 hours to 3.5 hours relative to traditional manual workflows, illustrating how faster, collaborative detection pipelines can shorten investigation cycles. These figures are specific to the datasets, imbalance ratios, and experimental setups used, so they should be treated as illustrative case studies rather than universal guarantees.

Regulatory compliance and auditability

Blockchain integration provides immutable audit trails essential for financial services compliance. Smart contracts automate regulatory reporting and ensure adherence to privacy regulations while enabling collaborative model development.

IoT and edge computing applications

IoT and edge computing environments present unique challenges for federated learning due to resource constraints, network variability, and security vulnerabilities that blockchain technology can address.

Smart city infrastructure

Deployments leverage blockchain-federated learning for collaborative intelligence across municipal systems. Traffic management systems, environmental monitoring, and public safety applications can share learning insights while maintaining data sovereignty and operational independence.

Industrial IoT applications

They utilize blockchain-federated learning for predictive maintenance and quality control across manufacturing networks. Federated learning enables equipment manufacturers and industrial operators to collaborate on predictive models while protecting proprietary operational data and trade secrets.

Autonomous vehicle networks

They implement blockchain-federated learning for collaborative perception and navigation improvement. NVIDIA's Autonomous Vehicles Federated Learning platform demonstrates cross-border model training that complies with regional data regulations while improving global autonomous vehicle performance.

Intrusion detection systems

For IoT networks to benefit from collaborative threat intelligence sharing through blockchain-federated learning. Systems achieve 99.8% data security while detecting 45% more attacks than traditional centralized approaches, with significant reductions in false positives and investigation time.

Transportation and mobility solutions

Transportation systems represent a rapidly growing application area for blockchain-federated learning, where safety-critical applications require robust collaborative learning with strong security guarantees.

Intelligent traffic management

Systems use blockchain-federated learning to optimize traffic flow and reduce congestion through collaborative learning across smart traffic infrastructure. Statistical heterogeneity and data sharing challenges are addressed through federated learning algorithms with server-side momentum optimization and blockchain-based model verification.

Vehicle-to-everything communication

Vehicle-to-everything (V2X) networks leverage federated learning for real-time traffic optimization and hazard detection, while blockchain ensures secure communication and incentivizes data sharing. Prototype implementations demonstrate feasibility, accuracy, and performance in real-world vehicular environments.

Cross-jurisdictional collaboration

Enables transportation authorities to share traffic patterns and safety insights without compromising sensitive infrastructure information. Blockchain-based systems provide transparent governance and automated compliance with varying regulatory requirements across jurisdictions.

Performance and security metrics

Demonstrate practical viability with systems achieving comparable accuracy to centralized approaches while providing enhanced security guarantees. Blockchain integration enables new models of trustless collaborative intelligence for safety-critical transportation applications.

Conclusion

This chapter has detailed how blockchain technology transforms federated learning from a centralized paradigm into a fully decentralized, trustless, and economically aligned system for collaborative artificial intelligence. We have traversed the complete architecture of BCFL: from foundational concepts (FL paradigms, blockchain coordination) through cryptographic primitives (homomorphic encryption, secret sharing, zero-knowledge proofs, differential privacy, secure multi-party computation) to practical engineering (TFF integration, performance optimization, production deployment). Real-world case studies demonstrated that healthcare consortia achieving superior diagnostic accuracy, financial networks detecting fraud across institutional boundaries, IoT ecosystems coordinating millions of edge devices, and autonomous fleets sharing perception models safely demonstrate that DAI is not theoretical; it is operational, delivering measurable business value while preserving privacy and democratizing participation.

Federated learning and blockchain are not merely a technical combination; they represent a paradigm shift in how humanity approaches artificial intelligence development. For decades, AI has been centralized; powerful models concentrated in the hands of large technology companies, trained on data extracted from individuals. DAI offers an alternative: collaborative intelligence where data remains with its owners, where benefits are shared equitably, and where development is governed by participants rather than gatekeepers.

The next chapter covers the operational architecture enabling robust, scalable model deployment in decentralized networks that transforms trained models into reliable, verifiable, and continuously improving systems serving real-world applications at a global scale.

CHAPTER 6
Model Deployment and Management

Introduction

In traditional Web2 MLOps, models are deployed into centrally controlled environments where a single organization owns the infrastructure, governs access, and unilaterally manages updates, monitoring, and rollback. In decentralized AI, those assumptions break down: infrastructure is contributed by independent parties, control is shared through on-chain governance, and models must operate across heterogeneous, partially trusted nodes. This makes deployment not just an engineering problem but also a coordination, incentive, and governance challenge that spans multiple organizations and jurisdictions. As a result, familiar MLOps practices must be rethought for environments where trust, ownership, and execution are enforced by cryptographic and economic mechanisms rather than by a single platform provider.

AI model deployment in decentralized networks revolutionizes traditional centralized paradigms through blockchain-enabled distributed systems featuring trustless sharing, community governance, and token-incentivized collaboration. Readers will master building robust infrastructure for model packaging, versioning, peer-to-peer distribution, runtime orchestration, serving architectures, load balancing, performance monitoring, seamless updates with rollbacks, and comprehensive quality assurance across global networks. The chapter tackles blockchain-specific challenges, including smart contract limitations, gas optimization, consensus delays, cryptographic privacy protocols, tokenomic incentives, **Decentralized Autonomous Organization** (**DAO**) decision making, and federated learning coordination to deliver secure, high-performance, democratically governed AI ecosystems.

Structure

The chapter covers the following topics:

- Model packaging and versioning
- Decentralized model distribution

- Runtime environment management
- Model serving infrastructure
- Load balancing and scaling
- Performance monitoring
- A/B testing in decentralized systems
- Automated rollback procedures
- Quality assurance and validation

Objectives

By the end of this chapter, learners will be able to design and implement a blockchain-integrated model packaging using **InterPlanetary File System** (**IPFS**) for content-addressable storage and smart contracts for immutable versioning. The chapter will enable building token-incentivized, peer-to-peer model distribution networks that use reputation, staking, and dynamic pricing to reward reliable service providers.

Readers will learn how to configure and operate DAO-governed runtime environments that use on-chain consensus for resource allocation, policy changes, and coordinated upgrades. They will also learn how to deploy privacy-preserving model serving pipelines that combine secure multi-party computation, zero-knowledge proofs, homomorphic encryption, and regulatory compliance controls.

The chapter establishes community-driven quality assurance processes using crowd-sourced validation, automated on-chain monitoring, and bias detection mechanisms. Readers will be able to design and implement consensus-based update and rollback systems that couple economic incentives with safe, coordinated cross-chain synchronization. This chapter aims to develop decentralized compliance frameworks that encode community audits, dispute resolution procedures, and cross-jurisdictional regulatory requirements into smart contract logic.

Model packaging and versioning

The deployment of AI models in decentralized networks fundamentally transforms how we approach model packaging and versioning. Unlike traditional centralized systems, where models exist within controlled environments, decentralized AI networks require sophisticated packaging strategies that enable secure, verifiable, and efficient distribution across untrusted nodes while maintaining immutable version histories through blockchain technology.

Model packaging in decentralized systems

The paradigm shift from centralized to decentralized AI model deployment has fundamentally altered how we approach model packaging. In centralized systems, models are typically deployed to homogeneous environments with predictable infrastructure characteristics. However, decentralized networks introduce significant complexity through heterogeneous hardware configurations, varying network conditions, and diverse operating environments that span from cloud data centers to edge devices.

Challenges of distributed model packaging

The primary challenge in decentralized model packaging stems from the need to ensure consistent model behavior across vastly different execution environments. Traditional packaging approaches that work well in controlled data center environments often fail when deployed to edge devices with limited computational resources, different operating systems, or varying hardware architectures. The containerization revolution has provided partial solutions, but decentralized systems require more sophisticated approaches that account for network partitioning, intermittent connectivity, and resource constraints.

Modern AI models, particularly large language models and deep neural networks, can range from gigabytes to terabytes in size, making their distribution across networks a significant challenge. The packaging strategy must consider not only the model artifacts themselves but also the entire dependency graph, including runtime environments, supporting libraries, and configuration files. This complexity is further amplified in decentralized systems where different nodes may have different capabilities and requirements.

One practical example illustrates how these challenges surface in real deployments. Imagine packaging a 7-billion-parameter language model so it can run both on edge GPUs with 16-24 GB of VRAM and on CPU-only validator nodes operated by community members. The deployment must support quantized variants, sharded weights, and hardware-specific runtimes while still guaranteeing that inference results remain within acceptable equivalence bounds across all nodes. This requires packaging not just the core model, but multiple optimized binaries, accelerator backends, configuration profiles, and fallback execution paths so that each node can select an appropriate execution plan without breaking deterministic behavior or consensus on model outputs.

Differences from centralized approaches

Centralized model packaging typically focuses on creating a single, comprehensive package that contains all necessary components for deployment. This approach works well when deploying to a known, controlled environment, but it becomes problematic in decentralized systems where nodes may have varying capabilities. Decentralized packaging must embrace modularity, allowing different nodes to receive and deploy only the components they need while maintaining model consistency and performance.

The versioning challenges in decentralized systems are also more complex than their centralized counterparts. While centralized systems can implement versioning through simple sequential updates, decentralized systems must handle scenarios where different nodes may be running different model versions simultaneously, requiring sophisticated conflict resolution and compatibility management strategies.

Blockchain-native model packaging

Model packaging in decentralized AI systems extends far beyond conventional containerization approaches to incorporate blockchain-specific requirements that ensure trustless operation and community governance. The fundamental challenge lies in creating package formats that can leverage blockchain immutability while maintaining the flexibility necessary for AI model evolution and optimization.

Content-addressable model artifacts

The foundation of decentralized model packaging begins with content-addressable storage systems, primarily leveraging the IPFS to create immutable, distributed model artifacts. When a model is packaged for deployment, its binary representation is processed through cryptographic hashing algorithms to generate a unique **content identifier** (**CID**) that serves as both a storage location and an integrity verification mechanism. A CID in IPFS is not just a hash of a single file blob, but the hash of a node in a **Merkle directed acyclic graph** (**Merkle DAG**) that encodes both the node's payload and the CIDs of its children. When a model artifact is added, IPFS chunks it into blocks, structures those blocks into a Merkle DAG (for example, using UnixFS), and then computes a cryptographic hash of the root node; this hash, combined with codec and multihash metadata, becomes the CID that uniquely identifies that entire DAG. As each node's hash commits to all descendant hashes, any bit-level change in the model weights or dependency tree produces a different CID, giving decentralized deployments a built-in integrity and provenance mechanism for model packages.

Smart contract integration for model registry

Blockchain smart contracts serve as the authoritative registry for model packages, providing immutable records of model ownership, versioning, and access permissions. In practice, ERC-721 is well-suited when each model instance or major version is treated as a truly unique asset with its own lifecycle and metadata, making ownership and transfer semantics simple and explicit. ERC-1155 becomes preferable when you need to manage families of related models or semi-fungible variants (for example, many identical edge-optimized copies of the same base model) in a single contract, gaining gas-efficient batch minting and transfer while still supporting distinct IDs for individual model versions.

Cryptographic verification and integrity

Model integrity in decentralized networks relies on multiple layers of cryptographic verification to prevent tampering and ensure authentic model deployment. The packaging process incorporates digital signatures using the model creator's private key, enabling anyone to verify the authenticity of a model package using the corresponding public key stored on-chain.

Immutable versioning on blockchain

Traditional software versioning systems rely on mutable repositories where version histories can be modified or deleted by administrators. Decentralized AI systems leverage blockchain immutability to create tamper-proof versioning records that provide permanent historical context for model evolution and enable sophisticated governance mechanisms for model updates.

On-chain version management

The implementation of on-chain version management begins with the design of smart contract data structures that can efficiently store and retrieve version information while minimizing gas costs. Version records typically include the IPFS hash of the model package, timestamp of publication, creator address, and metadata describing the changes from the previous version.

Fork management and branching

Decentralized development naturally leads to model forking, where different teams or communities create divergent versions of models to serve different purposes or incorporate different improvements. The blockchain versioning system must accommodate this organic evolution while maintaining clear relationships between different development branches.

Governance integration and community curation

Version management in decentralized systems extends beyond technical considerations to incorporate community governance mechanisms that enable democratic decision-making about model evolution. The versioning system integrates with DAOs that can vote on version approval, funding allocation, and development priorities.

Container orchestration for decentralized deployment

The orchestration of containerized AI models across decentralized networks requires sophisticated coordination mechanisms that can handle the heterogeneous nature of distributed infrastructure while maintaining performance and reliability guarantees. This orchestration must account for varying computational capabilities, network connectivity patterns, and economic incentives across different network nodes.

Container specifications in decentralized systems often include multiple optimization variants of the same model, enabling the orchestration system to select the most appropriate version for each deployment target. These variants might include quantized models for low-memory environments, pruned models for **central processing unit** (**CPU**)-only deployment, or specialized formats optimized for particular hardware accelerators.

Economic incentive integration

Container orchestration in decentralized networks must incorporate economic mechanisms that incentivize node operators to provide reliable computational resources while ensuring fair compensation for their contributions. The orchestration system interfaces with token economics to implement payment systems, performance bonuses, and penalty mechanisms for unreliable service.

Consensus-based coordination

Orchestration decisions in decentralized systems often require consensus among multiple network participants to ensure transparency and prevent centralized control. The orchestration system implements consensus mechanisms that enable distributed decision-making about resource allocation, deployment priorities, and network configuration changes.

These consensus mechanisms must balance decision-making speed with democratic participation, often implementing delegated proof of stake systems where token holders delegate their voting power to technical experts who can make rapid operational decisions. These delegated proof of stake arrangements trade off wider direct participation for operational agility: a small, elected validator set can coordinate upgrades and orchestration quickly, but coin-weighted delegation risks plutocratic capture or low voter turnout if large holders dominate or fail to re-delegate actively. Alternative governance schemes such as quadratic voting and optimistic governance favor broader, preference-sensitive participation or **approve-by-default** workflows, which can better surface minority views and reduce voting overhead, but they generally introduce more complex **user experience** (**UX**), parameter tuning, and veto or challenge processes that may slow down time-critical infrastructure decisions.

Automated deployment pipelines

The implementation of automated deployment pipelines in decentralized AI networks requires sophisticated integration between traditional DevOps practices and blockchain-specific workflows. These pipelines must handle the complexities of distributed consensus, economic coordination, and community governance while maintaining the speed and reliability expected in modern deployment systems.

Smart contract-driven automation

Deployment automation in decentralized systems leverages smart contracts to implement programmable deployment logic that executes automatically based on predefined conditions and community governance decisions. These smart contracts serve as the orchestration layer that coordinates between traditional **continuous integration/continuous deployment (CI/CD)** systems and blockchain-based coordination mechanisms.

The automation pipeline begins with code and model updates being committed to distributed version control systems, triggering smart contract functions that initiate the deployment process. The smart contract logic includes validation steps that verify model quality, check compliance with community standards, and ensure that all necessary approvals have been obtained before proceeding with deployment.

Multi-chain deployment coordination

Modern decentralized AI systems often operate across multiple blockchain networks to leverage different capabilities and optimize for various use cases. The deployment pipeline must coordinate deployments across these different chains while maintaining consistency and handling the complexities of cross-chain communication.

The coordination system implements bridge protocols and oracle networks that enable smart contracts on different chains to communicate and synchronize deployment states. In practice, these cross-chain layers introduce additional security risks: bridge contracts have been a major source of protocol-draining exploits, and poorly designed message formats can allow replayed payloads or mis-sequenced messages to be accepted more than once or in the wrong order. Robust multi-chain deployment, therefore, needs explicit replay protection (chainscoped nonces and domain separation), finality and ordering guarantees, and idempotent receive logic so that out-of-order, duplicate, or stale cross-chain deployment messages cannot corrupt the global view of which model version is live on each network.

Decentralized model distribution

The distribution of AI models across decentralized networks represents a fundamental departure from traditional centralized **content delivery networks (CDNs)** and application stores. In blockchain-enabled AI ecosystems, model distribution must account for economic incentives, trustless verification, community governance, and the diverse computational capabilities of distributed nodes while maintaining security and performance standards comparable to centralized alternatives. *Figure 6.1* details the peer-to-peer infrastructure, content-addressing mechanisms, and specialized storage protocols required for decentralized model distribution. It also illustrates how the system enforces privacy-preserving distribution and robust cryptographic access control across large-scale AI networks.

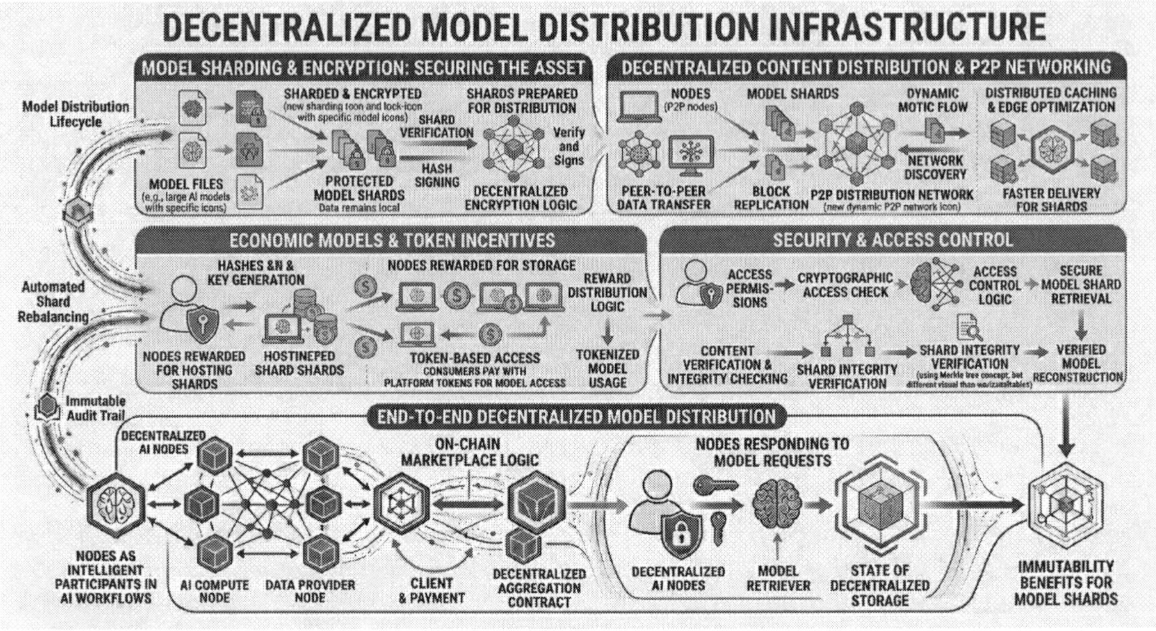

***Figure 6.1**: Decentralized model distribution infrastructure*

Peer-to-peer distribution networks

The architecture of **peer-to-peer (P2P)** distribution networks for AI models leverages the collective bandwidth and storage resources of network participants to create scalable, resilient distribution systems that eliminate single points of failure while providing economic incentives for participation.

Token-incentivized content distribution

Peer-to-peer distribution in decentralized AI networks implements sophisticated tokenomic mechanisms that reward network participants for storing and serving model content. Unlike traditional P2P systems that rely on altruistic participation, blockchain-enabled networks create direct economic incentives for providing reliable distribution services.

Distributed hash table implementation

The technical foundation of the P2P model distribution relies on **distributed hash tables (DHTs)** that provide efficient content discovery and routing without requiring centralized coordination. The DHT implementation for AI models must handle the unique characteristics of model artifacts, including large file sizes, complex dependency relationships, and the need for cryptographic verification.

The DHT structure maps content identifiers (typically IPFS hashes) to network node locations, enabling efficient content discovery across the distributed network. For AI models, this mapping includes metadata about model characteristics, computational requirements, and optimization variants to enable intelligent routing decisions. Nodes can preferentially route requests to other nodes that have specialized hardware or optimized implementations for specific model types.

Cross-chain distribution protocols

Modern decentralized AI ecosystems often span multiple blockchain networks, each with different capabilities, performance characteristics, and economic models. Cross-chain distribution protocols enable seamless model sharing across these different networks while maintaining security and performance guarantees.

IPFS integration and content addressing

The IPFS serves as the foundational storage layer for decentralized AI model distribution, providing content-addressable, distributed storage that naturally integrates with blockchain verification and incentive systems. The integration of IPFS with AI model distribution requires specialized approaches to handle the unique characteristics of machine learning artifacts.

Optimized storage for large AI models

Traditional IPFS implementations face challenges when handling the large file sizes typical of modern AI models, which can range from hundreds of megabytes to several gigabytes. Optimized storage strategies break these large models into smaller chunks that can be distributed and retrieved in parallel, improving both distribution performance and fault tolerance.

The storage system also implements tiered storage strategies that automatically move less frequently accessed model chunks to lower-cost storage tiers while maintaining hot caches for popular content. This optimization balances storage costs with performance requirements while ensuring that the most valuable models remain highly available.

Content verification and integrity checking

IPFS content addressing provides natural integrity verification through cryptographic hashing, but AI models require additional verification mechanisms to ensure not only data integrity but also model authenticity and compliance with quality standards. The verification system extends IPFS capabilities to provide comprehensive model validation.

Cryptographic signatures embedded in model metadata enable verification of model creator identity and prevent tampering with model contents. The signature verification process integrates with blockchain identity systems to provide strong authentication guarantees while enabling the community to track model provenance and establish trust in model sources.

Distributed caching and edge optimization

Effective model distribution requires sophisticated caching strategies that account for the geographic distribution of users, the heterogeneous nature of network infrastructure, and the economic incentives for cache participation. The caching system optimizes for both performance and cost-effectiveness while ensuring fair compensation for cache providers.

Edge optimization specifically targets deployment scenarios where models need to be cached on resource-constrained devices or networks with limited connectivity. The caching system implements dynamic cache management that automatically adjusts cache contents based on demand patterns, economic incentives, and node capabilities.

Economic models for model distribution

The economic framework supporting a decentralized model distribution must balance multiple competing objectives, including fair compensation for contributors, affordability for users, quality incentives for model creators, and long-term network sustainability. This requires sophisticated tokenomic design that creates a sustainable economic equilibrium while promoting network growth and quality improvement.

In a single inference cycle, a user or dApp sends a request and pays in the network's native or AI-specific token into a payment contract, which escrows or streams value for the duration of the call. The contract then routes a portion of these tokens to the model creator as a royalty on each successful invocation, allocates another portion to the node operator(s) who actually execute the inference (proportional to their verifiable compute contribution or stake-weighted reputation), and optionally diverts a small protocol fee to a treasury to fund audits, upgrades, and ecosystem grants, creating a closed-loop flow of value between users, model IP owners, infrastructure providers, and the network itself.

These tokenized incentive systems with dynamic pricing, stake-weighted reputation, and growth-aligned rewards create sustainable distribution economics that balance contributor compensation, user affordability, and network expansion:

- **Pricing mechanisms and market dynamics**: Dynamic pricing for model distribution services creates market-driven efficiency while ensuring fair compensation for network participants. The pricing system must account for multiple factors, including bandwidth costs, storage requirements, computational complexity, and demand patterns, while maintaining predictable costs for end users.
- **Staking and slashing for service quality**: Service quality assurance in decentralized networks relies on economic mechanisms rather than traditional service level agreements enforced by legal contracts. Staking and slashing systems create strong economic incentives for reliable service provision while providing recourse for users who experience service failures.

- **Incentive alignment for network growth**: Long-term network sustainability requires incentive structures that promote network growth, quality improvement, and community development rather than just short-term profit maximization. The incentive design must align individual participant interests with overall network health and growth objectives.

Security and access control

Security in decentralized model distribution encompasses multiple layers of protection, including cryptographic security, economic security, and social security mechanisms that work together to create robust protection against various attack vectors while maintaining the openness and accessibility that make decentralized systems valuable.

Cryptographic security frameworks

The cryptographic foundation of secure model distribution begins with strong encryption and authentication mechanisms that protect model content and verify the identity of all participants. This includes both data-at-rest encryption for stored models and data-in-transit encryption for distribution activities, implemented using state-of-the-art cryptographic protocols.

Access control and permissions

Decentralized access control systems must balance openness with appropriate restrictions while maintaining the efficiency and scalability required for practical model distribution. The access control framework implements multiple layers of permissions that can be combined to create sophisticated access policies.

Token-based access control uses blockchain tokens to represent access rights and permissions, enabling fine-grained control over who can access specific models or services. In practice, revocation for tokengated access is handled at the authorization layer rather than by migrating contracts: the access control contract maintains its own registry of which token IDs, addresses, or token holdings currently confer rights, and can invalidate them by flipping a flag, updating a role mapping, or enforcing timelimited or epoch-based entitlements even if the underlying tokens remain transferable. Systems that need stronger guarantees often issue non-transferable or soulbound access tokens, or separate ownership NFTs from short-lived capability tokens, so that an admin can revoke or let capabilities expire (for example, by burning or blacklisting specific capability tokens or ranges) without touching the core ownership contract or forcing a global migration.

Attribute-based access control (**ABAC**) enables sophisticated permission policies based on user attributes, model characteristics, environmental conditions, and dynamic factors. The access control system also implements delegation mechanisms that enable rights holders to grant specific permissions to other parties without transferring full ownership.

Privacy-preserving distribution

Privacy protection in model distribution must address multiple stakeholder concerns, including user privacy, model creator intellectual property, and compliance with data protection regulations across multiple jurisdictions. The privacy framework implements multiple complementary techniques to provide comprehensive protection.

Runtime environment management

Runtime environment management in decentralized AI networks requires sophisticated orchestration capabilities that can coordinate model execution across heterogeneous, distributed infrastructure while maintaining consistency, security, and performance. Unlike traditional centralized deployments, where runtime conditions can be precisely controlled, decentralized environments must adapt to diverse hardware configurations, varying network conditions, and dynamic node participation patterns while ensuring reliable model execution through blockchain-coordinated governance.

Containerized model execution

The deployment of AI models in containerized environments across decentralized networks extends traditional containerization approaches to incorporate blockchain-specific requirements for trustless execution, economic coordination, and community governance. The containerization strategy must balance security isolation with performance optimization while enabling efficient resource utilization across diverse infrastructure environments.

Blockchain-coordinated container orchestration

Container orchestration in decentralized AI networks leverages smart contracts to coordinate deployment decisions, resource allocation, and lifecycle management across distributed infrastructure. Decentralized orchestration implements consensus-based decision-making, unlike traditional orchestration systems that rely on centralized control planes. This enables community participation in infrastructure management while maintaining operational efficiency.

The orchestration smart contracts maintain comprehensive registries of available compute resources, including detailed capability profiles that describe hardware specifications, performance characteristics, geographic location, and economic requirements for each participating node. The orchestration system also implements sophisticated health monitoring and failure detection mechanisms that can automatically detect and respond to node failures, performance degradation, or malicious behavior.

Heterogeneous hardware adaptation

Decentralized networks typically encompass a wide range of hardware configurations, from high-performance cloud instances with specialized AI accelerators to resource-constrained edge devices and consumer hardware. The runtime environment management system must dynamically adapt model execution to match available hardware capabilities while maintaining consistent behavior and performance guarantees.

The adaptation system maintains comprehensive performance profiles for different hardware-model combinations, enabling predictive placement decisions that can estimate execution performance and resource requirements before deployment.

Cross-platform compatibility frameworks

Ensuring consistent model behavior across diverse runtime environments requires sophisticated compatibility frameworks that can abstract away platform-specific differences while maintaining optimal performance on each target platform. The compatibility system implements multiple layers of abstraction that handle differences in operating systems, hardware architectures, and software dependencies.

The framework includes comprehensive dependency management systems that can automatically resolve and install required software components while ensuring version compatibility and security compliance. This includes AI framework libraries, specialized hardware drivers, and system-level dependencies that may vary across different deployment environments.

Distributed resource management

Effective resource management in decentralized AI networks requires sophisticated algorithms and economic mechanisms that can efficiently allocate computational resources across distributed infrastructure while maintaining fairness, security, and economic sustainability. The resource management system must handle dynamic capacity changes, varying demand patterns, and complex optimization objectives while operating in a trustless environment.

Dynamic capacity planning and allocation

Capacity planning in decentralized networks faces unique challenges due to the voluntary and potentially unreliable nature of distributed infrastructure. The planning system must continuously monitor resource availability, predict future capacity requirements, and implement allocation strategies that optimize for multiple objectives, including performance, cost, reliability, and community benefit.

Dynamic scaling mechanisms can automatically adjust resource allocations based on real-time demand and performance metrics. This includes horizontal scaling that distributes workloads across multiple nodes for improved performance, vertical scaling that allocates additional resources to existing deployments, and load balancing that optimizes resource utilization across the network.

Economic resource optimization

Resource optimization in decentralized networks must balance technical efficiency with economic considerations, creating allocation strategies that minimize costs while maintaining required performance levels and ensuring fair compensation for resource providers. The optimization system implements sophisticated economic models that account for complex market dynamics and participant incentives.

Resource pooling strategies aggregate computational capabilities across multiple nodes to create virtual resources that can be allocated as a unified capacity. This pooling approach enables more efficient utilization of distributed resources while providing users with simplified resource management interfaces and predictable performance characteristics.

Quality of service guarantees

Providing reliable QoS guarantees in decentralized environments requires sophisticated coordination mechanisms that can handle the inherent unreliability of distributed infrastructure while maintaining service commitments. The QoS system implements multiple layers of guarantees and compensation mechanisms that protect users while incentivizing reliable service provision.

Security and isolation in distributed environments

Security in decentralized AI model execution requires comprehensive approaches that protect against various threat vectors while maintaining the performance and accessibility that make decentralized systems valuable. The security framework must address both traditional cybersecurity concerns and unique threats that arise from the distributed, trustless nature of decentralized networks.

Trusted Execution Environments

Trusted Execution Environments (TEEs) provide hardware-based security guarantees that enable secure model execution even on untrusted infrastructure. TEE integration with blockchain verification creates powerful security frameworks that can prove correct execution without requiring trust in individual node operators.

The TEE framework enables secure enclaves where AI models can execute with cryptographic guarantees about code integrity, data confidentiality, and execution correctness. In practice, these guarantees are realized by concrete technologies such as Intel SGX, which creates process-level encrypted enclaves inside the CPU, and AMD SEV and its SEV-SNP extensions, which encrypt and attest entire virtual machines so that model weights and user data remain protected even from a malicious hypervisor or cloud operator.

Sandboxing and process isolation

Process isolation mechanisms create security boundaries that prevent malicious or buggy AI models from compromising host systems or affecting other workloads running on the same infrastructure. The isolation framework implements multiple layers of protection that work together to create comprehensive security coverage.

Cryptographic protection of model assets

Cryptographic protection mechanisms ensure that valuable AI model assets are protected from unauthorized access, copying, or modification throughout the execution lifecycle. The protection framework integrates with blockchain systems to provide verifiable security guarantees while maintaining practical usability for legitimate model deployment scenarios.

Performance optimization and monitoring

Performance optimization in decentralized AI environments requires sophisticated monitoring and optimization techniques that can handle the complexities of distributed execution while providing actionable insights for improving system performance and resource utilization.

Distributed performance profiling

Performance profiling across distributed infrastructure creates unique challenges due to the heterogeneous nature of execution environments and the need to correlate performance data across multiple independent systems. The profiling system must collect comprehensive performance metrics while minimizing overhead and preserving privacy.

Real-time performance analytics provide immediate feedback about system performance while enabling rapid response to performance issues or optimization opportunities. The analytics system includes anomaly detection algorithms that can identify unusual performance patterns and automated alerting mechanisms that notify relevant stakeholders about performance issues requiring attention.

Adaptive optimization strategies

Adaptive optimization systems automatically adjust execution parameters and resource allocation based on observed performance characteristics and changing system conditions. These systems enable continuous performance improvement without requiring manual intervention while maintaining stable service delivery.

Machine learning-based optimization uses historical performance data to predict optimal execution parameters for different models and environment combinations. These predictions enable proactive optimization that can improve performance before issues become apparent while reducing the need for reactive optimization responses.

Community-driven performance enhancement

Performance enhancement in decentralized networks benefits from community participation and collaborative optimization efforts that leverage the collective knowledge and resources of network participants. The enhancement framework creates incentives for community contribution while ensuring that improvements benefit the entire network.

Performance benchmarking initiatives enable community members to contribute standardized performance tests and optimization techniques that can be shared across the network. These benchmarks create common reference points for evaluating performance while enabling fair comparison across different hardware and software configurations.

Model serving infrastructure

Model serving infrastructure in decentralized AI networks represents a fundamental reimagining of how AI models are made available for inference, moving from traditional client-server architectures to distributed, blockchain-coordinated systems that leverage community resources while providing strong guarantees about service quality, security, and economic fairness. This infrastructure must handle the complexities of trustless operation while maintaining the performance and reliability characteristics expected in production AI systems.

Decentralized API gateways and service discovery

The implementation of API gateways in decentralized environments requires sophisticated coordination mechanisms that can provide unified interfaces to distributed services while maintaining the decentralization properties that make blockchain-enabled systems valuable. Decentralized gateways distribute functionality across multiple nodes while providing consistent service interfaces, unlike traditional API gateways that operate as centralized chokepoints.

Smart contract-mediated service registration

Service discovery in decentralized AI networks leverages smart contracts as authoritative registries that maintain comprehensive information about available AI models and their hosting infrastructure. The registration system creates immutable, transparent records of service capabilities while enabling dynamic updates as services come online or offline.

The registration smart contract maintains detailed metadata about each available AI model, including model architecture, input/output specifications, performance characteristics, pricing information, and quality guarantees.

Service health monitoring is integrated with the registration system through automated uptime reporting and performance metrics collection. Nodes hosting AI models must regularly submit attestations about their operational status and performance characteristics, with failure to provide these attestations resulting in automatic service deregistration.

Distributed load balancing and traffic routing

Load balancing in decentralized systems must account for the heterogeneous nature of distributed infrastructure while ensuring fair distribution of traffic and compensation across service providers. The load balancing system implements sophisticated algorithms that optimize for multiple objectives, including performance, cost, reliability, and fairness.

Geographic routing optimization directs user requests to nearby service providers to minimize latency while accounting for network topology and infrastructure capabilities. Capability-based routing ensures that requests are directed to infrastructure that is optimized for specific model types or performance requirements. This includes routing **graphics processing unit (GPU)**-intensive models to nodes with appropriate acceleration hardware, directing low-latency requests to edge infrastructure, and balancing computational requirements with available capacity across the network.

In practice, the router can compute a composite score for each candidate node by combining normalized metrics such as estimated latency L_n, marginal cost C_n, and historical reliability into a single objective, for example $S_n = \alpha \cdot \hat{L}_n + \beta \cdot \hat{C}_n - \gamma \cdot \hat{R}_n$, and then route to the node(s) with the lowest score. Here $\hat{L}_n$, $\hat{C}_n$, and $\hat{R}_n$ are scaled into comparable ranges, while the weights α, β, γ are tuned by governance or per-tenant policy to express how much the network should prioritize latency, price, or reliability when placing each inference request.

Cross-chain service coordination

Modern decentralized AI ecosystems often span multiple blockchain networks, requiring sophisticated coordination mechanisms that can handle cross-chain service discovery and request routing. The coordination system must account for different consensus mechanisms, transaction costs, and performance characteristics across different blockchain platforms.

Consensus-based model execution verification

Verification of model execution results in trustless environments requires sophisticated consensus mechanisms that can validate AI model outputs without relying on trusted central authorities. The verification system must balance computational efficiency with security guarantees while providing practical solutions for real-world AI applications.

Multi-node execution and result consensus

Consensus-based execution involves running AI models on multiple independent nodes and comparing results to detect errors, manipulation, or inconsistencies. The consensus system must handle the inherent variability in AI model outputs while providing strong guarantees about result correctness.

Parallel execution coordination distributes identical requests across multiple service providers who execute the same model independently. The coordination system handles the complexities of request distribution, result collection, and consensus determination while ensuring that all participants receive fair compensation for their computational contributions.

Byzantine fault tolerance mechanisms ensure that consensus can be reached even when some participating nodes behave maliciously or produce incorrect results. The consensus algorithm can tolerate a specified fraction of malicious participants while still producing correct results, providing strong security guarantees for critical AI applications.

Zero-knowledge proof integration

ZK proofs enable verification of model execution correctness without revealing sensitive information about model parameters, input data, or intermediate computations. This technology is particularly valuable for protecting intellectual property while enabling trustless verification of AI model execution.

Execution proof generation creates cryptographic proofs that demonstrate correct model execution without revealing the specific computations performed. These proofs can verify that a model was executed correctly on specific inputs, that the model parameters match registered specifications, and that no unauthorized modifications were made during execution.

Verification efficiency optimizations reduce the computational overhead of generating and verifying ZK proofs for AI model execution. This includes specialized proof systems optimized for machine learning computations, batch verification techniques that amortize verification costs across multiple executions, and hardware acceleration for proof generation and verification.

Privacy-preserving verification enables model execution verification while protecting the confidentiality of both input data and model parameters. This is particularly important for applications involving sensitive data or proprietary models where traditional verification approaches would compromise confidentiality requirements.

Quality assurance through community validation

Community-driven quality assurance leverages the collective intelligence and resources of network participants to validate model execution quality and identify potential issues. The validation system creates economic incentives for community participation while providing comprehensive quality coverage.

Economic models for model serving

The economic framework supporting the decentralized model must create sustainable incentives for service provision while ensuring affordable access for users and fair compensation for all network participants. The economic design must account for the unique characteristics of AI workloads and the distributed nature of blockchain-enabled networks. These models leverage blockchain's programmability to create dynamic, self-regulating economic systems tailored for distributed AI inference:

- **Usage-based pricing and micropayments**: Usage-based pricing models charge users based on their actual consumption of AI services, creating efficient market signals while ensuring that service providers are compensated proportionally to their contributions. The pricing system must handle the high-frequency, low-value transactions typical of AI inference requests while minimizing transaction costs and latency.
- **Staking models for service providers**: Staking mechanisms create economic incentives for reliable service provision while providing security deposits that can be used to compensate users for service failures or quality issues. The staking system must balance capital efficiency with security guarantees while providing fair risk-reward profiles for service providers.
- **Revenue sharing and governance participation**: Revenue-sharing models distribute income from AI service fees across various network participants. This includes model creators, infrastructure providers, governance participants, and community contributors. The distribution mechanism must fairly compensate all stakeholders while creating sustainable incentives for network growth and development.

Performance optimization and caching

Performance optimization in decentralized model serving requires sophisticated techniques that can handle the latency and bandwidth limitations inherent in distributed systems while maintaining the quality and consistency expected in production AI applications. The optimization framework must balance multiple competing objectives, including speed, cost, security, and decentralization. The following core strategies leverage distributed caching, edge integration, and adaptive resource allocation to achieve centralized performance levels in decentralized environments:

- **Distributed caching strategies**: Intelligent caching systems can dramatically improve performance by storing frequently accessed models and results closer to users while reducing computational load on serving infrastructure. The caching strategy must account for the economic incentives and technical constraints of decentralized networks.
- **Edge computing integration**: Edge computing integration brings AI model serving capabilities closer to end users while leveraging distributed edge infrastructure that

may be owned and operated by various organizations and individuals. The integration must handle the heterogeneous nature of edge infrastructure while providing consistent service quality.

- **Adaptive QoS**: Adaptive QoS systems automatically adjust service parameters based on current network conditions, user requirements, and resource availability. This enables efficient resource utilization while maintaining acceptable service quality under varying operating conditions.

Load balancing and scaling

Load balancing and scaling in decentralized AI networks require sophisticated algorithms and economic mechanisms that can efficiently distribute computational workloads across heterogeneous, distributed infrastructure while maintaining performance guarantees and fair compensation for all participants. Unlike traditional load balancing that operates within controlled data centers, decentralized load balancing must account for voluntary participation, varying reliability, economic incentives, and the trustless nature of blockchain-enabled networks.

Intelligent load distribution algorithms

The design of load distribution algorithms for decentralized AI networks must account for multiple complex factors, including node capabilities, economic incentives, geographic distribution, and quality requirements, while optimizing for both system-wide efficiency and individual participant satisfaction. These algorithms must operate in real-time while making decisions based on incomplete and potentially unreliable information about network state.

Multi-criteria decision making for request routing

Request routing in decentralized networks involves complex multi-criteria optimization that must balance competing objectives, including performance, cost, reliability, and fairness. The routing algorithm must make decisions based on real-time information about node capabilities, current load, historical performance, and economic factors while ensuring that no single criterion dominates the decision-making process inappropriately.

Machine learning-based routing prediction uses historical data and real-time metrics to predict the likely performance outcomes of different routing decisions. These predictions enable proactive optimization that can anticipate performance issues and optimize routing decisions before problems become apparent to users.

Geographic and network topology awareness

Geographic distribution and network topology play critical roles in determining optimal routing decisions for decentralized AI workloads. The routing system must consider physical proximity, network path characteristics, and regulatory constraints when making placement decisions while optimizing for both performance and compliance requirements.

Predictive load balancing with machine learning

Predictive load balancing uses machine learning techniques to anticipate future demand patterns and proactively adjust resource allocation and routing decisions to maintain optimal system performance. This approach enables more efficient resource utilization while reducing the impact of demand spikes and system variability. These advanced **machine learning (ML)** models enable proactive capacity management by forecasting demand, detecting anomalies, and continuously optimizing resource distribution across decentralized serving nodes:

- Demand forecasting models analyze historical usage patterns, seasonal trends, and external factors to predict future resource requirements across different time horizons.
- Anomaly detection algorithms identify unusual demand patterns or system behaviors that may indicate emerging issues or opportunities for optimization.
- Dynamic rebalancing algorithms automatically adjust resource allocation and routing decisions based on predicted demand patterns and current system performance.
- Learning from feedback mechanisms continuously improves prediction accuracy by analyzing the outcomes of routing decisions and adjusting algorithms based on observed performance. To avoid model drift and runaway bias toward already well-provisioned nodes, the routing controller periodically retrains on fresh traffic and outcome data, incorporates explicit exploration terms (for example, multi-armed-bandit style randomization), and enforces fairness constraints so that lower resource but reliable nodes continue to receive a calibrated share of traffic for evaluation and capacity growth.

Horizontal and vertical scaling strategies

Scaling strategies in decentralized AI networks must account for the voluntary and potentially unreliable nature of distributed infrastructure while providing predictable performance and capacity growth. The scaling framework must implement both horizontal scaling across multiple nodes and vertical scaling within individual nodes while maintaining economic efficiency and quality guarantees. The following hybrid scaling approaches combine elastic resource provisioning, dynamic node orchestration, and cross-chain coordination to achieve seamless capacity expansion across heterogeneous decentralized infrastructure:

- **Elastic resource allocation**: Elastic resource allocation enables automatic scaling of computational resources based on demand patterns while maintaining cost efficiency and performance guarantees. The allocation system must coordinate across multiple independent resource providers while ensuring fair compensation and preventing resource monopolization.

- **Dynamic node participation management**: Managing dynamic node participation in decentralized networks requires sophisticated coordination mechanisms that can handle nodes joining and leaving the network while maintaining service continuity and quality. The participation management system must provide incentives for reliable participation while gracefully handling unreliable or malicious participants.
- **Cross-chain scaling coordination**: Scaling across multiple blockchain networks requires sophisticated coordination mechanisms that can leverage the unique capabilities of different blockchain platforms while maintaining consistent performance and service quality. Cross-chain scaling enables access to broader resource pools while optimizing for different performance and cost characteristics.

Community-driven scaling governance

Scaling decisions in decentralized networks benefit from community input and governance oversight to ensure that scaling strategies align with community values and long-term network sustainability. The governance framework must balance technical efficiency with democratic participation while enabling responsive scaling decisions. These DAO-based governance models empower community stakeholders to collectively determine scaling policies, capacity thresholds, and resource allocation priorities through transparent, incentive-aligned voting mechanisms:

- **Decentralized capacity planning**: Community-driven capacity planning leverages the collective intelligence and diverse perspectives of network participants to develop scaling strategies that account for multiple stakeholder interests and usage scenarios. This approach ensures that scaling decisions reflect the actual needs and priorities of the network community.
- **Economic governance of scaling decisions**: Economic governance mechanisms ensure that scaling decisions consider the economic impact on all network participants while maintaining fair compensation and sustainable network economics. The governance framework must balance efficiency with equity while preventing economic manipulation or exploitation.

Performance-based auto-scaling

Performance-based auto-scaling systems automatically adjust network capacity based on real-time performance metrics and user quality requirements while maintaining economic efficiency and participant satisfaction. These systems must balance responsiveness with stability while accounting for the economic and technical constraints of decentralized infrastructure. These intelligent auto-scaling leverages real-time monitoring, algorithmic triggers, and community feedback to dynamically optimize capacity while ensuring predictable performance SLAs across volatile decentralized networks:

- **Real-time performance monitoring integration**: Real-time performance monitoring provides the data foundation for auto-scaling decisions by continuously tracking system performance across multiple dimensions and providing early warning of capacity or performance issues. The monitoring system must collect comprehensive data while minimizing overhead and maintaining privacy protection.
- **Algorithmic scaling triggers and thresholds**: Auto-scaling algorithms must implement sophisticated trigger mechanisms that can distinguish between normal system fluctuations and conditions that require scaling responses. The trigger system must balance sensitivity with stability while accounting for the time and cost implications of scaling actions.
- **Community feedback integration**: Community feedback provides valuable input for auto-scaling decisions by incorporating qualitative assessments and user preferences that may not be captured by automated monitoring systems. The feedback integration system must process diverse input while preventing gaming or manipulation of scaling decisions.

Performance monitoring

Performance monitoring in decentralized AI networks requires comprehensive observability frameworks that can track system behavior across distributed, heterogeneous infrastructure while providing actionable insights for optimization and issue resolution. Unlike traditional centralized monitoring systems, decentralized monitoring must handle the challenges of voluntary participation, varying reliability, privacy protection, and economic coordination while maintaining the detailed visibility necessary for managing complex AI workloads.

Distributed monitoring architecture

The architecture of monitoring systems for decentralized AI networks must balance comprehensive data collection with privacy protection, economic efficiency, and the practical constraints of distributed infrastructure. The monitoring framework must provide real-time visibility while enabling historical analysis and predictive insights that support proactive system management. The following layered monitoring architectures combine blockchain telemetry, privacy-preserving aggregation, and cross-chain coordination to deliver comprehensive observability across heterogeneous decentralized AI ecosystems:

- **Blockchain-integrated telemetry collection**: Telemetry collection in decentralized AI networks leverages blockchain technology to create tamper-proof, transparent monitoring records while providing economic incentives for accurate data reporting. The collection system must handle high-volume monitoring data while maintaining the security and integrity guarantees that blockchain systems provide.

- **Privacy-preserving metrics aggregation**: Metrics aggregation in decentralized systems must protect the privacy of individual participants while providing network-wide visibility into system performance and behavior. The aggregation framework implements sophisticated privacy-preserving techniques that enable collective intelligence while protecting individual operational information.
- **Cross-chain monitoring coordination**: Modern decentralized AI ecosystems often span multiple blockchain networks, requiring monitoring systems that can provide unified visibility across different platforms while handling the technical and economic differences between blockchain systems. Cross-chain monitoring coordination enables comprehensive system observability while respecting the autonomy and characteristics of different blockchain networks.

Real-time analytics and alerting

Real-time analytics capabilities enable immediate detection and response to performance issues, security threats, and operational anomalies while providing continuous optimization insights that can improve system performance and efficiency. The analytics framework must balance computational efficiency with analytical sophistication while operating across a distributed infrastructure.

Stream processing for live metrics

Stream processing systems enable real-time analysis of high-volume monitoring data as it arrives from distributed nodes, providing immediate insights and rapid alert generation without the latency associated with batch processing approaches. The stream processing framework must handle varying data rates and quality while maintaining analytical accuracy.

The event processing system implements complex event pattern recognition that can identify sophisticated attack patterns, performance degradation scenarios, and system optimization opportunities. These distributed stream processing architectures deliver real-time analytics through fault-tolerant checkpointing and efficient on-edge inference, enabling instantaneous response to dynamic network conditions:

- The processing system implements checkpointing and recovery mechanisms that can handle node failures without losing analytical state or monitoring data.
- The inference system must balance model complexity with computational efficiency while providing accurate analytical results in real-time.

Machine learning-based anomaly detection

ML-based anomaly detection systems automatically identify unusual patterns in monitoring data that may indicate performance issues, security threats, or optimization opportunities. The detection system must adapt to changing system conditions while minimizing false-positive alerts that could overwhelm system operators.

Automated alert management and escalation

Automated alert management systems process monitoring alerts to prevent information overload while ensuring that critical issues receive appropriate attention and response. The alert management framework must balance comprehensiveness with operator efficiency while providing clear escalation paths for different types of issues.

Community-driven quality assurance

Quality assurance in decentralized AI networks benefits from community participation and collective intelligence while maintaining appropriate standards and preventing gaming or manipulation. The quality assurance framework must create incentives for valuable community contributions while ensuring that quality standards remain objective and reliable. Token-incentivized governance harnesses community expertise for crowd-sourced validation and decentralized benchmarking, creating objective, adaptive quality standards across diverse deployment environments:

- **Crowd-sourced performance validation**: Community-driven performance validation leverages the collective expertise and resources of network participants to assess AI model performance and system quality across diverse usage scenarios and deployment conditions. The validation framework must coordinate community contributions while maintaining quality standards and preventing bias or manipulation.

- **Decentralized quality metrics and benchmarking**: Decentralized quality metrics systems enable the development and maintenance of quality standards through community consensus while ensuring that quality measures remain relevant and useful for assessing AI model performance. The metrics framework must balance standardization with flexibility while accommodating diverse use cases and requirements.

Performance optimization insights

Performance optimization in decentralized AI networks requires sophisticated analysis capabilities that can identify optimization opportunities across multiple dimensions, including computational efficiency, economic cost, user satisfaction, and network-wide resource utilization. The optimization framework must provide actionable insights while accounting for the constraints and opportunities unique to decentralized systems.

Predictive performance analytics

Predictive analytics capabilities enable proactive optimization by forecasting future performance issues and identifying optimization opportunities before they become critical problems. The predictive system must handle the complexities of distributed systems while providing accurate and actionable predictions. These systems leverage historical performance data, usage patterns, and external factors to generate forecasts that inform capacity planning, resource allocation, and preventive maintenance strategies. Advanced machine learning models continuously improve prediction accuracy through feedback loops that incorporate real-world outcomes and evolving network conditions.

ML-driven forecasting models analyze temporal patterns, resource utilization trends, and external variables to deliver precise capacity predictions and preemptive optimization recommendations across decentralized infrastructure.

Resource utilization optimization recommendations

Resource utilization optimization provides specific recommendations for improving the efficiency of computational resource usage while maintaining or improving service quality. The optimization system must consider both individual node efficiency and network-wide resource allocation patterns. These recommendations analyze GPU/CPU utilization rates, memory consumption patterns, and idle time across distributed nodes to identify underutilized capacity and inefficient workloads. The system generates actionable strategies, including workload redistribution, model compression techniques, and hardware-specific optimizations tailored to heterogeneous decentralized infrastructure.

Intelligent optimization engines deliver granular recommendations for workload redistribution, model pruning, and hardware-specific tuning to maximize resource efficiency across diverse decentralized compute pools.

Continuous improvement feedback loops

Continuous improvement mechanisms ensure that performance optimization insights are systematically applied to improve system performance over time while creating learning systems that adapt to changing conditions and requirements. The improvement framework must balance automation with human oversight while ensuring that improvements actually provide expected benefits. These automated feedback systems with rigorous testing, rollback safety nets, and stakeholder validation ensure optimization changes deliver measurable value while maintaining system stability and participant trust:

- The automation system includes rollback capabilities and performance monitoring that can detect and reverse optimization changes that do not provide the expected benefits.
- The testing system must account for the distributed nature of the network while providing statistically valid results about optimization effectiveness.
- The feedback system helps ensure that optimization efforts focus on improvements that provide real value to network participants.
- The baseline system must account for changing system conditions and usage patterns while providing stable reference points for performance evaluation.

A/B testing in decentralized systems

A/B testing in decentralized AI systems presents unique challenges that extend far beyond traditional web application experimentation. The distributed nature of modern AI deployments, combined with the statistical complexities of machine learning model evaluation, creates sophisticated requirements for experimental design, data collection, and statistical analysis. In decentralized environments, these challenges are amplified by network effects, geographic distribution, varying infrastructure capabilities, and the need to maintain experimental validity across heterogeneous deployment conditions. This section explores comprehensive frameworks for designing, implementing, and analyzing A/B tests in distributed AI systems while addressing the unique statistical and operational challenges inherent in decentralized experimentation.

To improve readability, this dense section can be restructured into four focused subsections that mirror how large-scale network experimentation is typically organized. This follows common practice in the A/B testing literature, which separates statistical design, randomization mechanics, organizational governance, and ethical or compliance concerns into distinct but related components:

- **Statistical foundations**: Briefly state that decentralized A/B tests must handle interference, clustered randomization, and non-IID traffic, and that classical Stable **Unit Treatment Value Assumption (SUTVA)** assumptions often fail in networked AI settings.
- **Randomization strategy**: Isolate 2-3 sentences on the unit of randomization (user, cluster, region, node), spillover-aware designs, and how assignments are propagated and logged across heterogeneous infrastructure.
- **Governance integration**: Pull out the pieces on who can start/stop experiments, how guardrails and kill-switches are encoded in on-chain or off-chain governance, and how experiment policies are reviewed or voted on.
- **Compliance considerations**: End with data residency, privacy, consent, and logging constraints for cross-jurisdiction experiments (e.g., different chains/regions), and how these limit sample pooling and metric definition.

A/B testing framework design

ML A/B testing frameworks for decentralized systems integrate advanced statistical foundations addressing complex multi-dimensional performance metrics through effect size measures, multiple testing corrections, and Bayesian inference, balancing statistical significance with practical impact, alongside experimental designs featuring stratified randomization, cluster-based approaches, and crossover strategies that maintain validity across geographic regions, infrastructure variations, network effects, and temporal dynamics. Comprehensive power analysis accounts for non-normal distributions, sequential testing, minimum detectable effects, and network dependencies using bootstrap methods and simulations, all enabled by deterministic hash-based, geographically-aware, load-balanced, and fault-tolerant randomization, ensuring experimental balance without centralized coordination. These frameworks incorporate blockchain timestamping for immutable experiment records, cryptographic commitments for tamper-proof randomization verification, and token-weighted governance for community-approved experimental protocols, enabling trustworthy, auditable ML experimentation across sovereign decentralized networks while supporting regulatory compliance through transparent, reproducible statistical processes.

Implementation strategies

Decentralized A/B testing implementation combines hash-based, weighted random, session-based, and infrastructure-aware traffic splitting for consistent experimental allocation across global node distributions; multi-armed bandit algorithms including epsilon-greedy, UCB, Thompson Sampling, and contextual bandits for adaptive optimization balancing exploration and exploitation while maximizing statistical efficiency; hierarchical cluster-adaptive randomization with cross-cluster validation and topology awareness to handle infrastructure dependencies and network effects; plus network interference mitigation through geographic isolation, temporal separation, statistical adjustments, and real-time detection mechanisms ensuring statistical independence. These strategies leverage blockchain oracles for tamper-proof experiment logging, smart contract-based allocation governance, and token-incentivized validator participation to maintain integrity across untrusted decentralized serving environments while enabling seamless scalability from pilot deployments to production-scale experimentation across heterogeneous blockchain ecosystems.

Measurement and analysis

Decentralized ML A/B testing measurement combines distributed logging, event streaming, local aggregation, and synchronization for fault-tolerant metrics collection across heterogeneous infrastructure; production statistical inference through sequential analysis, non-parametric methods, robust variance estimation, and practical significance testing; advanced causal inference using instrumental variables, difference-in-differences, mediation analysis, and heterogeneous treatment effects beyond simple comparisons; plus comprehensive bias correction addressing selection, survivorship, measurement, and temporal biases through balance tests, propensity analysis, and longitudinal modeling. Smart contract-based metrics oracles provide tamper-proof data integrity, token-incentivized validator consensus ensures statistical result verification, and blockchain audit trails enable reproducible analysis across decentralized networks, supporting regulatory compliance through immutable experiment provenance and community-governed statistical standards for production ML deployments.

Advanced testing scenarios

Decentralized ML experimentation employs multi-variant A/B/C/n testing with multiple comparison adjustments, factorial designs, hierarchical testing, and simulation-based power analysis for efficient multi-model optimization; sequential testing featuring group sequential designs, futility analysis, adaptive sample sizing, and continuous monitoring to optimize efficiency while controlling error rates; contextual bandits enabling context-aware policy learning, online adaptation, and off-policy evaluation for personalized experimentation across diverse user/system contexts; plus long-term effect measurement through cohort analysis, longitudinal modeling, attribution techniques, and holdout groups to assess sustained ML model impact beyond immediate experimental periods. DAO-governed experiment approval processes ensure community alignment, blockchain oracles provide tamper-proof outcome verification, and token-incentivized validator networks deliver consensus-based statistical validation, enabling scalable, trustworthy experimentation across global decentralized AI ecosystems with immutable audit trails for regulatory compliance and reproducible scientific validation. Model updates and rollbacks.

Model updates and rollbacks in decentralized AI networks require sophisticated coordination mechanisms that can manage the complexities of distributed consensus, economic incentives, and community governance while ensuring system reliability and continuity of service. Unlike traditional centralized systems, where updates can be coordinated through a central authority, decentralized networks must implement consensus-based update procedures that balance innovation with stability and enable community participation in model evolution decisions.

Consensus-based update mechanisms

The implementation of model updates in decentralized networks requires consensus mechanisms that can coordinate changes across distributed infrastructure while ensuring that updates are properly validated, economically sustainable, and aligned with community governance decisions. The consensus framework must balance update speed with safety while providing appropriate safeguards against malicious or problematic updates.

Governance-driven update approval processes

Update approval in decentralized AI networks leverages community governance mechanisms to ensure that model changes reflect the needs and priorities of network participants while maintaining appropriate quality and security standards. The approval process must balance democratic participation with technical expertise while enabling timely updates for critical improvements.

The proposal system must provide comprehensive information for community evaluation while maintaining accessibility for non-technical participants. The voting system must ensure adequate participation while preventing manipulation or capture by special interests. The impact analysis helps ensure that update decisions consider the needs of all stakeholders while identifying potential concerns or objections.

Smart contract-orchestrated deployment coordination

Deployment coordination in decentralized networks uses smart contracts to automate update distribution and installation while ensuring that all network participants implement updates consistently and according to approved schedules. The coordination system must handle the technical complexities of distributed deployment while maintaining security and reliability guarantees. The phased approach enables early detection of issues while minimizing the impact of potential problems on the broader network.

The compatibility system must handle complex dependency relationships while providing clear migration paths. The atomic system provides rollback capabilities if updates cannot be completed successfully. The economic system ensures fair compensation while creating incentives for timely update adoption.

Cross-chain update synchronization

Update synchronization across multiple blockchain networks requires sophisticated coordination protocols that can handle the different consensus mechanisms, timing characteristics, and governance procedures of different blockchain platforms while maintaining consistency in model versions and functionality. These multi-chain coordination protocols with conflict resolution, secure bridges, and adaptive scheduling enable consistent model updates across diverse blockchain ecosystems while preserving individual chain autonomy:

- The coordination system must handle conflicts and inconsistencies that may arise from different governance outcomes.
- The bridge system must verify the authenticity of cross-chain communications while handling the technical differences between blockchain platforms.
- The scheduling system must account for network-specific constraints while maintaining overall coordination.

Automated rollback procedures

Automated rollback capabilities provide essential safety mechanisms for decentralized AI deployments by enabling rapid restoration of previous model versions when issues are detected with new deployments. The rollback system must operate quickly and reliably while maintaining data consistency and minimizing service disruption.

Failure detection and automatic rollback triggers

Failure detection systems monitor deployed models for various types of issues that may require automatic rollback, including performance degradation, quality issues, security vulnerabilities, and operational failures. The detection system must balance sensitivity with specificity to provide a rapid response to genuine issues while avoiding unnecessary rollbacks.

For example, rollback policies can encode explicit quantitative triggers such as revert if median or P95 endtoend latency degrades by more than 5-10% relative to the previous version for at least N consecutive evaluation windows or revert if the new model's primary accuracy or reward metric shows a statistically significant drop (for instance, $p < 0.01$ with a pre-specified minimum effect size) in online A/B traffic. In decentralized settings, these thresholds are enforced by on-chain or off-chain controllers that compare canary and baseline metrics across multiple nodes, only triggering a network-wide rollback when both performance SLO breaches and statistical tests agree that the degradation is real rather than noise.

The following multi-layered detection, combining automated monitoring, statistical validation, security analysis, and community verification, triggers precise rollback responses while minimizing false positives across decentralized deployments:

- The monitoring system must account for normal performance variations while detecting genuine degradation that indicates model problems.
- The quality monitoring system must provide objective assessment criteria while accounting for the probabilistic nature of AI model outputs.
- The security monitoring system must detect various types of security threats while distinguishing between genuine attacks and normal operational variations.
- The reporting system must validate community reports while preventing false reporting that could trigger unnecessary rollbacks.

Graceful degradation and service continuity

Graceful degradation strategies ensure that rollback procedures maintain service continuity while transitioning from problematic updated models to previous versions. The degradation system must balance service quality with availability while providing clear communication about temporary service limitations. The redirection system must maintain load balancing and performance optimization while ensuring that users receive reliable service during rollback procedures. These progressive degradation protocols with intelligent traffic management, state preservation, and health validation ensure seamless service continuity during automated rollback operations:

- The state management system must handle complex data relationships while preventing data loss or corruption during rollback procedures.
- The fallback system must provide acceptable service quality while clearly communicating limitations to users.
- The restoration system must validate system health before returning to normal operation while providing monitoring for potential recurring issues.

Data consistency and state management during rollbacks

Data consistency during rollback operations requires sophisticated coordination mechanisms that can maintain the integrity of the system state while reverting model functionality to previous versions. The consistency framework must handle complex data relationships while providing transactional guarantees for rollback operations. The isolation system must provide appropriate locking and coordination mechanisms while minimizing performance impact. The migration system must account for schema changes and compatibility issues while ensuring data integrity. The checkpoint system must balance storage efficiency with recovery speed while providing reliable restoration capabilities. The audit system must capture detailed information about rollback triggers, procedures, and outcomes while maintaining privacy and security protections.

Version control and branching strategies

Version control in decentralized AI networks extends traditional software version control concepts to handle the unique characteristics of AI models, including large binary artifacts, complex dependency relationships, and community-driven development processes. The version control framework must support collaborative development while maintaining security and quality standards. This blockchain-enhanced version control with cryptographic signing, content-addressable storage, and governance-gated branching enables a secure collaborative model evolution across distributed networks:

- **Distributed version control for AI models**: Distributed version control systems for AI models must handle the challenges of large file sizes, complex metadata, and collaborative development across potentially untrusted participants. The version control system must provide efficient storage and transfer mechanisms while maintaining complete version histories and enabling sophisticated branching and merging strategies.
- **Community-driven model evolution**: Model evolution in decentralized networks benefits from community participation and collective intelligence while maintaining appropriate quality standards and governance oversight. The evolution framework must create incentives for valuable contributions while preventing malicious or low-quality modifications.
- **Compatibility management and migration paths**: Compatibility management ensures that model updates maintain appropriate backward compatibility while enabling innovation and improvement. The compatibility framework must balance stability with evolution while providing clear migration paths for users and dependent systems.

Emergency response and incident management

Emergency response procedures provide rapid reaction capabilities for handling critical issues with deployed AI models, including security breaches, severe performance problems, and safety-critical failures. The emergency response framework must enable a fast response while maintaining appropriate governance oversight and community communication. These predefined escalation protocols with automated safeguards and multi-channel community coordination enable rapid, transparent crisis resolution while preserving network trust and stability:

- **Rapid response protocols for critical issues**: Rapid response protocols enable immediate action when critical issues are detected with deployed AI models while maintaining appropriate safeguards against hasty decisions that could cause additional problems. The response system must balance speed with safety while providing clear escalation and coordination mechanisms.

- **Community communication during emergencies**: Community communication during emergencies ensures that network participants receive timely, accurate information about critical issues while maintaining transparency and building trust in emergency response procedures. The communication framework must balance comprehensive information sharing with the need for rapid response.

Quality assurance and validation

Quality assurance and validation in decentralized AI networks require comprehensive frameworks that can ensure model reliability, performance, and safety across distributed infrastructure while leveraging community participation and blockchain-based verification mechanisms. Unlike traditional centralized quality assurance that relies on controlled testing environments and centralized authority, decentralized quality assurance must coordinate validation activities across multiple independent participants while maintaining objectivity and preventing gaming or manipulation.

Decentralized testing frameworks

The implementation of testing frameworks for decentralized AI networks must balance comprehensive validation coverage with the practical constraints of distributed participation, economic incentives, and community coordination. The testing framework must provide reliable quality assessment while enabling community participation and ensuring that testing activities are fairly compensated and appropriately incentivized.

Community-driven test case development

Community-driven test case development leverages the collective expertise and diverse perspectives of network participants to create comprehensive testing coverage that reflects real-world usage scenarios and edge cases that may not be anticipated by centralized testing teams. The test development framework must ensure test quality while preventing malicious or biased test cases.

Distributed test execution and coordination

Distributed test execution coordinates testing activities across multiple independent nodes while ensuring consistent test conditions and reliable result aggregation. The execution framework must handle the heterogeneous nature of distributed infrastructure while maintaining test reliability and preventing result manipulation.

Test orchestration mechanisms coordinate test execution across multiple nodes while ensuring that tests are distributed fairly and executed under consistent conditions. The orchestration system must handle node availability fluctuations while maintaining comprehensive test coverage and preventing single points of failure in test execution.

Automated quality assessment pipelines

Automated quality assessment pipelines provide continuous evaluation of model quality across multiple dimensions while integrating with community-driven testing and providing real-time feedback about model performance and reliability. The assessment framework must balance automation efficiency with comprehensive quality evaluation.

Multi-dimensional quality metrics evaluate models across various quality aspects, including accuracy, fairness, robustness, efficiency, and compliance with community standards. The metrics system must provide a comprehensive assessment while being computationally efficient and economically sustainable for continuous evaluation. Continuous integration with deployment pipelines ensures that quality assessment is integrated throughout the model lifecycle while preventing the deployment of models that fail to meet quality standards. Regression testing capabilities automatically detect quality degradation when models are updated or modified, while providing a detailed analysis of performance changes. Performance benchmarking provides a standardized evaluation of model performance against established baselines and competitor models while ensuring fair and objective comparison.

Consensus-based model validation

Consensus-based validation mechanisms leverage the collective intelligence and diverse expertise of network participants to evaluate model quality and performance while preventing manipulation and ensuring objective assessment. The validation framework must coordinate multiple independent evaluations while maintaining the integrity and reliability of validation results.

Multi-party model evaluation

Multi-party evaluation engages multiple independent evaluators to assess model quality while providing redundancy and objectivity in validation results. The evaluation system must coordinate multiple participants while ensuring that evaluations are independent and unbiased. This approach leverages diverse perspectives and computational resources across the network to create comprehensive quality assessments that mitigate individual biases and errors. The framework implements cryptographic commitments, stake-weighted consensus, and incentive alignment to ensure honest participation and reliable aggregate results for production deployment decisions.

Decentralized evaluation protocols coordinate stake-weighted, cryptographically-committed assessments from diverse validators to deliver robust, bias-resistant quality verification across global participant pools.

Zero-knowledge proof validation

Zero-knowledge proof validation enables verification of model properties and performance characteristics without revealing sensitive information about model architecture, training data, or proprietary techniques. This approach provides strong verification guarantees while protecting intellectual property and sensitive information. Training data validation proofs can verify that models were trained on appropriate datasets without revealing the actual training data, enabling validation of data quality and compliance while protecting data privacy and proprietary datasets. The validation system must provide strong guarantees about training data characteristics while maintaining privacy protection.

Community consensus mechanisms

Community consensus mechanisms enable collective decision-making about model quality and validation standards while ensuring that decisions reflect the diverse perspectives and needs of network participants. The consensus framework must balance democratic participation with technical expertise while enabling efficient decision-making.

Voting mechanisms for quality standards enable community participation in establishing and updating quality criteria while ensuring that standards reflect the actual needs and priorities of network users. The voting system must balance expert knowledge with community input while preventing capture by special interests.

Compliance and regulatory validation

Compliance validation in decentralized AI networks must address complex regulatory landscapes while providing transparent verification of regulatory compliance across multiple jurisdictions and regulatory frameworks. The compliance framework must balance regulatory requirements with the distributed nature of decentralized networks while providing clear accountability and verification mechanisms.

Multi-jurisdictional compliance frameworks

Multi-jurisdictional compliance addresses the challenge of operating across different regulatory environments while ensuring that AI models comply with applicable laws and regulations in all relevant jurisdictions. The compliance framework must handle conflicting requirements while providing practical compliance solutions. Regulatory requirement mapping identifies applicable regulations and compliance requirements for different types of AI models and use cases while accounting for geographic deployment patterns and user populations. The mapping system must stay current with evolving regulatory landscapes while providing clear guidance for compliance activities.

Cross-border compliance coordination ensures that models deployed across multiple jurisdictions comply with all applicable regulations while handling conflicts between different regulatory requirements. The coordination system must provide practical solutions for complex multi-jurisdictional scenarios while maintaining legal compliance. Regulatory update monitoring tracks changes in applicable regulations while providing timely notification of new requirements that may affect deployed models. The monitoring system must provide comprehensive coverage while filtering relevant changes from the broader regulatory environment.

Automated compliance monitoring and reporting

Automated compliance monitoring provides continuous verification that deployed models maintain regulatory compliance while generating comprehensive documentation for regulatory reporting and audit purposes. The monitoring framework must balance automation efficiency with regulatory rigor while providing reliable compliance verification.

Audit trail generation creates comprehensive records of compliance activities, including monitoring results, validation procedures, and corrective actions, while ensuring that audit trails meet regulatory requirements for completeness and integrity. The audit system must provide reliable documentation while protecting sensitive information.

Regulatory reporting automation generates required compliance reports while ensuring accuracy and timeliness of regulatory submissions. The reporting system must handle diverse regulatory requirements while maintaining consistency and reliability across different reporting obligations.

Blockchain-based compliance verification

Blockchain-based compliance verification leverages immutable ledger technology to create tamper-proof records of compliance activities while providing transparent verification of regulatory compliance for all network participants. The blockchain verification framework must balance transparency with privacy while providing reliable compliance documentation.

Immutable compliance records create permanent, tamper-proof documentation of compliance verification activities while ensuring that compliance evidence cannot be modified or deleted. The record system must provide comprehensive documentation while maintaining appropriate privacy protections for sensitive compliance information.

Smart contract compliance automation implements programmable compliance checking that can automatically verify regulatory requirements while providing transparent and auditable compliance verification. Cryptographic compliance proofs enable verification of regulatory compliance without revealing sensitive information about model implementation or deployment details. Multi-party compliance verification enables independent verification of compliance claims by multiple parties while providing redundancy and objectivity in compliance assessment.

Continuous quality improvement

Continuous quality improvement mechanisms ensure that model quality and validation processes improve over time while incorporating lessons learned from deployment experience and evolving best practices. The improvement framework must balance stability with innovation while ensuring that improvements provide real value for network participants.

Feedback loop integration

Feedback loop integration connects quality assessment results with model development and improvement processes while creating systematic mechanisms for incorporating quality insights into model evolution. The integration framework must provide actionable feedback while maintaining appropriate separation between quality assessment and model development activities.

User feedback aggregation collects and analyzes user experiences with deployed models while providing insights for quality improvement and validation enhancement. Performance monitoring integration connects real-world performance data with quality assessment activities while providing continuous validation of quality predictions and assessments. Developer feedback incorporation ensures that model developers receive meaningful feedback from quality assessment activities while creating channels for developers to contribute to quality improvement processes. Community insight integration leverages collective community intelligence to identify quality improvement opportunities while ensuring that improvement suggestions are properly evaluated and prioritized.

Iterative quality enhancement

Iterative quality enhancement implements systematic improvement processes that continuously refine quality assessment methods, validation procedures, and performance standards based on experience and evolving best practices. The enhancement framework must balance improvement with stability while ensuring that changes provide real benefits.

The evolution system must balance improvement with historical continuity while ensuring that quality metrics remain relevant and useful. The improvement system must balance efficiency with thoroughness while ensuring that process changes provide real benefits.

The best practice system must balance standardization with innovation while ensuring that practices remain current and effective. The education system must be accessible and effective while keeping pace with evolving technologies and practices.

Conclusion

Decentralized AI deployment transforms models from centralized control to blockchain coordinated ecosystems through comprehensive frameworks for packaging, distribution, serving, monitoring, and governance that prove technical feasibility and practical viability comparable to or exceeding centralized systems in performance, reliability, and cost effectiveness, while adding fault tolerance, geographic distribution, and democratic governance.

Key achievements include smart contract orchestration with IPFS distribution and cryptographic verification for technical viability; token incentives aligning participant interests for economic sustainability; and strategic advantages like distributed resources, collaborative development, new business models, enhanced security, privacy compliance, and immutable audit trails.

While technical infrastructure is essential, the next chapter addresses sustainable networks that require well-designed token economies and incentives to motivate quality contributions, ensure fair compensation, and enable global scaling.

Chapter 7
Tokenomics, Incentive Mechanisms and Decentralized Governance

Introduction

Decentralized AI (**DAI**) networks enable global collaboration among data providers, compute contributors, model developers, validators, and users, replacing centralized control with distributed participation. Tokenomics, the economic framework governing these tokens, coordinates resources through price signals, aligns incentives via rewards and penalties, and captures value from network success while addressing challenges in data quality assurance, compute resource efficiency, model validation, and economic security.

This chapter provides a comprehensive technical framework for designing sustainable DAI tokenomics ecosystems, focusing on economic design principles rather than exhaustive regulatory or implementation details. It covers token design principles, including utility versus governance models, supply dynamics from fixed to inflationary schedules, sophisticated allocation and vesting strategies, and proven economic security mechanisms. Through real-world case studies like the ASI merger and the practical HEALTHAI hypothetical, readers gain actionable insights for building networks that scale while maintaining decentralization, fairness, and basic regulatory compliance. These tokenomics frameworks support long-term viability and stakeholder alignment for data marketplaces, AI service platforms, or federated learning networks.

Structure

The chapter covers the following topics:

- Token design principles
- Utility vs. governance tokens
- Incentive mechanism design
- Staking and delegation models
- Reward distribution algorithms

- Economic security and attack resistance
- Market making and liquidity
- Token metrics and analytics
- Regulatory compliance
- Governance framework design
- Case studies and examples

Objectives

By completing this chapter, readers will gain specific competencies in decentralized AI tokenomics, including designing emission schedules, evaluating staking models, and analyzing reward distribution algorithms. You will learn to identify and apply the three essential dimensions of coordination, incentives, and value capture that distinguish these systems from traditional centralized models. The chapter provides technical guidance on token architecture, covering optimal supply models from fixed to dynamic schedules and the rationale for multi-function tokens, balancing transactional utility with governance authority.

Readers will develop expertise in advanced incentive design, applying behavioral economics and game theory to encourage high-quality data contributions while countering threats like Sybil attacks and model poisoning. You will understand how to implement secure staking protocols, graduated slashing mechanisms, and reward distribution strategies, including proportional, quality-weighted, and reputation-based systems. The text covers critical market infrastructure such as bonding curves and automated market makers for liquidity provision, plus network health evaluation through analytics dashboards. Finally, you will navigate regulatory complexities, understanding compliance frameworks like the Howey Test within decentralized AI contexts.

Token design principles

This section explores the foundational concepts behind effective tokenomics in decentralized AI networks, emphasizing the importance of defining the token's purpose as an economic operating system that facilitates payments, resource coordination, and governance. It highlights the necessity of aligning token mechanics with network goals, ensuring utility-driven value creation, and leveraging network effects to foster positive feedback loops. Additionally, it covers critical decisions on supply dynamics such as fixed, inflationary, or adaptive and strategic token allocation, including vesting mechanisms that promote long-term commitment and stability for AI ecosystems.

DAI token lifecycle framework

This framework, as shown in *Figure 7.1*, illustrates the complete token lifecycle from minting through circulation, staking rewards, and deflationary mechanisms, anchoring token design decisions to measurable economic flows within DAI networks:

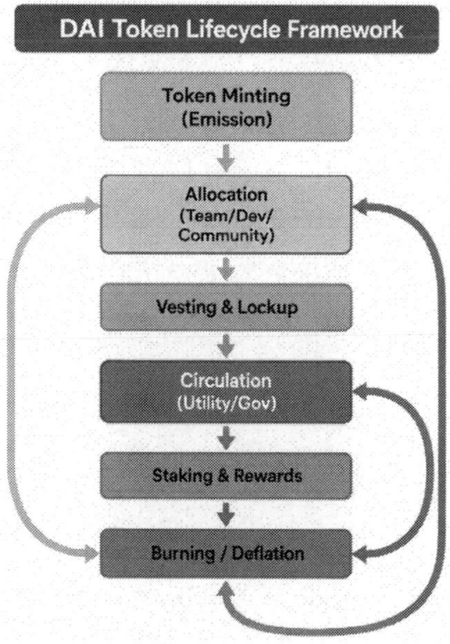

Figure 7.1: *DAI lifecycle framework*

Defining purpose and value capture

The foundation of any successful tokenomics model begins with clearly defining the token's purpose and establishing mechanisms for value capture and retention. In decentralized AI networks, tokens typically serve multiple interconnected functions: facilitating payments for AI services, coordinating resource allocation, enabling governance participation, and aligning long-term incentives across stakeholders.

Value capture model

Token value follows from the quantity theory of money adapted for networks:

$$MV=PQ$$

Here, M is the token supply, V is velocity (transactions per period), P is the price level, and Q is transaction volume. Lower velocity increases the price for fixed demand, but high-utility transactions can drive Q growth.

Key principles include:

- **Value alignment with network goals**: The token's economic mechanics must directly support the network's core objectives. For an AI data marketplace, tokens should incentivize high-quality data contribution, accurate curation, and efficient discovery mechanisms. For a distributed compute network, tokens should reward computational contributions while penalizing malicious behavior or poor performance.
- **Utility-driven value creation (with caveats)**: Tokens derive value from ecosystem utility like premium model access or fee discounts, though speculative dynamics and market inefficiencies can decouple price from utility. Greater fool trading often dominates early adoption. The key principle is ensuring that token value grows in correlation with network adoption and utility.
- **Network effects and positive feedback loops**: Effective token design creates virtuous cycles where increased participation enhances network value, which in turn attracts more participants. For example, as more data providers join an AI network, the diversity and quality of available datasets increase, making the platform more attractive to AI researchers and enterprises, thereby increasing demand for the token used to access these resources.

Multi-function token architecture

DAI tokens serve multiple functions simultaneously, including payments for AI services, resource coordination, governance participation, and economic security. These functions create interconnected value flows that sustain network growth. At the systems level, tokens operate as a unified protocol layer that orchestrates decentralized coordination through signaling, incentive alignment, and state synchronization across network nodes.

Key principles of multi-function design include:

- **Transaction function**: Users spend tokens to purchase AI services, access datasets, or use computational resources. This creates direct token demand proportional to network usage.

  Token flow in AI transaction:

  - User | pays 100 AITOKEN | AI service provider
  - AI service provider | 80 AITOKEN (service payment) | 20 AITOKEN (ecosystem fees)

- **Staking function**: Network participants stake tokens to earn rewards for securing the network, validating data quality, or maintaining infrastructure.

  Validator staking is as follows:

  - Validator stakes 10,000 AITOKEN.
  - Earns 5% annual reward = 500 AITOKEN per year.
  - **Risk**: Slashed if it behaves maliciously.

- **Governance function**: Token holders vote on protocol changes, fee structures, and allocation of treasury resources.

  Governance proposal flow:

  - **Proposal**: Increase data validation rewards from 2% to 3%.
  - Token holders vote (voting power = token balance).
  - If more than 50% approve, the change is implemented.

- **Value accrual function**: As network economic value grows, token holders benefit through appreciation. This creates long-term holding incentives and attracts capital to support network development.

- **Composability function**: Tokens integrate with external DeFi protocols, enabling lending, borrowing, and liquidity provision. This expands token utility beyond the native network.

These functions create reinforcing dynamics. As more users transact (transaction function), the network becomes more valuable (value accrual function). Token holders, motivated by appreciation potential, vote to improve governance and security (governance function). The improved governance attracts validators who stake more tokens (staking function), enhancing network security and attracting more users.

This virtuous cycle of transaction to value, to governance, to staking, to security, to adoption forms the foundation of sustainable tokenomics.

The following are design trade-offs:

- Transaction users prefer stable prices for predictable costs.
- Stakers want high rewards and slashing protection.
- Governance participants seek concentrated voting power.
- Long-term holders prioritize appreciation potential.

Successful tokenomics balances these competing demands through carefully calibrated parameters, vesting schedules, and governance mechanisms.

Supply dynamics

One of the most critical tokenomics decisions is the supply emission curve. This determines how many new tokens are created over time and how they are distributed. Token supply mechanisms fundamentally shape the economic incentives and long-term sustainability of decentralized AI networks. The choice between fixed, inflationary, or deflationary supply models has profound implications for participant behavior, value accrual, and network growth dynamics. Three primary approaches exist for DAI networks, each with distinct advantages and trade-offs. Token supply emission curves critically shape economic incentives and network sustainability in decentralized AI systems. Fixed, inflationary, and dynamic models each carry distinct trade-offs for participant behavior and value accrual.

Emission schedule examples:

- **Linear emission**:

  $E_t = R$ (constant rate R per epoch) provides predictable rewards but risks oversupply.

- **Bitcoin-style halving**:

  $E_t = E_0/2^{(t/4)}$ creates programmed scarcity through periodic halvings every 4 years.

- **Exponential decay**:

  $E_t = E_0 \cdot \alpha^t$, where $0 < \alpha < 1$, rewards early participants while tapering emissions.

- **Dynamic adjustment**:

  $Inflation_t = Base\ rate \times (1 - Network\ activity_t / Max\ activity)$ reduces emissions during high utilization.

Key supply models include:

- **Fixed supply models**: Networks employing fixed token supplies create inherent scarcity that can drive value appreciation as adoption increases. This model works well for mature networks with established utility and predictable demand patterns. However, fixed supplies can create deflationary pressures that discourage spending and limit the network's ability to reward new participants during rapid growth phases.

- **Inflationary supply with emission schedules**: Many successful decentralized networks employ controlled inflation through predetermined emission schedules. These schedules can follow various patterns: linear emission provides predictable rewards but may lead to oversupply; exponential decay mirrors Bitcoin's halving mechanism, creating scarcity over time; sigmoid curves allow for rapid early growth followed by stabilization. The key is balancing reward adequacy for current participants with long-term scarcity to maintain value.

  These schedules follow distinct mathematical patterns:

  - Linear emission provides constant rewards ($E_t = R$) but risks oversupply over time.

  - Exponential decay mirrors Bitcoin's halving mechanism every 210,000 blocks (roughly 4 years); the block reward halves from its prior level (50 | 25 | 12.5 | 6.25 BTC), creating programmed scarcity that reduces new supply issuance by 50% each cycle.

  - Sigmoid curves enable rapid early growth followed by stabilization as emissions asymptotically approach a cap.

  - The key challenge remains balancing short-term reward adequacy with long-term scarcity preservation.
  - This Bitcoin halving chart illustrates how rewards have declined across four cycles, demonstrating the mechanism's effect on supply issuance.

- **Dynamic supply adjustment**: Advanced tokenomics models incorporate algorithmic supply adjustments based on network conditions. For instance, the supply inflation rate might decrease during periods of high network utilization to prevent dilution of rewards or increase during growth phases to incentivize new participation. These mechanisms require sophisticated economic modeling and governance structures to prevent manipulation.

Allocation strategies

Initial token distribution significantly impacts network decentralization, community building, and long-term success. Effective allocation strategies balance the need to reward early contributors, fund development, build community, and maintain adequate treasury reserves, creating a foundation for sustainable growth and stakeholder alignment.

Key allocation categories include:

- **Community and ecosystem development**: A substantial portion of tokens should be allocated to community building and ecosystem development. This includes airdrops to early adopters, grants for developers building on the platform, rewards for quality data contributors, and incentives for validators securing the network. Research suggests that allocating 40-60% of tokens to community and ecosystem development creates stronger network effects and more sustainable growth.
- **Team and advisor allocations**: While necessary to incentivize core contributors, team allocations should be carefully structured with appropriate vesting schedules to prevent early dumping and signal long-term commitment. Typical allocations range from 10-20% with vesting periods of 2-4 years, often including performance milestones tied to network adoption metrics.
- **Strategic partnerships and integration**: Allocating tokens for strategic partnerships can accelerate adoption and integration with existing systems. This might include allocations for AI research institutions, data providers, enterprise customers, or complementary blockchain networks. These allocations should include lock-up periods and performance requirements to ensure genuine value creation.

Vesting and lock-ups

Vesting schedules and lock-up periods are critical tools for aligning long-term incentives and preventing market manipulation. Well-designed vesting mechanisms protect against early token dumps while ensuring continued commitment from key stakeholders, creating sustainable economic alignment throughout the network lifecycle.

Key vesting approaches include:

- **Progressive vesting structures**: Rather than simple linear vesting, progressive structures can better align incentives with network development milestones. For example, team tokens might vest faster as the network achieves adoption targets, or data provider rewards might increase based on the quality and usage of their contributions over time.
- **Performance-based unlocking**: Advanced vesting mechanisms tie token unlocks to specific performance metrics such as network adoption, revenue generation, or quality benchmarks. This ensures that token recipients have ongoing incentives to contribute to network success rather than simply waiting for vesting periods to complete.
- **Market-responsive vesting**: Some networks implement vesting schedules that adjust based on market conditions or network health. During periods of high volatility or network stress, vesting might slow to provide stability, while during growth phases, vesting might accelerate to reward successful contributors. Market-responsive vesting adjusts token release schedules based on real-time network conditions through smart contract oracles.

  For example, a DAI network contract might monitor seven-day price volatility (σ_p) and **total value locked** (**TVL**):

```
if (volatility > 30% OR TVL < threshold) {
    vestingMultiplier = 0.5  // Slow release during stress
} else if (activeUsers > target) {
    vestingMultiplier = 1.5  // Accelerate during growth
}
uint256 vestingRate = baseRate * vestingMultiplier;
             tokensReleased = vestingRate * timeElapsed;
```

  This approach slowed releases by 40-60% during the 2022 bear market for projects like Arbitrum, preventing sell pressure while accelerating 20-30% during 2023-2024 bull phases when TVL doubled.

  During high volatility *(σp>30%)* or TVL drops, vesting halves to stabilize markets; during user growth phases, it accelerates to reward contributors.

Token utility design for AI-specific functions

Unlike generic blockchain tokens, AI tokens must specifically enable AI ecosystem participation, creating specialized utility functions that reflect the unique economics of decentralized AI development and deployment. These functions go beyond standard payments to address AI-specific challenges like quality assurance, resource coordination, and model verification.

AI service payment layer

Tokens serve as the native currency for AI service transactions. The economic model should incentivize efficient resource utilization while remaining competitive with centralized alternatives.

The tiered pricing structure ensures providers earn returns proportional to resource intensity while users pay fair market rates. Prices reflect actual costs (energy, hardware depreciation, opportunity costs) and dynamically adjust based on supply/demand, creating efficient resource allocation without central planning.

AITOKEN pricing by service type is as follows:

- **Model inference**:
  - **Small model (<1B parameters)**: 0.01 AITOKEN per inference
  - **Medium model (1-7B parameters)**: 0.05 AITOKEN per inference
  - **Large model (7B-70B parameters)**: 0.20 AITOKEN per inference
  - **Multimodal model (>70B parameters)**: 1.0 AITOKEN per inference
- **Data access**:
  - **Public dataset**: 0.001 AITOKEN per sample
  - **Premium dataset**: 0.05 AITOKEN per sample
  - **Proprietary dataset**: Variable (auction-based)
- **Compute resources**:
  - **GPU hours**: 0.1 AITOKEN per GPU-hour
  - **TPU hours**: 0.15 AITOKEN per TPU-hour
  - **Storage (per GB-month)**: 0.001 AITOKEN

These prices reflect actual resource costs, create predictable economics for providers, and ensure network sustainability through competitive pricing.

Quality verification layer

Tokens gate access to quality-verified resources, creating economic incentives for excellence and preventing garbage-in-garbage-out problems inherent in decentralized systems.

The quality-gated token economics is an escrow-based system that creates skin-in-the-game for contributors and economic rewards for honest validators. Quality becomes profitable while poor contributions incur real costs, which creates self-improving network quality without a central authority.

A data provider workflow is as follows:

- Submit dataset with 10,000 AITOKEN escrow.
- Network validators assess data quality (consensus-based).
- **If approved**:
    - Escrow returned + quality bonus
    - Dataset listed in the marketplace
    - Provider earns 0.05 AITOKEN per access
- **If rejected**:
    - Escrow retained as validator reward
    - Feedback provided for improvement

A model developer workflow is as follows:

- Submit AI model with 50,000 AITOKEN escrow.
- **Network testers evaluate the model**:
    - Accuracy metrics
    - Safety benchmarks
    - Efficiency analysis
- **If approved**:
    - Escrow returned + quality bonus
    - Users pay fees to use the model
    - Developer earns revenue share
- **If rejected**:
    - Escrow distributed to assessors
    - Improvement recommendations provided

This creates self-reinforcing quality standards where high-quality contributions earn premium returns while poor quality incurs economic penalties.

Utility vs. governance tokens

The distinction between utility and governance tokens represents one of the most important architectural decisions in tokenomics design. Each approach offers different benefits and challenges, and the choice significantly impacts user behavior, regulatory considerations, and long-term network evolution. Refer to the following table:

Dimension	Utility tokens	Governance tokens
Primary role	Provide access to products, services, or protocol features; function as a medium of exchange within the network[1].	Convey voting power over protocol parameters, treasury, upgrades, and other governance decisions.
Regulatory risk	Often positioned as consumption assets, but may still face scrutiny if expectations of profit or revenue sharing are explicit[2].	Higher likelihood of being viewed as investment-like when tightly coupled to treasury control, fee flows, or protocol cash flows[3].
User experience	Simple mental model for end users: spend to use, stake to earn, low cognitive load for non-technical participants.	Higher cognitive load: users must understand proposals, voting mechanisms, and delegation; participation tends to be more niche[4].
Economic design focus	Demand for network services, pricing, and sink mechanisms (fees, burns, staking) drives value and circulation[5].	Distribution, concentration of voting power, and alignment between influence and long-term commitment dominate design concerns[6].
Network evolution impact	Strongly tied to product-market fit and usage growth, value tracks utility adoption more than governance quality.	Directly shapes protocol roadmap, risk profile, and treasury strategy; poorly designed governance can stall or capture the network.

***Table 7.1**: Key trade-offs*

Functional roles and use cases

Tokens in decentralized AI networks typically serve dual roles in utility and governance, and each addresses different economic needs and creates distinct value propositions. Understanding these functional distinctions enables designers to create balanced architectures that serve both immediate transactional needs and long-term strategic governance.

Key functional roles include:

- **Utility tokens**: These tokens primarily serve functional purposes within the network ecosystem. In DAI networks, utility tokens facilitate access to AI services, enable payment for computational resources, provide priority access to premium models, or unlock advanced features. The value proposition is clear: holders can use tokens to

1 https://www.c-sharpcorner.com/article/governance-tokens-vs-utility-tokens/
2 https://101blockchains.com/governance-token-vs-utility-token/
3 https://www.linkedin.com/pulse/utility-vs-governance-security-tokens-which-one-should-jade-mckinley-box7c/
4 chrome-extension://efaidnbmnnnibpcajpcglclefindmkaj/https://arxiv.org/pdf/2102.10096
5 chrome-extension://efaidnbmnnnibpcajpcglclefindmkaj/https://arxiv.org/pdf/2008.02538
6 chrome-extension://efaidnbmnnnibpcajpcglclefindmkaj/https://arxiv.org/pdf/2102.10096

access tangible services or benefits.

The utility-driven approach creates direct demand pressure as users must acquire tokens to access services. Examples of utility functions include:

- Paying for AI model inference requests.
- Purchasing access to proprietary datasets.
- Renting computational resources for model training.
- Accessing premium analytical tools.
- Receiving priority customer support.

- **Governance tokens**: These tokens grant holders voting rights and decision-making power over protocol development, parameter adjustments, treasury management, and strategic direction. Governance tokens represent ownership and influence, enabling stakeholders to shape network evolution. These tokens create long-term alignment by giving participants decision-making power over critical network parameters.

  The value proposition centers on influence and potential future benefits rather than immediate utility. Governance functions typically include:

  - Voting on protocol upgrades.
  - Adjusting economic parameters like reward rates or fees.
  - Deciding treasury fund allocation.
  - Selecting network validators or node operators.
  - Determining partnerships or strategic initiatives.

Dual-token architectures

Many sophisticated DAI networks employ dual-token architectures that separate utility and governance functions. This separation provides several advantages: reduced regulatory risk by clearly distinguishing utility from investment-like governance rights, improved user experience by allowing pure utility access without governance complexity, better economic design by optimizing each token for its specific purpose, and enhanced flexibility in adjusting tokenomics for different functions. Real-world implementations demonstrate proven effectiveness.

Key examples:

- **Axie Infinity (AXS/SLP)**: AXS handles governance and staking (fixed supply), while SLP serves unlimited in-game transactions, preventing volatility spillovers.
- **VeChain (VET/VTHO)**: VET acts as governance/collateral; VTHO covers transaction fees, generated proportionally to VET holdings for stable pricing.

- **CENNZnet (CENNZ/CPAY)**: CENNZ secures the network; CPAY provides predictable gas fees for developers, shielding dApps from token price swings.

These models delivered 3-5x better price stability during the 2022 bear markets compared to single-token peers, while maintaining independent utility/governance incentives.

Key dual-token approaches include:

- **Utility-governance token pairs**: In this model, users acquire utility tokens for day-to-day network interactions while simultaneously earning or purchasing governance tokens for participation in network decision-making. The two tokens often have different supply mechanisms, vesting schedules, and market dynamics optimized for their respective functions.

- **Conversion and interoperability mechanisms**: Effective dual-token systems include mechanisms for converting between tokens or using them jointly for enhanced benefits. For example, users might stake governance tokens to receive discounts on utility token transactions, or burn utility tokens to acquire governance tokens, creating dynamic relationships that benefit active participants.

Balancing power and participation

This addresses the critical challenge of designing governance systems that prevent power concentration while encouraging broad, meaningful participation from diverse stakeholders. Effective governance requires balancing the legitimate interests of large token holders with the need for inclusive decision-making that represents the entire network ecosystem.

Key mechanisms for balanced governance include:

- **Preventing plutocracy**: One of the primary concerns with governance tokens is the risk of plutocracy, where wealthy participants gain disproportionate influence over network decisions. Several mechanisms can mitigate this risk, including quadratic voting, where voting power increases with the square root of tokens held rather than linearly; delegation systems that allow smaller holders to pool their voting power; time-weighted voting that rewards long-term holding over short-term speculation; and minimum participation thresholds that require broad community involvement for decisions to be valid.

- **Encouraging diverse participation**: Successful governance systems actively encourage participation from diverse stakeholder groups, including technical contributors, data providers, end users, and domain experts. This can be achieved through specialized voting tracks for different types of decisions, rotating leadership roles, educational initiatives to increase governance awareness, and rewards for constructive participation in governance discussions.

Incentive mechanism design

The design of effective incentive mechanisms requires a deep understanding of behavioral economics, game theory, and the specific dynamics of DAI networks. These mechanisms must motivate desired behaviors like high-quality data contribution and honest validation while discouraging harmful actions like Sybil attacks or model poisoning, all within a transparent and fair framework. Unlike traditional centralized systems, where managers direct behavior, decentralized networks rely entirely on codified incentives to coordinate thousands of independent actors toward a common goal.

Behavioral economics foundations

Behavioral economics provides the psychological toolkit for designing incentives that resonate with human motivation. Rather than assuming participants are purely rational profit-maximizers, effective tokenomics acknowledges cognitive biases and emotional drivers, crafting mechanisms that leverage these psychological realities to guide network behavior.

Key behavioral principles include:

- **Psychological incentive structures**: Human behavior in decentralized networks is influenced by both rational economic considerations and psychological factors. Loss aversion suggests that participants are more motivated by avoiding losses than by achieving equivalent gains, implying that penalty mechanisms may be more effective than pure reward systems. Framing effects show how the way incentives are presented significantly impacts participation rates.
- **Social proof and network effects**: Participants are more likely to engage in behaviors they observe others performing successfully. Incentive mechanisms should leverage social proof through leaderboards, reputation systems, public recognition, and community rewards. Creating visible success stories helps establish behavioral norms and encourages wider participation.
- **Temporal considerations**: The timing of rewards significantly impacts their effectiveness. Immediate rewards drive short-term engagement, while delayed rewards encourage long-term thinking and network loyalty. Optimal incentive design often combines both immediate and delayed rewards to satisfy different psychological needs and time preferences.

Kahneman and *Tversky's prospect theory* (1979) demonstrates that participants deviate from rational profit-maximization due to cognitive biases, requiring tokenomics to leverage these realities. The core principles are:

- **Loss aversion**: *Kahneman* and *Tversky* showed losses feel 2x more painful than equivalent gains ($v(x)=x^{\alpha}$ *for gains*, $-(-x)^{\beta}$ *for losses*, $\lambda \approx 2.25$), making slashing penalties more effective than rewards alone.

- **Framing effects**: How incentives are presented alters participation; avoiding 90% failure boosts engagement by 20-30% over 10% success in A/B tests.
- **Social proof**: *Cialdini's* principle explains why leaderboards increase activity 3-5x by signaling normative behavior.

Mechanism taxonomy

Mechanism design offers a structural framework for structuring economic interactions. Different network activities require distinct reward structures; routine maintenance benefits from predictability, while scarce resource allocation benefits from market-based pricing. Choosing the right mechanism for each activity is crucial for efficiency.

Primary mechanism types include:

- **Fixed reward systems**: These provide predictable compensation for specific actions or contributions. Fixed rewards work well for routine tasks with clear quality metrics, such as data validation, basic computational tasks, or network maintenance. The predictability helps participants plan their involvement and builds trust in the system.
- **Auction-based mechanisms**: These allow market forces to determine optimal reward levels for different types of contributions. Participants bid for opportunities to provide services or contribute resources, with rewards adjusting dynamically based on supply and demand. This approach is particularly effective for heterogeneous resources like computational power or specialized datasets where quality and costs vary significantly.
- **Dynamic bounty systems**: These adapt reward levels based on network needs, urgency, and participant availability. Bounties might increase for scarce resources or critical tasks, then decrease as supply normalizes. This flexibility helps networks efficiently allocate resources and respond to changing conditions.

Sybil resistance and fairness

Security and fairness are the twin pillars of sustainable decentralized networks. Without strong defenses against identity manipulation (Sybil attacks) and transparently fair distribution rules, trust can erode quickly, leading to participant exodus and network collapse.

Essential protection mechanisms include:

- **Identity verification mechanisms**: Decentralized networks must prevent participants from gaming the system by creating multiple fake identities to claim excess rewards. Solutions include stake-based identity systems where participants must commit economic resources to establish credibility, reputation-based systems that build trust over time through consistent good behavior, and cryptographic proof systems that establish a unique identity without revealing personal information.

- **Quality assessment systems**: Beyond identity verification, networks need mechanisms to assess the quality and value of contributions. This might involve peer review systems where participants evaluate each other's work, algorithmic quality scoring based on usage patterns and outcomes, or hybrid approaches that combine automated assessment with human validation.
- **Fair distribution algorithms**: Reward distribution must be perceived as fair to maintain long-term participation. This requires transparent algorithms, consistent application of rules, appeals processes for disputed decisions, and regular auditing of distribution outcomes. Unfair distribution can quickly undermine network trust and participation.

Feedback loops and adaptive incentives

Static incentive systems inevitably fail as network conditions and participant behaviors evolve. Adaptive systems create resilience by creating feedback loops where network data, like participation rates, quality metrics, and security levels, automatically inform and adjust incentive parameters, ensuring the economic model remains optimized over time.

Core adaptive components include:

- **Performance monitoring**: Effective incentive systems continuously monitor network performance and participant behavior to identify optimization opportunities. Key metrics include participation rates across different stakeholder groups, quality trends for various contribution types, network security and stability indicators, and economic health measures like token velocity and concentration.
- **Algorithmic adjustment mechanisms**: Based on monitoring data, incentive systems can automatically adjust reward parameters, redistribution rules, quality thresholds, and participation requirements. These adjustments should be gradual and predictable to avoid disrupting participant expectations while allowing the network to adapt to changing conditions.

Staking and delegation models

Staking mechanisms serve multiple crucial functions in DAI networks: they provide economic security by requiring participants to commit capital, create alignment between individual and network interests, and establish a basis for governance participation and reward distribution.

Fundamentals of staking

At its core, staking transforms digital tokens from passive assets into active collateral that guarantees operational integrity. It creates a direct financial interface between personal behavior and network health, ensuring that trust is derived from economic value rather than centralized reputation.

Core staking principles include:

- **Economic security through collateralization**: Staking requires participants to lock up tokens as collateral, creating economic incentives for honest behavior. In AI networks, stakers might include validators securing the network, data providers guaranteeing quality, compute providers ensuring availability, or curators filtering and organizing resources.

  The amount of required stake typically correlates with the potential impact of the participant's role. Validators securing critical network infrastructure require higher stakes than individual data contributors. This graduated approach balances accessibility with security requirements.

- **Reward mechanisms**: Stakers earn rewards through various mechanisms, including block rewards for validators, usage fees from network activity, inflation-based token emissions, and performance bonuses for exceptional contributions. The reward structure should provide competitive returns while maintaining network sustainability.

- **Risk and slashing**: Staking involves risk through slashing mechanisms that penalize malicious or negligent behavior. In AI networks, slashable offenses might include providing false data, failing to maintain computational availability, violating privacy protocols, or attempting to manipulate consensus mechanisms. Slashing parameters must be carefully calibrated to deter misconduct without creating excessive risk for honest participants.

Delegation architectures

Not every token holder possesses the technical expertise or hardware infrastructure to operate as a full network node. Delegation architectures solve this participation gap by allowing everyday users to assign their economic weight to trusted operators. This thereby democratizes security and ensures that a wider distribution of tokens contributes to consensus.

Key delegation mechanisms include:

- **Delegated proof-of-stake systems**: Many networks allow token holders to delegate their stake to professional validators rather than operating the infrastructure themselves. This delegation increases network participation while leveraging specialized expertise for critical operations. Delegation mechanisms typically involve:

  - **Validator selection processes** where token holders choose whom to delegate to based on performance, fees, and reputation.

  - **Reward sharing agreements** where validators distribute earnings to delegators after deducting operational fees.

  - **Flexible delegation** that allows delegators to move their stake between validators based on performance.

- **Liquid staking derivatives**: Advanced networks offer liquid staking where participants receive tradeable tokens representing their staked assets. This approach allows participants to earn staking rewards while maintaining liquidity for other activities. Liquid staking is particularly valuable in AI networks where participants might need tokens for various utility functions while maintaining staking positions.

Slashing and penalty mechanisms

While rewards incentivize participation, the integrity of a decentralized network ultimately relies on the credible threat of economic loss for malpractice. Slashing mechanisms act as the network's automated judicial system, enforcing rules and imposing financial consequences on actors who violate protocols or compromise data integrity. In Ethereum, an isolated slashing event typically costs a validator around 1 ETH out of a 32 ETH stake (about 3% of their deposit), with additional penalties for correlated attacks that can escalate toward total stake loss in extreme cases. Cosmos Hub slashes roughly 5% of a validator's bonded stake for severe offenses like double-signing and around 0.01% for prolonged downtime, pairing financial loss with jailing or permanent removal from the validator set to deter repeated violations.

Essential slashing components include:

- **Misbehavior detection**: Effective slashing requires robust mechanisms to detect and verify malicious behavior. In AI networks, this might involve:
  - Algorithmic monitoring of validator performance and behavior patterns.
  - Peer reporting systems where network participants can flag suspicious activity.
  - Cryptographic proof systems that provide verifiable evidence of misconduct.
  - Appeals processes that prevent false accusations from causing unjust penalties.
- **Graduated penalty systems**: Rather than binary slashing decisions, sophisticated networks employ graduated penalties that scale with the severity and frequency of infractions. Minor violations might result in warnings or small penalty fees, while major breaches could lead to significant stake slashing or network exclusion.
- **Recovery and rehabilitation**: Progressive slashing systems often include mechanisms for participants to rehabilitate their reputation and reduce penalties over time through consistent good behavior, additional stake requirements, or community service contributions.

Stake weighting and governance influence

The relationship between economic stake and decision-making power defines the political character of a decentralized network. Stake weighting algorithms determine how raw capital translates into governance influence, balancing the rights of large investors with the need to prevent centralization and ensure that long-term commitment is valued over short-term speculation.

Primary weighting approaches include:

- **Proportional vs. quadratic influence**: Different staking systems use various approaches to translate stake amounts into governance influence. Proportional systems give voting power directly proportional to stake size, while quadratic systems use the square root of stake to reduce the influence of large holders and encourage broader participation.
- **Time-weighted staking**: Some networks implement time-weighted staking, where longer commitment periods increase voting power or rewards. This approach encourages long-term thinking and reduces the influence of short-term speculators on network governance.
- **Multi-dimensional staking**: Advanced systems consider multiple factors beyond stake size when determining influence, including contribution history, community reputation, technical expertise, and participation consistency. This multidimensional approach creates more nuanced and fair governance systems.

Reward distribution algorithms

The algorithm used to distribute rewards among network participants fundamentally shapes incentive alignment and long-term sustainability. Different distribution mechanisms suit different network goals and participant types. *Figure 7.2* details how diverse reward distribution algorithms are structured to align long-term incentives and ensure network sustainability:

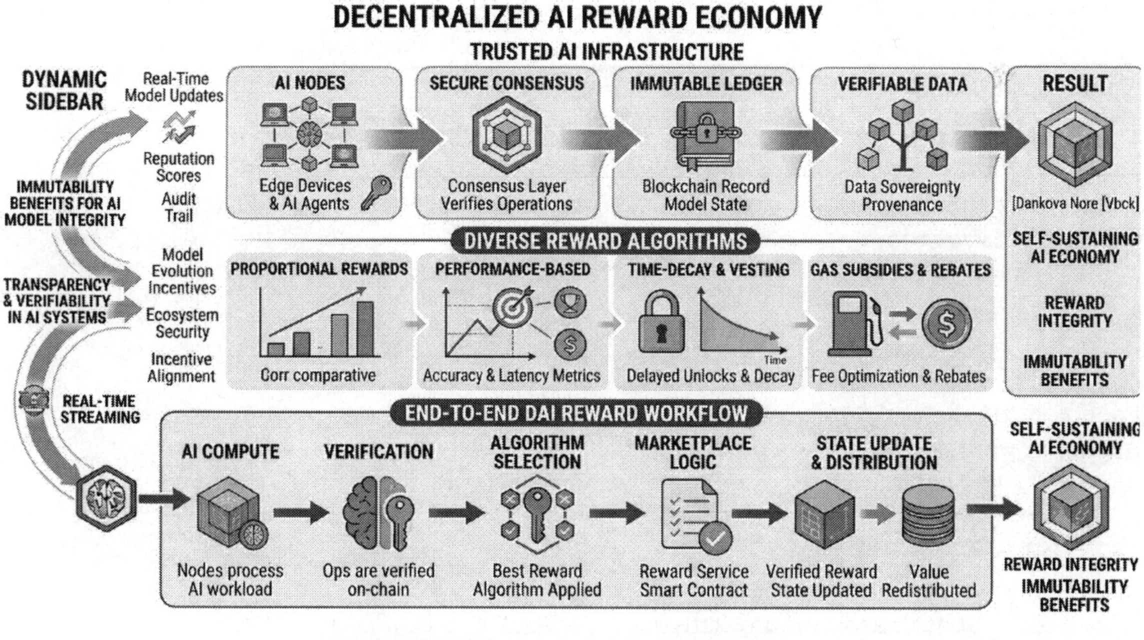

***Figure 7.2**: DAI rewards distribution algorithms*

Proportional vs. curated rewards

The tension between rewarding volume and rewarding value defines the core challenge of distribution design. Simple quantitative metrics are easy to verify but prone to gaming, while qualitative assessments are harder to implement but crucial for maintaining high standards.

Key distribution approaches include:

- **Simple proportional distribution**: The most straightforward approach distributes rewards in direct proportion to contributions or stake. For computational resources, this might mean rewards proportional to processing power contributed. For data providers, rewards might correlate with dataset size or usage frequency.

  While simple to implement and understand, pure proportional distribution can create several issues, such as:

  - It may not account for quality differences between contributions.
  - It might not incentivize innovation or improvement.
  - It could lead to a race to the bottom in terms of contribution quality if quantity is rewarded over value.

- **Curated distribution systems**: More sophisticated systems incorporate curation mechanisms where expert participants or algorithmic systems assess contribution quality and adjust rewards accordingly. Curation can involve: peer review processes where participants evaluate each other's contributions, algorithmic quality scoring based on usage patterns and user feedback, hybrid systems that combine automated assessment with expert review, and market-based curation where users vote with their usage patterns.

- **Bonding curve mechanisms**: Some networks implement bonding curves that automatically adjust reward rates based on supply and demand dynamics. As more participants join a particular activity, the reward rate might decrease, encouraging diversification. Conversely, scarce or high-demand contributions might receive premium rewards.

Time-decay and vesting rewards

Economic sustainability requires aligning reward distribution with the network's long-term health. Temporal mechanisms prevent farm-and-dump behavior by linking the full realization of rewards to continued network participation and stability.

Temporal reward strategies include:

- **Temporal reward structures**: The timing of reward distribution significantly impacts participant behavior and network stability. Immediate rewards encourage short-term participation and provide quick gratification, while delayed rewards promote long-term commitment and network stability.

- **Vesting schedules**: Many networks implement vesting periods for rewards to encourage continued participation and prevent immediate selling pressure. Vesting might be linear over time, milestone-based, tied to continued participation or performance targets, or cliff-based, with rewards unlocking after minimum commitment periods.
- **Compound reward systems**: Advanced networks allow participants to reinvest rewards automatically to compound their earning potential. This approach encourages long-term commitment while providing exponential growth opportunities for dedicated participants.

Meritocratic and performance-based models

In an AI ecosystem, the value of a contribution, whether data, compute, or code, varies wildly. Meritocratic models move beyond basic participation rewards to explicitly value excellence, creating an upward spiral where the highest-quality contributors capture the most value.

Performance-based strategies include:

- **Quality-based distribution**: Rather than purely quantitative metrics, performance-based systems reward the quality and impact of contributions. For AI networks, this might involve:
    - Accuracy metrics for data quality or model performance, usage-based rewards where frequently accessed contributions earn more.
    - Innovation bonuses for novel or groundbreaking contributions.
    - Community recognition systems that factor in peer evaluation.
- **Reputation integration**: Sophisticated reward systems integrate reputation scores that evolve over time based on consistent performance. High-reputation participants might receive: bonus multipliers on base rewards, access to premium earning opportunities, governance privileges, or preferential treatment in resource allocation decisions.
- **Competitive elements**: Some networks introduce competitive elements where participants compete for limited reward pools based on performance metrics. This approach can drive innovation and quality improvement, but must be balanced to avoid discouraging new participants or creating unsustainable competitive pressures.

Gas subsidies and fee rebates

High friction in blockchain interactions can stifle AI network adoption, especially for microtransactions common in data labeling or inference. Subsidies and rebates remove these barriers, ensuring that economic utility gas costs drive participation.

Fee mitigation strategies include:

- **Transaction cost management**: High blockchain transaction costs can significantly impact network participation, particularly for smaller contributors. Effective networks implement various subsidy mechanisms:
  - Direct gas subsidies for certain types of transactions, fee rebates for active participants, and batch transaction processing to reduce individual costs.
  - Alternative payment methods that allow fee payment with earned rewards rather than requiring upfront capital.
- **Merit-based subsidies**: Rather than universal subsidies that might be abused, networks can provide fee relief based on contribution history, stake levels, reputation scores, or participation in network governance. This targeted approach reduces costs for valuable participants while maintaining barriers against spam or abuse.

Economic security and attack resistance

Economic security represents the cornerstone of any successful tokenomics design, particularly in DAI networks where valuable data, models, and computational resources are at stake. The cost of attacking the network must exceed the potential benefits, creating a strong economic deterrent against malicious behavior.

Threat landscape

Decentralized networks operate in an adversarial environment where any profitable attack vector will inevitably be exploited. Understanding the specific threats facing AI networks, from consensus manipulation to data poisoning, is the first step in designing robust economic defenses.

Primary attack vectors include:

- **51% attacks and consensus manipulation**: Traditional blockchain networks face the risk of majority attacks where malicious actors gain control of consensus mechanisms. In AI networks, these attacks might involve:
  - Manipulating model training data to introduce biases or backdoors, censoring specific types of data or participants.
  - Redirecting rewards to colluding participants.
  - Halting network progress on competitive AI models.
- **Oracle manipulation**: AI networks often rely on external data feeds and oracles to function properly. Attackers might manipulate these data sources to influence reward calculations, bias model training outcomes, trigger automated actions based on false information, or create arbitrage opportunities in token pricing mechanisms.

- **Economic attacks**: Beyond technical attacks, networks face purely economic threats, including flash loan attacks that manipulate token prices or governance outcomes temporarily, wash trading or artificial volume to manipulate reward calculations, coordinated token dumps to destabilize the network economically, and Sybil attacks using multiple identities to claim excess rewards.

Capital requirements and attack costs

The primary defense against economic attacks is making them prohibitively expensive. By requiring participants to lock significant capital as collateral, networks create a security budget that scales with the value being secured.

Security scaling strategies include:

- **Stake-based security**: Networks that require a significant stake for participation create natural economic barriers to attack. The cost of acquiring enough stake to mount a successful attack often exceeds the potential benefits, particularly when including the risk of slashing penalties.
- **Dynamic security scaling**: As network value increases, security requirements should scale proportionally. This might involve:
  - Automatic adjustment of minimum stake requirements based on network value.
  - Increasing slashing penalties for higher-stakes roles.
  - Implementing progressive security measures that activate as network value crosses thresholds.
  - Diversifying security mechanisms to avoid single points of failure.
- **Multi-layered defense**: Robust networks employ multiple overlapping security mechanisms rather than relying on single approaches. This layered defense might include:
  - Economic barriers through stakeholder requirements.
  - Technical safeguards through cryptographic proofs.
  - Social mechanisms through reputation systems.
  - Governance oversight through community monitoring.

Game-theoretic analysis

Designing secure networks requires modeling rational behavior under adversarial conditions. Game theory provides the mathematical framework to ensure that honest participation remains the dominant strategy for all actors, even when they are purely self-interested.

Fundamental game-theoretic principles include:

- **Incentive compatibility**: Network mechanisms should be designed so that following the intended behavior is the most profitable strategy for rational participants. This requires careful analysis of potential attack vectors and ensuring that honest behavior always provides better expected returns than malicious alternatives.
- **Nash equilibrium considerations**: The network should reach stable equilibria where no participant can improve their position by unilaterally changing their strategy. This stability requires:
    - Balanced reward structures that do not create excessive competition or cooperation.
    - Penalties that make defection unprofitable.
    - Governance mechanisms that allow for peaceful resolution of conflicts.
- **Mechanism robustness**: Security mechanisms must remain effective under various network conditions, including periods of high volatility, rapid growth or contraction, changing participant compositions, and external economic pressures. Stress testing and scenario analysis help identify potential vulnerabilities before they can be exploited.

Solutions and mitigations

Identifying threats is insufficient; networks must implement concrete mechanisms to detect, prevent, and mitigate attacks. These solutions combine cryptographic controls with economic incentives to create resilient systems. Proven mitigation strategies include:

- **Time-Locking and commitment schemes**: Require participants to commit resources for extended periods, making attacks more expensive and easier to detect. Time-locked stakes cannot be quickly withdrawn, giving the network time to respond to malicious behavior.
- **Multi-signature governance**: Critical network decisions and treasury management should require consensus from multiple independent parties. This prevents single points of failure and makes coordinated attacks more difficult to execute.
- **Monitoring and alert systems**: Automated monitoring systems can detect unusual patterns that might indicate attacks in progress, such as rapid changes in stake distribution, abnormal transaction patterns, coordinated behavior across multiple accounts, or deviations from expected network metrics. Early detection enables rapid response and mitigation.

Market making and liquidity

Adequate liquidity is essential for token utility and network growth. Without sufficient liquidity, tokens cannot function effectively as mediums of exchange, stores of value, or governance mechanisms. Well-designed liquidity systems ensure that participants can enter and exit positions efficiently while maintaining price stability.

Importance of liquidity for token utility

Liquidity is not just a financial metric; it is the lubricant that allows the diverse gears of a decentralized AI network to mesh and turn. Without deep markets, the friction of entering or exiting the ecosystem becomes too high for practical usage, rendering the token's utility theoretical rather than actual.

Critical liquidity requirements include:

- **Functional liquidity requirements**: For tokens to serve their intended utility functions, sufficient liquidity must exist at multiple levels: primary markets where tokens are initially distributed or earned, secondary markets where tokens can be traded for other assets, utility markets where tokens are exchanged for network services, and governance markets where voting rights can be delegated or transferred.
- **Price discovery and stability**: Adequate liquidity enables efficient price discovery, reducing volatility and making tokens more suitable for utility functions. High volatility makes it difficult to price services consistently and creates uncertainty for both providers and consumers of network services.
- **Network effects and adoption**: Liquid tokens are more attractive to potential participants because they reduce the risk of being locked into illiquid positions. This liquidity premium encourages broader adoption and participation in the network ecosystem.

Automated market makers

In decentralized networks, traditional order books are often replaced by **automated market makers (AMMs)**, algorithmic protocols that allow digital assets to be traded automatically and without permission. These smart contracts act as the primary liquidity infrastructure, ensuring that trades can always be executed regardless of whether a specific counterparty is immediately available.

Core AMM mechanisms include:

- **Constant product formula**: The most common AMM design uses the constant product formula ($x \times y = k$), where x and y represent token reserves and k remains constant. This mechanism provides continuous liquidity but creates a price impact that increases with trade size. The most common AMM design uses $x \times y = k$, where and are token reserves in the pool and stays fixed during trades. Intuitively, this acts like a rubber band: swapping token A for B shrinks A's reserve and expands B's, but their product remains constant, automatically pushing prices toward balance.

  Example:

- Start with 100 ETH (x) and 200,000 USDC (y), so k=20M. Alice swaps 1 ETH: new x=101, so y=20M/101≈198,020 USDC. She receives ~1,980 USDC, and the price impact rises with larger trades.
- This curve shows how reserves shift while maintaining the xy=k invariant, creating continuous liquidity without order books.

- **Advanced AMM designs**: More sophisticated AMMs address limitations of the basic constant product model through:
    - Concentrated liquidity that focuses liquidity around current market prices.
    - Dynamic fee structures that adjust based on volatility or market conditions.
    - Multiple asset pools that enable complex trading relationships.
    - Oracle integration that helps maintain price accuracy.
- **Impermanent loss management**: Liquidity providers in AMMs face impermanent loss when token prices diverge. Networks can mitigate this risk through impermanent loss insurance funded by protocol fees, dynamic fee structures that compensate for higher risk periods, and liquidity mining rewards that offset potential losses.

Liquidity mining and yield farming

To bootstrap liquidity in the early stages of a network, protocols often employ liquidity mining strategies that distribute tokens to users who provide capital. This mechanism effectively rents liquidity from the market, but must be designed carefully to ensure that it builds long-term network loyalty rather than attracting mercenary capital that flees once rewards dry up.

Essential liquidity mining components include:

- **Incentive alignment**: Liquidity mining programs reward participants for providing liquidity to trading pools. These programs must be carefully designed to:
    - Attract sufficient liquidity for network operations.
    - Avoid creating unsustainable reward expectations.
    - Target productive liquidity rather than mercenary capital.
    - Maintain rewards even after initial incentive periods end.
- **Program design**: Successful liquidity mining programs typically include: gradual reward decay to prevent cliff effects when programs end, performance-based bonuses for consistent participation, multi-pool incentives that encourage liquidity across different token pairs, and governance integration that gives long-term liquidity providers additional network influence.
- **Sustainability considerations**: Liquidity mining programs must be economically sustainable for the network. This requires careful modeling of reward costs versus

network benefits, diverse funding sources beyond token inflation, integration with network revenue streams, and exit strategies that maintain liquidity after incentive periods.

Managing impermanent loss

Impermanent loss is the primary risk factor for liquidity providers, occurring when the price ratio of deposited tokens changes after they are deposited in a pool. Understanding and mitigating this mathematical inevitability is crucial for retaining long-term liquidity providers who might otherwise find that simply holding the token yields better returns than supporting the network.

Loss mitigation approaches include:

- **Risk assessment**: Liquidity providers must understand and price impermanent loss risk when participating in AMM pools. Networks can help by:
    - Providing clear risk disclosures and education.
    - Offering tools to calculate potential losses under different scenarios.
    - Creating insurance options for risk-averse participants.
    - Designing token mechanisms that reduce correlation risk.
- **Mitigation strategies**: Various approaches can reduce impermanent loss, including single-sided staking that avoids correlation risk, stable coin pairs that minimize price divergence, dynamic rebalancing mechanisms that adjust pool weights, and fee structures that compensate for increased risk during volatile periods.

Token metrics and analytics

Comprehensive analytics and monitoring systems are essential for understanding network health, participant behavior, and the effectiveness of tokenomics mechanisms. These systems provide the data necessary for informed governance decisions and ongoing optimization.

Key performance indicators

Metrics form the foundation of network health assessment, providing objective measures of tokenomics performance and identifying areas requiring attention or adjustment.

Essential **key performance indicators (KPIs)** include:

- **Supply and distribution metrics**: Fundamental metrics include circulating supply versus total supply, token distribution concentration across holders, vesting schedule progress and future unlock dates, and inflation rates and their impact on supply growth. These metrics help assess tokenomics health and potential future price pressures.

- **Network activity indicators**: Transaction volumes and frequency indicate network adoption and usage patterns. Key metrics include daily and monthly active users, transaction volumes in both token terms and USD equivalents, gas usage and fee generation, and network throughput and capacity utilization.
- **Economic health metrics**: Financial sustainability indicators include token velocity and holding patterns, staking participation rates and duration, reward distribution efficiency and fairness, and correlation between network usage and token value. These metrics help identify potential economic imbalances or sustainability issues.

On-chain analytics tools

On-chain data provides the most reliable and transparent source of network truth. Analytics tools transform this raw data into actionable insights that reveal patterns invisible to casual observation. Primary analytics tools include:

- **Blockchain explorers**: Basic analytics start with blockchain explorers that provide transaction history, address activity, and smart contract interactions. Advanced explorers offer:
    - Token holder analysis and distribution charts.
    - Transaction flow visualization.
    - Smart contract interaction mapping.
    - Historical price and volume data integration.
- **Custom analytics platforms**: Sophisticated networks develop custom analytics platforms that track network-specific metrics such as:
    - AI model usage and performance statistics.
    - Data quality and curation metrics, compute resource utilization, and efficiency.
    - Governance participation and voting patterns.
- **Real-time monitoring**: Continuous monitoring systems track key metrics in real-time and alert administrators to potential issues, including:
    - Unusual transaction patterns that might indicate attacks.
    - Sudden changes in staking or delegation patterns, governance proposals, and voting progress.
    - Economic metrics that deviate from expected ranges.

Economic health dashboards

Dashboards consolidate complex metrics into intuitive visualizations that enable rapid decision-making by diverse stakeholders. Well-designed dashboards democratize access to network intelligence while providing context-specific views for different user needs.

Core dashboard functionalities include:

- **Stakeholder visibility**: Transparent dashboards provide different stakeholders with relevant information, including public dashboards showing network growth and adoption metrics, governance dashboards displaying proposal status and voting results, participant dashboards showing individual rewards and performance, and developer dashboards tracking ecosystem development activity.
- **Predictive analytics**: Advanced dashboards incorporate predictive modeling to forecast: token supply changes and their price impact, network growth trajectories and capacity requirements, reward sustainability under different scenarios, and governance proposal outcomes based on current voting patterns.

Predictive modeling

Forward-looking analytics enable proactive decision-making rather than reactive firefighting. Predictive models synthesize historical patterns with current trends to forecast future network states, allowing governance to act before problems materialize.

Key predictive approaches include:

- **Network growth forecasting**: Statistical models can predict network adoption and growth based on historical patterns, external market conditions, competitive landscape analysis, and technological development milestones. These forecasts help with capacity planning and tokenomics adjustments.
- **Economic scenario modeling**: Comprehensive models simulate network behavior under different economic conditions, including:
    - Market crashes or booms
    - Regulatory changes
    - Competitive threats
    - Internal parameter adjustments

  This scenario planning helps design robust tokenomics that perform well under various conditions.

Regulatory compliance

The regulatory landscape for tokens and decentralized networks continues to evolve rapidly, with significant implications for tokenomics design and network operation. Understanding and proactively addressing regulatory requirements is essential for long-term sustainability, ensuring that innovation does not come at the cost of legal peril.

Securities law considerations

Navigating securities regulations is often the most critical legal challenge for token projects, as misclassification can lead to enforcement actions and existential threats to the network.

Key securities considerations include:

- **Token classification**: The classification of tokens as securities, commodities, or utility assets has profound implications for regulatory requirements. Key factors influencing classification include:
    - How tokens are marketed and sold to investors.
    - The degree of decentralization in network governance and operation.
    - Whether token holders have reasonable expectations of profit from others' efforts.
    - The functional utility vs. investment characteristics of the token.
- **Regulatory clarity**: Different jurisdictions provide varying levels of clarity on token classification. The U.S. SEC has taken an increasingly aggressive stance on token enforcement, while other jurisdictions like *Switzerland* and *Singapore* have provided clearer frameworks for compliant token operations. Networks must consider their target markets and design compliance strategies accordingly.
- **Safe harbor provisions**: Some regulatory frameworks provide safe harbor provisions for truly decentralized networks or utility tokens. To qualify for these protections, networks typically must demonstrate: genuine decentralization of control and governance, clear utility functions rather than pure investment characteristics, transparent operations and fair token distribution, and compliance with applicable disclosure requirements.

KYC or AML and data privacy

As decentralized networks intersect with traditional finance and global commerce, they face increasing pressure to prevent illicit financial flows while respecting user privacy rights.

Primary compliance requirements include:

- **Identity verification requirements**: Many jurisdictions require some form of identity verification for participants in token networks, particularly those involving large transactions or governance functions. Networks must balance regulatory compliance with privacy protection through risk-based **know your customer (KYC)** that applies stronger requirements to higher-risk activities, privacy-preserving identity solutions that verify identity without revealing personal information, and jurisdiction-specific compliance that adapts to local requirements.

- **Anti-money laundering compliance**: AML requirements typically include transaction monitoring for suspicious patterns, reporting of large or unusual transactions, maintaining audit trails for regulatory examination, and implementing sanctions screening for prohibited persons or entities.
- **Privacy protection**: While complying with regulatory requirements, networks must also protect participant privacy through:
  - Data minimization that collects only necessary information.
  - Secure storage and transmission of personal data.
  - User control over personal information sharing.
  - Compliance with privacy regulations like the **General Data Protection Regulation (GDPR)**.

Tax implications for participants

The tax treatment of crypto assets remains complex and varied, creating a significant compliance burden for both network operators and individual participants.

Major tax categories include:

- **Income tax considerations**: Token rewards and airdrops may constitute taxable income in many jurisdictions, requiring:
  - Clear documentation of reward values and timing.
  - Participant education about tax obligations.
  - Integration with tax reporting tools and services.
  - Coordination with tax authorities where required.
- **Capital gains treatment**: Token trading and disposal may trigger capital gains obligations, requiring:
  - Accurate cost basis tracking for token acquisitions.
  - Reporting of trading gains and losses.
  - Integration with tax calculation tools.
  - Compliance with holding period requirements for preferential tax treatment.

- **Reporting obligations**: Networks may have reporting obligations to tax authorities, including:
    - Participant identity information for large transactions.
    - Transaction details for audit purposes.
    - Aggregate network statistics for regulatory monitoring.
    - Compliance with information-sharing agreements between jurisdictions.

Jurisdictional variations

The decentralized nature of blockchain networks often conflicts with the strictly territorial nature of national laws, necessitating a sophisticated multi-jurisdictional strategy.

Key jurisdictional challenges include:

- **Regulatory arbitrage**: Different jurisdictions offer varying regulatory environments, leading some networks to engage in regulatory arbitrage by:
    - Incorporating in favorable jurisdictions.
    - Structuring operations to minimize regulatory burden.
    - Providing different services in different markets based on local requirements.
- **Compliance complexity**: Operating across multiple jurisdictions creates compliance complexity requiring:
    - Legal expertise in each target market.
    - Systems that can adapt to different regulatory requirements.
    - Ongoing monitoring of regulatory changes.
    - Relationships with local compliance partners.
- **Future regulatory evolution**: The regulatory landscape continues evolving rapidly, requiring networks to:
    - Monitor regulatory developments proactively.
    - Engage with regulators and industry groups.
    - Design flexible systems that can adapt to changing requirements.
    - Maintain legal reserves for compliance and potential enforcement actions.

Governance framework design

A healthy decentralized governance framework starts with a precise purpose statement, such as: *Uniting global compute providers to collaboratively train open-source AI models*, paired with a scope matrix that maps decision rights, vote, propose, advisory, across stakeholders, token holders, node operators, research partners, and areas like protocol upgrades, treasury spending, and membership. It is anchored in transparency via public on-chain records, inclusivity through accessible grants, auditability with formal verification, and resilience from timelocks and multi-signature guardians. It also harmonizes on-chain elements, voting, and execution with off-chain tools, forums, and snapshot polls. MakerDAO exemplifies a focused scope on collateral and risk parameters, whereas optimism showcases a layered design with health dashboards.

Practical templates, a stakeholder scope matrix table, security checklist covering unit tests, static analysis, and timelock validation, plus a three-layer model, on-chain, off-chain, monitoring, facilitate secure, scalable deployment.

Voting mechanisms and systems

DAI networks use voting mechanisms to convert individual preferences into collective decisions while balancing simplicity, fairness, and security. Direct voting grants one vote per token for permissionless participation but risks whale control, whereas reputation-weighted systems link influence to verified contributions, such as compute provision or code commits. Quadratic voting requires n^2 token for n votes to empower minority intensity, as demonstrated by *Gitcoin Grants*, while liquid democracy allows fluid delegation with reclaim options (Gnosis Safe). Conviction voting builds power over time to reward sustained support (Moloch DAO), safeguarded by zero-knowledge proofs, commit-reveal protocols, and slashing for vote buying.

Essential metrics, including turnout rate, engagement depth, Gini coefficient for vote concentration, and delegation ratio, provide health insights through dashboards monitoring proposal activity and distribution. Hybrid models optimize outcomes by blending quadratic voting for passion, delegation for expertise, and protections like randomized scheduling to deliver representative, attack-resistant results.

Voting mechanisms comparison

DAI networks balance simplicity, fairness, and security across diverse voting systems. *Table 7.2* compares key approaches with their strengths, weaknesses, and real-world implementations:

System	Mechanism	Strengths	Weaknesses	Examples
Direct voting	1 token = 1 vote	Simple, permissionless	Whale dominance (Gini > 0.8 typical)	Compound, Uniswap
Reputation-weighted	Votes ∝ verified contributions	Merit-based, sybil-resistant	Subjective scoring, capture risk	Gitcoin Passport, Hop Protocol
Quadratic voting	n2 tokens for n votes	Amplifies minority intensity	Complex UX, credit limits	Gitcoin Grants (>$50M allocated)
Liquid democracy	Delegatable votes with recall	Expertise routing, flexible	Delegation cascades	Gnosis Safe, Polkadot OpenGov

System	Mechanism	Strengths	Weaknesses	Examples
Conviction voting	Power = stake/ (time since vote)	Rewards conviction	Momentum bias	MolochDAO, MetaCartel

***Table 7.2**: Voting mechanisms*

Proposal and decision processes

Robust proposal processes advance ideas through four distinct phases:

- Ideation via open forum brainstorming to surface concepts.
- Drafting with formal templates detailing technical specifications and resource needs.
- Risk assessments and community feedback during a structured 14-day window, supported by version control and change tracking.
- Final ratification plus execution through secure on-chain voting followed by a mandatory 48-hour timelock.

Eligibility criteria demand minimum token stakes or verified reputation scores to effectively filter spam and low-quality submissions. At the same time, quorum requirements such as 5% eligible voter participation validate proposals, employing adjustable curves that impose stricter thresholds for high-stakes constitutional changes versus routine operational updates.

Timelines incorporate standard timelocks for deliberate review, fast-track supermajority approval requiring two-thirds consensus for urgent 12-hour execution windows, and guardian veto mechanisms with structured appeal processes to balance security and responsiveness. Communication standards mandate comprehensive templates covering background context, detailed rationale, step-by-step implementation plans, quantified risks, and impact analysis; these integrate with decentralized repositories for immutable records, regular town hall discussions, automated notification bots across platforms, and multilingual accessibility features. This comprehensive framework delivers exceptional clarity, ironclad accountability, and operational agility essential for thriving DAI governance ecosystems.

Delegation and representative systems

DAI networks blend direct participation with scalable expertise through delegation systems that prevent voter fatigue while curbing elite capture. Structured models include revocable delegation for instant reclaim, permanent locks for stability, caps such as a 5% maximum vote power with dynamic adjustments based on network growth, and tiered hierarchies where local working groups elect higher-level councils for federated representation. Accountability relies on public dashboards displaying voting records, participation rates, proposal success metrics, alongside recall votes triggered by poor performance and mandatory periodic reports through on-chain attestations or community calls.

Hybrid architectures integrate on-chain delegation for binding decisions like treasury allocations and protocol upgrades with off-chain advisory councils comprising technical experts, legal advisors, or researchers who vet complex proposals. Council recommendations, published on decentralized forums for community feedback, enrich delegate choices without binding authority, creating iterative loops that bridge specialized insight and broad input. Real-world examples like Optimism's citizen assemblies demonstrate how such systems sustain engagement and informed governance at scale.

Dispute resolution mechanisms

Disputes in DAI networks over proposals, parameters, or misconduct demand structured frameworks, including on-chain arbitration. Kleros employs stake-based jurors who earn fees or face slashing for dishonest rulings. Aragon Court deploys random jurors supplemented by judges to establish binding precedents. Mediation paths progress methodically from self-resolution in public forums, through advocate-facilitated dialogue with neutral facilitators, to formal arbitration appeals requiring progressively higher stakes. Tiered escalation ensures efficiency by resolving most conflicts informally while reserving on-chain adjudication for irreconcilable disputes. Advocates earn reputation multipliers for successful compromises that preserve community harmony.

Enforcement operates automatically and credibly through slashing mechanisms that redistribute or burn offender tokens, dynamic reputation score adjustments reflecting dispute outcomes, and smart contract execution of remedies such as parameter resets, fund clawbacks, or membership revocations. The standardized dispute submission form captures dispute title, involved parties, detailed timeline with evidence links, requested remedy, prior mediation attempts, and escalation level to streamline intake and transparency. Real-world effectiveness shines in networks like optimism, where integrated dispute systems maintain protocol integrity amid rapid evolution.

Implementation with DAOs

Implementation converts governance designs into operational DAOs through proven frameworks:

- Aragon provides intuitive permissions and voting interfaces.
- DAOstack enables conviction voting with advanced analytics.
- Colony streamlines task-based reputation bounties.
- Snapshot delivers gasless off-chain polls for rapid consensus.

Smart contracts emphasize modularity by separating voting logic, treasury management, and execution modules; proxy upgrades leverage OpenZeppelin UUPS or Transparent patterns for seamless evolution; rigorous testing employs Truffle, Hardhat, and MythX alongside formal verification to guarantee security and governance-approved upgradability.

DAO framework selection criteria

Choose DAO tools based on governance complexity, team expertise, and execution needs. The matrix shown in *Table 7.3* matches Aragon, DAOstack, Colony, and Snapshot to specific use cases:

Framework	Best for	Technical skill	Voting types	Execution	Scalability	Community
Aragon	General-purpose, permissions	Low-medium	Token, multi-sig	On-chain	High (L2 native)	Largest
DAOstack	Complex governance, conviction	High	Holographic, Reputation	Modular plugins	Very high	Smaller
Colony	Task/reputation bounties	Low-medium	Reputation-based	Native payments	Medium	Growing
Snapshot	Gasless signaling, rapid polls	Very Low	Token, quadratic	Off-chain only	Highest	Massive

***Table 7.3**: DAO framework selection criteria*

Deployment follows a disciplined path from comprehensive testnet pilots simulating real-world scenarios to independent audits by Trail of Bits or ConsenSys Diligence, culminating in phased mainnet rollout:

- Phase 0 launches token distribution and Snapshot integration.
- Phase 1 activates proposal submission and basic voting.
- Phase 2 introduces execution capabilities with timelocks and emergency pauses.
- Phase 3 grants full privileges once a 20% token holder turnout is achieved.

Continuous monitoring utilizes real-time dashboards tracking participation rates, Gini coefficients for vote concentration, proposal execution times, and dispute frequency, augmented by structured feedback loops, quarterly governance workshops, and 24-month rolling roadmaps that drive iterative evolution and adaptation to emerging needs.

Case studies and examples

Examining real-world implementations of tokenomics in decentralized AI networks provides valuable insights into successful strategies and common pitfalls. These case studies illustrate how theoretical principles translate into practical systems.

Leading DAI protocols

Leading DAI protocols demonstrate how carefully designed tokenomics can coordinate data, compute, and AI services at scale while aligning incentives for developers, users, and infrastructure providers. These networks move beyond speculative tokens, embedding economic mechanisms directly into AI marketplaces, autonomous agent frameworks, and privacy-preserving data exchanges.

Prominent implementations include:

- **SingularityNET (AGIX | ASI)**: SingularityNET pioneered the concept of DAI marketplaces, creating a platform where developers can monetize AI services and users can access diverse AI capabilities through a unified interface. The AGIX token served multiple functions, including payment for AI services, staking for network security, and governance participation.

  The network's tokenomics evolved significantly over time. Initially, AGIX tokens were used primarily for payment, with a simple proportional reward distribution to service providers. As the network matured, more sophisticated mechanisms were introduced, including:

  - Reputation-weighted rewards that favored high-quality service providers.
  - Staking mechanisms that allowed users to earn rewards for network security.
  - Governance features that gave token holders control over network development.
  - Cross-chain compatibility that expanded accessibility.

- **Fetch.ai (FET)**: Fetch.ai focuses on autonomous economic agents that can interact and transact independently. The FET token facilitates these interactions and provides the economic incentives for agent development and deployment. The network's tokenomics emphasize utility over speculation, with clear use cases for token consumption.

  Key design elements include:

  - Agent registration and discovery fees paid in FET.
  - Computational resources purchased with FET tokens.
  - Reputation systems that affect agent earning potential.
  - Developer incentives for creating valuable autonomous agents.

  The network successfully demonstrated real-world applications in energy optimization, supply chain coordination, and mobility services.

- **Ocean Protocol (OCEAN)**: Ocean Protocol created a decentralized data marketplace that enables secure data sharing while preserving privacy and ownership rights. The OCEAN token coordinates data transactions and incentivizes quality data contribution.

Ocean's tokenomics innovations include:

- o Datatokens that represent access rights to specific datasets.
- o Compute-to-data functionality that allows AI training without exposing raw data.
- o Curation markets where token holders stake on valuable datasets.
- o Revenue sharing between data providers and curators.

This approach successfully addresses the challenge of monetizing data while maintaining privacy.

DAO governance models

Real-world implementations both illuminate the transformative potential and expose critical pitfalls of DAI governance. By rigorously analyzing proven successes, dissecting high-profile failures, and strategically adopting cutting-edge innovations, practitioners can engineer governance frameworks that robustly scale alongside rapidly evolving network demands and technological paradigms.

Successful DAO governance models include the following:

- **Uniswap** masterfully utilizes **Unique Network Identifier** (**UNI**) governance tokens to empower community votes on protocol upgrades, dynamic fee structures, treasury grants, and ecosystem initiatives. The streamlined process originates with community forum proposals, advances through efficient Snapshot off-chain sentiment polls for broad participation, and concludes with secure on-chain execution protected by timelock multisig architecture.

  This sophisticated hybrid model elegantly balances rapid experimentation with ironclad security controls, enabling Uniswap to swiftly iterate critical features like concentrated liquidity pools in v3 and temperature-controlled fee mechanisms within months of community consensus.

- **Optimism collective** pioneers a sophisticated two-tier **citizen house** governance architecture that elegantly separates strategic allocation from tactical execution. **Optimism** (**OP**) token holders exercise authority over high-level budget frameworks, protocol parameter boundaries, and constitutional amendments. At the same time, randomly selected, time-limited citizens' assemblies, drawn from verified active participants, deliberate on complex strategic research grants and public goods funding.

  This fusion of token-weighted democracy and sortition-driven expertise ensures genuinely broad engagement while systematically surfacing domain-specific knowledge essential for optimal resource allocation, establishing a sustainable model for public goods financing.

- **MakerDAO** exemplifies institutional-grade risk management embedded within decentralized governance through its autonomous risk core unit. MKR token holders strategically delegate on-chain voting authority to specialized risk analysts who rigorously assess prospective collateral types using proprietary quantitative models, comprehensive stress testing frameworks, and scenario analysis. Only collateral assets passing these stringent safety thresholds advance to formal governance proposals for parametric deployment.

  This demonstrates how curated representative expertise can operate seamlessly within transparent, token-governed decision frameworks while maintaining protocol solvency under extreme market conditions.

Artificial superintelligence alliance merger

In 2024, SingularityNET, Fetch.ai, and Ocean Protocol announced their merger to form the **artificial superintelligence alliance (ASI)**, creating a unified token and combining their complementary technologies. This merger provides insights into how mature tokenomics systems can be integrated and evolved.

Key merger aspects include:

- **Token migration strategy**: The merger involved a carefully orchestrated token migration process with defined conversion rates between the original tokens (FET, AGIX, OCEAN) and the new ASI token and a phased migration timeline that allowed for an orderly transition. This has maintained functionality during the transition period and clear communication to all stakeholder groups.
- **Unified tokenomics design**: The new ASI token combines the best features of the predecessor tokens, including:
  - Comprehensive utility covering AI services.
  - Data access and autonomous agents.
  - Enhanced governance rights reflecting the expanded network scope.
  - Improved liquidity through token consolidation.
  - Integrated reward mechanisms that incentivize cross-platform activity.
- **Lessons learned**: The successful merger demonstrates several important principles, including the importance of community alignment and communication during major changes, the value of technical compatibility between merging systems, the need for clear value propositions for all stakeholder groups, and the benefits of combining complementary capabilities rather than competing directly.

Success stories and pitfalls

Analyzing both triumphs and failures in decentralized AI tokenomics reveals actionable patterns for sustainable network design. Success stories demonstrate that utility-first approaches combined with adaptive governance create resilient economic systems, while common pitfalls highlight the dangers of speculation-driven models and inadequate security planning.

Key observations from real-world implementations include:

- **Successful implementations**: Analysis of successful DAI tokenomics reveals common patterns, including:
    - Clear utility-driven value propositions rather than purely speculative models.
    - Gradual evolution of tokenomics based on user feedback and network growth.
    - Strong community governance that includes diverse stakeholder groups.
    - Sustainable reward mechanisms that do not rely solely on token inflation.
    - Proactive regulatory compliance that builds trust with institutions.
- **Common pitfalls**: Failed or struggling projects often exhibit predictable problems, including:
    - Over-reliance on speculative token appreciation rather than utility value.
    - Inadequate security mechanisms that allow exploitation or manipulation.
    - Poor governance structures that concentrate power or exclude key stakeholder groups.
    - Unsustainable reward systems that create boom-bust cycles.
    - Neglect of regulatory compliance leading to enforcement actions.
- **Evolution patterns**: Successful networks typically follow similar evolution patterns, starting with simple tokenomics focused on basic utility, gradually adding governance and staking mechanisms as the community matures. This has implemented more sophisticated reward and curation systems as usage grows and is developing cross-chain and interoperability features for broader adoption.

Hypothetical design walkthrough

This hypothetical walkthrough demonstrates how tokenomics principles can be applied to create a DAI network for healthcare research, coordinating sensitive data sharing, computational resources, and AI model training while maintaining privacy and regulatory compliance. The design illustrates a practical implementation of multi-function tokens, sophisticated incentive mechanisms, and adaptive governance structures tailored to specific industry requirements.

Key design elements would include:

- **AI data marketplace scenario**: Consider designing tokenomics for a new AI data marketplace that enables privacy-preserving data collaboration between healthcare institutions. The network requires a careful balance of incentives for data providers, AI researchers, validators, and end users.

  This real-world scenario demonstrates the practical application of tokenomics principles to solve complex coordination problems in sensitive industries. The design must address healthcare-specific challenges, including regulatory compliance, data privacy, institutional participation, and long-term sustainability, while creating positive-sum economic incentives for all stakeholders.

- **Token utility design**: The native token (HEALTHAI) would serve multiple functions, including payment for data access and computational services, staking requirements for data providers to guarantee quality and compliance, governance rights for network parameter adjustment and partnership decisions, and reward distribution for data contribution, validation, and curation activities.

- **Incentive structure**: The reward system would incorporate quality-weighted rewards based on data usage and research outcomes, privacy compliance bonuses for meeting regulatory standards, collaborative incentives for institutions that contribute to multi-party research projects, and long-term vesting to encourage sustained participation rather than short-term extraction.

- **Governance framework**: Given the sensitive nature of healthcare data, governance would include: specialized committees with domain expertise in healthcare, privacy, and AI; multi-stakeholder representation, including patients, researchers, and institutions; transparent decision-making processes with public proposal and voting systems; and emergency governance procedures for addressing security or compliance issues.

- **Security and compliance**: The network would implement robust security and compliance mechanisms, including:
  - Mandatory KYC for institutional participants, automated compliance monitoring for data usage.
  - Cryptographic proofs for data quality without exposing sensitive information.
  - Integration with healthcare regulatory frameworks like HIPAA.

Conclusion

Tokenomics establishes the economic foundation for DAI networks, coordinating resource allocation, incentive alignment, and value distribution through utility, governance, and security functions without centralized authority. Successful designs prioritize genuine utility over speculation, ensure honest participation proves most profitable via precise mechanism design, and sidestep pitfalls like misaligned incentives, inadequate vesting, and regulatory oversights. The frameworks detailed throughout this chapter, from token utility models and staking systems to reward algorithms, governance tokenomics, and real-world implementations such as the ASI merger, offer complete blueprints for production-ready DAI economies. These proven systems convert economic theory into scalable coordination mechanisms that operate globally while preserving decentralization and security.

Mastering tokenomics empowers developers, researchers, and organizations to create sustainable AI networks coordinating data, compute, and intelligence across borders and institutions. These economic foundations support the privacy-preserving techniques and advanced security architectures covered in the next chapter.

CHAPTER 8
Privacy-preserving AI Techniques

Introduction

In decentralized AI networks, where data and computation span multiple untrusted parties without centralized control, traditional security models fail. This chapter presents the cryptographic and architectural foundation for privacy-preserving AI. These techniques enable powerful machine learning while mathematically guaranteeing data confidentiality, input privacy, and regulatory compliance.

We examine the full spectrum of advanced privacy technologies purpose-built for distributed AI environments, including homomorphic encryption for computing directly on encrypted data without decryption, ZKF to verify computations without revealing underlying data, secure multi-party computation for collaborative model training without data sharing, differential privacy offering mathematical guarantees against individual data leakage, and TEEs providing hardware-isolated secure computation.

Beyond theory, the chapter delivers implementation roadmaps with production frameworks like Microsoft SEAL, MP-SPDZ, and Zokrates; quantitative performance analysis revealing real-world trade-offs; regulatory mapping to GDPR, CCPA, and HIPAA requirements; and cross-industry case studies demonstrating viable deployments in healthcare, finance, and beyond. Architects and developers will gain the practical knowledge to select, combine, and optimize these techniques for specific threat models, transforming privacy from a constraint into a competitive advantage for next-generation decentralized AI systems.

Structure

The chapter covers the following topics:

- Privacy requirements in decentralized AI
- Homomorphic encryption for AI
- Zero-knowledge proofs and zk-SNARKs

- Secure multi-party computation
- Differential privacy mechanisms
- Trusted execution environments
- Privacy-preserving data sharing
- Implementation examples
- Performance trade-offs
- Compliance and regulations

Objectives

This chapter equips readers with comprehensive mastery of advanced privacy-preserving techniques critical for deploying secure AI systems across decentralized networks lacking centralized trust. Readers will gain a deep understanding of core privacy requirements like data confidentiality, user anonymity, robust trust models, and defenses against sophisticated privacy threats. At the same time, they will master the mathematical foundations and practical implementations of these technologies. Key learning outcomes include proficiency in homomorphic encryption for direct computation on encrypted data, balancing security guarantees with efficiency trade-offs; zero-knowledge proofs and zk-SNARKs enabling verifiable computations.

Through hands-on implementation examples featuring production toolkits like Microsoft SEAL, IBM HELib, and MP-SPDZ, paired with real-world case studies, readers will evaluate performance trade-offs in computational overhead, latency, scalability, and model accuracy. The chapter provides strategic mapping to compliance frameworks such as GDPR and CCPA, demonstrating how these techniques generate auditable evidence of regulatory adherence. Ultimately, readers will emerge equipped to design, audit, and optimize privacy-preserving AI architectures that harmonize ironclad privacy guarantees with operational performance in decentralized ecosystems, while anticipating emerging research frontiers.

Privacy requirements in decentralized AI

Decentralized AI networks fundamentally reshape privacy demands by distributing data and computation across untrusted nodes without centralized authority, creating heightened risks of leakage, inference attacks, and unauthorized access that traditional security models cannot address. This section dissects the core privacy pillars—confidentiality, anonymity, and trust minimization while mapping regulatory requirements and outlining cryptographic countermeasures essential for resilient, compliant systems. *Figure 8.1* details how privacy-preserving AI techniques maintain absolute data confidentiality across untrusted nodes while protecting user anonymity. The figure details how the system enforces global regulatory compliance mandates and preserves user data integrity under adversarial conditions:

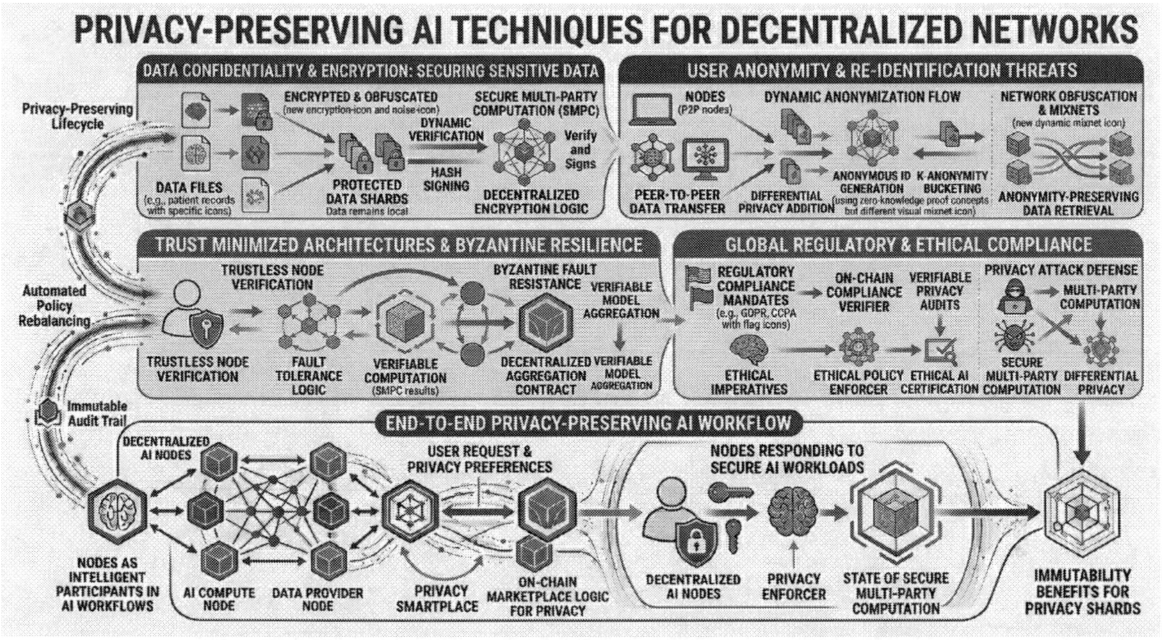

Figure 8.1: *Privacy-preserving AI techniques for decentralized networks*

Data confidentiality across untrusted nodes

In contrast to centralized systems with single-point trust, decentralized AI scatters sensitive data across heterogeneous devices and entities, amplifying exposure through breaches, side-channel metadata leaks, or compromised intermediaries. Robust protection demands end-to-end encryption for data at rest and in transit, coupled with privacy-preserving computation techniques detailed in the earlier section, enabling AI inference and training directly on ciphertext or secret shares without ever exposing plaintext.

User anonymity against re-identification threats

Beyond direct identifiers, decentralized systems face sophisticated deanonymization via correlation attacks, behavioral inference, or auxiliary data linkage, particularly in high-stakes domains like healthcare and finance. Effective countermeasures combine pseudonymization to unlink identifiers, differential privacy, injecting calibrated noise for mathematical indistinguishability guarantees, and zero-knowledge proofs enabling identity-agnostic verification of contributions or compliance without revealing underlying attributes or transaction details.

Trust minimized architectures and Byzantine resilience

Lacking central authorities, decentralized AI requires explicit trust models, from honest-but-curious to fully adversarial, underpinning protocols resilient to malicious nodes, Byzantine failures, and collusion. Cryptographic guarantees ensure confidentiality, computation integrity, and verifiable execution, often anchored by blockchain-based audit logs or distributed consensus mechanisms that provide tamper-proof provenance and dispute resolution even among partially compromised participants.

Threats and privacy attacks

Decentralized AI amplifies privacy vulnerabilities through distributed trust, enabling sophisticated attacks like data leakage, inference reconstruction, node collusion, and identity manipulation that bypass traditional defenses. Mitigation demands layered cryptographic primitives, adversarial protocol design, and runtime threat detection.

The decentralized architecture lacking centralized oversight intensifies exposure to targeted privacy attacks, where untrusted nodes can exploit partial views of data or computation to undermine confidentiality guarantees.

Prominent threats include:

- **Data leakage vectors**: Raw datasets, intermediate model gradients, or partial computation outputs risk exposure through misconfigurations, node compromises, or transmission intercepts, directly violating input privacy even when aggregated statistics appear secure.
- **Inference and reconstruction attacks**: Adversaries leverage model predictions, shadow training, or membership inference to reverse-engineer sensitive training attributes—such as medical diagnoses from healthcare models or user demographics from recommendation systems often achieving high-fidelity reconstruction with sufficient query access.
- **Collusion and multi-node exploitation**: Coordinated subsets of nodes can pool secret shares, partial decryptions, or auxiliary metadata to defeat threshold protocols, reconstructing private inputs that individual participants could not access alone.
- **Sybil and influence manipulation**: Attackers flood networks with fake identities to skew federated learning aggregates, amplify malicious contributions, or systematically collect user data across pseudonymous interactions, eroding statistical privacy protections.

Effective countermeasures integrate proactive defenses, proactive secret sharing refresh, verifiable computation attestations, anomaly detection in contribution patterns, and economic disincentives, ensuring resilience across diverse threat models while preserving system utility.

Regulatory and ethical considerations

Decentralized AI must navigate stringent global regulations like GDPR alongside ethical imperatives for user autonomy and fairness, embedding privacy-by-design to deliver verifiable compliance and transparent data governance without centralized oversight.

Privacy requirements in decentralized AI extend beyond technical defenses to encompass binding regulatory frameworks and ethical principles that demand proactive protection of personal data, transparency in processing, and respect for individual rights.

Global regulatory compliance mandates

Legislation such as GDPR, CCPA, and emerging AI Acts enforce data minimization, purpose limitation, and user rights, including access, rectification, portability, and erasure, across distributed nodes lacking unified controllers, requiring auditable mechanisms like zero-knowledge compliance proofs and decentralized consent ledgers to demonstrate adherence.

Ethical imperatives beyond legal minimums

Responsible deployment prioritizes user autonomy through granular control over data usage, algorithmic fairness to prevent biased outcomes in heterogeneous training, and harm prevention by mitigating societal risks like surveillance amplification or discriminatory inference, often addressed through interdisciplinary governance frameworks.

Decentralized systems achieve this through privacy-by-design integration: transparent policies encoded in smart contracts, verifiable audit trails via cryptographic receipts, and user-empowering tools like self-sovereign identity wallets, ensuring legal compliance doubles as an ethical foundation while fostering trust in untrusted environments.

Homomorphic encryption for AI

Homomorphic encryption (HE) enables direct computation on encrypted data without decryption, providing unbreakable confidentiality for decentralized AI processing across untrusted nodes and eliminating exposure risks during model inference or training.

Homomorphic encryption represents a revolutionary cryptographic primitive that transforms privacy-preserving AI by allowing complex computations ranging from linear algebra to neural network operations directly on ciphertext, ensuring sensitive data remains confidential throughout processing in decentralized environments lacking trusted intermediaries.

Fundamentals of homomorphic encryption

At its core, homomorphic encryption allows a party to encrypt data and send it to an untrusted processor (such as a cloud or decentralized AI node), which can then compute on the ciphertext. The result, still encrypted, is sent back to the data owner, who decrypts it to obtain the final output as if the computation were performed on the original plaintext. This ensures that no information about the data is exposed during computation, effectively maintaining confidentiality end-to-end.

Mathematical foundations

HE schemes rest on four essential algorithms: key generation, creating public/private key pairs; encryption, converting plaintext to ciphertext; homomorphic evaluation, applying algebraic operations (additions, multiplications) on ciphertexts to mirror plaintext results; and decryption, recovering plaintext from evaluated ciphertext. This homomorphic property, where $Decrypt(Eval(Enc(m), op)) = op(m)$, underpins **fully homomorphic encryption (FHE)** capable of arbitrary computation depth, though practical implementations balance security with efficiency through leveled or bootstrapping approaches.

Mathematically, a homomorphic encryption scheme comprises four main algorithms:

- **Key generation**: Generates a public and private key pair.
- **Encryption**: Transforms plaintext data into ciphertext using the public key.
- **Evaluation**: Performs algebraic operations on ciphertext to produce a new ciphertext representing the result.
- **Decryption**: Converts the resultant ciphertext back into plaintext using the private key.

The critical property is that the decryption of the evaluated ciphertext matches the result of the plaintext operations.

Types of homomorphic encryption

HE schemes are classified by the breadth and depth of ciphertext operations they support, directly impacting their suitability for privacy-preserving AI workloads ranging from linear models to deep neural architectures.

HE schemes are generally categorized based on the nature and extent of operations they support, such as:

- **Partially homomorphic encryption (PHE)**: Supports either addition or multiplication on ciphertexts but not both. For example, RSA supports homomorphic multiplication, and Paillier encryption supports homomorphic addition. While useful for specific tasks, PHE's limited operational scope restricts its applicability in complex AI computations.

- **Somewhat homomorphic encryption (SHE)**: Supports a limited number of additions and multiplications but is constrained by noise growth that accumulates with each operation, eventually making the ciphertext undecryptable.

- **Fully homomorphic encryption (FHE)**: Supports arbitrary depth of additions and multiplications, allowing the evaluation of any Boolean or arithmetic circuit on encrypted data. FHE is the holy grail for privacy-preserving AI but remains computationally intensive despite recent optimizations.

Application in AI computations

HE transforms AI workflows by enabling matrix operations, activations, and gradient updates directly on ciphertext, supporting secure inference on user data and distributed training across nodes while preserving end-to-end input privacy for decentralized systems.

AI computations from matrix multiplications and non-linear activations to backpropagation gradients traditionally expose raw data to processors, but homomorphic encryption relocates this vulnerability by executing the entire pipeline on encrypted inputs, ensuring service providers or peer nodes deliver accurate results without plaintext access. Homomorphic encryption powers diverse AI scenarios through the following specialized implementations:

- **Encrypted inference workflows**: A deployed neural network processes ciphertext-encoded user inputs (e.g., medical images or financial profiles), producing encrypted predictions that decrypt only to the data owner, ideal for privacy-sensitive prediction-as-a-service in healthcare diagnostics or personalized recommendations, where model weights may remain public, but inputs stay confidential.
- **Distributed encrypted training**: Collaborative learning aggregates encrypted gradient updates from siloed datasets across nodes, enabling federated-style model refinement without central data pooling; this supports vertical or horizontal partitioning scenarios while thwarting reconstruction attacks through additive homomorphic properties.
- **Scheme selection for AI workloads**: Approximate computations in neural networks favor **Cheon-Kim-Kim-Song** (**CKKS**) for its real-number encoding and noise-tolerant arithmetic, while exact-integer operations in decision trees or cryptographic protocols leverage **Brakerski-Gentry-Vaikuntanathan** (**BGV**) for precise arithmetic; practical libraries like Microsoft SEAL support both schemes with optimized packing strategies to bridge theoretical guarantees with production-scale performance.

Zero-knowledge proofs and zk-SNARKs

Zero-knowledge proofs (**ZKPs**) constitute a powerful cryptographic paradigm that enables one party, the prover, to convince another party, the verifier, that a particular statement is true without revealing any additional information beyond the validity of the statement itself. This property, proving knowledge without disclosure, is crucial for preserving privacy in decentralized AI systems where sensitive data and models must often be validated or verified without exposing private information.

Principles of zero-knowledge proofs

ZKPs are widely applicable in verifying AI model computations, compliance, and data integrity, where revealing internal details could compromise intellectual property or user privacy.

A ZKP protocol must satisfy three integral properties:

- **Completeness**: If the statement is true, an honest prover can convince the verifier of its truth.
- **Soundness**: If the statement is false, no dishonest prover can convince the verifier otherwise, except with negligible probability.
- **Zero-knowledge**: No information about the statement beyond its validity is revealed to the verifier.

These properties ensure privacy and trust without explicit data sharing.

zk-SNARKs

Among ZKPs, **zero-knowledge succinct non-interactive arguments of knowledge** (**zk-SNARKs**) represent an advanced form that is particularly suited for decentralized and blockchain-integrated.

AI applications. zk-SNARKs offer:

- **Succinctness**: The proof size and verification time are very small, often on the order of a few hundred bytes and milliseconds, respectively, regardless of the computational complexity of the statement being proven.
- **Non-interactivity**: They require no back-and-forth communication between prover and verifier, making them efficient in decentralized environments.
- **Proof of knowledge**: They demonstrate that the prover knows the secret witness (e.g., the private inputs) corresponding to a public statement.

These features make zk-SNARKs practical for verifying AI computations carried out off-chain or on untrusted nodes without leaking model or data specifics.

Applications in privacy-preserving AI

zk-SNARKs deliver succinct, verifiable proofs of correct AI computation without exposing inputs, models, or data, perfectly suiting decentralized systems where blockchain efficiency meets privacy needs, from model validation to regulatory audits across healthcare, finance, and supply chains.

In decentralized AI ecosystems, zk-SNARKs enable trustless verification of complex computations while preserving confidentiality, leveraging their constant-size proofs and non-interactive verifier properties for seamless blockchain integration.

Core AI verification use cases

AI nodes prove accurate inference or training execution against committed parameters without parameter disclosure; validate training data quality and compliance without raw data exposure; generate auditable evidence of regulatory adherence (e.g., GDPR data minimization); and attest to off-chain AI workloads, minimizing on-chain computational costs while maintaining chain-level trust.

zk-SNARKs power essential privacy-preserving functions across the AI lifecycle:

- **Model validation**: Provers (e.g., AI nodes) can demonstrate that AI inference or training steps are performed correctly based on committed model parameters without revealing those parameters.
- **Data privacy assurance**: zk-SNARKs can prove that data used in model training meets quality and compliance constraints without exposing the raw data.
- **Regulatory compliance**: zk-SNARKs enable the demonstration of adherence to privacy policies and legal requirements in an auditable yet privacy-respecting manner.
- **Secure off-chain computation**: Complex AI computations can be offloaded from costly on-chain environments to decentralized nodes, with zk-SNARKs providing lightweight proofs for verifier trust.

Healthcare applications

zk-SNARKs enable hospitals to collaboratively train diagnostic AI models across siloed patient datasets, proving model accuracy, fairness, and regulatory compliance without ever sharing protected health information, revolutionizing secure medical AI in federated environments.

Hospitals leverage zk-SNARKs for secure collaborative training of diagnostic models such as cancer detection from imaging or predictive analytics for rare diseases, where each institution contributes encrypted gradient updates or model validations without exchanging raw patient records.

Financial services

Banks harness zk-SNARKs to validate fraud detection and risk models trained on proprietary transaction data, delivering verifiable performance proofs to regulators and auditors while concealing sensitive financial records, enabling compliant AI innovation without data exposure.

Banks deploy zk-SNARKs to cryptographically attest to the integrity and efficacy of AI models trained on siloed transaction histories, customer behavioral profiles, and market signals, ensuring fraud detection systems achieve high precision without compromising account-level confidentiality.

Supply chain transparency

zk-SNARKs validate AI-driven supply chain optimization models trained on proprietary operational data, generating compliance proofs for trade regulations and sustainability standards without exposing competitive intelligence, cost structures, or strategic sourcing details.

Enterprises deploy zk-SNARKs to cryptographically verify the accuracy and regulatory adherence of AI models optimizing logistics, inventory forecasting, and supplier selection across global networks, ensuring end-to-end visibility without revealing sensitive commercial information.

Federated learning verification

zk-SNARKs cryptographically validate federated learning aggregations, confirming accurate model updates from distributed client devices across heterogeneous data sources, ensuring privacy-preserving global convergence without exposing individual contributions or enabling malicious interference.

zk-SNARKs provide zero-knowledge guarantees for federated learning rounds, where edge devices compute local updates on private data and servers aggregate them into global models, verifying correctness against protocol specifications without reconstructing participant inputs.

Construction and technical overview

Building zk-SNARKs involves translating computational statements into arithmetic circuits, representing mathematical operations as polynomials over finite fields. This conversion facilitates the creation of cryptographic proofs that the computation was carried out correctly.

Key components in zk-SNARK architectures include:

- **Setup phase**: Generates a proving key and a verification key. The setup must be trusted or downloadable, as a compromise can undermine security.
- **Prover algorithm**: Uses the proving key and the secret witness to generate a proof.
- **Verifier algorithm**: Uses the verification key and the proof to confirm correctness efficiently.

Recent cryptographic research has enhanced zk-SNARK efficiency with innovations such as pairing-based cryptography and polynomial commitment schemes. However, trusted setups remain a subject of scrutiny, inspiring alternative proof systems like zk-STARKs (scalable transparent arguments of knowledge), which omit the setup at the cost of larger proofs.

Integration with blockchain and decentralized AI networks

zk-SNARKs are frequently integrated into blockchain platforms that underpin many decentralized AI systems. Through smart contracts, verifiers on-chain can validate zk-SNARK proofs submitted by AI nodes, ensuring transparent and verifiable computations without direct data access. This integration fosters secure collaboration and auditability in multi-party AI networks where trust is decentralized and privacy is mandatory. zk-SNARK-enhanced AI platforms support confidential model sharing, verifiable machine learning, and decentralized privacy-preserving marketplaces.

Secure multi-party computation

Secure multi-party computation (**SMPC** or **MPC**) is a foundational cryptographic technique that enables multiple parties to jointly compute a function over their private inputs while keeping those inputs confidential from one another. This ability to collaboratively derive conclusions without exposing raw data makes SMPC a cornerstone technology for privacy-preserving AI in decentralized networks, where trust among participants cannot be assumed.

Core concepts and objectives

SMPC represents the gold standard for enabling collaborative AI in environments where no single party can be trusted with raw data. By mathematically guaranteeing that private inputs remain confidential throughout distributed computation, SMPC unlocks the potential for cross-organizational AI development while addressing fundamental trust barriers in decentralized networks.

The primary goal of SMPC is to enable a group of mutually distrusting parties to compute a shared output based on their individual inputs, such that:

- No party learns anything beyond what can be inferred from its own input and output.
- The computed result is correct and verifiable.
- The privacy of each party's input is preserved even if some participants behave maliciously.

Achieving these objectives demands carefully designed protocols with rigorous security proofs, ensuring confidentiality, correctness, and robustness even in adversarial settings.

Protocols and techniques

SMPC protocols rely on sophisticated cryptographic primitives that enable secure distributed computation while preserving input privacy. These foundational building blocks transform complex AI functions into privacy-preserving operations across multiple untrusted parties, forming the technical core of collaborative machine learning in decentralized environments.

SMPC protocols employ various cryptographic building blocks to secure computations, including secret sharing, oblivious transfer, and garbled circuits:

- **Secret sharing**: Each participant splits their private input into multiple shares distributed among other parties. No single share reveals information about the input, but when combined, they enable computation of the desired function. Shamir's secret sharing and additive secret sharing are popular schemes.
- **Garbled circuits**: A protocol where one party transforms a function into an encrypted Boolean circuit (garbled circuit) and another party evaluates it without learning the inputs. This technique is useful for secure two-party computations and has been extended to multi-party settings.
- **Oblivious transfer**: A method where a sender transmits information to a receiver but remains oblivious as to which piece of information was sent, supporting secure data exchanges in MPC protocols.

These techniques are often combined into hybrid protocols tailored for specific AI functions.

Application in decentralized AI

In decentralized AI, SMPC allows distributed model training and inference without exposing raw data. For example, multiple healthcare providers can collaboratively train a predictive model on private patient data without sharing sensitive health records. Similarly, SMPC enables privacy-preserving aggregation of model updates in federated learning.

SMPC protocols can compute a range of AI functions, including:

- **Linear algebra operations** (matrix multiplication, dot products) essential for neural network computations.
- **Non-linear functions** approximated securely with polynomial or piecewise-linear approximations.
- **Gradient calculations** for secure model optimization.

This makes SMPC highly adaptable to the requirements of various AI algorithms.

Security models and adversary assumptions

SMPC protocols must operate effectively across diverse threat landscapes, requiring explicit definitions of adversary capabilities and behaviors. Security models and adversary assumptions form the foundation for protocol design, ensuring appropriate protection levels based on real-world trust assumptions in decentralized AI networks.

SMPC protocols are designed against different adversary models, each defining the capabilities and intentions of malicious parties:

- **Semi-honest (honest-but-curious)**: Parties follow the protocol but try to learn additional information.
- **Malicious**: Parties may deviate arbitrarily from the protocol, attempting to subvert privacy or correctness.
- **Covert**: A middle ground where parties may cheat but aim to avoid detection.

Protocols ensuring security under malicious models are more complex and computationally expensive, but necessary for high-trust applications.

Performance and scalability challenges

SMPC implementations face fundamental performance hurdles that limit their adoption in large-scale, real-time AI applications. The inherent need for cryptographic coordination across multiple parties introduces substantial computational overhead, network latency, and resource demands that challenge practical deployment in production decentralized AI systems.

SMPC often involves significant communication overhead and computational cost due to repeated cryptographic operations and coordination among participants. Latency grows with the number of parties and the complexity of the computed function. Efficient implementations leverage:

- **Preprocessing**: Generating correlated randomness offline to accelerate online computations.
- **Batching**: Processing multiple computations simultaneously.
- **Hybrid techniques**: Combining SMPC with homomorphic encryption or trusted execution environments.

Despite these optimizations, tailoring SMPC to large-scale, real-time AI systems remains an active research area.

Real-world implementations and frameworks

SMPC has matured from theoretical cryptography to production-ready frameworks that enable practical privacy-preserving AI deployments across industries. These battle-tested libraries and platforms demonstrate how SMPC can scale from research prototypes to enterprise-grade solutions handling sensitive data processing in regulated environments.

Several software libraries provide platforms for building SMPC-enabled AI applications, including:

- **MP-SPDZ**: Supporting various MPC protocols with high flexibility.
- **Sharemind**: A commercial framework for privacy-preserving data analytics.
- **SEAL-embedded MPC**: Combining homomorphic encryption with MPC for hybrid solutions.

Real deployments demonstrate SMPC's potential in financial fraud detection, collaborative healthcare analytics, and cross-organizational AI initiatives where data privacy is paramount.

Differential privacy mechanisms

Differential privacy (DP) has emerged as a rigorous mathematical framework designed to provide strong privacy guarantees when analyzing and sharing data. Its central objective is to ensure that the output of a computation does not reveal sensitive information about any individual data record, thereby protecting privacy even in the presence of adversaries with extensive auxiliary information. This property makes differential privacy especially valuable in decentralized AI systems, where data is often drawn from diverse sources and involves personally identifiable information.

Fundamentals of differential privacy

Differential privacy defines privacy loss in terms of the indistinguishability of outputs when a single record in the dataset is modified or removed. Formally, a randomized algorithm A is said to provide ϵ-differential privacy if for all datasets D and D′ differing in one element, and for all outputs $S \subseteq \text{range}(A)$:

$$Pr[A(D) \in S] \leq \epsilon \times Pr[A(D') \in S]$$

Here, ϵ is the privacy loss parameter controlling the level of privacy; smaller values of ϵ indicate stronger privacy guarantees but typically at the cost of lower utility.

This definition ensures that the presence or absence of any individual data sample has a limited effect on the output distribution, making it difficult for adversaries to infer specific information about that individual.

Noise addition mechanisms

The key mechanism to enforce differential privacy is adding noise to the output of queries or computations to mask the contribution of individual records. The type and scale of noise depend on the **global sensitivity** Δf of the function, formally defined as $\Delta f = \max_{D\sim D'} \| f(D) - f(D') \|_1$, where the maximum is over neighboring datasets D,D' (differing by one record) and $\|\cdot\|_1$ is the ℓ_1 norm representing the maximum output change from altering a single record.

Two prevalent mechanisms are:

- **Laplace mechanism**: Draws noise from Laplace($\Delta f/\epsilon$) for ϵ-DP, ideal for scalar numeric queries like sums or means where exact privacy budgeting is required.
- **Gaussian mechanism**: Applies $\mathcal{N}(0,\sigma^2)$ noise with $\sigma = \Delta f\sqrt{2\ln(1.25/\delta)}/\epsilon$, supporting (ϵ,δ)-DP for high-dimensional outputs or when a small failure probability δ is acceptable.

In AI applications, these mechanisms calibrate noise to gradients, parameters, or query results during training/inference, obscuring individual contributions while preserving aggregate learning signals.

Application in AI training and inference

Differential privacy has evolved from theoretical privacy guarantees to practical integration within core machine learning pipelines, enabling organizations to train accurate models while providing mathematically provable protection against individual data leakage. This section explores how DP mechanisms are specifically adapted for AI workflows, balancing privacy preservation with model utility across training, inference, and distributed learning scenarios.

Differential privacy mechanisms are increasingly integrated into machine learning workflows to build models that respect individual privacy:

- **Differentially Private Stochastic Gradient Descent (DP-SGD)**: Trains neural networks by adding noise to gradient updates and clipping gradients to bound sensitivity. This procedure ensures that the resultant model retains privacy guarantees about its training data.
- **Privacy-preserving inference**: At inference time, noise can be added to model outputs, preventing reverse engineering of training data or extraction of sensitive attributes.
- **Aggregation in federated learning**: Differential privacy protects individual device contributions when aggregating model updates from multiple clients, thwarting adversarial reconstruction attacks.

Balancing privacy and utility

A principal trade-off in differential privacy pits stronger privacy guarantees (smaller ϵ) against data utility, as increased noise degrades model accuracy and analytical insights. Privacy budget allocation demands careful calibration against application sensitivity, regulatory mandates, and user expectations, leveraging **sequential composition** (where k ϵ-DP queries yield $k\epsilon$-DP) and **parallel composition** (where disjoint dataset queries on the same preserve ϵ-DP overall).

Advanced techniques like privacy amplification by subsampling (reducing effective through data sampling) and moment accountant tracking (tightly bounding cumulative Gaussian privacy loss), optimize multi-iteration budgets for practical DP-SGD in AI training, enabling thousands of epochs within feasible privacy constraints.

Differential privacy in decentralized AI

In decentralized AI systems, differential privacy addresses privacy at the algorithmic level, enabling nodes to share intermediate results or model updates with formal guarantees about individual data protection. The decentralized context poses additional challenges:

- **Heterogeneous data and trust levels**: Nodes may have varying data distributions and trust settings, requiring adaptive privacy mechanisms.
- **Communication constraints**: Noise addition must be efficient and minimal to prevent excessive degradation of communication efficiency.
- **Compliance with local policies**: Nodes may enforce distinct privacy regulations, necessitating flexible privacy budgets and accountability.

Practical frameworks implement differential privacy as part of privacy-by-design architectures, combining it with cryptographic tools to reinforce end-to-end privacy.

Trusted execution environments

Trusted execution environments (TEEs) are specialized, hardware-based secure areas within a processor that provide an isolated execution environment for sensitive computations. By guaranteeing both the confidentiality and integrity of code and data during execution, TEEs offer a robust security solution for privacy-preserving AI, especially in decentralized networks where nodes and infrastructures may not be fully trusted.

Architecture and core principles

At the heart of a TEE is a separate processor or a trusted area within a main processor that isolates code and data from the rest of the system, including the operating system and hypervisor. This isolation prevents unauthorized access or tampering by malicious software, privileged users, or physical attackers.

Key features of TEEs include:

- **Isolated execution**: Code running inside a TEE cannot be observed or interfered with by processes outside the enclave.
- **Secure storage**: Data inside a TEE is encrypted and protected even when stored in untrusted memory or persistent storage.
- **Remote attestation**: TEEs can produce cryptographic proofs of their integrity and trustworthiness to remote verifiers, enabling trustworthy computations in distributed environments.
- **Sealed storage**: Allows data to be encrypted and securely stored so that only the same TEE instance can decrypt it later.

These capabilities shift security trust explicitly from unverified software stacks to the hardware vendor and microcode/firmware implementing the TEE root of trust, establishing physical and architectural security foundations rather than software-alone assurances.

Popular TEE implementations

TEE has evolved into mature, industry-standard hardware security solutions with widespread adoption across cloud infrastructure, edge devices, and enterprise servers. This section examines the leading TEE implementations that power privacy-preserving AI deployments, comparing their architectural approaches, security features, and practical applicability for securing distributed AI workloads.

Several mainstream TEE technologies have been developed and widely adopted:

- **Intel Software Guard Extensions (SGX)**: SGX provides enclaves, protected areas in memory, with hardware-enforced isolation. It supports attestation protocols and is actively used for securing AI workloads.
- **ARM TrustZone**: TrustZone partitions the processor into secure and normal worlds, facilitating secure environment creation for embedded and mobile devices.
- **AMD Secure Encrypted Virtualization (SEV)**: Extends security to virtual machines by encrypting VM memory and isolating execution.

Each implementation varies in security guarantees, performance overhead, developer accessibility, and ecosystem support, influencing its suitability for specific AI applications.

Role in privacy-preserving AI

TEEs provide a compelling balance between efficiency and security in decentralized AI systems by enabling sensitive data and AI computations to reside securely even on potentially compromised infrastructure.

Privacy-preserving AI applications hosted inside TEEs benefit from:

- **Confidential model execution**: AI models and data inputs can be processed inside TEEs without exposure, protecting proprietary models as well as user privacy.
- **SMP collaboration**: Different stakeholders can contribute data or model components to TEEs, reassuring participants of confidentiality.
- **Trusted verification**: Remote attestation allows external parties to verify that computations were executed in a secure enclave without tampering.

These attributes reduce the reliance on heavyweight cryptographic techniques alone, enabling faster and more scalable privacy-preserving AI.

Challenges and limitations

Despite their powerful security guarantees, TEEs face practical deployment challenges that impact their effectiveness in diverse decentralized AI scenarios. Understanding these limitations is crucial for architects designing robust privacy-preserving systems that balance hardware security with real-world operational constraints.

While TEEs offer significant advantages, several challenges remain:

- **Side-channel attacks**: TEEs have been vulnerable to sophisticated attacks leveraging CPU side channels like cache timing or speculative execution (e.g., Specter and Meltdown), requiring continual mitigation.
- **Limited memory and computational power**: TEEs usually impose restrictions on memory size and processing capabilities, which can constrain large AI workloads.
- **Platform dependency**: TEEs depend on specific hardware architectures, making portability across diverse decentralized nodes challenging.
- **Complex development**: Writing secure applications for TEEs requires specialized programming models and careful handling of enclave transitions to minimize attack surfaces.

Emerging standards and tools aim to address these limitations by improving usability, standardizing APIs, and hardening against attacks.

Hybrid architectures combining TEEs and cryptography

TEEs provide performance advantages but face limitations in cryptographic strength and distribution capabilities, making hybrid architectures with advanced cryptographic protocols essential for comprehensive privacy-preserving AI. These combined approaches leverage hardware isolation for efficiency while cryptographic methods ensure end-to-end confidentiality across decentralized networks.

To leverage their complementary strengths, TEEs are increasingly combined with cryptographic methods such as homomorphic encryption and secure multi-party computation. Hybrid architectures can offload sensitive parts of computation to TEEs while encrypting data in transit or at rest, achieving strong privacy guarantees with improved performance and flexibility.

Privacy-preserving data sharing

Privacy-preserving data sharing is a critical enabler for decentralized AI systems, where multiple stakeholders, often with competing interests, need to collaboratively access and utilize data without compromising privacy. The objective is to design protocols and frameworks that allow controlled, secure, and privacy-respecting data exchange among distributed actors while preventing unauthorized information leakage.

Need for privacy-preserving data sharing

Data is the lifeblood of AI, but in many scenarios, especially those involving sensitive or regulated information such as healthcare, finance, or personal user data, direct sharing of raw data is either legally restricted or ethically unacceptable. Decentralized AI networks often span multiple organizations or users who wish to jointly benefit from their data without exposing it to others. Privacy-preserving data sharing mechanisms thus ensure collaborative AI model training and inference without sacrificing confidentiality, facilitating richer insights while upholding privacy rights.

Protocols and cryptographic frameworks

Privacy-preserving data sharing relies on sophisticated cryptographic protocols that enable secure information exchange across untrusted decentralized networks. These frameworks provide the technical foundation for controlled data collaboration, ensuring confidentiality while supporting AI model training and inference across organizational boundaries.

Various cryptographic and access control techniques and adversary models form the backbone of privacy-preserving data sharing:

- **Attribute-based encryption (ABE)**: Enables fine-grained access control where data is encrypted with policies tied to the attributes of users or systems. Only authorized recipients possessing matching attributes can decrypt the data, allowing secure selective sharing.

- **Secret sharing**: Distributes a secret (e.g., sensitive data) among multiple participants such that only authorized subsets can reconstruct it, enabling collaborative operations without revealing full data to any single party.

- **SMPC**: Allows joint computations on private data contributed by multiple parties without revealing their inputs, facilitating federated learning or collective data analysis.

- **DP**: Adds noise to shared data or aggregate statistics to prevent the identification of individual records, preserving privacy in shared datasets or model updates.
- **ZKPs**: Enable parties to prove compliance with access policies or data integrity conditions without revealing underlying data.

Privacy techniques adversary model comparison

ABE suits access control against outsiders, SMPC collaborative threats, DP statistical inference attacks, ZKP untrusted verification, select per workflow (e.g., DP+SMPC hybrids for federated AI). Refer to the following table:

Technique	Primary adversary model	Decentralized AI context	Key assumptions/limits
ABE	Unauthorized colluders lacking attributes; colluding attribute authorities[1].	Model/data sharing with role-based access	IND-CPA/CCA security; vulnerable to authority compromise
SMPC	Semi-honest/malicious participant subsets ($t < n/2$ or $t < n/3$)[2].	Federated learning aggregation	Honest majority; high comms overhead for malicious case
DP	Curious observers/analysts inferring individuals from aggregates.	Noisy model updates/queries	Bounded sensitivity; privacy-utility trade-off via ε,δ
ZKP	Malicious verifiers extracting info beyond proof validity[3].	Verifiable computation/model integrity	Computational soundness; prover/verifier separation

***Table 8.1**: Privacy techniques adversary model comparison*

Collectively, these frameworks ensure data confidentiality, integrity, and controlled access while enabling useful computations.

Data anonymization and sanitization

Data anonymization techniques serve as essential preprocessing steps that complement cryptographic protocols by fundamentally altering datasets to prevent re-identification while preserving analytical utility. These methods address privacy risks that persist even with encryption, providing defense-in-depth protection against linkage attacks and supporting regulatory compliance requirements for de-identified data sharing.

[1] //efaidnbmnnnibpcajpcglclefindmkaj/https://pdfs.semanticscholar.org/ef75/a3b0236ff1f1e19731f6fc2472020efe24bf.pdf
[2] https://www.emergentmind.com/topics/secure-multi-party-computation-smpc
[3] https://arxiv.org/html/2502.03773v1

Complementing cryptographic methods, data anonymization and sanitization techniques mask or remove personally identifiable information to reduce privacy risks during sharing. This includes:

- **K-anonymity**: Ensures that any individual's data is indistinguishable from at least k others in the dataset.
- **L-diversity and T-closeness**: Improve upon k-anonymity by ensuring diversity and distributional similarity in sensitive attributes.
- **Data perturbation**: Modifies data points to prevent exact re-identification while preserving utility.

Key limitations: These methods remain vulnerable to **linkage attacks** (cross-referencing with auxiliary data) and background knowledge inference; they prove particularly weak against high-dimensional data where uniqueness emerges via the curse of dimensionality, demanding hybrid approaches with DP or encryption.

Effective anonymization reduces the risk of de-anonymization attacks and inference risks while supporting legal compliance.

Decentralized data marketplaces and incentives

Decentralized data marketplaces represent the economic evolution of privacy-preserving data sharing, creating sustainable ecosystems where data owners can monetize valuable information while maintaining strict privacy controls. By integrating blockchain infrastructure with privacy-preserving protocols, these platforms enable novel business models for collaborative AI development across diverse stakeholders.

Privacy-preserving data sharing also underpins emerging decentralized data marketplaces where data owners can monetize their contributions without compromising privacy. Blockchain and smart contracts are frequently integrated to provide:

- **Immutable audit trails**: Ensuring transparency and accountability in data transactions.
- **Automated enforcement**: Enforcing access controls, payments, and policy compliance programmatically.
- **Incentive mechanisms**: Encouraging data owners to share valuable data securely through tokenization or revenue-sharing.

Such marketplaces enable new economic models for data-driven AI while prioritizing privacy, creating sustainable ecosystems where data providers receive fair compensation for privacy-preserving contributions to collective intelligence.

Challenges and practical considerations

Deploying privacy-preserving data sharing at scale requires overcoming significant technical, operational, and regulatory hurdles that span system architecture, performance optimization, and legal compliance. These challenges determine the feasibility of production-grade implementations across diverse decentralized AI ecosystems with varying stakeholder requirements and threat models.

Designing privacy-preserving data sharing solutions involves addressing several challenges:

- **Scalability**: Efficient protocols are required to handle large volumes and high-velocity data across multiple participants.
- **Interoperability**: Diverse systems and data formats necessitate standardized protocols and APIs.
- **Trust management**: Balancing cryptographic guarantees with practical trust relationships between participating entities.
- **Regulatory alignment**: Ensuring that data sharing practices comply with relevant privacy laws and consent requirements.

Addressing these factors requires multidisciplinary approaches involving cryptography, system design, and legal frameworks to create a robust, production-ready privacy-preserving data sharing infrastructure for decentralized AI applications.

Implementation examples

This section explores real-world applications and software toolkits that embody the principles of privacy-preserving AI techniques covered in this chapter. By examining practical implementations, both in academic research and industry, a clearer understanding emerges of how cryptographic and privacy frameworks can be effectively applied to decentralized AI systems, demonstrating their feasibility, challenges, and benefits.

The implementation landscape of privacy-preserving AI is rich and rapidly evolving, combining cryptographic libraries, hardware technologies, and software frameworks. These real-world examples demonstrate that while challenges in computation cost and complexity persist, practical deployment of secure, privacy-respecting AI in decentralized environments is becoming increasingly viable, opening new horizons for data collaboration and trustworthy AI services.

Homomorphic encryption in practice

Homomorphic encryption frameworks have reached production maturity, enabling encrypted AI inference and training across regulated industries where data cannot leave secure boundaries. These libraries transform theoretical FHE concepts into practical tools for privacy-preserving machine learning.

Microsoft **Simple Encrypted Arithmetic Library (SEAL)** delivers optimized **Brakerski-Fan-Vercauteren (BFV)** and CKKS implementations, powering secure medical image classification where patient scans remain fully encrypted during diagnostic AI analysis. IBM HELib supports fully homomorphic operations for financial risk modeling, processing sensitive transactional data without ever exposing plaintext values.

Key capabilities and challenges are as follows:

- **Advanced HE capabilities**: Both libraries implement critical optimizations, including ciphertext batching for parallel operations, relinearization to manage noise growth, and key switching for efficient homomorphic operations. These features enable the practical deployment of encrypted neural network inference and limited training scenarios.
- **Deployment realities**: Production implementations reveal HE's substantial computational overhead, often 100-1000x slower than plaintext processing, and high memory demands. Success requires algorithmic redesign, GPU acceleration, and hybrid architectures combining HE with TEEs to achieve viable performance for real-world privacy-preserving AI applications.

Zero-knowledge proof frameworks

Zero-knowledge proof libraries have matured into accessible frameworks that enable developers to integrate privacy-preserving verification into decentralized AI applications. Zokrates and libsnark provide comprehensive toolkits for constructing zk-SNARK circuits and generating proofs that validate AI computations while maintaining complete confidentiality over sensitive inputs and proprietary algorithms.

Key applications and deployments are as follows:

- **Privacy-preserving model auditing**: These frameworks power critical use cases such as secure model validation, where AI service providers generate succinct proofs demonstrating correct execution of training or inference pipelines. Clients verify model integrity on permissionless blockchains without accessing underlying intellectual property or training datasets, enabling trustless deployment of black-box AI services.
- **Machine learning (ML) marketplaces**: Production deployments include privacy-centric ML marketplaces where providers attest compliance with data governance policies through zero-knowledge proofs. This approach satisfies regulatory audits while protecting competitive advantages, with platforms leveraging standardized proof formats for seamless interoperability across decentralized AI ecosystems.
- **Deployment considerations**: While significantly more efficient than earlier ZKP schemes, zk-SNARKs require meticulous circuit design optimization and trusted setup ceremonies. These complexities demand specialized expertise, though ongoing tooling improvements and universal setup solutions continue to lower barriers to practical adoption in enterprise-grade privacy-preserving AI systems.

Secure multi-party computation platforms

SMPC frameworks have evolved into robust platforms that bridge theoretical cryptography with practical AI deployments, enabling secure collaborative computation across untrusted participants in decentralized environments. MP-SPDZ and Sharemind provide comprehensive toolkits supporting diverse cryptographic protocols with configurable security models, facilitating joint model training, inference, and analytics without exposing raw sensitive data.

Key applications and deployments are as follows:

- **Federated learning integration**: These platforms power real-world federated learning implementations where mobile devices securely aggregate model updates through MPC protocols, ensuring individual contributions remain confidential while improving global model performance.
- **Healthcare and enterprise deployments**: In healthcare consortia, SMPC enables multi-institutional research through encrypted statistical analysis and distributed machine learning over siloed patient datasets, satisfying stringent regulatory requirements while accelerating medical AI innovation.
- **Performance optimization advances**: Although SMPC introduces communication and computational overheads, continuous improvements in preprocessing techniques, communication-efficient protocols, and hybrid cryptographic approaches are making these solutions viable for production-scale privacy-preserving AI applications.

Differential privacy libraries and applications

Differential privacy has transitioned from a theoretical construct to an operational cornerstone in modern AI systems, particularly where user-level data protection and regulatory compliance are non-negotiable. This section highlights mature software frameworks and concrete deployments that demonstrate how DP can be embedded into end-to-end machine learning pipelines without entirely sacrificing model utility.

The following key areas capture how differential privacy is operationalized in practice:

- **Production DP frameworks**: Google's Differential Privacy Library and TensorFlow Privacy provide battle-tested implementations that seamlessly integrate differential privacy into production AI pipelines, enabling organizations to train models with mathematically provable privacy guarantees against individual data reconstruction.
- **DP-SGD and privacy-preserving ML**: These frameworks power **Differentially Private Stochastic Gradient Descent (DP-SGD)** implementations that clip gradients and inject calibrated noise during training, ensuring released models cannot leak training data even under sophisticated membership inference attacks. DP-SGD powers Differentially Private Stochastic Gradient Descent by applying per-sample gradient clipping, specifically, L2 norm clipping, where each individual sample's gradient vector g_i is scaled if $\| g_i \|_2 > C$:

$$\mathbf{g}_i' = \mathbf{g}_i \cdot \min\left(1, \frac{C}{\| \mathbf{g}_i \|_2}\right)$$

It is followed by averaging clipped gradients across the batch and adding calibrated Gaussian noise $\mathcal{N}(0, \sigma^2 C^2 \mathbf{I})$. This bounds the per-sample influence on sensitivity C, ensuring released models resist membership inference attacks even from sophisticated adversaries.

- **Real-world deployments**: Applications span personalized recommendation engines protecting user behavior profiles, smart device telemetry safeguarding IoT sensor data, and natural language models preventing sensitive query reconstruction. Service providers like search engines and mobile platforms use DP to comply with privacy regulations while maintaining recommendation quality.
- **Privacy-utility optimization**: Production deployments continuously advance privacy budget accounting, noise scale calibration, and utility-preserving mechanisms. Balancing epsilon privacy loss with model accuracy remains an active research frontier, driving innovations in adaptive DP algorithms and composition theorems for complex multi-stage AI workflows.

Trusted execution environment integrations

TEEs have become a practical backbone for securing sensitive AI workloads where both data and model confidentiality are critical. TEEs such as Intel SGX are used to run AI training and inference inside isolated enclaves, with systems like VC3 combining hardware-backed isolation and remote attestation to provide verifiable guarantees about code integrity and data protection.

Decentralized marketplaces and collaborative learning platforms increasingly embed TEEs into their architectures to establish trust among mutually untrusted parties without exposing raw inputs or proprietary models. By executing privacy-critical logic inside enclaves, TEEs significantly reduce the performance overhead associated with purely cryptographic approaches, enabling faster private computation while maintaining strong confidentiality assurances.

However, real-world use also exposes limitations, including constrained enclave memory, ecosystem-specific dependencies, and exposure to advanced side-channel attacks. Ongoing hardware revisions, improved SDKs, and hardened runtimes are steadily enhancing TEE robustness, making them more suitable as a key component in scalable privacy-preserving AI deployments.

Cross-technology hybrid implementations

Emerging solutions often combine multiple privacy-preserving techniques to leverage their respective strengths. For example, a system might employ homomorphic encryption for secure data preprocessing, followed by SMPC for joint training and TEEs for secure final model evaluation. Similarly, differential privacy can be integrated with cryptographic protocols to augment data privacy beyond basic encryption. These hybrid architectures aim to balance computational efficiency, scalability, and privacy guarantees, providing tailor-made solutions according to application demands and threat models.

Performance trade-offs

Privacy-preserving AI techniques in decentralized systems entail vital trade-offs between privacy guarantees and performance metrics such as computational cost, latency, scalability, and accuracy. Understanding these trade-offs is critical for practitioners and researchers to effectively design systems that balance security with practical usability and efficiency.

Computational and communication overhead

Privacy-preserving AI techniques, especially cryptographic approaches such as HE, ZKPs, and SMPC, inherently introduce substantial performance costs at both the compute and network layers. These methods trade raw efficiency for strong security and privacy guarantees, which directly impacts their suitability for latency-sensitive or large-scale deployments.

Fully homomorphic encryption allows arbitrary operations on encrypted data, but each ciphertext operation is far more expensive than its plaintext counterpart, and additional work is required to control noise growth within ciphertexts. As a result, end-to-end execution times can be several orders of magnitude slower than conventional computation, and memory consumption is significantly higher. Likewise, zk-SNARK generation and verification, although succinct on-chain, rely on heavy arithmetic over elliptic curves and often require trusted setup procedures, adding complexity and computational overhead.

SMPC-based protocols amplify these costs on the communication side. Parties must repeatedly exchange encrypted shares, masks, or garbled circuit components, and this interaction grows with both the number of participants and the complexity of the target function. The resulting communication complexity can create severe latency bottlenecks and increased bandwidth usage, which is particularly problematic for real-time or near-real-time AI workloads that require rapid inference or frequent model updates.

Latency and throughput considerations

In privacy-preserving AI systems, end-to-end latency is shaped by a combination of heavy cryptographic computation, additional communication steps, and underlying hardware constraints. Hardware-based approaches, such as TEEs, can offer relatively low-latency secure computation, but they are limited by enclave memory size, context-switching overhead, and available processing power. By contrast, cryptographic techniques like homomorphic encryption and secure multi-party computation generally introduce much higher latency, yet they deliver stronger, more formal privacy guarantees that may be essential in high-risk or highly regulated scenarios.

The throughput, i.e., the volume of queries, inferences, or training batches that can be processed per unit time, also tends to degrade when strong privacy protections are applied. DP can require repeated training runs or additional secure aggregation steps to maintain acceptable accuracy, significantly increasing total compute effort. Homomorphic encryption may use batching and ciphertext packing to improve throughput, but these optimizations add complexity to system design and require careful management of encrypted data layouts to avoid new performance bottlenecks.

Accuracy and utility trade-offs

Privacy-preserving techniques do not come for free: they often reduce the predictive power or analytical usefulness of AI models. DP, for example, protects individuals by injecting carefully calibrated noise into training or outputs, but if the privacy budget (often expressed through the parameter ϵ) is set too conservatively, the resulting model can suffer noticeable drops in accuracy. Finding an acceptable compromise between strong privacy guarantees and usable model performance requires careful tuning of privacy budgets and sensitivity analyses tailored to each application.

Similar trade-offs arise with cryptographic methods. HE schemes, particularly approximate schemes such as CKKS, represent real-valued computations with fixed-point encodings, which naturally introduce rounding and approximation errors. Models and training procedures must be redesigned to remain robust under this numerical noise. In secure multi-party computation, operations are frequently quantized or approximated to reduce cost, and complex non-linear functions are replaced with simpler polynomial or piecewise-linear surrogates, which can subtly distort model behavior and reduce fidelity if not engineered with care.

Scalability challenges

Scalability is a central constraint for privacy-preserving, decentralized AI, where systems must cope with many participants, large models, and constantly changing network conditions. As deployments move from laboratory prototypes to real-world settings, the overheads introduced by cryptography, coordination, and communication become increasingly difficult to manage.

Privacy-preserving protocols must be capable of supporting large-scale collaborations, sustaining hundreds or even thousands of participants without collapsing under excessive message exchange, synchronization delays, or coordination complexity. They must also handle high-dimensional data and complex models, such as deep neural networks with millions of parameters, in a way that keeps computation and memory usage within practical limits. In addition, decentralized environments impose dynamic network conditions, requiring protocols to remain robust when nodes join or leave, behave adversarially, or experience fluctuating latency and bandwidth.

To address these pressures, researchers and practitioners explore techniques such as hierarchical or layered SMPC architectures, federated learning augmented with differential privacy, and hybrid designs that combine TEEs with cryptographic protections. While these approaches can significantly improve scalability, they also demand sophisticated orchestration, careful resource allocation, and thoughtful protocol engineering to achieve reliable, efficient operation at scale.

Cost-benefit and technology selection

Choosing the right privacy-preserving technique is fundamentally a risk-reward and resource-capability decision, and must be aligned with application goals, latency constraints, and regulatory pressure rather than driven by technology novelty alone. Each approach offers a different balance between protection strength, implementation complexity, and operational cost, so architects should map techniques explicitly to their threat models and performance budgets.

For latency-sensitive systems (such as real-time inference services), TEEs paired with relatively lightweight encryption can often deliver an effective compromise, providing strong isolation with modest overhead. In highly regulated or high-risk environments that demand maximum confidentiality, such as healthcare, finance, or critical infrastructure, HE and ZKP offer stronger formal guarantees, albeit at significantly higher computational cost. When many organizations or devices with varying trust levels must collaborate, secure multi-party computation with rigorous adversary models is typically preferred, even though it increases communication and protocol complexity.

Differential privacy is particularly suitable for large-scale analytics and model training over aggregated data, where moderate accuracy loss is acceptable in exchange for rigorous individual-level protection. In practice, hybrid architectures that combine several of these techniques are often the most effective, allowing engineers to fine-tune trade-offs and apply the strongest (and most expensive) methods only where they are strictly necessary.

Compliance and regulations

Privacy-preserving AI techniques must be developed and deployed within the framework of existing and emerging legal and regulatory requirements that govern data protection and ethical AI practices. Compliance not only ensures adherence to laws but also builds trust among users and stakeholders, particularly in decentralized AI environments where data ownership and control are distributed.

Key regulatory frameworks

Global privacy regulations create a complex compliance landscape that fundamentally shapes the design, deployment, and operation of AI systems. These laws establish mandatory requirements for data handling, user rights, and organizational accountability that privacy-preserving techniques must explicitly satisfy.

Several influential data privacy laws shape the compliance landscape for AI systems:

- **General Data Protection Regulation** (**GDPR**), the EU's landmark legislation, imposes stringent requirements on personal data processing, including explicit consent, data minimization, purpose limitation, and individual rights to access, rectification, and erasure. AI developers must ensure full transparency in data usage, implement robust security measures, and enable user control over automated decision-making systems.

- **California Consumer Privacy Act** (**CCPA**) grants California residents unprecedented control over their personal information, including rights to disclosure, deletion, and opting out of data sales. This legislation drives privacy-by-design principles into AI architectures, requiring accessible mechanisms for data subject requests and clear data provenance tracking.

- **Health Insurance Portability and Accountability Act** (**HIPAA**) governs **protected health information** (**PHI**) in healthcare AI applications, mandating administrative, physical, and technical safeguards alongside strict breach notification protocols. Medical AI systems processing patient data must integrate HIPAA-compliant encryption, access controls, and audit trails.

- **Emerging AI governance frameworks** from international standards bodies and national regulators increasingly emphasize ethical AI principles like fairness, explainability, and accountability, which complement traditional privacy laws, requiring privacy-preserving AI to demonstrate both technical robustness and societal responsibility.

Privacy compliance in decentralized AI

Decentralized AI architectures introduce novel compliance complexities that centralized systems rarely face. Without single points of control or authority, ensuring regulatory adherence across distributed data flows, diverse jurisdictions, and multiple organizational boundaries demands entirely new approaches to governance and accountability.

Decentralized AI systems face unique compliance challenges due to their distributed nature:

- **Data sovereignty challenges**: Distributed datasets often span multiple legal jurisdictions with conflicting privacy obligations. Compliance requires sophisticated data flow mapping, automated geofencing controls, and dynamic policy enforcement that adapts to data location and cross-border movement.

- **Decentralized consent management**: Traditional consent mechanisms fail in peer-to-peer environments. Systems must implement interoperable, node-agnostic consent protocols with granular revocation capabilities, transparent policy propagation, and verifiable proof of user control across the entire network.

- **Distributed auditability requirements**: Regulatory compliance demands complete visibility into data processing activities. Decentralized systems achieve this through immutable audit trails, cryptographic provenance tracking, and blockchain-based logging that maintain tamper-proof records across all participating nodes.

- **Multi-party governance frameworks**: Cross-organizational collaborations require standardized legal agreements specifying data usage boundaries, liability allocation, breach response protocols, and privacy obligation sharing. Smart contracts increasingly automate these complex multi-stakeholder arrangements while maintaining regulatory transparency.

Technical measures supporting compliance

Privacy-preserving AI techniques directly address regulatory requirements by embedding compliance-enabling capabilities into their core architectures. These technologies transform legal obligations into verifiable technical properties, providing auditors and regulators with concrete evidence of adherence.

Privacy-preserving AI technologies inherently support compliance:

- **Data minimization through encrypted processing**: HE and SMPC enable powerful analytics on encrypted data, satisfying data minimization principles by eliminating the need to expose raw datasets during processing and dramatically reducing unauthorized disclosure risks.
- **Re-identification protection**: DP and advanced anonymization techniques meet legal definitions of de-identified data by providing mathematical guarantees against individual re-identification, even when adversaries possess extensive auxiliary information or correlation attacks.
- **Verifiable policy compliance**: ZKPs generate succinct, publicly verifiable attestations of regulatory compliance, demonstrating that AI models were trained on compliant datasets, respect access policies, or satisfy fairness constraints, without revealing proprietary algorithms or sensitive training data.
- **Hardware-rooted security controls**: TEEs provide tamper-proof execution environments with remote attestation capabilities, offering regulators hardware-authenticated proof of security controls, encryption usage, and data protection measures.

When integrated throughout the AI lifecycle, data ingestion through model deployment and monitoring these measures creates auditable systems that can automatically generate compliance evidence, streamlining regulatory reviews while maintaining operational confidentiality and competitive advantage.

Challenges and future directions

Even as privacy-preserving AI technologies mature, significant hurdles remain in achieving seamless regulatory alignment across diverse global jurisdictions and rapidly evolving legal landscapes.

Despite technological advances, challenges persist in aligning privacy-preserving AI with compliance demands:

- **Legal and technical misalignments**: Ambiguous regulatory definitions, such as what constitutes anonymized data, pseudonymization, or data controller responsibilities, create implementation uncertainty, forcing organizations to navigate conservative interpretations that sacrifice technical optimality.
- **Regulatory velocity outpacing technology**: The accelerating pace of privacy legislation and AI governance frameworks demands privacy architectures with modular, upgradable components that can adapt to new mandates without requiring complete system redesigns.
- **Missing standardization ecosystem**: Without universally accepted evaluation metrics, certification schemes, and interoperability standards for privacy-preserving AI, organizations struggle to demonstrate compliance to regulators and build market trust through independent validation.
- **Ethics beyond mere compliance**: Legal adherence alone cannot guarantee responsible AI deployment. Technical privacy solutions must integrate with fairness, bias mitigation, and societal impact assessments to address the broader ethical dimensions that regulations increasingly emphasize.

Future progress requires international standards bodies to establish unified evaluation frameworks, governments to create regulatory sandboxes for privacy-preserving AI innovation, and cross-disciplinary collaboration between cryptographers, legal experts, and ethicists to bridge the widening gap between technological capability and governance requirements.

Conclusion

This chapter showed how decentralized AI can remain powerful while rigorously protecting sensitive data. It outlined how homomorphic encryption, zero-knowledge proofs, secure multi-party computation, differential privacy, and TEEs together provide a toolbox for confidential computation, verifiable processing, and controlled data sharing in untrusted, distributed settings. It also highlighted the practical realities of performance overheads, accuracy impacts, and the need to align with evolving regulatory frameworks.

Readers should now be able to choose and combine appropriate privacy techniques based on threat models, application requirements, and compliance needs, designing systems where privacy is built in rather than added later.

Chapter 9, Security and Threat Detection, shifts focus from protecting data privacy to safeguarding system security. It will cover adversarial threats to decentralized AI, intrusion and anomaly detection, model and data poisoning attacks, consensus and network-layer threats, and real-time monitoring and response mechanisms.

CHAPTER 9
Security and Threat Detection

Introduction

Security in decentralized AI and blockchain systems cannot be retrofitted. It must be architected into every layer, from cryptographic primitives securing transactions to governance mechanisms authorizing protocol changes. Unlike centralized architectures with clear perimeters protecting concentrated assets, decentralized networks lack boundaries: participants join dynamically, code executes autonomously on public infrastructure, smart contracts expose logic to all attackers, and AI models train on untrusted data contributions.

The attack surface becomes a distributed, adversarial environment requiring navigation rather than defense. Consider *Beanstalk Farms* (2022), where a flash loan attacker temporarily acquired 2/3 governance power via manipulated voting, passing a proposal that drained $182M from the protocol in seconds, exposing how economic incentives and visible code amplify risks absent perimeter controls. This chapter examines the threat landscape, attack vectors, layered defenses, monitoring, incident response, and governance/compliance practices essential for resilient systems. Technical safeguards alone prove insufficient without encoded responsibility and evolution mechanisms that adapt to emerging threats. Key differences from centralized security include the absence of a single perimeter to defend, with assets distributed across autonomous smart contracts, dynamic participants contributing models and data at varying trust levels, visible source code enabling sophisticated attackers to study and exploit logic flaws, and economic incentives that can turn insiders like validators and stakers into rational adversaries.

Structure

The chapter covers the following topics:

- Security threat landscape
- Attack vectors and vulnerabilities
- Defense mechanisms and countermeasures

- Anomaly detection systems
- Incident response procedures
- Smart contract security auditing
- Network security monitoring
- Cryptographic security practices
- Compliance and risk management
- Security principles for DAI and blockchain systems

Objectives

Security in decentralized AI and blockchain systems demands technical precision and strategic foresight, positioning this chapter as both a tactical reference and strategic guide for practitioners building resilient infrastructure. Readers will master the unique threat landscape defined by protocol openness, autonomous execution, and value concentration, gaining systematic frameworks to analyze attack vectors from smart contract exploits and model poisoning to network-level disruptions and human factors. The chapter equips teams to design layered defenses spanning formal verification, Byzantine-resilient federated learning, multi-signature governance, differential privacy, and continuous monitoring systems that leverage blockchain transparency for superior behavioral anomaly detection compared to centralized architectures.

Practical skills include implementing structured incident response protocols optimized for blockchain's irreversibility, conducting comprehensive smart contract audits combining manual expertise with formal methods, and deploying network security monitoring across mempools, cross-chain correlations, and validator health metrics. Cryptographic foundations receive rigorous treatment, covering zero-knowledge proofs, threshold schemes, and post-quantum readiness as prerequisites for higher-level controls. Compliance integration transforms regulatory requirements into structural allies, demonstrating how GDPR, financial services standards, and AI governance reinforce technical safeguards when architected with intent rather than resentment.

Ultimately, this chapter cultivates a security-first culture recognizing that resilient decentralized AI emerges from continuous, community-driven responsibility rather than one-time technical fixes. Readers emerge equipped not merely to implement security controls, but to lead organizations that treat security as the prerequisite for sustainable protocol innovation across the full lifecycle of decentralized AI systems.

Security threat landscape

The threat landscape for decentralized AI and blockchain systems is best understood not as a list of attack types but as a topology, a map of the structural vulnerabilities that arise from the specific properties of these systems. Three properties define this topology more than any others: openness, autonomy, and value concentration.

Openness means that blockchain networks are public by design. Their transaction histories, smart contract code, and node communication patterns are visible to anyone. This transparency is a security asset; it enables public auditability and community-based vulnerability detection, but it is simultaneously a security liability because attackers have the same visibility as defenders. A vulnerability in a smart contract that manages hundreds of millions of dollars in assets is visible to every security researcher and every malicious actor simultaneously.

Autonomy means that smart contracts and AI agents execute code without human review of individual operations. When a smart contract contains a vulnerability or an AI model is manipulated, the harm can propagate instantly and at scale before any human can intervene. The irreversibility of blockchain transactions amplifies this: unlike a database where a compromised operation can sometimes be rolled back, a blockchain transaction that drains a smart contract treasury is permanent unless the network reaches social consensus to reverse it, a process that is itself politically contentious and technically complex, as the 2016 Ethereum DAO fork demonstrated.

Value concentration means that successful decentralized systems aggregate significant economic value in smart contracts and protocol treasuries. The Ethereum DeFi ecosystem alone has managed over $100 billion in **total value locked** (**TVL**) at peak periods, such as March 2026, when it crossed this threshold amid market recovery. This concentration creates attack incentives that dwarf those facing most conventional software systems. A sophisticated attacker investing months of effort and millions of dollars in an attack is economically rational when the target holds hundreds of millions in assets.

Figure 9.1 explores how modern digital systems intertwine artificial intelligence, blockchain, and network infrastructures, revealing the hidden vulnerabilities that emerge when these layers converge. It offers a unified framework for understanding cross-layer threat propagation, adversarial manipulation, and systemic risk.

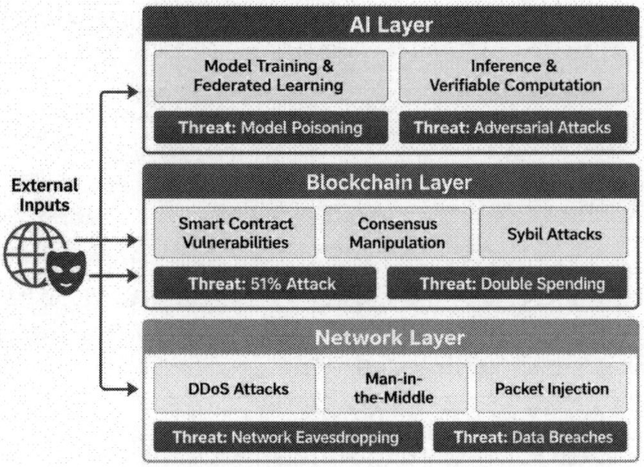

***Figure 9.1**: Integrated threat landscape across AI, blockchain, and network layers*

Human element

Technical threat analysis often underweights the human element, and decentralized AI and blockchain systems are no exception. Using the **Spoofing, Tampering, Repudiation, Information Disclosure, Denial of Service, Elevation of Privilege** (**STRIDE**) threat modeling framework: human layer threats primarily manifest as Spoofing (identity impersonation) and Elevation of Privilege (abusing trusted access).

Social engineering attacks, phishing campaigns targeting developers with protocol admin keys, impersonation on governance forums, and insider threats from privileged team members have caused massive losses. The *Ronin bridge hack* (March 2022) stole $625 million via spear phishing that compromised validator keys (Spoofing). BadgerDAO (December 2021) lost $120 million when a compromised Cloudflare API key enabled frontend manipulation (Elevation of Privilege). In both cases, blockchain infrastructure performed correctly. Failures stemmed from human and operational security gaps.

For AI systems, human risks extend to the model pipeline. Developers become targets for supply chain attacks, substituting malicious weights, tampering with training data, or corrupting updates (Tampering). These threats, increasingly documented in security literature, grow acute as deployed AI models hold escalating economic value.

Threat actor taxonomy

Understanding who attacks decentralized AI and blockchain systems and why is essential context for designing effective defenses. The threat actor landscape is more diverse than conventional cybersecurity frameworks acknowledge.

Nation-state actors have become significant participants in blockchain theft. The *Lazarus Group*, associated with North Korea's intelligence services, is believed to be responsible for over $3 billion in cryptocurrency theft across multiple years, using the proceeds to fund the country's weapons programs. Nation-state actors bring resources, patience, and technical sophistication that exceed those of most private criminal organizations.

Financially motivated criminal organizations pursue opportunistic and targeted attacks against protocols with significant value locked. These range from sophisticated teams that invest in deep protocol analysis to identify novel vulnerabilities to less sophisticated actors who replicate published exploits against protocols that have not applied available patches.

Competitive actors, including rival protocols and their supporters, have been implicated in governance attacks, where large token acquisitions are used to push through governance proposals that benefit the attacker at other participants' expense. The line between aggressive competition and malicious attack is contested in decentralized governance contexts, but the economic harm to affected participants is real regardless of categorization.

Researchers and white-hat hackers represent a threat actor category with ambiguous intent. Responsible disclosure of vulnerabilities by security researchers has prevented numerous significant exploits; less responsible handling of discovered vulnerabilities has preceded others. Bug bounty programs and responsible disclosure frameworks, discussed in the defense mechanisms section, are the primary mechanisms for channeling this community's capabilities toward protective rather than harmful ends.

Malicious insiders, developers, validators, and administrators with privileged access represent a threat that is structurally different in decentralized systems than in conventional organizations. When a decentralized protocol's governance is managed by a small founding team that controls privileged keys, the insider threat surface is concentrated and consequential. As protocols mature and governance is genuinely decentralized, the insider threat surface is reduced, reducing the impact of any single insider compromise but complicating the detection of coordinated insider activity.

Table 9.1 is an overview of understanding who attacks decentralized AI and blockchain systems and why it is essential context for designing effective defenses. The threat actor landscape is more diverse than conventional cybersecurity frameworks acknowledge.

Threat actor	Capability	Motivation	Typical attack vectors
Nation-state (e.g., Lazarus Group)	High (sophisticated tooling, persistence)	State funding (e.g., $3B+ stolen since 2017 for DPRK weapons) thehackernews+1.	Supply chain compromises, validator key theft, and DeFi exploits.
Financial criminals	Medium to high	Direct profit	Flash loan attacks, contract exploits, and unpatched vulnerability replication.
Competitive rivals	Medium	Market share / governance control	Token accumulation for malicious proposals, DDoS on competitors.
Researchers / White-Hats	Variable	Reputation / bounty rewards	Vulnerability disclosure (protective or harmful if mishandled).
Malicious insiders	High (privileged access)	Personal gain, coercion	Key abuse, model tampering, and governance collusion.

Table 9.1: *Threat actor taxonomy*

Technical classification of threats

A rigorous understanding of security threats in decentralized AI requires a structured framework capable of capturing the full range of adversarial behaviors across distributed systems. One of the most widely accepted models for threat classification is STRIDE, which categorizes adversarial actions into six core dimensions: Spoofing, Tampering, Repudiation, Information Disclosure, Denial of Service, and Elevation of Privilege. Applying STRIDE to decentralized AI provides a systematic method for mapping threats to specific failure modes, enabling practitioners to analyze risks consistently across models, smart contracts, consensus mechanisms, and data pipelines. *Table 9.2* maps each STRIDE category to representative decentralized AI threats and impacted layers:

STRIDE category	Decentralized AI threat examples	Layer impacted
Spoofing	Validator key phishing (*Ronin*, 2022); fake model provenance claims.	Network, AI model
Tampering	Model poisoning in federated learning; smart contract bytecode swaps.	AI model, Blockchain
Repudiation	Unsigned model updates; anonymous malicious governance proposals.	Blockchain governance
Information Disclosure	Private training data leakage via side channels; oracle input exposure.	AI model, Network
Denial of Service	Mempool flooding; resource exhaustion in inference nodes.	Network, AI i nference
Elevation of Privilege	Flash loan governance takeover (Beanstalk); admin key abuse.	Blockchain, Governance

***Table 9.2**: STRIDE threat model mapping*

In decentralized AI systems, threats rarely occur in isolation. They emerge across interacting layers of infrastructure, each introducing its own attack surface. These layers include the AI model layer (training, inference, and model governance), the blockchain execution layer (smart contracts, consensus, and state transition logic), and the networking layer (peer-to-peer communication, validators, and data propagation). When these layers combine, they form a complex, interdependent system in which weaknesses at one level can cascade into broader systemic failures. Understanding threats through a structured lens is therefore essential for designing resilient architectures.

Threats in decentralized AI fall into the following major categories:

- **External attacks**: External adversaries target weaknesses in publicly exposed components of the system. In decentralized AI, these attacks exploit the network's openness, the transparency of smart contract logic, and the accessibility of API endpoints.

  The network-level exploits attackers often begin at the networking layer, exploiting exposed RPC endpoints, unprotected API gateways, or misconfigured validator interfaces. Common threats include:

  - **Exploited RPC endpoints**: Attackers inject malicious requests to manipulate node behavior, drain funds through replay attacks, or trigger logic faults in inference nodes.
  - **DoS and DDoS attacks**: Validator networks face sustained traffic floods that exceed 100 Gbps, overwhelming bandwidth and CPU resources and causing honest nodes to fall out of sync.
  - **Eclipse attacks**: By isolating an honest node's view of the network, an attacker can feed it manipulated state data, delay its messages, or force it into accepting a fork under adversarial control. For decentralized AI, this can corrupt model updates, distort oracle inputs, or trigger false governance decisions.
- **Protocol-level attacks**: Attackers exploit the permissionless nature of decentralized networks to inject malicious transaction payloads that target AI-integrated smart contracts processing model outputs, inference requests, or reward distributions, often using flash loans to trigger reentrancy or logic flaws in real-time. Oracle manipulation compounds these threats by corrupting external data feeds that power on-chain AI systems, enabling attackers to deliver falsified price signals or market data that produce incorrect model inferences, mispriced incentives, or cascading liquidations. These protocol exploits thrive precisely because any node can broadcast disruptive payloads, weaponizing open access to poison data flows, manipulate economic engines, and drain liquidity before defenses react.
- **Insider threats**: Decentralized AI networks assume honest behavior from validators, stakers, and governance participants, yet insiders with privileged access pose acute risks through economic incentives to subvert protocol rules. Malicious validators can double-sign blocks to create conflicting histories, collude to manipulate governance votes favoring their interests, or inject poisoned model updates that corrupt federated learning convergence. Oracle operators and key holders exacerbate threats by feeding biased price data that misleads AI risk engines or by abusing admin privileges to alter model weights and inference parameters for private gain. These insider attacks prove especially devastating because perpetrators already possess established legitimacy, token stakes, and protocol-level access, making detection and prevention far harder than for external threats.
- **Systemic risks**: Systemic threats in decentralized AI networks emerge from inherent protocol design flaws, consensus mechanism limitations, and misaligned incentives rather than isolated exploits, potentially cascading failures across interconnected layers. Consensus-level vulnerabilities include costly 51% attacks on PoW chains that reorganize history to rewrite model lineages or censor federated learning updates, long-range attacks on PoS systems exploiting stale private keys to invalidate historical AI provenance, and nothing-at-stake problems where validators cheaply vote on multiple forks to destabilize consensus and disrupt inference attestation. Cross-layer cascades amplify damage; a consensus fork corrupts global model aggregates;

compromised oracles poison AI risk models, triggering economic meltdowns; and validator cartels reorder requests to bias decentralized outcomes. Economic attacks further exploit reward structures for model sabotage, governance capture, or arbitrage, while misaligned incentives among model providers, compute operators, data owners, and token holders create fragile market dynamics that undermine overall protocol resilience.

Attack vectors and vulnerabilities

Smart contracts are programs that execute autonomously on blockchain networks, managing assets and enforcing rules without human oversight of individual operations. Their security properties are therefore exceptional in their consequence: a vulnerability in a smart contract managing significant value can be exploited instantly, completely, and irreversibly. The history of smart contract exploits is a rich source of lessons about the specific vulnerability classes that practitioners must understand and defend against.

Reentrancy attacks

These attacks represent the vulnerability class most famously exploited in the 2016 DAO hack, which resulted in the theft of 3.6 million ETH (approximately $60 million at the time) and triggered the Ethereum hard fork that created Ethereum Classic. A reentrancy vulnerability occurs when a smart contract calls an external contract before updating its internal state, allowing the external contract to call back into the original contract before the state update is complete. The attacker can repeatedly withdraw funds before the contract's balance is decremented, draining the treasury in a recursive loop.

The following example illustrates a classic reentrancy vulnerability in a simple bank contract, where an external call is made before the contract updates its internal balance, allowing an attacker to repeatedly withdraw funds by re-entering the function during execution:

```
// Simplified DAO-style reentrancy vulnerability
contract VulnerableBank {
    mapping(address => uint256) public balances;
    function deposit() public payable {
        balances[msg.sender] += msg.value;
    }
    function withdraw(uint256 amount) public {
        require(balances[msg.sender] >= amount, "Insufficient balance");

        // Vulnerable: External call BEFORE state update
        (bool success, ) = msg.sender.call{value: amount}("");
        require(success, "Transfer failed");
        // State updated AFTER call - attacker can reenter
```

```
        balances[msg.sender] -= amount;
    } }
```

The reentrancy vulnerability is well understood and has clear remediation patterns: updating state before making external calls, using reentrancy guard modifiers, and following the checks-effects-interactions pattern. Yet reentrancy variants continue to appear in production contracts, sometimes in subtle forms that pass automated auditing tools. The persistence of known vulnerability classes in deployed code reflects a recurring pattern in smart contract security: the gap between theoretical understanding of a vulnerability and consistent practical application of its remediation.

Integer overflow and underflow

Integer overflow and underflow vulnerabilities arise when arithmetic operations produce results that exceed the storage capacity of their data type, wrapping around to unexpected values. In early Solidity versions (before 0.8.0), arithmetic operations did not include overflow protection by default. The **BeautyChain** (**BEC**) token attack of 2018, in which an integer overflow allowed an attacker to generate an arbitrarily large token balance from nothing, illustrates the consequences. Solidity ≥0.8.0 explicitly enforces safe arithmetic by default through built-in overflow checks that revert transactions on underflow/overflow, making these vulnerabilities rare in modern contracts compiled with recent versions. Developers must still audit legacy code, unchecked {} blocks, or low-level assembly, where manual safeguards like SafeMath libraries remain essential.

Logic errors and business logic flaws

They represent a vulnerability class that automated tools are ill-equipped to detect because they require understanding the intended behavior of the contract, not just its formal properties. A contract that correctly implements its written code may still behave in ways that allow value extraction if the code does not correctly reflect the designer's intent. The Compound protocol's $150 million over-distribution of COMP tokens in September 2021, caused by a logic error in a contract upgrade, illustrates how logic errors can produce large unintended transfers even without malicious exploitation.

Access control vulnerabilities

They arise when contracts do not correctly restrict which addresses can call privileged functions. The *Parity multisig wallet* hack of November 2017, in which an attacker exploited an uninitialized library contract to claim ownership and subsequently self-destruct it, rendering approximately $300 million in ETH permanently inaccessible, resulted from an access control flaw that allowed any address to initialize an uninitialized library contract. Access control in smart contracts requires deliberate design: every privileged function must have explicitly specified access restrictions, and the ownership and key management infrastructure that controls privileged access must be secured with the same rigor as the contracts themselves.

Consensus protocol exploits

Consensus mechanisms lie at the core of decentralized systems, but they also introduce distinct classes of vulnerabilities that adversaries can exploit at scale. These attacks target the economic and structural assumptions of PoW and PoS protocols, enabling malicious actors to rewrite history, manipulate finality, or undermine network stability. Understanding these exploit pathways is essential for designing resilient decentralized AI and blockchain architectures that can withstand both short-term operational threats and long-term systemic risks.

Key exploit types:

- **51% attacks (PoW)**: $15-200M/hour hashpower rentals (NiceHash data 2025)
  - **Double-spend window**: 6 confirmations Ethereum, 60+ Bitcoin
  - **Selfish mining**: 33% hashpower | 51% revenue capture
- **Long-range attacks (PoS)**:
  - Historical state rewrite from the genesis block
  - **Mitigation**: Checkpointing contracts + finality gadgets
- **Nothing-at-stake problem**:
  - Validators sign conflicting forks (zero slashing cost)
  - **Fix**: Economic finality via slashing + inera bonds

AI-specific attack vectors

The AI components of decentralized AI systems introduce a distinct set of vulnerabilities that are separate from, though often interacting with, the smart contract vulnerabilities previously discussed.

Adversarial examples

They are inputs crafted to cause AI models to produce incorrect outputs, misclassifying images, generating false fraud alerts, or producing incorrect risk assessments. In centralized AI deployments, adversarial attacks are typically constrained by the attacker's limited access to the model. In decentralized systems where model weights are publicly accessible, white-box adversarial attacks, which exploit complete knowledge of the model's architecture and parameters to craft maximally effective adversarial inputs, are available to any participant.

For AI systems that make consequential decisions, such as fraud detection in financial networks, diagnostic support in healthcare, and risk assessment in supply chain finance, adversarial attacks can produce targeted incorrect decisions that benefit the attacker. A fraud detection model that misclassifies fraudulent transactions as legitimate when those transactions have specific characteristics can be exploited by attackers who understand the model's decision boundary and craft their fraud accordingly.

Real-world example of credit card fraud evasion: In real-world credit card fraud detection, attackers apply subtle perturbations to transaction features like tweaking amounts, times, or merchant codes using algorithms such as **Zeroth Order Optimization** (**ZOO**), causing ML models to misclassify fraudulent spend as legitimate and approve it. Studies on datasets like the **Machine Learning Group** (**MLG**) Kaggle show that even simple random perturbations outperform complex attacks in evading deployed fraud classifiers, highlighting practical vulnerability in production systems.

Model poisoning attacks

These attacks target the training process rather than the deployed model. In federated learning systems, where multiple participants contribute gradient updates to a shared model, a malicious participant can submit crafted gradients that shift the model's behavior in the attacker's desired direction, causing the model to misclassify specific inputs, embedding a backdoor triggered by a chosen pattern, or degrading overall model performance to reduce competitors' advantage. Byzantine-robust federated learning aggregation algorithms, including Krum, Coordinate-wise Median, and FLTrust, provide partial protection against poisoning, but no aggregation algorithm provides complete protection against all poisoning strategies, particularly when the attacker controls a significant fraction of participating nodes.

Data poisoning attacks

They operate upstream of the federated learning process, corrupting the training data at its source. In decentralized AI systems that draw training data from blockchain-anchored data registries, an attacker who can contribute fraudulent data entries, sensor readings, financial records, and medical observations can influence the resulting model's behavior without directly manipulating the training process. The blockchain's immutability prevents the poisoned data from being altered after submission, which paradoxically makes data poisoning attacks harder to remediate. Poisoned data records cannot be deleted, only identified and excluded from training runs.

Model extraction attack

These attacks use a series of carefully crafted queries to a deployed model to reconstruct the model's architecture, weights, or decision logic with sufficient fidelity to mount more effective adversarial attacks or to replicate the model's commercial value without authorization. In decentralized AI networks where model inference is provided as a service and billed through smart contracts, model extraction attacks are economically motivated; an attacker who can reconstruct a valuable model can offer competing inference services without paying for the original model's development.

Sybil attacks

Sybil attacks against decentralized AI networks involve creating multiple pseudonymous identities to gain disproportionate influence over federated learning, governance votes, or data marketplace dynamics. A participant who controls many nodes in a federated learning network can contribute a higher fraction of gradient updates, increasing their influence over model behavior. Sybil resistance mechanisms, such as PoS (which requires economic commitment per identity), PoW (which requires computational expenditure), and decentralized identity systems (which tie node identities to verifiable real-world credentials), provide partial protection but involve tradeoffs between Sybil resistance, participation accessibility, and privacy.

Network-level attack vectors

51% of attacks occur when a single actor gains control of a majority of a blockchain network's consensus resources, hash power in PoW networks, or staked tokens in PoS networks. With majority control, an attacker can rewrite recent transaction history, executing double-spend attacks in which the same tokens are spent in two conflicting transactions, with only one recorded on the canonical chain. Smaller blockchain networks, where the total consensus resources are limited and therefore cheaper to acquire majority control of, are the primary targets. Ethereum and Bitcoin, whose consensus resources are sufficiently large that a 51% attack would require billions of dollars of investment, are considered practically resistant to this attack vector; smaller networks have suffered multiple successful 51% attacks.

Eclipse attacks

Eclipse attacks isolate a target node from the legitimate network by surrounding it with attacker-controlled peers, controlling all of the target's incoming and outgoing network communications. An eclipsed node can be fed manipulated blockchain data, selectively withheld information about new transactions or blocks, or deceived into accepting an attacker-controlled fork as the canonical chain. Eclipse attacks are particularly relevant to light client nodes that do not store the complete blockchain and rely on peers to provide honest summaries and on validators in PoS networks whose vote on block validity depends on seeing an accurate view of the current chain state.

Transaction ordering manipulation

Also known in DeFi as **maximal extractable value** (**MEV**), it involves reordering, inserting, or censoring transactions within a block to extract value at other participants' expense. Miners and validators who propose new blocks have discretion over transaction ordering within the block, and this discretion can be monetized by including or excluding specific transactions in ways that benefit the block proposer. Flash loan attacks, sandwich attacks on DEX trades, and liquidation front-running are all MEV extraction strategies that have collectively extracted billions of dollars from DeFi users. MEV represents a structural vulnerability of transparent mempool blockchains that requires both technical mitigations (encrypted mempools, fair ordering protocols, MEV auctions) and economic design responses.

Cross-chain bridge vulnerabilities

Cross-chain bridge vulnerabilities have become one of the most consequential attack surfaces in the blockchain ecosystem. Bridges that allow tokens to move between different blockchain networks must lock assets on one chain and issue corresponding representations on another, creating a custody mechanism that, if compromised, allows an attacker to drain the locked assets without invalidating the issued representations. The Ronin bridge hack ($625 million), the Wormhole hack ($320 million), and the Nomad bridge hack ($190 million) were all bridge exploits that collectively represent some of the largest individual thefts in the history of any technology industry.

Defense mechanisms and countermeasures

Secure development lifecycle: The most effective defense against smart contract vulnerabilities is not detection after deployment but prevention before deployment. A rigorous, secure development lifecycle for smart contracts incorporates security considerations at every stage from design through deployment and ongoing operation.

The design stage should include explicit threat modeling; systematic identification of assets to be protected, actors who might attack them, and attack paths they might use. Threat models that are created by security specialists working alongside protocol designers, rather than imposed as a checkbox requirement after design decisions are made, produce architectures that are structurally more resistant to attack. The principle of minimal privilege, that every component should have only the permissions it needs to perform its function, should be applied consistently: administrative functions should be restricted to explicitly authorized addresses; upgradeable contracts should require multi-signature authorization; and privileged operations should be subject to time-locks that provide a delay between authorization and execution.

The development stage should apply established secure coding patterns consistently. The checks-effects-interactions pattern eliminates reentrancy vulnerabilities. SafeMath libraries (now integrated into modern Solidity by default) prevent integer overflow. Pull-over-push payment patterns (where recipients withdraw their funds rather than having funds pushed to them) reduce the exposure of payment logic to reentrancy and denial-of-service attacks. These patterns should be enforced through code review checklists and, where possible, through static analysis tools integrated into the development pipeline.

Testing for smart contracts must go beyond functional correctness to include adversarial testing, deliberate attempts to exploit the contract's logic by individuals who did not write it. Unit tests verify that functions behave correctly under normal conditions; property-based tests and fuzzing verify that invariants hold across large numbers of automatically generated inputs; formal verification provides mathematical proof that specific security properties hold for all possible inputs. Each layer of testing catches different vulnerability classes; a comprehensive testing program incorporates all three. *Figure 9.2* details the multi-layered defense mechanisms and operational countermeasures required to maintain system-wide cryptographic security. The figure shows how the system combines automated threat reactions with community-driven bug bounties to ensure an immutable, self-defending AI ecosystem:

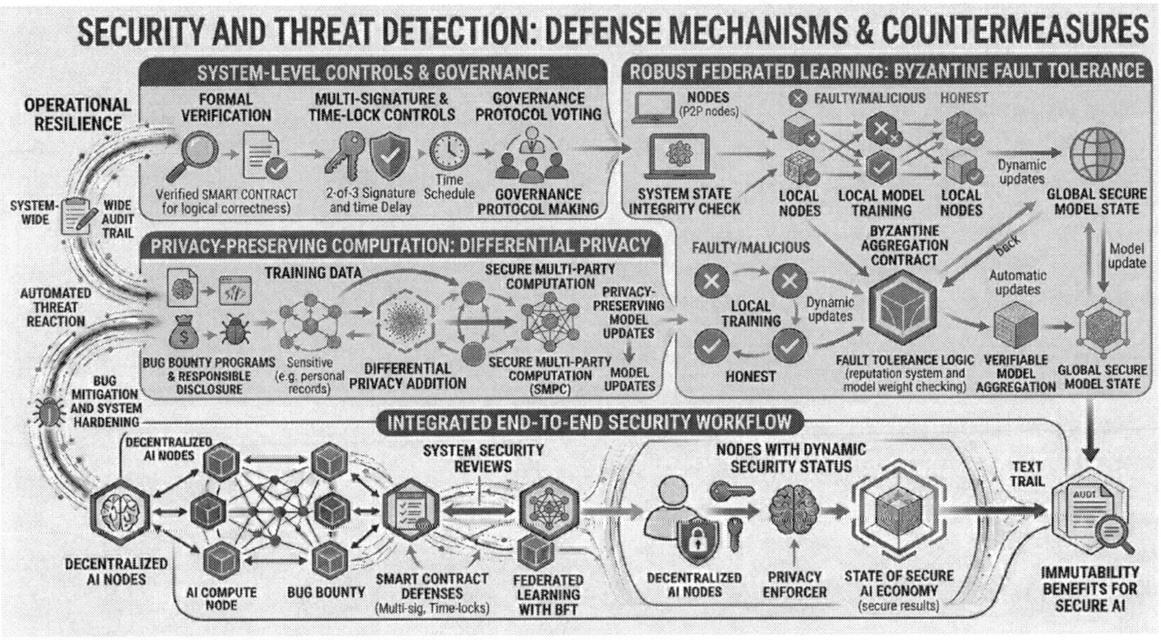

Figure 9.2: *Defense mechanisms and countermeasures*

Formal verification

Formal verification applies mathematical proof techniques to establish that a smart contract satisfies formally specified security properties. Unlike testing, which samples the contract's behavior across a finite number of inputs, formal verification provides guarantees about all possible inputs and execution paths. For smart contracts managing significant value, formal verification of critical security properties, such as no reentrancy, no unauthorized state transitions, and conservation of token balances, is increasingly considered standard practice by leading security teams.

Tools including Certora Prover, Echidna, and K-EVM enable formal verification of Solidity and other smart contract languages. These tools require security engineers to specify the properties to be verified in formal languages, a process that itself surfaces ambiguities and implicit assumptions in the protocol design. The Aave, Compound, and MakerDAO protocols have all incorporated formal verification into their development processes; the Ethereum Foundation has used formal verification extensively in the development of the Ethereum consensus layer specifications.

The limitations of formal verification are important to understand. Formal verification proves that a contract satisfies its specified properties, but the specification must be correct and complete for the proof to be meaningful. A formally verified contract that satisfies an incomplete specification may still contain vulnerabilities in the unspecified dimensions. Formal verification is most powerful when combined with expert security review, which can identify specification gaps and verify that the formal model accurately represents the intended protocol behavior.

Multi-signature and time-lock controls

Administrative controls for decentralized protocols, the ability to upgrade contracts, modify parameters, pause operations, and manage protocol treasuries must be protected with access control mechanisms that resist both external compromise and insider abuse. Multi-signature schemes, which require a threshold number of designated signers to authorize privileged operations, distribute the compromise risk: an attacker must compromise multiple independent key holders rather than a single administrator to gain unauthorized access.

The 3-of-5 multi-signature configuration, where any three of five designated signers must authorize a transaction, has become a common baseline for protocol treasuries. More sophisticated configurations specify different signing requirements for different operation types: low-risk parameter adjustments might require 2-of-5 signatures, while high-risk operations like contract upgrades require 4-of-5. The distribution of signing authority across geographically separated, institutionally diverse signers who use different key management approaches reduces the risk of coordinated compromise.

Time-locks add a temporal dimension to administrative control: privileged operations are executed not immediately upon authorization but after a specified delay, typically 24 to 72 hours. This delay provides a window during which the community can observe a pending operation, verify its legitimacy, and take countermeasures if it appears malicious. The combination of multi-signature authorization and time-lock execution has become the standard governance security model for mature DeFi protocols; protocols that lack either control are considered high-risk by security-conscious users.

Byzantine fault tolerant federated learning

For decentralized AI systems that use federated learning, defense against gradient poisoning attacks requires aggregation algorithms that are robust to Byzantine participants –those who submit arbitrary, potentially malicious updates. The standard federated averaging algorithm (FedAvg) is not Byzantine robust: a single sufficiently influential participant can shift the aggregated model significantly by submitting crafted gradients.

Byzantine-robust aggregation algorithms take different approaches to identifying and excluding anomalous updates. Krum selects the single gradient update that is most similar to its nearest neighbors, effectively excluding outlier updates from aggregation. Coordinate-wise Median replaces coordinate-wise averaging with coordinate-wise median, which is statistically robust to outliers at each dimension. FLTrust requires a small trusted dataset at the aggregating server, uses it to evaluate the trustworthiness of each participant's update, and weights updates proportionally to their measured trustworthiness. *Table 9.3* compares Krum, Median, and FLTrust across accuracy on clean data, Byzantine tolerance, and compute cost:

Algorithm	Accuracy (Clean data)	Robustness (% Byzantines tolerated)	Compute cost
Krum	High (82-90%) isprs-archives.copernicus+1	Good (≤20%) ndss-symposium+1	High (O(n^2d) pairwise distances) ndss-symposium
Median	Medium (75-85%) isprs-archives.copernicus	Medium (≤25%, coord-wise) nature	Medium (O(nd log n) per dim) themoonlight
FLTrust	High (85-95%) ndss-symposium+1	High (≤33%, trust-scored) ndss-symposium	Medium-High (trusted eval + weighting) ndss-symposium

Table 9.3: *Byzantine-robust aggregation comparison*

Each algorithm involves tradeoffs between Byzantine robustness, model accuracy under non-Byzantine conditions, and computational overhead. No single algorithm dominates across all scenarios; the appropriate choice depends on the expected fraction of Byzantine participants, the heterogeneity of legitimate participant data, and the computational resources available at the aggregation layer. Blockchain integration enhances Byzantine-robust aggregation by recording each participant's update commitment on-chain, enabling forensic analysis of poisoning attacks after the fact and providing an auditable basis for excluding identified malicious participants from future training rounds.

Differential privacy

Differential privacy provides a formal mathematical framework for quantifying and bounding the privacy leakage from AI model training. Intuitively, ε (epsilon) measures how much your personal data influences the model's output, like a privacy leakage dial where ε=0 means zero risk of identification (perfect privacy, but impractical), and smaller ε means tighter privacy with less data influence.

A differentially private training algorithm guarantees that the probability of any particular output, including the trained model weights, changes by at most a multiplicative factor of e^ε when any single training example is added or removed. The parameter ε (epsilon) quantifies the privacy guarantee: smaller values of ε provide stronger privacy protection at the cost of model accuracy.

In federated learning systems, differential privacy is typically applied by adding calibrated noise to gradient updates before they leave the participant's local environment. The noise magnitude is chosen to satisfy the desired ε guarantee given the sensitivity of the gradient computation. The blockchain layer records the ε values used in each training round, providing an auditable privacy budget that external parties can verify.

The practical challenge of differential privacy is the accuracy-privacy tradeoff: the noise required to achieve strong privacy guarantees (small ε) can significantly degrade model accuracy, particularly for small datasets or complex models. Current research on adaptive differential privacy mechanisms, which apply noise more precisely based on the actual sensitivity of each training round rather than a fixed worst-case bound, is gradually improving this tradeoff. For decentralized AI systems in regulated industries like healthcare, financial services, and telecommunications, where regulatory frameworks are beginning to incorporate differential privacy requirements, investing in high-quality differential privacy implementation is increasingly a compliance necessity as well as a security best practice.

Bug bounty programs and responsible disclosure

The open-source nature of most blockchain protocols means that the global security research community can examine protocol code for vulnerabilities. Bug bounty programs create economic incentives for security researchers to report discovered vulnerabilities to the protocol team rather than exploiting them or selling them to malicious actors. Effective bug bounty programs specify clear scope (which components are in scope for bounty rewards), clear severity classifications (with corresponding reward tiers), and clear disclosure timelines (how long the protocol team has to remediate before a researcher may disclose publicly).

Immunefi, the leading bug bounty platform for blockchain protocols, has facilitated the payment of over $100 million in bounties and claims to have prevented over $25 billion in potential hack proceeds through its programs. Several individual bounty payments have exceeded $10 million, a reflection of both the value at risk in major protocols and the program designers' accurate recognition that paying researchers is far less costly than absorbing an exploit.

The most effective bug bounty programs combine competitive rewards with a reputation for honest engagement, paying claimed bounties promptly, treating researchers with respect, and crediting them publicly for their contributions. Programs that dispute valid findings, delay payments, or characterize researcher behavior as malicious when researchers have followed responsible disclosure procedures are corrosive to the trust that makes responsible disclosure attractive as an alternative to exploitation.

Anomaly detection systems

Decentralized AI and blockchain systems require continuous, real-time monitoring to detect anomalous activity that may indicate an attack in progress, a system malfunction, or an emerging vulnerability. The monitoring challenge in decentralized systems differs from conventional infrastructure monitoring in several important ways.

First, the attack surface is public. Every transaction, every smart contract call, and every governance action is visible on-chain. This means that monitoring systems can observe the complete operational history of a protocol, a significant advantage compared to conventional systems, where attackers operate in logs that may be incomplete or tampered with. It also means that monitoring must process very high volumes of public data to distinguish malicious patterns from legitimate activity.

Second, the response window is often extremely narrow. Smart contract exploits can drain large amounts of value in a single transaction or a small number of transactions occurring within seconds. Effective anomaly detection must be able to identify suspicious activity and trigger circuit-breaker responses within the time constraints of a blockchain's block production interval, typically 12 seconds on Ethereum's mainnet.

Third, the relevant anomalies span multiple layers simultaneously. An attack may involve smart contract manipulation at the protocol layer, unusual network communication patterns at the node layer, and anomalous gradient submissions at the AI model layer. Effective monitoring requires correlation of signals across layers to detect attacks that would not be apparent from any single layer's data stream. The Anomaly detection systems for a secure and decentralized AI economy are shown in *Figure 9.3*:

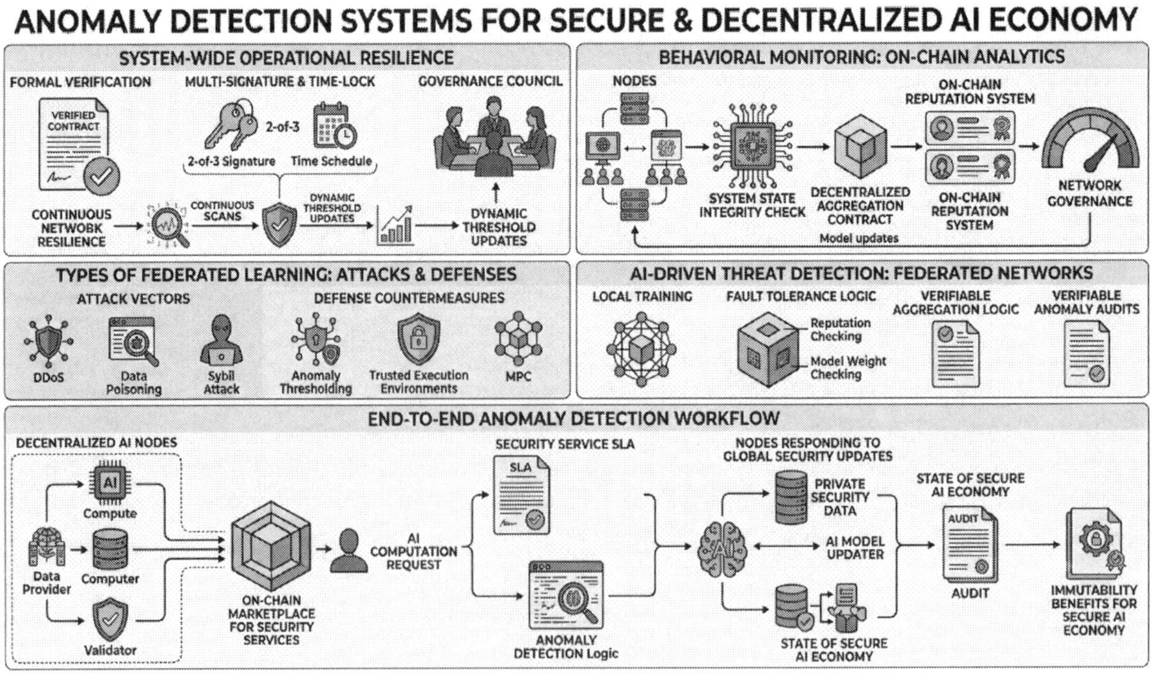

Figure 9.3: *Anomaly detection systems for a secure and decentralized AI economy*

On-chain analytics for behavioral monitoring

On-chain analytics platforms, including Chainalysis, Nansen, Dune Analytics, and Arkham Intelligence, have developed sophisticated tooling for behavioral monitoring of blockchain networks. These platforms ingest raw blockchain transaction data and apply machine learning models to identify patterns associated with known attack types: large, sudden outflows from smart contract treasuries, unusual sequences of DEX trades that match known MEV extraction patterns, governance token accumulations that precede contested governance votes, and bridge transaction patterns consistent with price manipulation.

Decentralized protocols can integrate on-chain analytics capabilities directly into their monitoring infrastructure through event subscriptions and smart contract hooks. A treasury contract can be configured to emit monitoring events when withdrawals exceed configurable thresholds; a governance contract can emit events when voting patterns deviate significantly from historical norms; a lending protocol can emit events when liquidation volumes surge. These events, consumed by off-chain monitoring systems, enable real-time alerting and automated circuit-breaker responses.

The machine learning models applied to on-chain data for anomaly detection face a domain-specific challenge: the concept drift problem. Attack patterns evolve as attackers respond to detection capabilities. Models trained on historical attack patterns will miss novel attack strategies that have not been observed before. Effective monitoring systems, therefore, combine rule-based detection (explicit encodings of known attack patterns) with anomaly detection models (that flag statistical deviations from baseline behavior regardless of whether they match known attack patterns) to maintain detection coverage as the attack landscape evolves.

AI-driven threat detection for federated networks

For decentralized AI networks specifically, anomaly detection must address threats to the AI system itself in addition to the blockchain infrastructure it runs on. Detecting gradient poisoning attacks in federated learning and identifying which participants are submitting anomalous updates that could shift model behavior requires statistical analysis that can distinguish genuine data heterogeneity (legitimate participants whose local data distributions differ from the population) from adversarial manipulation.

Several detection approaches have been proposed and implemented. Gradient similarity monitoring compares each participant's gradient update to the aggregated update from previous rounds and to the current round's population distribution. Participants whose updates are consistently outliers with a high cosine distance from the population mean or high variance across training rounds are flagged for further investigation. Activation pattern analysis evaluates the behavior of individual neurons in response to validation inputs, identifying backdoor attacks that manifest as unusual activation patterns triggered by specific input features.

Blockchain integration provides a critical enhancement to these detection approaches: the ability to maintain a persistent, tamper-evident record of each participant's gradient update history. When a participant is identified as potentially malicious through statistical analysis, their complete contribution history can be retrieved from the blockchain for forensic analysis. Patterns that are not apparent in individual rounds may become evident across the full history, identifying, for instance, a slow poisoning attack designed to shift model behavior gradually over many rounds in a way that would not trigger round-by-round anomaly detection.

Circuit breakers and automated response

The narrow response window available during many blockchain attacks has motivated the development of automated circuit-breaker mechanisms that can pause protocol operations when anomalous activity is detected, without requiring human decision-making in critical moments.

Circuit breakers are implemented as smart contract-level controls that monitor specific operational metrics and trigger protective actions when those metrics exceed configured thresholds. A lending protocol's circuit breaker might pause new borrowing when the protocol's collateralization ratio falls below a threshold. A bridge's circuit breaker might pause withdrawals when the volume of outbound transfers exceeds a threshold relative to the protocol's total value locked. A token contract's circuit breaker might pause transfers when a single address attempts to transfer more than a configured fraction of the total supply in a short time window.

Example false positive in DEX TWAP: During rapid 50% market crashes, DEX-based TWAP circuit breakers can lag real-time prices, generating false positives that disable liquidations or deposits unnecessarily precisely when they are needed most. This unintended consequence highlights calibration risks, as overly sensitive thresholds disrupt legitimate activity amid volatility.

The design of circuit breakers requires careful calibration. Thresholds set too conservatively will trigger false positives, pausing legitimate user activity during periods of genuine high demand or volatility. Thresholds set too aggressively will miss attacks. The optimal calibration depends on the specific protocol's operational characteristics and risk tolerance and should be informed by historical operational data and adversarial simulation. Several protocols have implemented graduated circuit-breaker responses, soft limits that trigger enhanced monitoring and delayed execution, followed by hard limits that trigger complete pauses to balance protection and availability.

Incident response procedures

Incident response in decentralized AI and blockchain systems must be planned before an incident occurs. The combination of rapid attack execution, irreversible blockchain transactions, and the reputational consequences of security failures creates time pressure and stress conditions that preclude effective improvisation. Teams that have documented, rehearsed, and tested their incident response procedures before an incident occurs respond faster, make fewer errors, and recover more completely than those that improvise under pressure.

An effective incident response plan for a decentralized AI and blockchain system addresses the following phases: detection and triage, containment, eradication, recovery, and post-incident review. Each phase has specific objectives, responsibilities, and time expectations that must be defined in advance.

The detection and triage phase begins when an anomaly is identified, whether by automated monitoring, a user report, a security researcher notification, or an external security firm's alert. The triage objective is to quickly determine whether the anomaly represents an active attack, a potential attack, a system malfunction, or a false positive, and to estimate the severity of the impact if an attack is underway. This assessment should be completed within minutes, not hours: the cost of an incorrect initial classification is acceptable if the triage process is fast; the cost of a slow triage during an active exploit is not.

Containment strategies

Containment in blockchain systems is more constrained than in conventional systems. Conventional incident response can involve isolating compromised systems from the network, reverting unauthorized file system changes, or suspending compromised user accounts, all actions that a system administrator can take unilaterally and immediately. Blockchain systems' decentralization means that containment options are limited to those encoded in the smart contract design and accessible through the existing governance mechanisms.

The most important containment tool for most protocols is a pause mechanism, a privileged function that halts specified protocol operations until the mechanism is explicitly lifted. Pause mechanisms should be accessible through a low-latency administrative path (a multi-signature with fewer signers than the normal governance path, or a single emergency key with appropriate safeguards) to enable rapid response. The tradeoff between response speed and governance security for pause mechanisms is a genuine design tension: a pause mechanism accessible through a single key is fast but creates a centralization risk; one that requires a multi-signature quorum with normal signing processes may be too slow to interrupt a fast-moving exploit.

Several protocols have addressed this tension through tiered emergency governance: a small security council with authority to pause operations immediately on detection of an active exploit, with a subsequent governance vote required to maintain the pause beyond a defined period. This design balances response speed against the decentralization principle, accepting temporary centralization of emergency response authority while preserving decentralized authority over the underlying protocol.

Communication protocols during incidents

Communication during a security incident in a decentralized protocol is uniquely challenging. Premature public disclosure of an active exploit can trigger a run on the protocol, causing users to rush to withdraw their funds, worsening the impact, or provide attackers with information that helps them move faster. Delayed disclosure can allow an exploit to continue longer than necessary and erodes community trust when the full timeline is revealed.

Effective communication protocols specify clear internal notification chains (who must be notified of a confirmed or suspected incident, through what channels, and within what timeframe), clear decision authority (who can authorize public communications at each stage), and clear templates for different communication scenarios (active exploit underway, potential vulnerability identified, incident contained, full post-mortem published).

Secure communication channels, encrypted messaging platforms, separate from the public community forums where discussion of suspicious activity might alert attackers, are essential for coordinating the internal response during an active incident. Several protocols maintain dedicated encrypted channels for security team communications that are distinct from their general operational communications.

The post-incident communication is as important as the in-incident communication. A comprehensive, honest post-mortem, detailing the timeline of events, the vulnerability exploited, the response actions taken, and the lessons learned, is the primary instrument for rebuilding community trust after a security incident. Post-mortems that minimize the severity of an exploit, obscure the timeline, or blame external parties rather than acknowledging internal failures are typically more damaging to long-term reputation than the incident itself. The protocols that have recovered most effectively from significant security incidents, including compound, Euler finance (which recovered the vast majority of stolen funds through negotiation with the attacker), and several others, have shared transparent, detailed post-mortems that the community received as evidence of honest accountability.

Recovery and remediation

Recovery from a security incident involves two distinct challenges: financial recovery and technical remediation. Financial recovery, restoring users who suffered losses to their pre-incident positions, is a governance challenge as much as a technical one. Several mechanisms have been used, including protocol treasury distributions, newly minted governance token allocations, insurance fund deployments, and, in several notable cases, negotiations with attackers that resulted in partial fund returns.

The *Euler Finance* exploit of March 2023, in which $197 million was stolen, resulted in the attacker returning the funds after a combination of on-chain messaging, negotiations, and the threat of on-chain forensics that could identify the attacker. The PolyNetwork hack of August 2021, in which $611 million was stolen across three chains at the time, the largest single theft in blockchain history, similarly ended with the attacker returning the funds, reportedly motivated by a combination of the logistical difficulty of laundering such a large sum and the protocol's offer of a bug bounty and security consultant role. These cases illustrate that financial recovery is sometimes achievable even after large exploits, particularly when the attacker's identity can be partially determined through on-chain forensics.

Technical remediation involves identifying the root cause of the vulnerability, deploying patched code, and verifying that the patch effectively closes the vulnerability without introducing new ones. In systems with upgradeable smart contracts, remediation can be deployed through a contract upgrade after the standard governance process. In systems with immutable contracts, remediation may require migrating to new contract versions, a process that involves coordinating users to transfer their assets to the new contracts, which presents its own risks and communication challenges.

Smart contract security auditing

Professional smart contract security auditing has evolved into a specialized discipline with its own methodologies, tools, and professional standards. Leading audit firms, including Trail of Bits, OpenZeppelin, ConsenSys Diligence, Certora, Halborn, and others, have developed deep expertise in the unique vulnerability patterns found in smart contract systems and have audited protocols that collectively manage hundreds of billions of dollars in assets.

A comprehensive smart contract audit involves multiple stages that collectively provide broad coverage of the vulnerability space. The initial review phase involves a thorough manual reading of the contract code, focusing on the protocol's overall architecture, the flow of assets and permissions, and the consistency between the code's implementation and the protocol's documentation. This phase focuses on identifying high-level design issues and architectural choices that introduce structural vulnerabilities, which automated tools often fail to detect.

The technical analysis phase then combines manual expert review with automated tooling to uncover specific instances of vulnerabilities. Manual review concentrates on issues that require contextual judgment, such as logic flaws, access control design, and the validity of economic invariants. Automated tools, including Slither for static analysis, Echidna for fuzz testing, and Mythril for symbolic execution, conduct systematic searches across the entire codebase to detect known vulnerability patterns, capturing issues that human reviewers may overlook in large and complex systems.

The validation phase verifies that the protocol's implementation satisfies its stated invariants: that assets cannot be created or destroyed without authorization, that state transitions follow the documented protocol rules, and that access controls prevent unauthorized operations. Where formal verification is applied, this phase includes the specification of formal properties and the verification proof.

Audit scope and limitations

Understanding what a smart contract audit does and does not guarantee is essential for interpreting audit reports accurately. An audit is not a certification that a contract is free of all vulnerabilities. It is a professional assessment that the contract, as reviewed, appears to satisfy its specified requirements and does not contain the vulnerability classes that the audit methodology covers, given the time and resources invested.

Several important limitations apply. Audits cover the code as submitted, not code changes made after the audit completes. Many protocols have suffered exploits because vulnerabilities were introduced during upgrades that did not receive the same level of scrutiny as the original deployment. Security audits typically concentrate on smart contract logic and often exclude off-chain components such as oracle systems, front-end interfaces, key management processes, and operational infrastructure that may contain weaknesses capable of compromising the protocol, even when the underlying smart contracts are secure.

The economic incentives of the auditing industry create a potential misalignment: audit firms are paid by the protocols they audit, and protocols that receive unfavorable audit findings may seek second opinions from less rigorous firms or deploy without completing remediation. Several high-profile exploits have occurred in protocols that received clean audits from reputable firms, illustrating that audit quality varies significantly and that a completed audit should not be conflated with verified security.

Continuous audit programs, in which a security firm provides ongoing review of protocol updates, governance decisions, and operational processes rather than conducting a single audit before launch, offer a far more resilient engagement model for protocols that manage substantial value. The cost is higher, but the coverage of post-launch changes and the depth of relationship-based understanding of the protocol's security posture provide substantially better protection than a point-in-time assessment.

Automated auditing tools and their limitations

The automation of smart contract analysis has advanced significantly, with several tooling categories now providing meaningful coverage of specific vulnerability classes. Static analysis tools, with Slither being the most widely used, examine contract code without executing it and identify patterns linked to known vulnerabilities through rule-based matching and data flow analysis. Slither can identify reentrancy patterns, access control issues, and many common coding errors at high speed across large codebases, making it valuable as a first-pass screening tool. Its limitations include high false positive rates on some checks and the inability to reason about the economic logic of a protocol.

Fuzzing tools, including Echidna and the fuzzer built into Foundry, execute the contract using automatically generated inputs in order to detect violations of expected invariants. Property-based fuzzing, in which developers define specific invariants that must hold for all possible inputs, enables focused testing of the contract's most security-critical behaviors. Fuzzing is particularly effective at finding edge cases in arithmetic operations and complex state machine transitions that manual review might miss.

Symbolic execution tools such as Mythril and Manticore examine all possible execution paths within a contract, offering a theoretically comprehensive view of its reachable state space. In practice, however, symbolic execution faces significant constraints. The first is path explosion, the exponential increase in the number of potential paths as contract complexity grows. The second is the difficulty of accurately modeling the broader execution environment, including interactions with external contracts, oracle inputs, and miner behavior, all of which influence how the contract may behave in real deployments. The appropriate use of automated tools is as systematic components of a broader security process, not as replacements for expert human judgment. Automated tools are fast and consistent; they do not miss vulnerability patterns they are programmed to detect, regardless of reviewer fatigue or time pressure. They cannot, however, understand the protocol's intended behavior, reason about the correctness of economic incentive designs, or detect vulnerability classes they were not programmed to search for.

Network security monitoring

The network infrastructure that supports decentralized AI and blockchain systems, including validators, nodes, bridges, oracle networks, and AI inference nodes, must be continuously monitored for signs of performance degradation, unusual communication patterns, and indicators of compromise that may signal or accompany attacks occurring at higher layers of the stack. Validator and node monitoring track the operational health of individual network participants: uptime, block production rate, attestation performance, peer connectivity, and resource utilization (CPU, memory, storage, and network bandwidth). Deviations from normal operational patterns, such as sudden increases in message volume, unexpected peer disconnections, or sharp spikes in resource usage, may signal network-level attacks, including eclipse attacks or distributed denial of service campaigns, or indicate operational issues that could undermine the security of the consensus process. For AI inference nodes in decentralized AI networks, monitoring extends to inference latency, output distribution characteristics, and the consistency of outputs across different nodes responding to the same query. Significant deviations in inference latency may indicate resource exhaustion attacks; unusual output distributions may indicate model substitution or drift; inconsistency across nodes may indicate that some nodes are running different (potentially compromised) model versions.

Mempool monitoring

The mempool, the set of submitted but not yet confirmed transactions waiting to be included in a block, offers a real-time view into pending network activity. Monitoring the mempool makes it possible to detect malicious or suspicious transactions before they are finalized, creating a narrow but potentially valuable window for defensive intervention.

Several security teams and protocol operators monitor mempools for transactions that interact with their contracts in ways consistent with known attack patterns: repeated calls to specific functions with parameter patterns that match exploit techniques, large flash loan initiations from addresses that have not previously used the protocol, or transaction sequences that would result in anomalous state transitions if confirmed.

When suspicious transactions are detected in the mempool, defensive responses available within the confirmation window include: front-running the attack transaction with a defensive transaction (a pause or parameter change that invalidates the attack), using MEV protection services to route defensive transactions directly to block builders without public mempool visibility, and activating automated circuit breakers that pause the protocol before the attack transaction is confirmed.

The effectiveness of mempool-based defense is limited by the narrow time window and the increasing use of private transaction channels (flashbots bundles, private mempools) by sophisticated attackers who specifically route their transactions to avoid mempool visibility. Nevertheless, several significant exploits have been partially or fully mitigated through mempool monitoring and rapid defensive response.

Cross-chain monitoring

The expansion of blockchain ecosystems to include multiple interconnected chains has created a cross-chain monitoring challenge: attacks that span multiple chains may be partially visible on each individual chain but fully apparent only to monitoring systems with simultaneous visibility across all chains.

Cross-chain bridge exploits, in particular, involve transactions on multiple chains that must be correlated to understand the full attack flow. A bridge exploit might involve a large deposit transaction on Chain A, followed by a fraudulent withdrawal claim on Chain B, with the attacker exploiting the time delay in cross-chain message verification to execute multiple withdrawals before the deposit transaction can be confirmed. Monitoring systems that watch only one chain will see either large deposits or large withdrawals, but not the causal relationship between them.

Multi-chain monitoring platforms that maintain real-time visibility across major blockchain networks, including the EVM-compatible chains (Ethereum, Polygon, Arbitrum, Optimism, and Avalanche), Solana, Cosmos ecosystem chains, and others, have become an important security infrastructure for protocols and their users. These platforms provide correlated alerts when activity patterns across chains match the signatures of known multi-chain attacks and maintain real-time dashboards of bridge liquidity, withdrawal volumes, and anomalous transaction patterns.

Cryptographic security practices

Private key compromise is the most common proximate cause of significant value loss in blockchain systems. Regardless of the sophistication of smart contract security, formal verification, and monitoring systems, a protocol whose signing keys are compromised is fully exposed to an attacker who can authorize arbitrary transactions in the protocol's name. Key management, the set of practices and infrastructure used to generate, store, use, and rotate cryptographic private keys, is the foundational layer of blockchain security.

For individual users, hardware wallets, which are physical devices that store private keys in tamper-resistant hardware and require a physical button press to authorize any transaction, offer the highest level of protection for personal digital assets.

For protocol operators who control administrative keys with authority over significant values, **hardware security modules (HSMs)** provide institutional-grade protection. These enterprise-level key storage devices combine physical and logical tamper resistance with detailed access logging and policy-enforced usage controls, ensuring that sensitive administrative keys remain secure even under sophisticated threat conditions.

Multi-party computation (MPC) key management has emerged as a complementary approach to hardware-based key security. MPC key management splits a private key into shares distributed across multiple custodians, requiring a threshold number of shares to reconstruct the key for signing operations. No single custodian ever holds the complete private key; an attacker must compromise multiple independent custodians to obtain signing authority. MPC key management is increasingly offered by institutional custody providers as the standard for large-value key management.

The operational security practices surrounding key storage are as important as the technical storage mechanism. Keys generated on internet-connected computers, stored in cloud environments, or accessible through automated software processes are exposed to compromise through malware, phishing, cloud provider breaches, and software supply chain attacks. Air gapped key generation, in which keys are created on computers that have never been connected to the internet, is considered the gold standard for generating high-value cryptographic keys. This method is used for the root keys of hardware wallets, certificate authorities, and administrative accounts that secure major blockchain protocols.

Zero-knowledge proofs and privacy-preserving cryptography

Zero-knowledge proofs (ZKPs) allow one party to prove the truth of a statement to another party without revealing any information beyond the truth of the statement itself. The applications in decentralized AI and blockchain security are extensive.

In blockchain transactions, ZKPs enable privacy-preserving proofs of asset ownership (proving you own sufficient funds to make a payment without revealing your balance), compliance (proving your transaction meets regulatory requirements without revealing the transaction details), and identity (proving you satisfy eligibility criteria without revealing your identity). Zcash, which implements zk-SNARKs for private transactions, is the most deployed implementation of ZKPs for blockchain privacy.

In decentralized AI, zero-knowledge proofs make it possible to verify that an AI model produced a specific output correctly, without exposing the model's weights or the input data used to generate that output. This enables verifiable AI in contexts where the model or the input is proprietary or sensitive. Projects, including Modulus Labs and EZKL, are developing **zero-knowledge machine learning** (**zkML**) infrastructure that makes this capability practical for real-world AI models, though the computational overhead of generating ZK proofs for large model inference remains a significant engineering challenge.

Threshold cryptography, in which a cryptographic operation can be performed only when a required subset of participants act together, provides a powerful foundation for governance functions that must be protected against both external attacks and internal misuse.

Threshold signature schemes, where a distributed signing ceremony produces a valid signature only when a threshold of signers cooperate, are increasingly used for protocol administrative keys, oracle aggregation, and cross-chain message signing.

Cryptographic agility and post-quantum readiness

The cryptographic algorithms underlying blockchain and decentralized AI systems, including the elliptic curve cryptography that secures transaction signing and the hash functions that underpin PoW and Merkle tree structures, were designed under computational hardness assumptions that hold against classical computers. The arrival of quantum computers capable of breaking modern cryptography machines, powerful enough to run Shor's algorithm against elliptic curve systems, would overturn the core security assumptions on which current cryptographic protocols rely.

The timeline for quantum computers capable of breaking modern cryptography remains uncertain, with expert predictions ranging anywhere from ten years to more than thirty. However, the *harvest now, decrypt later* threat, where adversaries capture encrypted data today with the intention of decrypting it once quantum computers become available, already applies to long-lived blockchain records whose confidentiality must be preserved for decades. This risk provides a strong incentive to invest in post-quantum cryptographic systems now, even though the quantum threat has not yet fully materialized.

The US National Institute of Standards and Technology completed its post-quantum cryptography standardization process in 2024, releasing standards for post-quantum key encapsulation mechanisms (ML KEM, based on lattice cryptography) and for digital signature schemes (ML DSA and SLH DSA). Decentralized AI and blockchain systems that are intended to operate over long time horizons should incorporate cryptographic agility, the capability to update cryptographic primitives without requiring major architectural changes, and should include post-quantum signature migration as a core element of their long-term security strategy.

Compliance and risk management

The relationship between regulatory compliance and security in decentralized AI and blockchain systems is far closer than it might initially seem. Many regulatory obligations, such as anti-money laundering and know your customer requirements, data protection mandates, audit logging rules, and breach notification standards, encode security best practices that protect both regulated entities and the individuals whose assets and information they handle. When compliance frameworks are understood and implemented as core components of the system's security architecture rather than as burdensome administrative tasks, the result is infrastructure that is both more secure and more aligned with regulatory expectations.

The **Financial Action Task Force** (**FATF**) Travel Rule, which requires financial institutions transmitting virtual asset transfers above a threshold to include originator and beneficiary identification information, has driven the development of compliant wallet screening and transaction monitoring infrastructure that simultaneously serves AML compliance and security monitoring purposes. Platforms that implement Travel Rule compliance have, in many cases, built the most sophisticated blockchain transaction monitoring capabilities in the industry, capabilities that provide security benefits extending well beyond the compliance use case.

GDPR and equivalent data protection regulations, as discussed in earlier chapters, mandate privacy-preserving computation approaches that are also security best practices. Organizations that implement federated learning and differential privacy to satisfy GDPR's data minimization and purpose limitation principles have also reduced their attack surface: systems that never centralize personal data cannot be breached for that data. Compliance and security are aligned rather than in tension when a privacy-preserving architecture is adopted as the design standard.

Risk management frameworks

Formal risk management frameworks provide the analytical infrastructure for making systematic, evidence-based decisions about security investment and risk tolerance. For decentralized AI and blockchain systems, the most applicable risk management standards are the NIST **Cybersecurity Framework** (**CSF**), the ISO 27001 information security management standard, and, for financial services applications, the FFIEC Cybersecurity Assessment Tool and the Bank for International Settlements' Principles for Operational Resilience.

Applying these frameworks to decentralized systems requires adaptations that account for the specific properties of these systems. The five core functions of the NIST Cybersecurity Framework—Identify, Protect, Detect, Respond, and Recover can be conceptually mapped to smart contract security: identifying vulnerabilities, protecting systems through secure development practices, detecting issues through continuous monitoring, responding through coordinated incident handling, and recovering through remediation and financial restoration. However, the specific controls associated with each function must be re-engineered for the blockchain environment, where immutability, decentralization, and autonomous execution fundamentally change how these activities must be implemented.

Risk quantification, the practice of expressing security risks in monetary terms to support cost-benefit analysis of security investments, is especially crucial for protocols that manage substantial user assets and must determine how best to allocate their security budgets across competing priorities. The expected loss from a specific vulnerability class can be estimated as the product of the probability of exploitation, the value exposed to that exploitation, and the fraction of exposed value likely to be lost. This framing enables rational prioritization: a high-probability, low-impact vulnerability class may warrant lower investment than a low-probability, high-impact class, depending on the specific numbers.

Insurance and financial risk transfer

Decentralized insurance protocols, with Nexus Mutual, InsurAce, and Unslashed Finance as leading examples, offer risk transfer mechanisms for smart contract users that operate in a manner similar to traditional insurance but are governed through mutual structures implemented on blockchain networks. Users pay premiums in exchange for coverage against smart contract exploits; claims are assessed and paid through decentralized governance processes.

The emergence of decentralized insurance has provided empirical data on smart contract exploit risk that has significant risk management value beyond the insurance use case. Premium pricing in competitive decentralized insurance markets reflects market participants' collective assessment of protocol-specific risk levels, providing information that is more specific and current than any static security assessment. Protocols with lower-priced coverage are, by this measure, assessed as more secure by a market that has a financial incentive to price risk accurately.

For enterprises deploying decentralized AI and blockchain systems, conventional cyber insurance policies are beginning to incorporate coverage for smart contract risks, though the terms are still evolving and the coverage often involves limitations and exclusions that require careful analysis. The creation of strong insurance markets, both decentralized and traditional, that cover blockchain and AI system risks is a crucial element of the financial risk management infrastructure needed for the ecosystem to reach true institutional scale.

Security principles for DAI and blockchain systems

Security and threat detection in decentralized AI and blockchain systems must be addressed from every angle, including technical, operational, governance-related, and regulatory. The breadth of these considerations reflects the breadth of the challenge itself. In systems where value, computation, and decision-making are distributed across networks of participants operating under different incentives and constraints, security cannot be treated as a single layer to be defended. Instead, it must be integrated into every aspect of system design.

The key themes that have emerged across this chapter deserve restatement as a unified set of principles:

- **The threat landscape is broad and adversarially dynamic**: Decentralized AI and blockchain systems contend with threats from highly capable adversaries, including nation states, organized criminal groups, competitive rivals, and malicious insiders, those actors with substantial resources and strong economic incentives to compromise these systems. The attack surface spans smart contract logic, AI model integrity, network infrastructure, and human factors, and attackers adapt their techniques in response to defensive improvements.
- **Defense requires depth and diversity**: No single security measure can address the full range of threats. Strong security emerges from layered defenses: secure development practices, formal verification, multi-signature governance, continuous monitoring, anomaly detection, circuit breakers, bug bounty programs, and well-rehearsed incident response procedures. Each layer compensates for weaknesses in the others.
- **Governance is a security property**: The mechanisms by which protocols are governed, how administrative keys are held, how parameter changes are authorized, and how emergency responses are triggered are not separate from security; they are central to it. Governance designs that concentrate administrative authority create high-value targets; those that distribute authority appropriately reduce the impact of any single compromise.
- **AI introduces novel security dimensions**: The integration of AI into blockchain systems extends the security challenge beyond smart contract vulnerabilities to include model poisoning, adversarial examples, data integrity, and model governance. Privacy-preserving computation, including federated learning with differential privacy and secure aggregation, is both the technical enabler of decentralized AI and a primary security mechanism for AI systems processing sensitive data.
- **Compliance and security are aligned**: Regulatory requirements in areas such as healthcare, financial services, and data protection encapsulate security best practices that benefit both compliance and system integrity. When implemented as genuine

security infrastructure rather than minimal procedural obligations, these frameworks create systems that are simultaneously more resilient and more aligned with regulatory expectations.

Conclusion

The security and threat detection landscape in decentralized AI networks represents one of the most critical domains for ensuring the viability, trustworthiness, and adoption of these transformative technologies. Throughout this chapter, we have examined the multifaceted challenges and comprehensive solutions necessary to protect decentralized AI ecosystems from an ever-evolving array of threats. From understanding the security threat landscape and attack vectors to implementing sophisticated defense mechanisms, anomaly detection systems, and incident response procedures, organizations must adopt a holistic, multi-layered approach to security.

Security, in the end, is a collective property of decentralized systems, one that no single participant can provide alone but that all participants can contribute to. The decentralized AI and blockchain systems that will matter most in the decade ahead will be those whose communities have taken that collective responsibility seriously from the beginning. The tools, frameworks, and practices described in this chapter are the foundation for doing so.

Emerging priorities in future research include strengthening zkML security to verify AI inferences on-the-chain without revealing models or data and developing defenses against autonomous AI agent attacks that exploit smart contracts or evade detection independently. Advancements in quantum-resistant cryptography for decentralized training and scalable Byzantine-robust aggregation are also critical areas demanding innovation.

The key open challenges lie in balancing the privacy-accuracy tradeoffs inherent in federated learning, safeguarding model provenance against poisoning risks in open marketplaces, and governing AI agents amid on-chain custody vulnerabilities. Advancing standardization across protocols for threat intelligence and achieving regulatory alignment for global deployment remain critical priorities.

The integration of smart contract security auditing, network monitoring, cryptographic security practices, and compliance frameworks demonstrates that security in decentralized AI is not a single-point solution but rather a continuous, adaptive process requiring vigilance, innovation, and community collaboration. As decentralized AI networks grow in complexity and adoption, the importance of proactive threat intelligence, rigorous testing, and rapid incident response cannot be overstated. By embedding security principles into the architecture and culture of decentralized AI systems, stakeholders can build platforms that are not only technologically advanced but also resilient, trustworthy, and aligned with emerging regulatory landscapes.

As we advance to *Chapter 10, Building Production Ready Systems*, readers will discover how to leverage the security principles and best practices covered here to architect scalable, resilient, decentralized AI systems capable of sustained operation in real-world environments.

CHAPTER 10
Building Production Ready Systems

Introduction

This chapter provides a roadmap for transforming decentralized AI from experimental prototypes into enterprise-ready systems. It focuses on building infrastructure that operates reliably under real-world conditions, addressing variable workloads, diverse environments, and regulatory demands. The chapter introduces architectural patterns that connect AI services, blockchain layers, storage, and enterprise platforms without creating single points of failure. In decentralized AI, a single point of failure can be a centralized aggregation server, a governance chokepoint, or a critical oracle dependency whose failure or compromise can interrupt model coordination, decision-making, or data delivery. It explores deployment strategies and continuous integration and deployment pipelines that automate the rollout of models, services, and smart contracts across independent nodes, embedding security, compliance, and governance directly into operational workflows.

Infrastructure requirements are examined across compute, storage, and networking, with emphasis on resilience and elasticity. Monitoring and observability frameworks capture system metrics, traces, and AI-specific signals such as drift and accuracy, enabling proactive optimization. Performance tuning, disaster recovery, and backup strategies ensure continuity and efficiency in distributed environments. Maintenance and updates are coordinated through decentralized governance, while scaling strategies combine horizontal expansion with Layer 2 enhancements to achieve global reach.

Enterprise integration aligns decentralized AI with identity, data, and operational systems, while cost management connects technical choices to sustainable economics. Together, these elements form a blueprint for building decentralized AI systems that are resilient, secure, and scalable for enterprise adoption.

Structure

The chapter covers the following topics:

- Production architecture design
- Deployment strategies and CI/CD
- Infrastructure requirements
- Monitoring and observability
- Performance optimization
- Disaster recovery and backup
- Maintenance and updates
- Scaling strategies
- Enterprise integration
- Cost management

Objectives

By the end of the chapter, readers will be able to design production-grade architectures that integrate AI compute layers, blockchain coordination, and enterprise systems with fault tolerance and scalability. They will learn to implement CI/CD pipelines for decentralized AI, covering model packaging, smart contract deployment, multi-node rollouts, and governance-driven release processes.

Readers will understand how to configure infrastructure across compute, storage, networking, and security to support heterogeneous nodes and compliance requirements. They will gain skills in building monitoring and observability systems that track distributed metrics, AI-specific signals, and blockchain events for proactive operations.

The chapter also equips readers to apply performance optimization techniques, develop disaster recovery and backup strategies, and establish maintenance workflows with decentralized governance and rollback mechanisms. Scaling strategies will be explored, combining node expansion, hardware optimization, federated learning, and Layer 2 blockchain solutions. Finally, readers will learn to integrate decentralized AI with enterprise IT ecosystems through APIs, identity federation, and compliance-aligned frameworks, while applying cost management practices to ensure sustainability and efficiency.

Together, these objectives provide actionable expertise for building secure, resilient, and scalable decentralized AI systems ready for enterprise deployment.

Production architecture design

Designing production-ready decentralized AI systems begins with a carefully structured architecture. This architecture must be resilient enough to address the inherent complexities of decentralized environments, seamlessly integrating AI model components with blockchain infrastructure across distributed networks. A well-conceived design ensures scalability, fault tolerance, security, and operational efficiency, while meeting enterprise-grade performance expectations as shown in *Figure 10.1*:

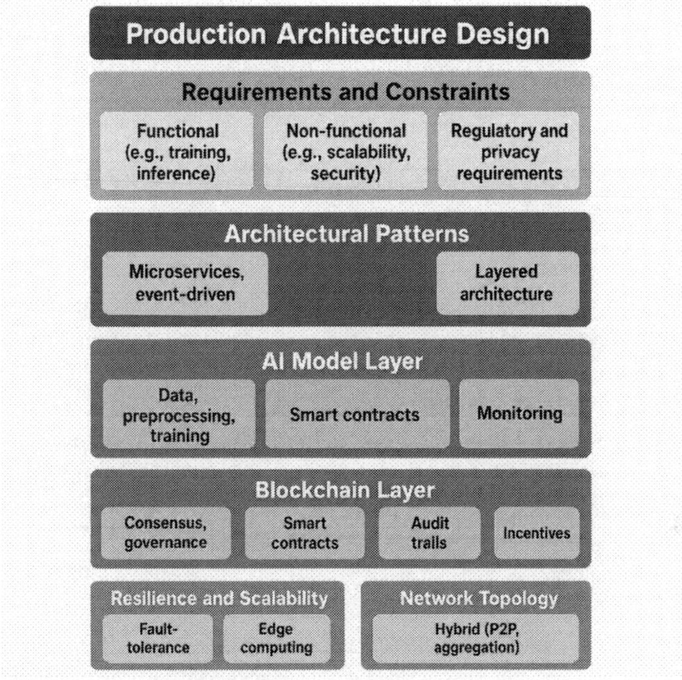

Figure 10.1*: Layered diagram showing AI layers, blockchain layers, and network topology*

Defining system requirements and constraints

The foundation of architectural design lies in clearly articulating both functional and non-functional requirements. Functional requirements encompass AI capabilities such as model training, inference, federated learning coordination, and smart contract interactions. Non-functional requirements include scalability, availability, latency, throughput, consistency, and security benchmarks, which should be translated into explicit **service level objective** (**SLOs**) and **service level agreement** (**SLAs**) that define measurable uptime, response time, and recovery targets for production systems. Regulatory compliance, privacy mandates, data sovereignty, and interoperability with enterprise systems must also be factored in. Constraints such as limited network bandwidth, heterogeneous node capabilities, and resource variability further shape architectural decisions.

Architectural patterns for decentralized AI

Decentralized AI benefits from modular and loosely coupled architectural patterns that allow independent evolution of components. Microservices architectures, where AI functions such as preprocessing, training, and serving are encapsulated into discrete services, provide flexibility and scalability. In this context, service mesh technologies such as Istio or Linkerd can strengthen secure service-to-service communication, improve observability, and enforce policy consistently across distributed microservices without changing application code. Event-driven architectures enable asynchronous communication between nodes, improving responsiveness and resilience. When blockchain is integrated, layered designs are often adopted, separating AI processing layers from ledger layers to maintain abstraction and establish clear interface contracts between models and decentralized state management.

Integrating blockchain with AI model layers

At the core of decentralized AI architecture is the interaction between AI components and blockchain networks. Blockchain layers provide trustless coordination, immutable audit trails, tokenized incentives, and governance mechanisms. AI layers manage data ingestion, training, inference, and monitoring. Secure smart contract interactions are essential to register models, validate contributions, and automate payments, while minimizing computational overhead. Middleware services and blockchain oracles are often employed to synchronize off-chain AI computations with on-chain state changes, but their design must clearly state the trust assumptions they rely on and the risks they introduce, since a compromised oracle can feed incorrect data into the system and undermine decentralized AI integrity.

Designing for fault tolerance and resilience

Decentralized architectures must anticipate node failures, network partitions, and inconsistent states. Strategies include replicating critical data and models across multiple nodes, employing **Byzantine fault tolerant** (**BFT**) consensus algorithms appropriate to the deployment context, and implementing automated recovery procedures. In permissioned environments, BFT protocols such as PBFT-style or validator-based variants are often used to support a known set of participants, while public decentralized networks typically rely on broader consensus designs that balance Byzantine resilience with openness and scalability. Components such as distributed consensus layers, gossip protocols for state dissemination, and health-check mechanisms ensure resilience and continuous availability of AI services.

Network topology considerations

Network topology directly influences performance, communication overhead, and scalability. **Peer-to-peer** (**P2P**) topologies promote decentralization through direct node-to-node communication but may introduce routing and latency challenges. Federated topologies simplify coordination via aggregation servers but risk partial centralization. Hybrid models blend P2P data exchange with aggregation services to balance decentralization with efficiency. A clear definition of node roles (trainers, aggregators, validators) and communication protocols is critical for optimizing data and model distribution.

Incorporating edge computing and resource utilization

Decentralized AI often leverages heterogeneous compute resources, including edge devices positioned closer to data sources. This reduces latency, optimizes bandwidth, and enhances privacy by keeping sensitive data local. Architects must support distributed workloads across edge and cloud nodes through resource-aware scheduling, load balancing, and data locality management. Edge nodes can perform preprocessing or inference tasks, alleviating pressure on central or blockchain nodes and improving overall throughput.

Case examples

Practical implementations highlight the balance between decentralization and production readiness. For instance, federated learning systems integrated with Ethereum smart contracts employ layered architectures where contracts manage participant registration and model versioning, off-chain nodes handle training and inference, and IPFS supports distributed storage. A real-world example is Ocean Protocol, which uses a compute-to-data model to keep data in place while enabling secure AI and machine learning workflows, showing how production systems can preserve privacy without sacrificing utility. Another example uses microservices deployed via Kubernetes, with a blockchain anchoring model hashes and facilitating secure payments. These cases demonstrate how production architectures combine decentralization with pragmatic requirements for performance, maintainability, and compliance.

Deployment strategies and CI/CD

Efficient and reliable deployment strategies are at the heart of building production-ready decentralized AI systems. Unlike traditional centralized AI deployments, decentralized AI involves complex networks of distributed nodes, blockchain interactions, and federated learning workflows, which together demand sophisticated automation and coordination mechanisms. **Continuous integration and continuous deployment** (**CI/CD**) pipelines tailored for decentralized AI environments enable rapid, secure, and consistent delivery of AI models, smart contracts, and system updates at scale.

Understanding the challenges in decentralized AI deployment

Deployment in decentralized AI systems fundamentally differs from traditional centralized approaches, introducing complexities that demand specialized strategies for reliable production operation.

These interconnected challenges of heterogeneous infrastructure, unreliable networks, coordination overhead, security risks, and versioning complexity require purpose-built deployment strategies that balance decentralization benefits with production reliability. Addressing them systematically enables decentralized AI systems to achieve the scalability, resilience, and security needed for enterprise-grade operations.

Deployment in decentralized AI systems presents unique challenges, including:

- **Multiple independent nodes**: Decentralized AI systems operate across diverse nodes that may be geographically distributed, running heterogeneous hardware and software environments.
- **Network variability**: Network variability also raises classic distributed-systems trade-offs around partition tolerance, meaning that during network partitions the system may need to choose between stronger consistency and higher availability, with decentralized AI deployments often accepting some eventual consistency to preserve operation across unreliable links. Nodes communicate over public or semi-public networks with variable latency and availability, requiring resilient deployment processes.
- **Coordination complexity**: Deployment must synchronously or asynchronously update AI models, federated learning protocols, smart contracts, and infrastructure components to maintain system consistency.
- **Security considerations**: Each deployment must safeguard against unauthorized alterations, ensuring that updates are signed, verified, and compliant with decentralized governance policies.
- **Version control and rollback**: Managing versions of AI models, smart contracts, and codebases across multiple nodes demands robust versioning and rollback mechanisms.

Key principles for deployment in decentralized AI

Successful decentralized AI deployment requires adherence to core principles that transform inherent challenges into operational strengths, ensuring reliability, security, and scalability across distributed environments.

These principles of automation, decentralized governance, security-first design, comprehensive observability, and deployment idempotency provide the foundation for production-grade decentralized AI systems that maintain decentralization benefits while achieving enterprise reliability.

Effective deployment strategies must adhere to:

- **Automation**: Manual deployment processes are impractical at decentralized scales. Automated CI/CD pipelines are essential for rapid iteration while minimizing human error.

- **Decentralized coordination**: Deployment orchestration must support decentralized control, potentially integrating governance-based approvals and multi-signature validations.
- **Security and compliance**: Enforce code signing, identity verification, and compliance checks at each deployment stage.
- **Observability**: Integrate monitoring for deployment health, enabling rapid detection and response to failures.
- **Idempotency**: Deployments must be repeatable without adverse effects to enable safe retries or rollbacks.

CI/CD pipelines

CI/CD pipelines form the automation backbone for decentralized AI, enabling rapid iteration across distributed networks while maintaining consistency, security, and reliability.

Traditional CI/CD transforms dramatically in decentralized AI environments, requiring blockchain-integrated verification, multi-signature approvals, and automated smart contract testing alongside conventional code validation. Pipeline stages must incorporate decentralized model validation, cross-chain compatibility checks, and federated testing across heterogeneous node configurations to ensure global consistency without central coordination. Immutable audit trails through blockchain logging provide tamper-proof deployment histories, while automated rollback mechanisms leverage consensus protocols for safe reversion across autonomous participants.

CI/CD pipelines in decentralized AI systems span numerous components:

- **Code integration**: Developers submit changes to AI algorithms, model training code, smart contract logic (e.g., Solidity), or infrastructure configurations. Automated builds and static analysis validate code quality.
- **Automated testing**: Unit, integration, and security tests are executed in simulated decentralized environments or testnets to verify correctness and performance.
- **Model packaging and versioning**: AI models and artifacts are packaged using container images or artifact repositories, with semantic versioning ensuring traceability.
- **Smart contract compilation and deployment**: Smart contracts undergo compilation, formal verification, third-party security auditing, and deployment to blockchain test environments before production deployment, as external audits are typically mandatory for production blockchain systems to identify vulnerabilities before irreversible deployment.
- **Multi-node rollout**: Deployment orchestration tools automate the release of AI models and updates across numerous decentralized nodes, handling network variance and node heterogeneity.

- **Governance integration**: On-chain governance mechanisms can trigger deployment approvals or rollbacks based on community votes or automated rules.
- **Monitoring and rollback**: Post-deployment monitoring assesses system health and AI model performance. Automated rollback procedures revert to previous stable versions upon anomaly detection.

Tools and frameworks supporting decentralized AI CI/CD

Specialized tools bridge traditional DevOps with Web3 requirements, enabling secure, automated model deployment across heterogeneous blockchain networks.

Key frameworks like Hardhat and Foundry provide smart contract testing with gas optimization and fuzzing capabilities essential for AI model governance contracts. GitHub Actions with `Web3.py` integration automates cross-chain deployments while Chainlink's automation network triggers decentralized oracle updates for model validation. IPFS pinning services combined with Arweave permanent storage ensure immutable model artifacts, while Cortex.ai and SingularityNET platforms offer native CI/CD for on-chain AI inference endpoints.

The following tools form a comprehensive ecosystem for implementing decentralized AI CI/CD pipelines, spanning containerization, blockchain development, federated learning, GitOps automation, traditional CI/CD platforms, and security validation:

- **Containerization and orchestration**: Docker and Kubernetes facilitate the packaging and scalable deployment of AI services across distributed environments.
- **Blockchain development suites**: Tools such as Hardhat, Truffle, and Remix streamline development, testing, and deployment of smart contracts, with Foundry increasingly dominant in Ethereum workflows due to its Rust-based speed and native testing capabilities.
- **Federated learning frameworks**: TensorFlow Federated or PySyft integrate into CI pipelines for federated model updates and validation.
- **GitOps and infrastructure as code**: Git-based declarative deployment combined with tools like Flux and ArgoCD enables automated infrastructure provisioning.
- **CI/CD platforms**: Jenkins, GitHub Actions, GitLab CI, and CircleCI provide extensible automation pipelines.
- **Security and compliance**: **Static Application Security Testing (SAST)**, dynamic analysis, and formal verification tools are integrated into CI/CD workflows.

Deployment strategies in practice

Proven deployment patterns adapted for decentralized AI ensure zero-downtime updates across global node networks while maintaining blockchain consensus and model integrity. Battle-tested patterns ensure zero-downtime updates across global decentralized AI networks while preserving blockchain consensus, model integrity, and continuous availability.

Blue-green deployments maintain parallel environments for safe smart contract and model validation before traffic switching, while canary releases gradually expose updates to node subsets with real-time performance monitoring. Rolling updates sequentially refresh infrastructure with minimal disruption, complemented by immutable deployments that guarantee full traceability through versioned container images and on-chain artifacts. On-chain coordination via multi-signature contracts and automated triggers provides trustless governance for synchronized global rollouts across heterogeneous networks.

These strategies combine traditional DevOps techniques with Web3-specific coordination mechanisms to achieve safe, observable rollouts in permissionless environments:

- **Blue-green deployments**: Maintain parallel production environments to test new AI models or smart contract versions safely before switching live traffic, complemented by shadow deployments or traffic mirroring that validate inference behavior under real production loads without affecting user-facing outputs.
- **Canary releases**: Gradually roll out updates to a subset of nodes or users, monitoring effects and expanding the rollout only upon performance validation.
- **Rolling updates**: Sequentially update nodes with minimal operational disruption, enabling continuous availability.
- **Immutable deployments**: Deploy immutable container images and smart contract versions, ensuring traceability and simplifying rollback.
- **On-chain coordination**: Use blockchain-based triggers and multi-signature contracts to govern deployment approvals and orchestrate synchronized updates.

Managing dependencies and versioning

Robust versioning prevents deployment failures across decentralized AI ecosystems where model, contract, and infrastructure incompatibilities cascade globally. Precise versioning and lock mechanisms safeguard decentralized AI pipelines against version drift, ensuring seamless interoperability across models, smart contracts, and distributed nodes.

Semantic versioning (**SemVer**) standardizes releases with **`MAJOR.MINOR.PATCH`** notation to signal breaking changes, additions, or fixes across AI models and immutable smart contracts. Dependency lock files like **`package-lock.json`** or Poetry locks combined with Docker image digests guarantee reproducible builds across heterogeneous environments, while backward compatibility guarantees enable safe incremental upgrades without network-wide disruptions. These practices cut deployment failures by up to 80% in multi-versioned blockchain-AI systems.

Comprehensive dependency management ensures that deployments do not produce incompatibilities:

- SemVer across AI models, codebases, and smart contracts clarifies compatibility.
- Dependency lock files and container image digests prevent drift between environments.
- Backward compatibility is maintained during incremental updates to avoid service disruption.

To sum up, deployment strategies combined with robust CI/CD pipelines form the backbone of operational excellence for decentralized AI systems. Automating complex, cross-node deployments while embedding rigorous security and governance ensures that decentralized AI networks remain agile, reliable, and secure, even as they scale globally. This capability enables organizations to confidently evolve their decentralized AI.

Infrastructure requirements

Building decentralized AI systems at production scale requires a carefully designed infrastructure that integrates distributed compute, storage, networking, security, and compliance capabilities. Unlike centralized architectures, where resources are tightly controlled within data centers, decentralized AI must operate across heterogeneous nodes that are often geographically dispersed and managed by diverse organizations. This environment demands infrastructure that is resilient, scalable, secure, and cost-effective, while remaining adaptable to the specialized needs of blockchain-integrated AI workflows.

Compute infrastructure

At the heart of decentralized AI lies the compute infrastructure, which provides the raw processing power required to train, deploy, and sustain intelligent systems across distributed environments. Unlike centralized architectures that rely on tightly managed clusters within data centers, decentralized AI must harness a diverse set of compute resources spanning edge devices, enterprise servers, cloud-based virtual machines, and specialized accelerators such as **graphics processing units** (**GPUs**) and **tensor processing units** (**TPUs**). This heterogeneity introduces both opportunities and challenges, requiring careful orchestration to achieve efficiency, scalability, and resilience.

The following compute infrastructure delivers the processing power essential for training, deploying, and maintaining AI systems in distributed networks:

- **Edge computing**: Edge devices such as **Internet of Things** (**IoT**) sensors, smartphones, and embedded systems enable localized inference, reducing latency and bandwidth consumption by processing data closer to its source. These nodes are critical for real-time applications like autonomous vehicles, industrial automation, and healthcare monitoring.

- **High-performance clusters**: GPU and TPU clusters provide the computational backbone for large-scale training workloads. Their parallel processing capabilities allow decentralized AI systems to handle massive datasets and complex models, ensuring rapid convergence and high accuracy.
- **Cloud and hybrid infrastructure**: Cloud-based virtual machines and containerized environments offer elasticity, enabling workloads to scale dynamically based on demand. Hybrid models combine on-premises resources with cloud platforms, balancing cost efficiency with performance and compliance requirements.
- **Scheduling and orchestration**: Efficient workload distribution across heterogeneous nodes requires advanced scheduling frameworks. Tools like Kubernetes and Ray orchestrate containerized AI services, ensuring portability, dynamic scaling, and optimal resource utilization across distributed environments.
- **Fault tolerance and resilience**: Compute nodes must be continuously monitored, with failover mechanisms in place to reroute tasks when nodes fail or become unavailable. Distributed checkpointing and redundancy strategies ensure that training and inference can continue seamlessly despite disruptions.

By integrating edge computing, high-performance clusters, cloud elasticity, and robust orchestration, decentralized AI compute infrastructure transforms a fragmented ecosystem into a cohesive and resilient platform. This foundation enables organizations to scale AI workloads across diverse environments while maintaining efficiency, reliability, and adaptability to evolving demands.

Storage infrastructure

In decentralized AI systems, storage plays a critical role in ensuring that data, models, and intermediate results can be accessed, shared, and updated across a distributed network of nodes. Unlike centralized environments where storage is consolidated in a single data center, decentralized AI requires a multi-layered storage architecture that balances performance, scalability, and security across heterogeneous participants.

Decentralized AI systems require storage solutions capable of managing large datasets, trained models, and transaction metadata across a distributed network. Key considerations include:

- **Distributed file systems**: Frameworks such as **Hadoop Distributed File System (HDFS)** or Ceph provide a unified namespace across geographically dispersed nodes, enabling large datasets to be partitioned and replicated for fault tolerance and parallel access.

- **Object storage**: Cloud-native solutions like Amazon S3 or MinIO are often used to store unstructured data such as images, video, and sensor streams. Their scalability and API-driven access make them ideal for decentralized AI workloads.
- **Blockchain-integrated storage**: Decentralized storage layers such as IPFS or Filecoin can be integrated with blockchain frameworks to ensure immutability, provenance, and verifiable access control for sensitive AI datasets.
- **Caching and edge storage**: To reduce latency, frequently accessed data and lightweight models can be cached at the edge, enabling real-time inference without constant reliance on centralized repositories.
- **Data versioning and model management**: Systems must support version control for datasets and models, ensuring reproducibility and traceability across distributed training cycles. Tools like **Data Version Control** (**DVC**) and MLflow are commonly employed for this purpose.

A well-architected storage layer ensures that decentralized AI systems can handle massive volumes of data while maintaining resilience, security, and compliance. By combining distributed file systems, object stores, blockchain-based storage, and edge caching, organizations can create a robust foundation for scalable AI workflows that operate seamlessly across diverse environments.

Network infrastructure

The effectiveness of decentralized AI systems depends heavily on the robustness of their underlying network architecture. Unlike centralized deployments, where communication flows within tightly controlled data centers, decentralized AI must operate across geographically dispersed nodes connected through heterogeneous networks. This introduces unique challenges in bandwidth management, latency reduction, security, and interoperability:

- **Bandwidth and latency**: Training and inference workloads often involve large volumes of data exchange. High-performance GPU clusters require fast interconnects, while edge devices rely on constrained wireless links. Network design must balance throughput with latency, ensuring real-time responsiveness for inference while supporting bulk transfers for training.
- **Interoperability**: Nodes may operate across diverse environments—enterprise LANs, public cloud networks, or mobile edge infrastructures. Protocols and APIs must be standardized to enable seamless communication, regardless of the underlying hardware or administrative domain.
- **Resilience and fault tolerance**: Decentralized AI networks must withstand node failures, intermittent connectivity, and dynamic topology changes. Techniques such as redundant routing, peer-to-peer overlays, and adaptive load balancing help maintain system continuity.

- **Security and privacy**: Since nodes may be managed by different entities, secure communication channels are essential. Encryption, authentication, and Zero Trust networking models ensure that sensitive data and model parameters remain protected during transmission.
- **Blockchain integration**: In workflows where blockchain is used for coordination or provenance, the network must support consensus protocols that require frequent message exchanges. This adds additional overhead, making efficient network design critical for scalability.

A well-architected network layer transforms decentralized AI from a fragmented set of nodes into a cohesive ecosystem. By combining high-throughput interconnects, resilient routing, secure communication, and standardized protocols, organizations can build networks that support scalable, trustworthy, and efficient AI operations across diverse environments.

Security and compliance infrastructure

Security and compliance are foundational pillars in the design of decentralized AI systems. Unlike centralized environments where governance is enforced within a single data center, decentralized AI operates across heterogeneous nodes managed by multiple organizations, often spanning jurisdictions with diverse regulatory frameworks. This distributed nature introduces unique risks that must be addressed through layered security and rigorous compliance strategies.

Production-ready decentralized AI infrastructure mandates robust security tooling embedded across compute, storage, and network layers:

- **Data security**: Sensitive datasets and model parameters must be protected during storage, transmission, and computation. Encryption at rest and in transit, **trusted execution environments** (**TEEs**) like Intel SGX, secure enclaves, and privacy-preserving techniques such as homomorphic encryption or differential privacy are essential to safeguard information across untrusted networks.
- **Identity and access management**: Nodes participating in decentralized AI must authenticate securely and enforce fine-grained access controls. Zero Trust models, role-based access, and decentralized identity frameworks ensure that only authorized entities can contribute to or consume AI services.
- **Compliance with regulations**: Operating across multiple geographies requires adherence to laws such as GDPR, HIPAA, or emerging AI-specific regulations. Compliance frameworks must be embedded into system design, ensuring auditability, explainability, and accountability for AI decisions.
- **Blockchain integration for trust**: Blockchain can serve as a trust layer, recording immutable logs of data access, model updates, and system events. This ensures provenance, transparency, and verifiable accountability across decentralized participants.

- **Monitoring and incident response**: Continuous monitoring of nodes and networks is critical to detect anomalies, intrusions, or compliance violations. Automated incident response mechanisms must be in place to isolate compromised nodes and restore system integrity without disrupting global operations.

By embedding security and compliance into every layer of the infrastructure, decentralized AI systems can achieve resilience and trustworthiness. This not only protects sensitive data and models but also ensures that organizations can scale AI deployments responsibly across diverse regulatory and operational environments.

Scalability and elasticity

Scalability and elasticity are defining characteristics of decentralized AI infrastructure, enabling systems to adapt seamlessly to fluctuating workloads and expanding demands. Unlike centralized environments, where scaling often involves adding capacity within a single data center, decentralized AI must orchestrate resources across a diverse and geographically dispersed network of nodes. This requires infrastructure that can dynamically expand, contract, and rebalance workloads without compromising performance, reliability, or compliance. These characteristics define decentralized AI infrastructure, enabling dynamic adaptation to varying workloads across global node networks:

- **Horizontal and vertical scaling**: Horizontal scaling involves adding more nodes, such as edge devices, servers, or GPU clusters, to increase capacity, while vertical scaling enhances the capabilities of individual nodes by upgrading hardware or accelerators. Decentralized AI often relies on a hybrid of both approaches to balance efficiency and cost.

- **Elastic resource allocation**: Elasticity ensures that compute, storage, and networking resources can be provisioned or released on demand. Cloud-native orchestration frameworks like Kubernetes and Ray enable containerized AI services to scale dynamically, responding to workload spikes or reductions in real time.

- **Load balancing**: Intelligent load balancing distributes tasks across heterogeneous nodes, optimizing throughput while preventing bottlenecks. Adaptive algorithms account for node availability, latency, and energy constraints, ensuring efficient utilization of resources across the network.

- **Resilience under scale**: As systems scale, resilience becomes critical. Fault-tolerant mechanisms such as distributed checkpointing, redundancy strategies, and automated failover ensure that scaling does not introduce fragility. Elastic scaling must be paired with robust monitoring to maintain system integrity.

- **Cost efficiency**: Elastic scaling allows organizations to align resource consumption with demand, avoiding over-provisioning while ensuring performance during peak workloads. This balance is essential for cost-effective decentralized AI deployments, especially when spanning multiple administrative domains.

By embedding scalability and elasticity into the compute, storage, and networking layers, decentralized AI systems can grow organically, adapt to dynamic workloads, and maintain resilience across diverse environments. This flexibility transforms decentralized AI from a static infrastructure into a living ecosystem capable of evolving alongside the complexity of modern applications.

Monitoring and management

Effective monitoring and management are essential to sustaining decentralized AI systems at a production scale. Unlike centralized environments where oversight is confined to a single data center, decentralized AI spans heterogeneous nodes distributed across geographies, administrative domains, and ownership boundaries. This complexity requires a comprehensive framework that ensures visibility, accountability, and operational continuity across the entire ecosystem:

- **Observability**: Unlike traditional monitoring, which tracks predefined metrics, observability enables teams to infer unknown system states from telemetry data (logs, traces, metrics), supporting root-cause analysis across decentralized nodes. Logs, traces, and performance indicators must be collected from diverse nodes, enabling holistic insights into workload execution, latency, and resource utilization. Tools like Prometheus and Grafana can provide real-time dashboards for system health.

- **Automated monitoring**: Continuous monitoring of compute, storage, and network layers is critical to detect anomalies, failures, or compliance violations. Automated agents can proactively identify bottlenecks, trigger alerts, and initiate corrective actions without human intervention.

- **Policy enforcement**: Management frameworks must enforce policies related to resource allocation, security, and compliance. This includes ensuring that workloads adhere to regulatory requirements, access controls, and organizational governance standards across distributed environments.

- **Lifecycle management**: Decentralized AI workloads evolve continuously, requiring lifecycle management for datasets, models, and services. Versioning, deployment pipelines, and rollback mechanisms ensure reproducibility and stability during updates.

- **Incident response and recovery**: When failures or breaches occur, rapid incident response is vital. Automated failover, distributed checkpointing, and recovery protocols allow systems to restore functionality while minimizing downtime and data loss.

- **Human-in-the-loop oversight**: While automation is central to monitoring and management, human oversight remains indispensable. Experts must validate alerts, interpret anomalies, and make strategic decisions in complex scenarios where automated systems may lack contextual judgment.

By embedding robust monitoring and management practices into decentralized AI infrastructure, organizations can achieve transparency, resilience, and trustworthiness. This ensures that systems not only scale effectively but also remain secure, compliant, and responsive to evolving operational demands.

Monitoring and observability

In decentralized AI systems, monitoring and observability serve as foundational pillars for maintaining operational integrity, security, and performance optimization. Unlike centralized architectures, decentralized environments span diverse geographic regions and administrative domains, making real-time visibility both complex and indispensable. A well-architected observability framework enables system health tracking, distributed troubleshooting, and continuous refinement of AI workflows across the network.

Understanding monitoring and observability

Monitoring involves the structured collection, processing, and visualization of metrics, logs, and events from distributed components to assess system status and detect anomalies. Observability goes further by enabling deep insights into internal system states through tracing, metadata correlation, and signal analysis, supporting root cause diagnostics and predictive issue detection.

Key telemetry dimensions include:

- Node availability and resource consumption.
- Network performance (latency, throughput, error rates).
- AI indicators (model accuracy, convergence, data drift).
- Blockchain metrics (transaction volume, smart contract execution).
- Security signals (access anomalies, cryptographic validations).

Architectural components and tooling

Monitoring in decentralized AI relies on a layered architecture that integrates agents, aggregators, telemetry storage, dashboards, and tracing frameworks. Together, these components provide end-to-end visibility, enabling operators to correlate signals across nodes, networks, and blockchain layers for real-time insights.

A distributed monitoring architecture must be layered and scalable:

- **Agent-based collection**: Lightweight agents deployed across nodes gather metrics, logs, and container statistics.
- **Aggregation frameworks**: Distributed message buses like Kafka or MQTT enable scalable telemetry ingestion, with local aggregation reducing bandwidth overhead.

- **Telemetry storage**: Time-series databases (Prometheus, InfluxDB) and log indexing systems (Elasticsearch) support high-volume data retention and querying.
- **Visualization dashboards**: Tools such as Grafana provide real-time, customizable dashboards for AI, network, and blockchain observability.
- **Tracing systems**: Distributed tracing frameworks (OpenTelemetry, Jaeger) link events across AI workflows and blockchain transactions, enabling end-to-end visibility.

AI-centric observability

Observability tailored to AI workflows ensures that training, inference, and data integrity are continuously tracked. By embedding AI-specific metrics into monitoring systems, organizations gain the ability to detect drift, bias, and inefficiencies, safeguarding model performance across distributed environments.

Observability must extend to AI-specific components:

- **Training metrics**: Track loss functions, gradient updates, training duration, and resource usage.
- **Inference performance**: Monitor latency, accuracy, confidence scores, and error rates per node.
- **Data drift detection**: MLOps platforms track feature drift (input distribution shifts), concept drift (target relationship changes), and data lineage to identify performance degradation in decentralized models, enabling proactive retraining across nodes.
- **Federated learning metrics**: Measure participation rates, update quality, and convergence across nodes.

Integrating AI telemetry with system observability helps surface subtle issues such as bias drift, stale data, or synchronization delays.

Security monitoring and threat detection

Security observability is indispensable in adversarial decentralized ecosystems. Continuous monitoring of transactions, consensus events, and node behaviors augmented by AI-driven anomaly detection provides early warning against cyberattacks, data poisoning, and unauthorized access.

Security observability is critical in adversarial decentralized environments:

- Detect anomalous transactions or compute behaviors that signal node compromise.
- Monitor blockchain consensus and contract execution for irregularities.
- Use AI-driven anomaly detection to identify cyberattacks, data poisoning, or insider threats.
- Automate alerting and incident response workflows with severity-based triggers.

Automation and feedback loops

Observability data fuels automation, enabling dynamic scaling, rollback of faulty updates, and proactive remediation. Feedback loops transform monitoring insights into actionable improvements, driving continuous optimization of models, resources, and governance processes.

Observability data powers intelligent automation:

- Dynamically scale compute or reroute network traffic based on load.
- Roll back or quarantine suspect model updates or smart contracts.
- Generate governance reports and developer insights.
- Enable continuous improvement cycles for retraining, tuning, and resource optimization.

Challenges and best practices

Building effective observability frameworks requires balancing telemetry volume with efficiency, ensuring privacy through encryption, and standardizing instrumentation across layers. Best practices emphasize compliance alignment, predictive monitoring, and fostering a proactive culture of resilience and innovation:

- Manage telemetry volume with efficient sampling and aggregation.
- Protect telemetry privacy through encryption and access controls.
- Standardize cross-layer instrumentation across AI, network, and blockchain.
- Align observability with compliance frameworks for auditability.
- Promote a proactive monitoring culture that drives predictive maintenance and innovation.

Monitoring and observability in decentralized AI are not just operational necessities; they are strategic enablers. By embedding telemetry across layers and integrating AI-centric insights, organizations can confidently scale, secure, and evolve decentralized AI systems with precision and agility.

Performance optimization

Performance optimization is a cornerstone of decentralized AI system design, ensuring that distributed networks operate efficiently at scale and deliver timely insights across heterogeneous environments. Unlike centralized deployments, decentralized AI faces unique challenges such as variable network latency, diverse computational capabilities, and the overhead introduced by blockchain operations. Addressing these demands requires holistic strategies that optimize compute, communication, storage, and algorithmic efficiency.

Defining key performance indicators

Establishing clear **key performance indicators** (**KPIs**) provides the foundation for optimization, aligning system goals with measurable outcomes such as latency, throughput, resource utilization, accuracy, and energy efficiency. Optimization begins with establishing clear metrics aligned to system objectives. Critical KPIs include:

- **Latency**: Execution time for tasks such as inference or training iterations, factoring in both local compute and network delays.
- **Throughput**: Volume of data processed or model updates applied per unit time across the network.
- **Resource utilization**: Efficiency of CPU, GPU, memory, and bandwidth consumption at each node.
- **Model accuracy and quality**: Sustaining high performance while balancing speed and cost.
- **Consensus finalization time**: Blockchain-specific measure of transaction or contract confirmation speed.
- **Energy efficiency**: Power consumption is particularly vital for edge devices with limited energy budgets.

Optimizing compute workloads

Efficient use of heterogeneous compute resources requires strategies like model compression, adaptive partitioning, asynchronous execution, and caching to balance performance with scalability. Decentralized workloads must leverage heterogeneous resources effectively:

- **Model compression**: Techniques such as pruning, quantization, and distillation reduce computational demand without major accuracy loss.
- **Adaptive partitioning**: Splitting models into subcomponents distributed across nodes to balance load and minimize data transfer.
- **Asynchronous execution**: Allowing nodes to compute independently improves throughput in high-latency networks.
- **Caching and memoization**: Reusing intermediate results reduces redundant processing.

Enhancing network communication

Reducing communication overhead is critical in decentralized AI, achieved through lightweight protocols, compression techniques, aggregation strategies, and adaptive bandwidth management. Communication overhead is a major bottleneck in decentralized AI:

- **Efficient protocols**: Lightweight peer-to-peer protocols minimize handshake delays and retransmissions.
- **Delta encoding and compression**: Transmit only incremental changes or compressed updates.
- **Aggregation strategies**: Hierarchical or federated aggregation reduces communication rounds.
- **Adaptive bandwidth management**: Prioritize critical transfers and adjust frequency dynamically.

Optimizing blockchain interactions

Blockchain introduces unique performance trade-offs, mitigated by off-chain computation, transaction batching, Layer 2 scaling solutions, and gas-efficient smart contract design. Blockchain introduces performance trade-offs that must be mitigated:

- **Off-chain computation**: Heavy tasks executed off-chain with results anchored on-chain reduce latency.
- **Batching transactions**: Combining updates into single transactions lowers costs.
- **Layer 2 solutions**: Optimistic rollups (assume validity, fraud proofs) and zk-rollups (validity proofs), alongside sidechains, improve throughput and reduce confirmation delays for AI workloads.
- **Gas optimization**: Efficient smart contract design minimizes computational and storage overhead.

Continuous monitoring and feedback

Performance optimization is iterative, relying on real-time telemetry, automated adjustments, and regression testing to sustain efficiency and adapt to evolving workloads. Optimization is iterative and requires ongoing monitoring:

- **Real-time telemetry**: Capture node and network metrics to identify bottlenecks.
- **Automated adjustments**: Redistribute workloads or tune communication parameters dynamically.
- **Regression testing**: Validate new models or infrastructure changes against performance baselines.

Balancing trade-offs

Optimization requires careful negotiation between competing priorities such as speed versus accuracy, latency versus security, and resource efficiency versus cost. Optimization must balance competing priorities:

- **Performance vs. accuracy**: Compression may reduce precision; trade-offs depend on application needs.
- **Latency vs. security**: Faster blockchain interactions must not compromise consensus integrity.
- **Resource efficiency vs. cost**: Maximizing utilization reduces expenses, especially in cloud or edge deployments.

Case examples and emerging techniques

Practical implementations highlight federated learning optimizations, energy-aware scheduling, and AI-driven predictive tuning as emerging approaches to enhance decentralized AI performance.

- **Federated learning optimization**: Algorithms like FedAvg reduce communication while maintaining convergence.
- **Energy-aware scheduling**: Workloads aligned with energy availability enhance sustainability.
- **AI-driven optimization**: Predictive models anticipate workload patterns and proactively adjust configurations.

To sum it up, performance optimization in decentralized AI is a multidimensional effort that integrates compute efficiency, communication strategies, blockchain scaling, and continuous monitoring. By balancing trade-offs and adopting emerging techniques, organizations can achieve scalable, cost-effective, and resilient AI deployments across diverse distributed networks.

Disaster recovery and backup

In decentralized AI systems, **disaster recovery (DR)** and backup are indispensable for ensuring continuity, safeguarding data integrity, and maintaining resilience against failures or malicious attacks. Unlike centralized infrastructures where backups reside within controlled data centers, decentralized AI operates across heterogeneous, autonomous nodes dispersed globally. This distributed nature introduces unique challenges and necessitates tailored strategies for effective recovery and protection.

Understanding disaster recovery in decentralized AI

DR in decentralized AI must address failures ranging from hardware breakdowns and network partitions to cyberattacks and regional outages. Unlike centralized systems, recovery here involves restoring distributed compute, AI models, training states, and blockchain consensus. A resilient DR plan ensures continuity of trust, performance, and collaboration across globally dispersed nodes.

Beyond technical restoration, disaster recovery in decentralized AI also requires maintaining system integrity and stakeholder confidence. As nodes are often managed by independent organizations, recovery strategies must account for heterogeneous environments, varying resource capacities, and diverse governance models. This means DR planning is not just about technical failover. It is about coordinating across multiple administrative domains to re-establish a consistent and verifiable system state.

Another critical dimension is time sensitivity. In decentralized AI, delays in recovery can lead to model drift, data inconsistency, or loss of consensus, which may compromise the accuracy of AI outputs or the validity of blockchain transactions. Therefore, DR frameworks must prioritize rapid detection, automated response, and synchronized restoration to minimize downtime and prevent cascading failures.

Finally, disaster recovery in decentralized AI is inseparable from security and compliance considerations. Recovery processes must ensure that sensitive data remains protected during restoration, that blockchain consensus is not undermined, and that regulatory requirements such as data sovereignty and auditability are upheld even under adverse conditions.

Backup strategies for robust data protection

Backups in decentralized AI must be designed for diversity and resilience. Distributed snapshots, incremental versioning, and encrypted storage protect against data loss while ensuring compliance. Geographic replication across multiple domains further strengthens availability, making backups resistant to localized disruptions and ensuring rapid restoration when needed. Backups form the backbone of DR planning and must be adapted to decentralized environments:

- **Distributed snapshots**: Capturing model and data states across multiple nodes reduces reliance on any single point of failure.
- **Versioned and incremental backups**: Tracking incremental changes enables efficient storage and rollback to specific states.
- **Encrypted storage**: Leveraging decentralized storage networks such as IPFS or Arweave ensures confidentiality and access control.
- **Redundant replication**: Copies distributed across geographic regions enhance resilience against localized outages.

Blockchain-integrated backup and recovery

Blockchain enhances disaster recovery by anchoring trust in immutable ledgers. Audit trails provide verifiable histories of state changes, while on-chain checkpoints validate off-chain data integrity. Governance mechanisms embedded in smart contracts automate recovery decisions, ensuring transparency and reducing human error during restoration. Blockchain strengthens DR by anchoring trust and transparency:

- **Immutable audit trails**: Ledgers record all state changes, transactions, and updates for verifiable recovery points.
- **State anchoring**: On-chain checkpoints validate off-chain data and model snapshots.
- **Governance mechanisms**: Smart contracts and multi-signature protocols automate recovery decisions and rollback approvals.

Recovery procedures and automation

Automated recovery workflows are essential for minimizing downtime. Health monitoring systems detect anomalies early, while orchestrated rollbacks restore validated model versions across nodes. Synchronization protocols rebuild consistent states across distributed environments, and regular DR drills validate readiness under diverse failure scenarios. Rapid recovery depends on automation and orchestration:

- **Health monitoring**: Continuous checks trigger preemptive DR actions before full downtime.
- **Orchestrated rollbacks**: Automated workflows restore validated model versions or configurations.
- **State synchronization**: Distributed parameters and blockchain states are rebuilt to ensure consistency.
- **Testing readiness**: Regular drills validate recovery mechanisms under diverse failure scenarios by ensuring alignment with enterprise disaster recovery standards, where the **recovery time objective** (**RTO**) defines the maximum acceptable downtime before systems must be restored and the **recovery point objective** (**RPO**) specifies the maximum acceptable data loss measured in time (such as the last backup point); testing should simulate both infrastructure failures and applicationlevel disruptions to verify that recovery processes meet defined RTO and RPO thresholds, while incorporating crossteam drills across engineering, operations, and compliance ensures readiness throughout organizational layers.

Compliance and data sovereignty

DR must align with regulatory frameworks such as GDPR and HIPAA. Policies ensure sensitive data remains within authorized jurisdictions, while audit logs provide transparency for compliance audits. By embedding sovereignty and auditability into DR strategies, organizations maintain both legal adherence and stakeholder trust. Regulatory frameworks shape DR and backup policies:

- **Data localization**: Sensitive backups must comply with sovereignty laws, remaining within authorized jurisdictions.
- **Auditability**: Detailed logs of backup and recovery actions support compliance and external audits.

Challenges and future directions

Decentralized AI faces challenges in managing massive data volumes, balancing availability with security, and ensuring cost-effective recovery. Emerging technologies such as homomorphic encryption and multi-party computation promise secure, privacy-preserving backups. Future directions emphasize scalable, intelligent DR systems that adapt dynamically to evolving risks.

- **Large-scale data**: The scale of AI workloads demands cost-effective, high-capacity backup systems.
- **Balancing availability and security**: Quick access must be achieved without compromising confidentiality or blockchain integrity.
- **Emerging technologies**: Homomorphic encryption and multi-party computation promise secure backups without exposing raw data.

To sum it up, DR and backup are vital to sustaining trust, resilience, and availability in decentralized AI. By combining distributed snapshotting, blockchain-anchored integrity, automated recovery workflows, and compliance-aware policies, organizations can protect their systems against disruption and ensure sustainable innovation.

Maintenance and updates

Maintenance and updates are essential for sustaining the long-term reliability, security, and adaptability of decentralized AI systems. Unlike centralized infrastructures, decentralized networks operate across autonomous nodes managed by diverse stakeholders. This distributed nature introduces unique challenges in coordinating system changes, applying updates, and ensuring stability without disrupting ongoing AI workflows or compromising trust.

Importance of maintenance in decentralized AI

Regular maintenance ensures that AI models, smart contracts, middleware, and infrastructure remain secure, performant, and aligned with evolving requirements. Activities include bug fixes, security patches, dependency upgrades, performance tuning, and feature enhancements. In decentralized ecosystems, maintenance also strengthens trust among participants, reinforcing the credibility of shared AI services and blockchain-based governance.

Types of updates and their management

Updates in decentralized AI span models, smart contracts, middleware, and infrastructure. Each update must be carefully versioned, validated, and deployed to maintain consistency across heterogeneous nodes. Effective management ensures accuracy, security, and seamless evolution of the system without disrupting ongoing workflows. Updates in decentralized AI span multiple domains:

- **AI model updates**: Retraining, fine-tuning, or replacing models to incorporate new data, improve accuracy, or mitigate bias.
- **Smart contract upgrades**: Revising logic to fix vulnerabilities, add features, or adapt to regulatory changes.
- **Software and middleware updates**: Keeping APIs, runtimes, and orchestration tools current.
- **Infrastructure adjustments**: Scaling resources, modifying network policies, or reconfiguring node parameters.

Each update requires version control, validation, and deployment protocols to maintain consistency across heterogeneous environments.

Coordination and governance for updates

Governance frameworks provide transparency and collective oversight in decentralized environments. On-chain voting, multi-signature approvals, and detailed upgrade proposals ensure that updates align with community interests, compliance mandates, and operational resilience. This coordination fosters trust among diverse stakeholders. Governance frameworks ensure updates are transparent and community-driven:

- **On-chain governance**: Proposals, voting, and consensus processes democratize decision-making.
- **Multi-signature authorization**: Critical updates require multiple trusted approvals, reducing risks of unilateral changes.
- **Upgrade proposals**: Detailed plans include risk assessments, testing outcomes, and rollback strategies.

These mechanisms align maintenance actions with community interests, compliance mandates, and operational resilience.

Technical approaches to applying updates

Applying updates requires robust technical strategies such as staged rollouts, backward compatibility, hot swapping, automated verification, and rollback mechanisms. These approaches minimize disruption, safeguard interoperability, and ensure that updates enhance system performance without introducing instability. Applying updates in decentralized AI requires careful orchestration through the following:

- **Staged rollouts**: Incremental deployment across nodes to monitor impact.
- **Backward compatibility**: Ensuring interoperability between old and new versions during transitions.

- **Hot swapping**: Live updates for certain components without downtime can enhance agility, but in blockchain ecosystems, proxybased upgrade patterns carry governance and security implications. Smart contract upgrades performed in production may expose systems to risks such as unauthorized logic changes, misaligned governance approvals, or attack surfaces in proxy contracts. Testing and governance controls must therefore ensure that hot swaps preserve integrity, comply with consensus rules, and maintain trust across stakeholders.
- **Automated verification**: Continuous integration, code reviews, and formal verification for smart contracts.
- **Rollback mechanisms**: Swift reversion to stable versions in case of faults.

Handling challenges in update processes

Decentralized systems face challenges including node heterogeneity, network latency, security risks, and coordination overhead. Addressing these requires adaptive pipelines, secure update channels, and efficient consensus models to maintain reliability across diverse environments. Decentralized environments face distinct hurdles, such as:

- **Node heterogeneity**: Diverse hardware and software stacks complicate uniform updates.
- **Network latency**: Propagation delays can cause temporary inconsistencies.
- **Security risks**: Updates must be safeguarded against malicious injection.
- **Coordination overhead**: Synchronizing large networks requires efficient communication and consensus.

Robust pipelines and adaptive strategies mitigate these challenges.

Monitoring and continuous improvement

Post-update monitoring validates deployment success and uncovers refinement opportunities through telemetry, logs, and feedback loops. Telemetry streams capture model drift, latency spikes, and resource anomalies in real-time, feeding AI-driven analytics for proactive optimization. Audit trails ensure on-chain verifiability of updates, while A/B testing compares new versions against baselines to quantify improvements in accuracy and efficiency. User feedback integrates via sentiment analysis on oracle-reported metrics, closing the loop for iterative enhancements that sustain long-term value without regressions.

Automation and tooling support

Modern DevOps practices and tooling, such as Kubernetes, Terraform, GitOps, and blockchain deployment frameworks, streamline maintenance workflows. Automation reduces human error, accelerates update cycles, and ensures reproducibility, enabling decentralized AI systems to evolve confidently. Modern DevOps practices are adapted for decentralized AI:

- IaC (Terraform, Ansible) ensures reproducibility.
- CI/CD pipelines streamline deployments.
- Container orchestration (Kubernetes, Docker) supports scalability.
- Blockchain deployment frameworks manage smart contract upgrades securely.

Automation reduces human error, accelerates update cycles, and fosters operational consistency across diverse nodes.

To sum it up, maintenance and updates are not one-time tasks but ongoing commitments that sustain decentralized AI systems. By combining governance, technical rigor, automation, and continuous monitoring, organizations can evolve their platforms confidently, delivering secure, scalable, and trustworthy AI services across dynamic, multi-stakeholder ecosystems.

Scaling strategies

Scaling is not a feature that can be added to a decentralized AI system after the fact; it is a design property that must be engineered into the architecture from the beginning. As participation grows, workloads intensify, and geographic reach expands, systems that were not designed with scaling in mind will encounter performance degradation, coordination failures, and economic inefficiencies that cannot be resolved through incremental infrastructure additions alone. In centralized AI architectures, scaling is primarily a resource provisioning problem: adding compute, storage, and network capacity within a controlled environment that a single organization manages. In decentralized AI systems, scaling requires orchestrating those resources across globally dispersed nodes operating under different organizational control, connected by networks of variable reliability, and coordinated through consensus mechanisms that impose their own scaling constraints. Meeting the scaling demands of production decentralized AI requires strategies that address compute, storage, networking, consensus, and economic sustainability as an integrated whole.

Horizontal and vertical scaling

The distinction between vertical and horizontal scaling in decentralized AI carries different implications than it does in centralized environments, and understanding both dimensions is necessary for designing scaling strategies that are practically effective.

Vertical scaling improves the capability of individual nodes by upgrading their hardware: more powerful CPUs, additional or higher-performance GPUs, expanded memory, or faster storage. These improvements increase the throughput and reduce the latency of workloads running on the upgraded node without requiring changes to network topology or coordination protocols. Vertical scaling is a practical and often cost-effective first response to performance pressure on nodes that are clearly resource constrained. Its fundamental limitation is that hardware improvement has a ceiling, and that ceiling is reached faster and at a higher cost than the scaling requirements of growing decentralized networks typically demand. Vertical scaling is a tactical tool, not a strategic foundation.

Horizontal scaling is the primary mechanism for decentralized AI systems, expanding network capacity by adding nodes that contribute additional compute, storage, and bandwidth to the collective system. Unlike vertical scaling, horizontal scaling has no inherent upper bound; the network can continue to expand as long as new participants can be onboarded and their contributions coordinated effectively. Realizing this potential requires careful engineering of the onboarding process, workload distribution mechanisms, and coordination protocols so that new nodes can be integrated without disrupting ongoing operations. Workloads must be dynamically redistributed to leverage newly available capacity, but scaling introduces coordination overhead that often grows in complexity as communication patterns approach $O(n^2)$ in large peertopeer networks. If coordination costs rise faster than the capacity new nodes contribute, the system risks hitting a scaling ceiling imposed not by resource availability but by communication inefficiency.

Dynamic resource management

The efficiency with which a decentralized AI network utilizes its available resources determines how effectively its scaling investments translate into performance improvements. A network that adds nodes but fails to distribute workloads intelligently across them will see diminishing returns from horizontal scaling investment. The following intelligent resource orchestration maximizes decentralized AI efficiency through dynamic workload allocation across heterogeneous global nodes:

- **Auto-scaling** mechanisms that monitor system load and dynamically provision or release resources in response to workload demand prevent both the underutilization costs of over-provisioning and the performance degradation costs of under-provisioning. In cloud-integrated decentralized AI deployments, auto-scaling policies can leverage elastic cloud infrastructure to absorb demand spikes without permanently expanding the node population, reducing the long-term cost of capacity that is only needed intermittently.

- **Workload scheduling** across heterogeneous nodes requires awareness of the specific capabilities and current load of each available node, assigning training tasks to nodes with appropriate GPU resources, inference tasks to nodes with low-latency network connectivity, and storage-intensive operations to nodes with sufficient capacity and throughput. Schedulers that optimize placement decisions based on real-time node telemetry achieve substantially higher resource utilization than static or round robin assignment policies.

- **Load balancing** distributes incoming requests and in-progress workloads across available nodes to prevent any single node from becoming a throughput bottleneck while others remain underutilized. In decentralized AI systems where nodes enter and leave the network dynamically, load balancers must continuously rebalance workload distribution in response to changing node availability rather than relying on static routing configurations.

- **Data locality management** ensures that computation is placed as close as possible to the data it requires, minimizing the volume of data that must traverse network connections during processing. In edge computing contexts where nodes are positioned at or near data sources, data locality management is particularly critical: routing edge-generated data to remote processing nodes for inference when local processing is feasible wastes bandwidth, introduces latency, and often violates the privacy rationale for edge deployment in the first place.

Federated learning scalability

Federated learning introduces scaling challenges that are distinct from those of conventional distributed computing, arising from the specific communication and aggregation patterns that federated training requires.

Communication efficiency

It becomes the primary scaling constraint in federated learning systems as the number of participating nodes grows. Each training round requires model updates to be transmitted from training nodes to the aggregation infrastructure and updated global models to be redistributed back to training nodes. Without compression and sparsification techniques that reduce the volume of data transmitted per round, communication costs grow proportionally with participant count and model size, eventually dominating total system cost. Gradient compression, quantization of model updates, and selective transmission of only the most significant update components reduce communication volume substantially without proportionate degradation in model convergence quality.

Aggregation strategy

It determines how individual node model updates are combined into updated global models, and the scalability of aggregation is directly affected by this choice. Centralized aggregation through a single aggregator is simple to implement but creates a throughput bottleneck and a single point of failure as participant count scales. Hierarchical aggregation, where updates are first combined within geographic or organizational clusters before being aggregated globally, distributes aggregation load across the network and reduces the volume of data that must traverse high-latency inter-cluster connections.

Participant selection

Participant selection for each training round balances the statistical quality of training data representation against the coordination overhead of involving large numbers of participants simultaneously. Selecting a representative subset of available participants for each round rather than requiring all participants to contribute simultaneously reduces coordination overhead and improves convergence speed by prioritizing participants whose local data provides the most informative updates for the current training state.

Robustness to dropouts

It is an essential scaling property for federated learning systems that operate at a scale where participant availability cannot be guaranteed. Training protocols that can tolerate a configurable fraction of selected participants failing to contribute their updates without stalling the training round or significantly degrading convergence quality enable the system to maintain training progress under the variable participation conditions that characterize large decentralized networks.

Blockchain scaling solutions

The blockchain coordination layer presents its own scaling challenges that are independent of but interact with the scaling requirements of the AI computation layers above it. Consensus protocols that provide strong security guarantees typically do so at the cost of throughput and latency properties that limit how frequently on-chain coordination can occur without becoming a bottleneck.

Layer 2 scaling solutions

They address blockchain throughput constraints by moving the majority of transaction processing off the main chain while preserving the security guarantees of the main chain for final settlement. State channels enable direct bilateral or multilateral transaction streams between participants that are settled on-chain only when participants choose to close the channel, reducing on-chain transaction volume by orders of magnitude for high-frequency coordination patterns. Rollup protocols batch large numbers of off-chain transactions into a single on-chain proof that can be verified without replaying individual transactions, achieving similar throughput improvements across a broader range of interaction patterns.

Sharding

It partitions the blockchain state and transaction processing workload across multiple parallel validator subsets, each responsible for a distinct shard of the overall state. Transactions that affect the state within a single shard are processed in parallel across shards, multiplying overall throughput by the number of shards. Cross-shard transactions that affect state in multiple shards require additional coordination but remain manageable when the proportion of cross-shard interactions is low relative to within-shard interactions.

Sidechains and application-specific chains

They enable decentralized AI workflows to operate on blockchain infrastructure optimized for their specific requirements, higher throughput, lower latency, or different consensus mechanisms, while maintaining the ability to interact with main chain assets and governance through bridge protocols. This approach allows the coordination layer to be tuned for AI workflow requirements without requiring changes to main chain protocols that affect all ecosystem participants.

Optimized consensus mechanisms

Optimized consensus mechanisms tailored to the trust assumptions and participant characteristics of specific decentralized AI deployments can achieve substantially better throughput and latency than general-purpose consensus protocols. Delegated proof of stake systems that concentrate validation among a smaller set of high-performance validators achieve faster finality at the cost of some decentralization. Byzantine fault tolerant consensus protocols optimized for known validator sets achieve high throughput in permissioned or semi-permissioned contexts where the participant population is stable and bounded.

Multi-cloud and edge integration

Decentralized AI systems that integrate across cloud and edge infrastructure gain scaling flexibility that neither environment provides alone, enabling workload placement decisions that optimize for performance, cost, compliance, and resilience simultaneously.

Cloud bursting

It extends decentralized AI workloads onto cloud infrastructure during demand spikes that exceed the capacity of on-premises or dedicated node infrastructure. By treating cloud capacity as an elastic extension of the permanent node network rather than a separate environment, cloud bursting enables systems to absorb demand variability without the capital expenditure of provisioning for peak load. Integration with multiple cloud providers reduces both cost through competitive pricing and risk through geographic and provider diversification.

Edge offloading

Edge offloading of inference workloads to nodes positioned close to data sources reduces round-trip latency for time-sensitive applications, reduces bandwidth consumption by processing data locally rather than transmitting raw inputs to central infrastructure, and enables operation in environments where connectivity to central infrastructure is intermittent or bandwidth-constrained. As edge hardware capabilities continue to improve, the class of AI workloads that can be effectively served at the edge expands, increasing the fraction of system load that can be handled without central infrastructure involvement.

Geographic distribution

Geographic distribution of node infrastructure across multiple regions and availability zones improves resilience by ensuring that regional infrastructure failures affect only a fraction of the overall system capacity. It also enables compliance with data residency requirements by allowing data to be processed within the jurisdictions where it was generated. Geographic distribution of training nodes additionally improves the diversity of data available for federated learning, potentially improving model generalization across the varied conditions that geographically distributed deployments encounter.

Enterprise integration

Integrating decentralized AI systems into enterprise environments is among the most strategically consequential steps an organization can take in its adoption of decentralized technology and among the most technically demanding. The promise of decentralized AI is compelling: immutable audit trails, trustless coordination, federated data collaboration, and tokenized incentive models that create new forms of value across organizational boundaries. But that promise is only realized when decentralized AI capabilities can operate in concert with the enterprise systems, workflows, and governance structures that organizations already depend upon. Bridging this gap requires more than technical connectors between old and new systems. It requires a deliberate integration architecture that aligns decentralized AI capabilities with organizational goals, compliance mandates, and operational realities while preserving the decentralization properties that make the investment worthwhile. *Figure 10.2* illustrates the multi-layered architectural approach through which this connectivity is achieved across API boundaries, middleware services, data federation layers, and hybrid deployment models:

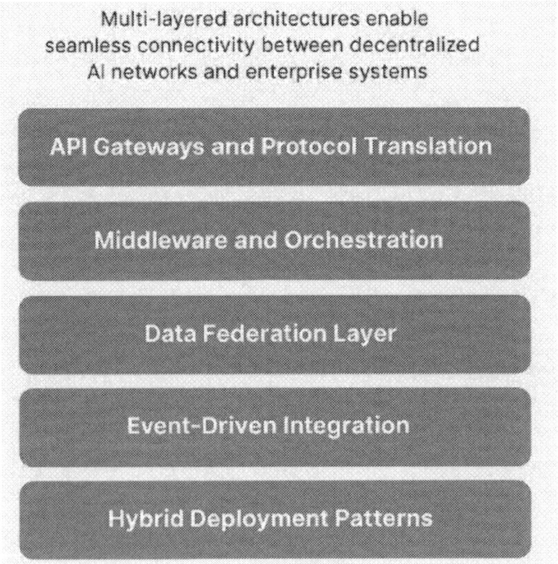

Figure 10.2: *Multi-layered enterprise integration architecture*

Understanding integration challenges

Enterprises are not blank slates awaiting decentralized transformation. They are complex, deeply interconnected ecosystems of established systems, entrenched processes, and accumulated governance obligations that have been built and refined over years or decades. Decentralized AI does not replace this ecosystem; it must integrate with it, which means confronting a set of challenges whose difficulty is easy to underestimate from the outside. These challenges are as follows:

- **Interoperability across heterogeneous systems** is the most immediately visible challenge. Enterprise environments typically include ERP platforms, CRM systems, data lakes, analytics infrastructure, and operational systems that were designed independently, use different data models, and expose different integration interfaces. Connecting decentralized AI workflows to this heterogeneous landscape requires integration layers capable of translating between the data formats, communication protocols, and consistency models of decentralized networks and the diverse interfaces of incumbent enterprise systems.

- **Legacy and modern hybridization** demand that integration strategies accommodate systems that cannot be replaced or significantly modified on the timescales of AI deployment projects. Core banking platforms, manufacturing execution systems, and healthcare record systems often carry decades of business logic that organizations cannot afford to retire. Integration architectures must allow decentralized AI capabilities to coexist with and augment these systems rather than requiring their replacement as a precondition for adoption.

- **Regulatory compliance** introduces constraints that vary by industry and jurisdiction and must be satisfied consistently across the full integrated system. Data residency requirements under GDPR, protected health information handling obligations under HIPAA, and financial data governance requirements impose specific constraints on where data can flow, how it must be protected, and what audit records must be maintained. Integration architectures that route data through decentralized networks without explicit compliance design will encounter regulatory barriers that block enterprise adoption.

- **Identity and access management** across the boundary between enterprise and decentralized systems is a persistent challenge with no single established solution. Enterprise systems rely on centralized identity providers and established access control frameworks. Decentralized AI networks rely on cryptographic identity and blockchain-based authorization. Bridging these models requires identity federation architectures that maintain security guarantees in both environments without creating administrative complexity that undermines operational manageability.

- **Enterprise-grade scalability and performance** requirements impose demands that many decentralized AI integrations initially fail to meet. Enterprise applications expect deterministic response times, high availability guarantees, and throughput capacities calibrated to organizational workload volumes. Integration layers that introduce unacceptable latency, availability dependencies on decentralized network conditions, or throughput bottlenecks will be rejected by enterprise operations teams regardless of the strategic value of the underlying capabilities.

Architectural approaches for enterprise integration

Successful enterprise integration of decentralized AI is achieved through multi-layered architectures that create clean abstraction boundaries between decentralized AI capabilities and enterprise consumption interfaces, enabling each layer to evolve independently without disrupting the others.

API and middleware layers

They form the primary integration boundary between decentralized AI networks and enterprise applications. Well-designed API gateways abstract the complexity of blockchain interactions, distributed node communication, and decentralized data access behind conventional REST or GraphQL interfaces that enterprise applications can consume without modification. Middleware services handle protocol translation, data format normalization, and consistency management between decentralized and centralized systems, insulating enterprise applications from the eventual consistency and distributed state characteristics of decentralized networks that would otherwise require changes to application logic.

Data federation and virtualization

They enable enterprise analytics and AI workloads to query and combine data that is physically distributed across decentralized storage networks without requiring data movement or centralization. Federated query engines construct unified views across distributed data sources, enabling enterprise reporting and AI training workflows to access decentralized data through familiar query interfaces while data governance policies enforce access controls and audit logging transparently at the federation layer.

Event-driven integration

It provides a real-time synchronization mechanism for enterprise workflows that must respond to state changes in decentralized AI systems as they occur. Event streaming platforms that subscribe to blockchain events, model update notifications, and decentralized governance decisions translate these signals into enterprise event formats that operational systems and monitoring infrastructure can consume. This bidirectional event integration enables decentralized AI state changes to trigger enterprise workflow actions and enterprise system events to initiate decentralized AI processes without tight coupling between the two environments.

Hybrid cloud and on-premises deployment

Hybrid cloud and on-premises deployment models allow enterprises to optimize the placement of integration components across available infrastructure. Latency-sensitive integration components can be deployed close to the enterprise systems they serve. Compliance-sensitive components can be deployed within organizational boundaries to satisfy data residency requirements. Compute-intensive AI workloads can be placed on cloud infrastructure to leverage elastic scaling capacity. Hybrid deployment architectures provide the flexibility to satisfy all of these requirements simultaneously rather than forcing a choice between them.

Security and compliance considerations

Security and compliance requirements do not diminish at the enterprise integration boundary; they intensify, because the integration layer is precisely where the trust boundaries between decentralized networks and enterprise systems must be carefully managed.

Identity federation

Identity federation using decentralized identity standards such as W3C **decentralized identifiers (DIDs)** and **verifiable credentials (VCs)** enables enterprise identity systems and blockchain ecosystems to recognize and validate each other's identity assertions without requiring a common central authority. By referencing these standards upfront, the architecture highlights how enterprise users can authenticate through familiar organizational identity providers and have their verified credentials recognized by decentralized AI systems, while blockchain participants can assert credentials that enterprise systems accept for access control decisions. This alignment with W3C standards reinforces interoperability, trust, and compliance across diverse ecosystems.

Fine-grained access control

Fine-grained access control enforced through smart contracts and policy engines ensures that every interaction between enterprise systems and decentralized AI networks is governed by explicit, auditable authorization policies. Smart contracts encode access rules that are enforced deterministically and transparently, while policy engines in the integration middleware layer apply enterprise governance policies to requests before they reach decentralized network components. The combination ensures that access controls are consistent across both environments and that neither can be bypassed through the other.

Immutable audit trails

Immutable audit trails created through blockchain logging of integration events provide the regulatory reporting foundation that enterprise compliance programs require. Every data access, model query, governance action, and system configuration change that crosses the integration boundary is recorded as a tamper-evident on-chain entry, creating an audit history that satisfies the record-keeping requirements of financial regulators, healthcare compliance frameworks, and data protection authorities without depending on the reliability of any single organization's logging infrastructure.

Privacy controls

Privacy controls, including end-to-end encryption, data anonymization, and differential privacy techniques, protect sensitive enterprise data as it flows through integration layers that may traverse infrastructure operated by multiple independent parties. Privacy-preserving computation techniques that enable AI model training on enterprise data without exposing the underlying data to decentralized network participants are particularly valuable for integrations involving regulated data categories.

Operational integration

Technical connectivity is a necessary but insufficient condition for successful enterprise integration. Decentralized AI capabilities must also be embedded into the organizational workflows, operational processes, and human systems through which enterprises actually function.

Beyond technical connectivity, the following operational integration embeds decentralized AI into enterprise workflows, processes, and teams for sustainable adoption:

- **Unified monitoring and alerting** that combine decentralized AI telemetry with enterprise observability infrastructure give operations teams a coherent view of system health across both environments. Rather than requiring operators to consult separate monitoring systems for decentralized and enterprise components, integrated dashboards and alerting pipelines surface decentralized AI signals, node health, model performance, blockchain transaction status, and consensus participation through the same tools and workflows that teams already use for enterprise system monitoring.
- **Change management** processes that govern the introduction of decentralized AI capabilities into enterprise workflows must address the organizational as well as technical dimensions of integration. Upgrade cycles that affect both decentralized network protocols and enterprise system interfaces require careful coordination to prevent incompatibilities. Conflict resolution procedures for situations where decentralized governance decisions conflict with enterprise operational requirements must be defined in advance rather than improvised when conflicts arise.
- **Training and capability development** programs that equip stakeholders across technical, operational, and business functions with the knowledge to work effectively with decentralized AI are essential for realizing the value of integration investments. Engineers need fluency in both decentralized and enterprise integration patterns. Operations teams need an understanding of decentralized system behaviors that differ

fundamentally from centralized system expectations. Business stakeholders need the conceptual frameworks to identify decentralized AI use cases and evaluate integration proposals.

Business value and innovation enablement

Enterprise integration of decentralized AI delivers business value that extends well beyond operational efficiency improvements, enabling new categories of capability that centralized architectures cannot support.

These decentralized AI integrations unlock transparency, collaboration, and tokenized models beyond centralized limits:

- **Transparency through immutable records** provides enterprises with audit and accountability capabilities that build stakeholder trust in ways that centralized record systems cannot match. Customers, regulators, and business partners can independently verify claims about data provenance, model behavior, and governance decisions rather than relying on organizational assurances, a capability that is increasingly valuable as regulatory scrutiny of AI systems intensifies.
- **Collaborative innovation through federated data sharing** enables organizations to derive AI insights from data that spans organizational boundaries without requiring data centralization, which raises privacy, competitive, and regulatory concerns. Federated learning architectures integrated with enterprise data infrastructure allow industry participants to train shared models on collectively owned data while each participant retains control of their contribution and receives proportional benefit from the shared capability.
- **New business models** enabled by tokenized incentives and decentralized marketplaces create revenue and value creation opportunities that conventional enterprise architectures cannot support. Organizations can monetize data assets, AI model capabilities, and compute resources through decentralized market mechanisms, reaching participants and customers that centralized distribution channels do not access.
- **Reduced vendor lock-in** through integration architectures built on interoperable open standards and portable infrastructure reduces the strategic and financial risks associated with dependence on single technology vendors. Organizations that invest in standards-based integration layers retain the flexibility to change underlying technology components without rebuilding integration infrastructure from scratch.

Cost management

Effective cost management is one of the most consequential and frequently underestimated disciplines in the production deployment of decentralized AI systems. In centralized AI architectures, cost control is primarily an infrastructure optimization problem: consolidating compute and storage within controlled environments, negotiating favorable cloud contracts, and tuning resource utilization within a well-understood cost model. Decentralized AI introduces a substantially more complex cost structure. Expenses are distributed across compute resources, storage systems, network bandwidth, blockchain transaction fees, operational overhead, and the incentive mechanisms that sustain participant engagement, each governed by different economic dynamics and subject to different optimization levers. Managing these costs without sacrificing the resilience, security, and decentralization properties that justify the architecture requires systematic strategies that span technical design, governance policy, and economic modeling.

Understanding cost drivers

Before cost can be managed effectively, it must be understood comprehensively. Decentralized AI systems incur expenses from six distinct categories, each with its own cost dynamics and optimization surface:

- **Compute resources** represent the largest and most variable cost category for most decentralized AI deployments. Continuous model training across distributed nodes consumes CPU, GPU, and specialized accelerator cycles whose costs accumulate continuously whether workloads are productive or idle. The distributed nature of computation means that inefficiency at any node level, underutilized accelerators, redundant recomputation, and poorly batched inference requests are multiplied across the full node population rather than absorbed within a single managed cluster.
- **Storage expenses** grow steadily as datasets, model artifacts, training checkpoints, and blockchain state accumulate over the system lifecycle. Replication strategies that provide fault tolerance and data availability across distributed nodes multiply raw storage volumes by the replication factor, and the immutability properties of blockchain storage mean that historical state cannot be pruned to control costs without careful architectural planning. Long-term storage costs are frequently underestimated during system design and become a significant operational burden as systems mature.
- **Network bandwidth** costs arise from the frequent data exchanges that decentralized AI requires: model update transmissions between training and aggregation nodes, consensus messaging between blockchain validators, data pipeline transfers between storage and compute infrastructure, and coordination signals between governance participants. In systems that span geographic regions or cloud providers, cross-boundary data transfer fees can represent a substantial and poorly predictable cost component.
- **Blockchain transaction fees** introduce a cost category with no equivalent in centralized AI systems. Every smart contract execution, token transfer, governance vote, and on-chain state update consumes gas whose price fluctuates with network congestion

in ways that are difficult to predict and budget. Systems that rely heavily on chain coordination without careful gas optimization can incur transaction costs that scale unfavorably with usage volume.

- **Operational overhead** encompasses the personnel, tooling, and infrastructure investments required to monitor, maintain, audit, and govern a production decentralized AI system. Security audits, compliance assessments, node operator support, and governance participation all represent ongoing costs that must be sustained throughout the system lifecycle rather than amortized over an initial deployment investment.
- **Incentive mechanisms** are a cost category unique to decentralized systems that rely on token economics or other reward structures to attract and retain participant contributions. Token-based rewards for data provision, model training, validation, and storage must be calibrated to sustain participation quality without creating inflationary pressure that undermines the economic model of the system as a whole.

Strategies for cost optimization

Decentralized AI demands targeted cost strategies focusing on resource efficiency, shared compute, and dynamic allocation to cut expenses while preserving performance. Understanding cost drivers creates the foundation for targeted optimization strategies that reduce expenses without degrading system capabilities. Leveraging idle global compute via decentralized networks can slash AI infrastructure costs by up to 80% compared to cloud monopolies. Tokenomics and incentive mechanisms align participant behaviors to favor low-cost, high-efficiency operations across the network.

Resource efficiency

Resource efficiency improvements reduce compute and storage demands at the algorithmic level, attacking costs at their source rather than simply provisioning cheaper infrastructure to run inefficient workloads. Model compression techniques, including quantization, pruning, and knowledge distillation, reduce the computational cost of inference without proportionate accuracy degradation. Adaptive model partitioning distributes model components across nodes in ways that match computational requirements to available resources, avoiding the waste of running large model components on hardware whose capacity they do not fully utilize.

Adaptive scaling

It matches infrastructure provisioning to actual workload demand in real time, eliminating the idle resource costs that result from static provisioning against peak demand estimates. Autoscaling policies that spin up additional compute capacity during training peaks and release it during inference-only periods can reduce compute costs substantially compared to always-on provisioning. Spot and preemptible compute instances available through cloud providers offer further cost reductions for workloads that can tolerate interruption, which many batch training jobs can accommodate with appropriate checkpointing.

Optimized communication

It reduces the bandwidth costs that model update exchanges and consensus messaging generate. Gradient compression techniques reduce the volume of data transmitted during distributed training without a significant convergence penalty. Increasing the interval between model update synchronizations reduces communication frequency at the cost of some convergence speed. Local aggregation within geographic clusters reduces the volume of data that must traverse expensive cross-region network connections before aggregation occurs at a higher level.

Blockchain layer optimization

It addresses the transaction fee costs that on-chain coordination generates. Layer 2 scaling solutions process transactions off-chain and settle aggregated results on the main chain, reducing per-transaction gas costs by orders of magnitude for high-volume coordination workflows. Transaction batching combines multiple logical operations into a single on-chain transaction, amortizing base transaction costs across multiple operations. Writing gas-efficient smart contracts through careful Solidity optimization and algorithmic design reduces the computational cost of each individual transaction.

Collaborative cost sharing

Collaborative cost sharing through transparent economic models distributes both costs and rewards across participants in ways that reflect actual contribution and consumption. Well-designed tokenomic models create aligned incentives where participants who contribute more valuable resources receive proportionally greater rewards, and participants who consume more system capacity bear proportionally greater costs. This alignment reduces free rider problems and ensures that the economic model remains sustainable as the participant population scales.

Monitoring and analytics

This provides the operational visibility needed to identify cost inefficiencies before they become entrenched. Granular cost tracking that attributes expenses to specific workloads, node operators, and system components enables informed optimization decisions. Predictive analytics models trained on historical cost and usage data can forecast future expenditures and identify emerging inefficiencies before they produce budget overruns.

Cost governance and transparency

Cost management in decentralized systems is not solely a technical optimization problem; it is also a governance challenge that requires transparent processes and shared accountability across independent participants. The following cost management demands transparent processes beyond pure optimization, fostering shared responsibility:

- **Community-driven budgeting** enables decentralized networks to allocate shared resources according to priorities that reflect the collective interests of participants rather than the preferences of any single controlling entity. Governance proposals for significant infrastructure investments or protocol changes that affect system costs are evaluated through the same on-chain governance mechanisms that govern other system decisions, ensuring that cost implications are visible and subject to community scrutiny before commitments are made.
- **Blockchain-based auditing** leverages the immutability and transparency of distributed ledgers to create cost audit trails that any participant can independently verify. Recording resource consumption, incentive distributions, and infrastructure expenditures as on-chain events ensures that cost reporting cannot be selectively manipulated and that regulatory compliance requirements for financial transparency can be satisfied without reliance on the honesty of any single reporting party.
- **Dynamic incentive adjustment** responds to real-time cost data by recalibrating token economics and reward structures to maintain economic sustainability as system conditions evolve. Automated adjustment mechanisms that respond to changes in participant numbers, workload volumes, or external economic conditions reduce the governance overhead of manual incentive management while maintaining the economic alignment that sustains participation quality.

Emerging trends in cost management

The cost management landscape for decentralized AI is evolving rapidly as new technologies and economic models create optimization opportunities that did not exist at the time most current production systems were designed.

The following landscape evolves with tech and models outpacing legacy systems:

- **Decentralized compute and data marketplaces** enable organizations to source AI infrastructure capacity through competitive markets that aggregate supply from diverse providers, driving prices toward their competitive equilibrium rather than the margin structures of established cloud vendors. Platforms that enable direct exchange of compute cycles, training data, and model artifacts between participants create economic mechanisms for matching supply and demand more efficiently than either centralized procurement or fixed bilateral agreements.

- **Green computing initiatives** are increasingly relevant to both cost management and corporate sustainability commitments. Energy-efficient neural network architectures, hardware accelerators optimized for inference efficiency, and workload scheduling strategies that favor renewable energy availability reduce both electricity costs and the carbon footprint of decentralized AI operations. As carbon pricing mechanisms mature across jurisdictions, the economic and environmental benefits of green computing will increasingly converge.
- **AI-driven cost optimization** closes the loop by applying machine learning to the cost management problem itself. Predictive models trained on historical resource utilization, transaction fee patterns, and workload characteristics can autonomously tune infrastructure provisioning, scheduling decisions, and communication strategies to minimize costs in real time, responding to changing conditions faster and more precisely than rule-based optimization policies allow. As these systems mature, they will enable decentralized AI deployments to maintain cost efficiency across a dynamic operational environment with substantially less manual intervention than current approaches require.

Conclusion

The disciplines explored throughout this chapter share a common purpose: transforming decentralized AI from an architectural concept into an operational reality that enterprises can depend upon. Production readiness is not achieved through any single design decision or technology selection; it emerges from the disciplined integration of production architecture, deployment automation, infrastructure resilience, observability, performance engineering, disaster recovery, governance-driven maintenance, scaling strategy, enterprise integration, and economic sustainability into a coherent whole. Each of these dimensions reinforces the others, and weakness in any one of them constrains the reliability and value that the system as a whole can deliver.

The frameworks and practices presented in this chapter reflect a fundamental conviction that runs throughout this book: that the principles of decentralization, trustless coordination, transparent governance, distributed resilience, and open participation are not obstacles to enterprise-grade performance but the foundation upon which a more robust and accountable class of AI infrastructure can be built. Realizing that potential requires the same engineering discipline and operational rigor that any production system demands, it is applied with a clear understanding of the specific challenges and opportunities that decentralized environments introduce.

With the production engineering foundation now established, the next chapter that follows builds upon it to explore the economic and governance dimensions that determine how decentralized AI systems sustain themselves over time and evolve in response to changing conditions. Tokenomics, governance design, and real-world implementation patterns each represent a layer of the larger architecture that this book constructs, and each will be more fully understood in light of the production engineering principles that this chapter has laid down.

CHAPTER 11
Case Studies and Future Trends

Introduction

The convergence of DAI and blockchain technology marks one of the most significant technological transformations of the twenty-first century. While earlier waves of digital innovation concentrated data, computational power, and decision-making within a few dominant platforms, this new paradigm disperses intelligence across networks of participants who cooperate without yielding authority to any single entity. The outcome is a generation of systems that are more resilient, transparent, and equitable than those that came before, with the capacity to reshape industries, governance models, and economic relationships in ways we are only beginning to understand.

This chapter explores that potential through real-world experience. Across sectors such as healthcare, financial services, supply chain operations, entertainment, and scientific research, practitioners have progressed beyond early experimental pilots to implement integrated decentralized AI and blockchain systems at a meaningful scale. Their work has produced not only technical advancements but also valuable lessons about governance, incentive structures, regulatory interaction, and the organizational complexities involved in building trust across institutional boundaries. These lessons are as essential as the underlying technology, and they form the foundation of the analysis presented here.

The chapter is structured to move from practical realities to broader possibilities. It begins with industry-specific case studies that ground the discussion in actual deployments, concrete data, and measurable outcomes, including failures that are often as instructive as successes. It then draws out the themes that cut across these implementations before examining emerging technologies and regulatory shifts that will define the next stage of this integration. The chapter concludes with a forward-looking discussion of the opportunities ahead, from new economic frameworks and cross-industry platforms to the wider societal implications of systems where intelligence and trust are intertwined at the protocol level. Whether readers engage with this material as technologists, business leaders, policymakers, or researchers, they will find both a clear view of the current landscape and guidance for navigating the path forward.

Structure

The chapter covers the following topics:

- Healthcare AI networks
- Financial services applications
- Supply chain and logistics
- Gaming and entertainment
- Scientific research collaboration
- Lessons learned and best practices
- Emerging technologies and trends
- Regulatory developments
- Future opportunities
- Recommendations

Objectives

By the end of this chapter, readers will gain a comprehensive understanding of how decentralized AI and blockchain integration drive transformation in the world's most data-intensive and trust-sensitive industries, including healthcare, financial services, supply chain, gaming, and scientific research. This chapter examines real-world case studies to illustrate practical applications and architectural patterns in decentralized AI and blockchain systems. It analyzes blockchain's role as a foundational layer for trust, transparency, auditability, and governance in AI-driven ecosystems through evidence-based assessments.

The chapter also identifies critical success factors such as governance design, incentive alignment, and stakeholder engagement. These often determine whether high-impact deployments succeed or fail. In addition, the chapter explores privacy-preserving technologies, including federated learning, secure multi-party computation, and zero-knowledge proofs. It demonstrates how integrating these technologies with blockchain enables secure data collaboration that may otherwise be legally or institutionally difficult.

The chapter surveys the evolving regulatory landscape across major jurisdictions and provides actionable compliance guidance for practitioners. It introduces emerging technologies and trends shaping the future of the field, such as edge AI, DAO-driven governance, autonomous AI agents, and next-generation consensus mechanisms. The chapter presents forward-looking opportunities in areas such as cross-industry AI platforms, decentralized data marketplaces, and token-incentivized AI development, which are positioned as the next frontier of value creation. Together, these objectives ensure readers depart not only informed about the current state of decentralized AI and blockchain but also equipped to contribute as builders, decision-makers, and advocates for technology that advances the public good.

Healthcare AI networks

The core problem for healthcare exists at the crossroads of two difficult truths. On one hand, medical AI systems achieve far better performance when trained on large and diverse datasets, the kind that no single hospital or research institution can provide. On the other hand, patient information is among the most sensitive data in the world, protected by strict regulations such as HIPAA in the United States, GDPR in Europe, PDPA in Southeast Asia, and numerous national equivalents, and further bound by deep ethical responsibilities. This creates a landscape where the information required to develop life-saving models is scattered across thousands of isolated institutions, each limited by legal and ethical barriers that prevent free data sharing.

Blockchain and federated learning together provide a way to resolve this tension in a manner that neither technology could achieve independently.

As illustrated in *Figure 11.1*, diverse vertical case studies range from healthcare to scientific research, alongside the critical emerging technologies driving the next phase of decentralized AI evolution. The figure shows how these converged vertical applications and decentralized governance design patterns unlock the full immutability and global-scale benefits of secure AI networks:

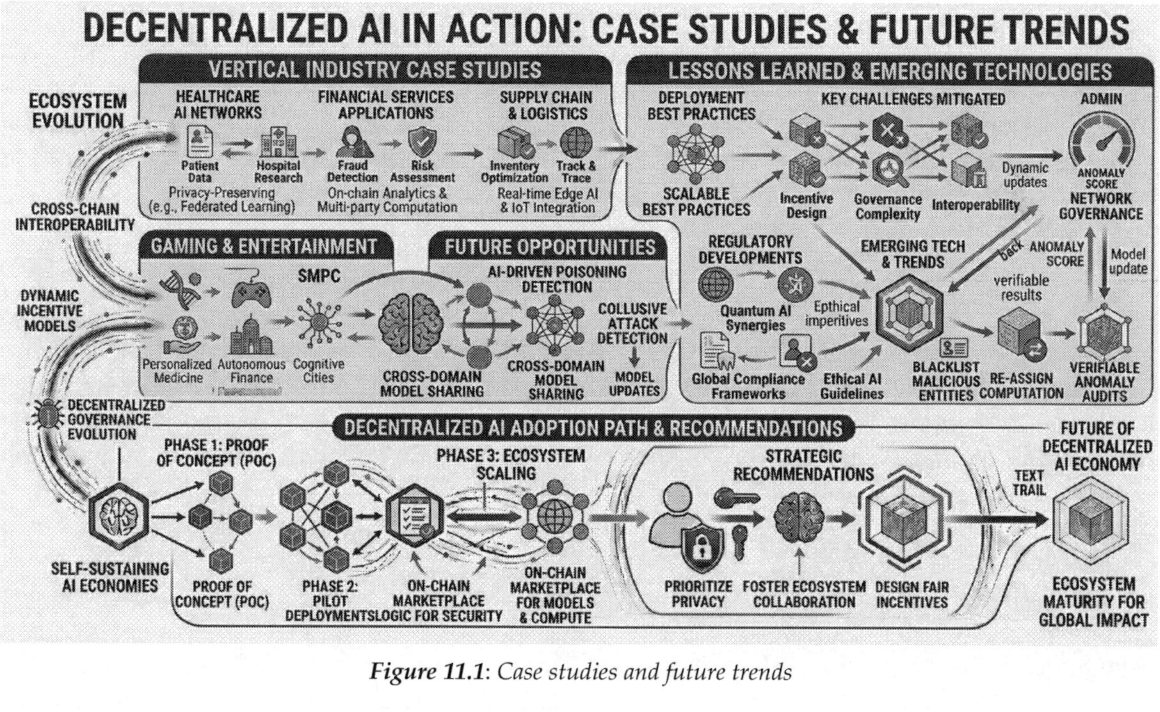

***Figure 11.1**: Case studies and future trends*

HealthChain consortium

Disclosure: This case study is based on a real implementation, with the consortium name and certain identifying details changed to protect participant confidentiality.

In 2021, a group of fourteen European hospitals and research organizations launched what would become one of the most thoroughly documented implementations of blockchain and federated learning in the healthcare sector. Operating within a framework later detailed in the HealthChain white paper, the project set out to create a shared oncology diagnostic model without requiring any institution to transmit raw patient data.

The system architecture relied on three core components. First, a permissioned blockchain built on Hyperledger Fabric acted as the coordination and audit layer. Every model update, every gradient aggregation round, and every participant's contribution were logged as immutable transactions. Second, a federated learning protocol distributed the training process across each hospital's local computing environment. Each institution trained its model on its own data, and only encrypted gradient updates were exchanged across the network. Third, a zero-knowledge proof mechanism enabled participants to confirm that peers were submitting valid gradient updates without revealing any underlying datasets used to generate them.

This blockchain layer addressed a challenge that traditional federated learning systems had struggled to overcome: transparency and accountability. In conventional federated setups, identifying the source of poisoned gradients, whether due to malicious intent or simple misconfiguration, can be extremely difficult. In contrast, the HealthChain consortium's immutable transaction log ensured that every submitted update was timestamped, hashed, and linked to its origin. When one participant experienced a local software misconfiguration in late 2022, the resulting anomalous gradients were detected within two aggregation cycles and traced back to their origin in a matter of hours, a process that would likely have taken days or even weeks in a standard federated environment.

Ultimately, the consortium's shared diagnostic model achieved 94.3 percent accuracy on a validation dataset assembled from patient populations across all fourteen institutions. No individual hospital had been able to approach this performance on its own, with the strongest locally trained model reaching only 87.1 percent. This difference demonstrated in concrete terms the value of collective learning enabled by a blockchain-secured federated architecture.

MedRec and patient data sovereignty

A different perspective on the use of blockchain in healthcare comes from MedRec, a project first developed at MIT and later expanded through various commercial deployments. Unlike systems focused on training AI models, MedRec tackles the question of who owns patient information and how access to medical records is controlled, a foundational requirement for any AI application that relies on patient consent.

Instead of storing data directly on a blockchain, the system keeps medical records on existing institutional servers while managing access permissions through a blockchain-based smart contract layer. Each patient holds a cryptographic key that determines who may view their records. When a healthcare provider, insurer, or research organization requests access, the patient's smart contract automatically approves or rejects the request based on predefined permissions. Every access event is recorded on the blockchain, creating a complete and tamper-evident audit trail.

The relevance to AI becomes clear when considering the downstream implications. When patients truly control their own information and can grant specific, limited, purpose-driven consent, they become active participants in AI training initiatives they might otherwise avoid. Several extensions of MedRec's architecture have introduced token-based incentive models in which patients receive small rewards for allowing their data to be used in approved research efforts. This creates a transparent, voluntary, and traceable marketplace for medical data that contrasts sharply with the opaque practices of current data broker networks.

Commercial implementations have highlighted important lessons about the divide between technical design and real clinical workflow. Early deployments faced strong pushback from hospital IT teams, not because the technology was flawed, but because blockchain-based access control required changes to established electronic health record integration practices. The key takeaway was not that blockchain was unsuitable for healthcare, but that successful adoption demands extensive stakeholder involvement and thoughtful change management, something technical teams often underestimate.

Estonia's e-health integrity at the national scale

Estonia secures the integrity and auditability of nearly all citizens' **electronic health records** (**EHRs**) using Guardtime's **keyless signature infrastructure** (**KSI**) blockchain, which anchors tamper-evident hashes from clinical systems to an independent, append-only ledger. Critically, no patient data is placed on-chain; only cryptographic evidence is published, enabling any authorized party to verify that records were not altered while preserving privacy. This model, deployed across the government's X-Road backbone, has operated for years, demonstrating how blockchain can provide population-level provenance and non-repudiation for clinical data workflows.

Blockchain-enabled health data networks

In the U.S., BurstIQ operates a HIPAA and GDPR-aligned, SOC-2 audited health data exchange where organizations share sensitive data with consent, governance, and policy automated via smart contracts, creating a LifeGraph of entities to support analytics and AI. This platform underpins research data collaborations and care coordination without centralizing raw records, an operational example of blockchain as the trust and policy layer for decentralized AI pipelines.

Federated learning for drug discovery

The pharmaceutical industry faces a distinctive version of the broader healthcare data challenge. Effective drug discovery depends on training models with molecular interaction data, clinical trial findings, and genomic information that companies consider highly confidential, competitive assets. Since no organization is willing to share this information openly, models trained on the data of any single company inevitably suffer from limited scope and insufficient diversity.

In response, several industry collaborations have begun exploring blockchain-anchored federated learning as a method for identifying promising drug candidates. One of the most prominent examples is the MELLODDY project, a joint effort involving ten major pharmaceutical companies under the coordination of the *Innovative Medicines Initiative*. Over the course of several years, the consortium conducted a large-scale federated learning study in which each participant contributed molecular activity data to a collective model without exposing its proprietary compound libraries.

Within this framework, the blockchain layer functioned mainly as a governance mechanism. Smart contracts established participation rules, managed gradient aggregation procedures, and enforced safeguards to detect and remove anomalous or suspicious contributions. The resulting models delivered measurable improvements in predicting high-value drug candidates when compared to models trained on any individual company's dataset. For an industry long known for deep competition and organizational silos, these results were compelling enough to support continued collaboration and further investment.

Key lessons from healthcare

Clear patterns emerge across real-world healthcare implementations. Privacy-preserving computation and blockchain-based auditability are not simply complementary ideas; they are fundamentally interdependent. Federated learning without a reliable audit mechanism exposes systems to risks such as gradient poisoning and free riding, while auditability without strong privacy safeguards makes participation impossible under current regulatory conditions. These technologies must be designed in tandem from the very beginning rather than assembled as separate components after the fact.

Engagement with regulatory bodies is just as essential. Some of the most technically sophisticated healthcare blockchain initiatives have struggled or stalled because early dialogue with data protection authorities was overlooked. Regulators in this domain are not uniformly opposed to innovation; several European data protection agencies, for example, have issued guidance that supports the use of federated learning as long as appropriate protections are implemented. Early and collaborative interaction with regulators typically results in workable, practical compliance frameworks, whereas adversarial or avoidant approaches often lead to delays, uncertainty, and increased costs.

Financial services applications

The financial sector was among the earliest to adopt AI at scale and among the first to encounter the challenges that arise when automated decision-making operates within a tightly regulated environment. Functions such as credit assessment, fraud detection, algorithmic trading, and compliance monitoring rely on models that must be explainable, auditable, and demonstrably free of discriminatory bias. These requirements naturally align with the qualities of transparency and immutability that blockchain technology provides.

The rise of decentralized finance has introduced an additional layer of complexity. Financial protocols that run without traditional intermediaries now depend on advanced AI systems to manage risk, identify attempts at manipulation, and optimize liquidity. All of this must occur in real time, on open public infrastructure, and without the safety net of a central operator who can intervene when problems emerge.

Federated fraud detection

Traditional fraud detection systems rely on centralized models trained on transaction data pooled from multiple institutions. This aggregation introduces significant privacy and competitive risks: financial organizations must share sensitive transaction patterns with a central authority, creating both a data monopoly and an attractive target for cyberattacks.

To address these challenges, a consortium of Nordic banks, working alongside a fintech research institute, implemented a blockchain-anchored federated learning system for collaborative fraud detection. This architecture has since become a widely referenced model in the field. Each bank trains its fraud detection model locally using its own transaction data. Encrypted model updates are then sent to a coordination layer, where secure multi-party computation combines the updates into a shared model. The blockchain logs every aggregation event, along with the cryptographic commitments of each participant's update and the verification proofs confirming that the computations were performed correctly.

The shared model delivered a thirty-one percent improvement in fraud detection compared with the individual models maintained by each institution. This gain was largely due to the behavior of fraudsters who operated across multiple banks, leaving patterns that no single institution could detect on its own. The blockchain-based audit trail also produced an unexpected compliance advantage. Regulators were able to verify that the federated model adhered to the required training protocols without accessing any bank's proprietary transaction data. This combination of transparency and confidentiality helped address key regulatory concerns, contributing to the system's approval by authorities who might otherwise have approached such an architecture with considerable caution.

On-chain threat detection as a decentralized AI network

The Forta Network runs a community of ML-powered detection bots and independent scan nodes monitoring transactions in real time across multiple chains. In 2024-25, Forta introduced a *firewall*, screening millions of transactions daily with sub-block latency and ML risk scoring to block malicious transactions before execution, a step-change from post incident alerts. Integrations span DeFi protocols, rollup-as-a-service providers (e.g., Conduit), and compliance partners (e.g., Solidus Labs ingests Forta's scam alerts for Web3 AML). This is decentralized AI + blockchain as security middleware for financial rails.

Smart contracts and AI-driven compliance

Regulatory compliance in financial services, including anti money laundering, **know your customer** (**KYC**) requirements, and transaction monitoring, remains one of the industry's most significant operational expenses. A 2023 survey estimated that global financial institutions were spending more than 206 billion dollars annually on financial crime compliance, much of it tied to manual review workflows that AI could greatly streamline.

The convergence of AI systems with smart contract infrastructure has introduced a new model for compliance automation. AI models evaluate transaction patterns and identify anomalies, while smart contracts encode the relevant compliance rules and automatically trigger predefined actions when certain thresholds are met. These actions may include freezing accounts, generating compliance reports, or escalating cases to human analysts. The blockchain records every compliance action along with the associated data inputs and the rules that were applied, producing an immutable audit trail that meets regulatory expectations and offers clear evidence during investigations or disputes.

A mature example of this architecture can be seen in the Axoni network, which is used by several major financial institutions for post-trade processing. AI components help optimize the sequence of settlements and detect potential settlement failures before they create broader disruptions. Smart contracts handle the settlement logic according to established institutional agreements, and the blockchain documents the complete lifecycle of each transaction from execution through final settlement. This integrated approach has reduced settlement failures by an estimated 47 percent compared with the earlier batch-based processing systems.

DeFi protocol risk management

Decentralized finance protocols control billions of dollars in assets through smart contracts that operate autonomously, without human intervention. This creates substantial risk exposure. Smart contract vulnerabilities, Oracle manipulation, flash loan exploitation, and liquidity shocks can drain a protocol's treasury in minutes. Traditional risk management frameworks, built for human-supervised systems with operational delays and manual override options, cannot be applied directly to this environment.

AI-driven risk management for decentralized finance has emerged as one of the most challenging and sophisticated areas within the decentralized AI ecosystem. Platforms such as *Gauntlet* and *Chaos Labs* use simulation-based AI models that continuously evaluate protocol-level parameters, including collateralization ratios, liquidation thresholds, and interest rate curves. These systems generate recommendations or execute automated parameter adjustments in response to evolving market conditions.

In this setting, blockchain integration is foundational rather than supplementary. The protocols being analyzed operate directly on blockchain infrastructure, and the governance processes that enact parameter changes are encoded in smart contracts. When an AI system produces a recommendation, it is submitted as a proposal to a decentralized governance framework, often a DAO structure explored later in this chapter. The blockchain records every step of the process, including the proposal, the community vote, and the final execution. The end result is a risk management architecture that is automated, transparent, and governed collectively by stakeholders, a structure with no direct equivalent in traditional finance.

The limitations of these systems have proven equally instructive. During the severe market turmoil of May 2022, several decentralized finance protocols that relied on AI-tuned risk parameters experienced rapid liquidation cascades that the models failed to foresee. Subsequent analysis showed that the models had been trained almost entirely on lower volatility conditions and systematically underestimated extreme tail risk. The takeaway was not that AI-based risk management is inherently flawed; human managers performed no better, but rather that decentralized AI systems must undergo the same adversarial stress testing and scenario analysis used in traditional finance, adapted to the distinct and sometimes unpredictable failure modes introduced by decentralized financial architectures.

Proof-of-reserve (PoR) is an automated control for collateralized assets. Chainlink's PoR feeds bring *cryptographic, on-chain attestations* of off-chain and cross-chain reserves, which protocols can wire directly into mint logic and circuit breakers (e.g., Kelp's rsETH Secure Mint, euro stablecoins like StablR, and real-world reinsurance pools via Re). Research notes PoR's role in mitigating bridge and stablecoin risks and supporting transparent DeFi collateral management.

Blockchain-based credit scoring

In many emerging markets, large segments of the population lack the formal credit history required by traditional scoring models. Blockchain-based identity systems and transaction records offer an alternative data foundation. Individuals who participate in decentralized finance protocols, make on-chain payments, or maintain blockchain-anchored financial activity develop a verifiable transaction trail that AI models can analyze to evaluate creditworthiness.

Projects such as Celo and Goldfinch have implemented AI-driven credit scoring frameworks that rely on behavioral data recorded on the blockchain. The blockchain supplies the underlying data layer, which is immutable, verifiable, and not controlled by any single institution. AI systems then interpret these raw transaction patterns to produce meaningful assessments of credit risk. This combination has expanded credit access for borrowers across sub-Saharan Africa, Southeast Asia, and Latin America who would otherwise remain invisible to conventional financial institutions.

However, these initiatives have revealed a significant challenge: on-chain behavior can be manipulated. Some sophisticated borrowers can design transaction patterns that appear favorable solely to influence AI scoring outputs. While this mirrors long-standing forms of credit score manipulation in traditional finance, the pseudonymous nature of blockchain addresses makes issues like identity verification and resistance to multiple fabricated identities more complex. The most resilient system designs incorporate cryptographic identity verification methods, including zero-knowledge proofs or decentralized identity standards, alongside transaction analysis. This creates a framework that protects user privacy while defending against identity fraud and synthetic borrower profiles.

Decentralized AI marketplaces and agent economies

Networks like Bittensor incentivize model providers (miners) across specialized *AI subnets*, with validators scoring model outputs and distributing the TAO token as an open neural internet for AI services. Meanwhile, Fetch.ai provides an agent platform and chain for autonomous economic agents in logistics, mobility, DeFi execution, and energy, including collective-learning pilots with Bosch and agent marketplaces/tooling for on-chain payments (FET). These projects illustrate a machine-to-machine economy where blockchain handles identity, payments, and provenance, and AI handles decision-making.

Supply chain and logistics

Modern supply chains are extraordinarily complex, distributed systems. A single consumer electronics product may incorporate components sourced from dozens of suppliers across multiple continents, assembled through several tiers of manufacturing partners, and distributed through logistics networks that hand the product off between dozens of carriers before it reaches a consumer. At each handoff, information about the product's origin, condition, and custody changes hands or fails to. The result is that supply chains are often opaque to the brands whose products they carry, to the regulators who govern them, and to the consumers who purchase from them.

Blockchain addresses the transparency problem by creating a shared, immutable ledger of custody transfers, sensor readings, and certification events. AI addresses the optimization problem by identifying patterns in supply chain data that humans cannot process at the necessary scale and speed. Together, they offer something that neither provides alone: a supply chain that is simultaneously transparent, trustworthy, and intelligent.

IBM Food Trust and AI-augmented traceability

IBM Food Trust, built on Hyperledger Fabric, was among the first large-scale commercial deployments of blockchain in supply chain management. Retailers, including *Walmart*, *Carrefour*, and *Nestlé*, joined the network to trace food products from farm to shelf. The initial blockchain deployment cut the time needed to identify the source of a contaminated food product from days or even weeks to just seconds, dramatically improving the speed and accuracy of food safety recalls.

The subsequent integration of AI augmented this capability significantly. Machine learning models trained on the network's accumulated data could identify anomalous patterns in temperature readings, custody chain gaps, or certification sequences that were statistically associated with quality issues before human reviewers would notice them. A model trained on years of cold chain data for seafood products, for instance, learned to flag shipments whose temperature logs showed patterns characteristic of partial thaw-refreeze cycles even when no individual reading exceeded the threshold that would automatically trigger a rejection.

The blockchain's role was essential: the AI model's training data and the inferences it produced both derived their value from the fact that the underlying records were tamper-evident. A temperature log that could be altered by any party in the chain would be worthless as training data and meaningless as evidence. The immutability guarantee was the prerequisite for the AI's analytical value.

Everledger and conflict mineral tracking

Everledger deployed blockchain tracking for diamonds and subsequently extended its platform to other high-value commodities, including rare earth metals, battery components, and luxury goods. The platform creates a digital passport for each tracked asset, recording provenance, certification, and custody history on a blockchain.

The integration of AI into Everledger's platform has focused on two applications. The first is anomaly detection: AI models analyze the network of transactions to identify patterns consistent with certificate fraud, where conflict minerals are laundered through false provenance claims. The second is demand forecasting: AI models trained on blockchain transaction data provide battery manufacturers and electronics companies with real-time visibility into supply availability, enabling more precise procurement planning.

The compliance dimension of this work has gained urgency as regulatory requirements around supply chain due diligence have strengthened. The EU **Corporate Sustainability Due Diligence Directive** (**CS3D**), enacted in 2024, imposes legal obligations on large companies to identify and address human rights and environmental risks in their supply chains. Blockchain-based provenance systems that can generate cryptographically verifiable audit trails are increasingly viewed not as optional enhancements but as compliance infrastructure.

AI-optimized logistics on distributed networks

The port congestion crises of 2021 and 2022 exposed with unmistakable clarity the vulnerability of logistics systems that operate without real-time visibility or adaptive routing capabilities. When the Suez Canal blockage coincided with widespread COVID-related port closures, disruptions rippled through global shipping networks faster than logistics operators could respond. Their information systems were too fragmented and too slow to support meaningful real-time adjustments.

In the aftermath, several logistics technology companies introduced blockchain-anchored AI systems designed to address these shortcomings. Maersk's TradeLens platform, prior to its discontinuation in 2023, attempted to create a unified information layer for container shipping. More recent platforms have taken a narrower but more targeted approach, applying blockchain's trust and verification properties to specific high-value data streams such as customs documents, phytosanitary certificates, and bills of lading. AI systems then build on this trusted data to optimize routing, predict delays, and reassign capacity dynamically.

The effectiveness of these AI systems depends heavily on the reliability and integrity of their data inputs. A routing model that incorporates arrival time predictions from multiple carriers is only as accurate as the forecasts it receives. If carriers consistently provide overly optimistic estimates to obtain better berth allocations, they introduce bias that undermines the entire model. Blockchain-based commitment mechanisms, where carriers stake reputation or financial collateral on the accuracy of their estimates, have emerged as a promising solution. Early deployments show that even relatively small stakeholder requirements significantly improve the precision of submitted estimates. This demonstrates how blockchain incentives can enhance the quality of data feeding AI models, rather than merely securing the outputs of those models.

TradeLens lessons on consortium governance challenge

The shutdown of TradeLens in December 2022 stands as one of the most revealing and instructive failures in the history of enterprise blockchain initiatives. When Maersk and IBM introduced TradeLens in 2018, they envisioned a global shared platform for managing container shipping documentation. The technical foundation was strong; the governance framework was not.

The central issue was that the platform's two primary sponsors, Maersk, the largest container shipping company in the world, and IBM, also held disproportionate governance authority over the system. For competing shipping lines, contributing their operational data to a platform partially controlled by Maersk represented an obvious strategic risk. This lack of trust prevented the platform from achieving the scale and network effects necessary for success. When Maersk announced the project's closure, it cited a clear reason: the level of industry-wide collaboration required to make TradeLens a viable and independent business was never realized.

For designers of decentralized AI and blockchain systems, the takeaway is essential: decentralizing data infrastructure also requires decentralizing governance. A blockchain platform whose governance is dominated by its most powerful stakeholders is not meaningfully decentralized, regardless of how distributed its technical architecture may be. The supply chain initiatives that have succeeded in attracting broad participation, such as the Global Shipping Business Network, an effort whose momentum increased following the failure of TradeLens, have prioritized neutral governance models in which no single party holds undue influence.

Gaming and entertainment

The gaming and entertainment industries have been among the earliest and most experimentally productive adopters of blockchain technology. The reason is structural: digital goods in games and entertainment have always had economic value to users, but the infrastructure for capturing and transferring that value has been tightly controlled by platform operators. Blockchain provides the first credible alternative.

Non-fungible tokens (**NFTs**) and fungible token economies have enabled game designers to create genuine digital ownership: in-game assets that players own at the cryptographic level, that can be transferred freely between players, and that exist independently of any single game operator's servers. The implications for decentralized AI are significant. When game assets exist on public blockchains, AI systems can interact with them, generate them, trade them, and manage them without requiring permission from a central platform.

Axie Infinity and the play-to-earn experiment

Axie Infinity, created by *Sky Mavis*, became one of the most closely examined early experiments in blockchain-based gaming. At its height in 2021, the game attracted more than 2.7 million daily active players, with large communities in the Philippines and Venezuela. Many participants earned meaningful income through the game's play-to-earn mechanics. Players generated **Smooth Love Potion** (**SLP**) tokens through gameplay, and these tokens carried real monetary value that could be exchanged for fiat currency.

Axie's trajectory offers both compelling validation and important cautionary lessons. On the positive side, blockchain enabled digital ownership that opened entirely new forms of economic participation. Players in lower-income regions gained access to earning opportunities through gameplay that traditional labor markets would not have provided. Scholarship arrangements emerged organically as NFT owners lent their assets to players who lacked the resources to purchase them, sharing the token-based earnings in return. This dynamic essentially created a decentralized capital allocation model that had no meaningful precedent in conventional gaming ecosystems.

However, the cautionary side of Axie's story is equally significant. The game's token economy functioned in a structurally unsound way: the earnings of existing players were largely funded by the capital inflows of new players. When user growth slowed, the economic model unwound predictably. The situation was further destabilized by the Ronin bridge hack in March 2022, where attackers stole 625 million dollars in cryptocurrency, accelerating the decline of the ecosystem. The lesson is not that token-based gaming models are intrinsically flawed, but rather that sustainable token economies must be grounded in economic fundamentals. Token value must come from genuine gameplay-driven demand, not speculative expectations. Games that have managed to sustain blockchain-enabled economies, such as Sorare and Stepn during certain periods, and a number of esports-oriented platforms have succeeded by anchoring token utility in real user engagement rather than in hopes of price appreciation.

AI-generated content and blockchain provenance

The proliferation of AI-generated content in entertainment has created an urgent provenance problem. When AI can generate photorealistic images, convincing deepfake videos, and narratively coherent written text at scale, the ability to distinguish authentic from synthetic content becomes critical for copyright enforcement, for combating misinformation, and for preserving the cultural and economic value of human creative work.

Blockchain-based content provenance systems have emerged as a primary technical response. The Coalition for **Content Provenance and Authenticity** (**C2PA**), a cross-industry initiative involving Adobe, Microsoft, Intel, BBC, and others, has developed a technical standard for attaching cryptographically signed provenance metadata to digital content. When content is produced, whether by a human photographer or an AI image generator, a signed attestation is embedded in the file that records the creation tool used, the time of creation, and, when applicable, the creator's cryptographic identity.

The integration with AI is bidirectional. AI systems can consume blockchain-verified provenance data to distinguish authentic from AI-generated content, filter misinformation, and respect copyright restrictions. AI systems can also produce blockchain-anchored provenance attestations as they generate content, creating an auditable record of AI involvement in content creation. Several major entertainment studios have deployed early versions of this infrastructure for their production pipelines, ensuring that AI-generated visual effects and AI-assisted script development are tracked through production in a way that satisfies both copyright compliance and emerging regulatory requirements around AI disclosure.

Decentralized AI-driven game mechanics

The frontier of gaming AI integration involves not just AI tools for human game designers but AI systems that participate autonomously in game economies and mechanics. Several blockchain games have deployed on-chain AI agents and autonomous programs that interact with game smart contracts, trade assets, manage resources, and compete with human players, creating hybrid human-AI game economies.

The design challenges are substantial. On-chain AI agents must execute deterministically (to produce the same result given the same inputs across all network nodes) while also being responsive to game state in ways that feel intelligent and non-trivial to human players. Several projects have addressed this by running AI inference off-chain while committing the inputs, outputs, and cryptographic proofs of correct computation to the blockchain, a pattern that mirrors the off-chain computation approaches used in DeFi (rollups, state channels) but applied to AI inference.

The economic implications extend beyond gaming. Blockchain-native AI agents that manage real digital assets represent the leading edge of the broader movement toward autonomous economic actors, software agents capable of owning, trading, and managing assets without human involvement in each transaction. The governance and regulatory implications of this trend are discussed in the emerging technologies section of this chapter.

Scientific research collaboration

Scientific research faces two related crises: the reproducibility crisis and the data silo problem. The first concerns replication: a substantial fraction of published findings cannot be independently reproduced, partly because the underlying data, code, and methodology are insufficiently documented or shared. The second concerns access: datasets that could enable significant scientific advances exist across institutional repositories, but a lack of interoperability, trust, and shared incentive structures prevents them from being used collaboratively.

Blockchain addresses both by providing immutable data provenance (supporting reproducibility) and shared data infrastructure with cryptographic access control (enabling collaboration across institutional boundaries). Decentralized AI makes it possible to analyze pooled datasets without bringing them together in a single location, using the same federated learning and secure multi-party computation frameworks that have proven effective in healthcare and are equally applicable to genomics, climate science, and particle physics.

Ocean Protocol and the scientific data marketplace

Ocean Protocol is a decentralized data marketplace that uses blockchain smart contracts to enable data owners to monetize their datasets while retaining control over access. Scientists and research institutions can publish datasets to the Ocean marketplace, set access conditions and pricing in smart contracts, and receive payments when qualified researchers access their data, all without surrendering custody of the underlying data to any central platform.

The integration with AI is explicit and central to Ocean's design. The platform includes a compute-to-data capability that allows AI models to be run against private datasets without the data ever leaving the data owner's infrastructure. A researcher at one institution can train a model on a dataset stored at another institution, use the resulting model and its outputs, and compensate the data provider with Ocean tokens, all without ever accessing the underlying raw data that informed the training process.

Several scientific research initiatives have adopted the Ocean as their data sharing infrastructure. A notable example involved climate science: a consortium of meteorological institutes across twelve countries created a shared model of ocean temperature patterns by running federated AI training against their local datasets through the Ocean compute-to-data framework. The blockchain provided the coordination layer: each contributing institution's dataset access permissions, model evaluation results, and token compensation were recorded on-chain. The resulting model achieved significantly stronger predictive accuracy for El Niño events than any model developed by a single institution, offering clear scientific evidence of the advantages created by a decentralized data architecture.

TrialChain and clinical research integrity

Clinical trial data integrity is one of the most consequential problems in medical science. When trial data can be altered, selectively reported, or fabricated, the consequences include ineffective drugs reaching the market, dangerous side effects going unreported, and the systematic distortion of the evidence base that clinical medicine depends on. The problem is not hypothetical: high-profile research fraud cases have involved alterations to trial data that were not detectable with existing audit mechanisms.

TrialChain, a blockchain-based clinical trial data management system, addresses this by timestamping and hashing trial data at the point of collection and recording these cryptographic commitments on a blockchain. Any subsequent alteration of the data is detectable through comparison with the original hash. AI models that analyze clinical trial data and are trained on blockchain-anchored datasets can therefore provide a level of data integrity assurance that conventional data management systems cannot.

Beyond data integrity, the blockchain layer enables pre-registration of statistical analysis plans, a practice that combats **Hypothesizing After Results are Known** (**HARKing**), where researchers adjust their analytical methodology after seeing the data to produce more favorable results. When analysis plans are committed to a blockchain before data collection begins, any deviation from the registered plan is detectable. AI systems can compare submitted analysis code against registered plans and flag deviations automatically, creating a scientific integrity monitoring capability that has historically depended entirely on peer reviewer vigilance.

Decentralized science movements

The **decentralized science** (**DeSci**) movement, or decentralized science, embodies a far more ambitious vision for blockchain's place in scientific research: not simply protecting data, but reshaping the entire incentive structure of academia through token-based economics and decentralized governance.

The current scientific publication system has well-documented problems. Access to published research is locked behind expensive journal paywalls. Peer review is performed for free by scientists who receive no formal recognition for the work. Research funding is concentrated through opaque grant-making processes. Negative results are rarely published, creating systematic bias in the literature.

DeSci projects propose blockchain-based alternatives to each of these structures. VitaDAO funds longevity research by issuing governance tokens to contributors, researchers, data providers, and funders who collectively vote on research priorities. AntidoteDAO funds rare disease research through a similar model. ResearchHub, modeled loosely on Reddit, distributes ResearchCoin tokens to scientists for publishing, reviewing, and reproducing research.

These projects are early, and the results are mixed. The funding amounts they have mobilized remain small relative to traditional grant mechanisms, and the quality of peer review within token-incentivized systems is uneven. But the structural problems they are addressing are real, and several of them have attracted serious scientific talent who see in the DeSci model a credible alternative to the dysfunctions of academic publishing and grant culture.

Lessons learned and best practices

The true measure of any transformative technology lies not in what it promises in theory but in what it delivers and what it demands in real-world practice. Across every industry explored in this chapter, the deployment of decentralized AI and blockchain systems has revealed a set of consistent lessons that no technical white paper fully anticipates. These lessons span organizational, economic, and regulatory dimensions, reflecting the challenge of building systems that must win the trust of stakeholders who operate under different incentives, legal constraints, and institutional cultures.

Some insights reaffirm what seasoned systems designers have long emphasized: governance, interoperability, and incentive alignment are not peripheral considerations but the foundational elements upon which technical architectures either succeed or fail. Other insights are unique to decentralized AI and blockchain systems themselves, including the oracle problem, the limitations of token-weighted governance, and the tension between immutability and accuracy, and require frameworks that the broader technology ecosystem is still working to develop.

What follows distills the most consequential lessons drawn from real-world deployments, presented as practical guidance for practitioners, enterprise leaders, and policymakers as they design, evaluate, and govern the next generation of decentralized AI and blockchain infrastructures.

Governance as the non-negotiable foundation

The single most consistent lesson across every domain examined in this chapter is that technical excellence is necessary but not sufficient. Projects that have truly succeeded, those that sustained user adoption, met their stated goals, and established lasting infrastructure, have consistently treated governance design with the same seriousness as their technical architecture. By contrast, many of the projects that faltered with TradeLens, as the most prominent example, were technologically advanced but lacked a mature approach to governance.

Effective governance for decentralized AI and blockchain systems requires clarity on several questions that are often deferred or underspecified in early-stage projects. These questions are as follows:

- Who has the authority to change the system's rules, and through what process?
- How are disputes between participants resolved?
- What happens when a participant behaves in ways that are harmful to others but technically within the rules?
- How are the benefits of the system distributed, and does the distribution mechanism remain fair as the system scales?

Token-based governance, in which voting power corresponds to the number of tokens held, has emerged as the prevailing model in decentralized systems. Its appeal is substantial: it is resistant to Sybil attacks, straightforward to measure, and aligns economic incentives with active participation in governance. However, pure token-weighted voting tends toward plutocracy and is vulnerable to governance attacks, where large token holders (including sophisticated adversarial actors who can acquire tokens cheaply) override the preferences of the broader user community. The most sophisticated governance designs have moved beyond simple token-weighted voting to incorporate reputation systems, time-locks, conviction voting, and multi-stakeholder structures that require buy-in from different constituencies before consequential changes can be executed.

Interoperability as strategic infrastructure

The network effects of decentralized systems are maximized when they interconnect with each other. A patient data system that operates exclusively within one hospital network provides limited value; one that interconnects with pharmacy chains, insurance providers, and research institutions provides transformative value. A supply chain transparency platform that covers one tier of a manufacturing process is a pilot project; one that spans the entire supply chain from raw material to retail is infrastructure.

Achieving interoperability requires technical standards, governance agreements, and legal frameworks that allow data and assets to flow between systems that were designed independently. The blockchain ecosystem has made notable advances in technical interoperability, with cross-chain bridges, atomic swaps, and interoperability frameworks such as Polkadot's XCMP and Cosmos's IBC enabling the transfer of both value and information across otherwise independent blockchain networks. The harder work is governance and legal interoperability: agreeing on data standards, liability frameworks, and dispute resolution mechanisms that span institutional and jurisdictional boundaries.

Projects that have prioritized interoperability from the very beginning, adopting open standards, participating in cross-industry governance groups, and deliberately planning for data exchange with complementary systems, have consistently outperformed those that built closed ecosystems and attempted to enforce interoperability through sheer market dominance.

Trust calibration and the Oracle problem

Blockchain systems are only as trustworthy as the data they record. The immutability of blockchain records is a profound guarantee about what was recorded, but it makes no guarantee about whether what was recorded was accurate. A temperature sensor that records fabricated data to the blockchain creates an immutable record of fabricated data. A hospital that submits fraudulent certification records creates a tamper-evident record of fraud.

This limitation, commonly referred to in the blockchain community as the oracle problem, named for the mechanisms that connect real-world data to on-chain systems, remains one of the most significant design constraints for practical applications. The technical responses include decentralized Oracle networks (Chainlink being the most deployed example), hardware security modules that attest to sensor data integrity, and cryptographic proofs that constrain the range of values a sensor can plausibly report.

AI adds another dimension to Oracle trust. When AI models generate inputs for blockchain systems such as risk scores, fraud alerts, or quality evaluations, the reliability of those inputs is tied directly to the integrity of the models that created them. Model governance, which involves tracking the exact model version used for each output, ensuring that models are not updated silently in ways that alter their behavior, and establishing accountability for model errors, functions as the AI-specific counterpart to the oracle problem. The most robust systems treat AI model outputs as untrusted inputs that require verification, not trusted facts that can be recorded directly to an immutable ledger.

Incentive design and long-run sustainability

Token economies that funded growth through speculative appreciation rather than genuine user value have uniformly failed. Axie Infinity's play-to-earn collapse, the broader NFT market deflation of 2022-2023, and the failures of numerous DeFi protocols that relied on high token emission rates to sustain artificially inflated yields all reflect the same underlying error: confusing token price appreciation with the creation of genuine economic value.

Sustainable token economies share several properties. They generate revenue through services that users would pay for regardless of token appreciation expectations. Token distribution is structured to reward meaningful contributions such as providing data, performing computational work, participating in governance, and ensuring quality, rather than simply holding tokens or engaging in speculation. The token supply mechanics are conservative, with clear mechanisms for value accrual that do not depend on continuously growing new entrant investment.

The Filecoin network, which pays storage providers in **Filecoin** (**FIL**) tokens for verifiably providing decentralized storage, represents a more sustainable model: the token economy is grounded in demand for a service (storage) that exists independently of token appreciation. The economic resilience of this model, through multiple crypto market cycles, provides an instructive contrast to the more speculative token designs that characterized the 2021-2022 period.

Emerging technologies and trends

Every generation of technological infrastructure gives rise to the next, building on established foundations while pushing beyond earlier limitations. The decentralized AI and blockchain ecosystem is no different. The systems operating today across healthcare, finance, supply chains, and scientific research, significant as they may be, represent only an early stage of what will become possible as the underlying technologies continue to mature, intersect, and reinforce one another in ways that current practitioners are only beginning to imagine.

The next wave of innovation will not emerge from a single breakthrough but from a set of parallel advances: more capable cryptographic tools that make privacy preserving computation faster and more cost effective, AI architectures that run efficiently at the network edge without compromising performance, governance models that embed collective intelligence into autonomous organizational structures, and consensus mechanisms that resolve long standing tensions among decentralization, throughput, and security.

Understanding these emerging technologies is far more than an academic exercise. Technologists define the design space for systems that will be built over the next three to five years. Business leaders identify the capabilities that will distinguish competitive infrastructure from platforms that quickly become outdated. For policymakers, they surface the regulatory questions that must be addressed before these technologies achieve widespread societal adoption.

This section examines each of these emerging directions with analytic clarity, evaluating not only what is technically feasible but also what is practically achievable, economically sustainable, and institutionally sound in the decentralized AI and blockchain landscape of the coming decade.

Federated learning maturity and next-generation privacy

Federated learning has matured significantly since its public introduction by Google in 2016. The technique has moved from research curiosity to production infrastructure, with deployments in mobile keyboards (Google GBoard), healthcare diagnostics, and financial fraud detection. The next generation of federated learning addresses limitations that earlier systems shared: vulnerability to gradient inversion attacks that can reconstruct training data from gradient updates, lack of formal privacy guarantees, and limited support for heterogeneous data distributions across participants.

Differentially private federated learning, which adds carefully calibrated noise to gradient updates before transmission, providing formal mathematical guarantees about the maximum information leakable about any individual training example, is becoming the default for privacy-sensitive deployments. Combining differential privacy with secure aggregation (where gradients are aggregated using cryptographic protocols that prevent the aggregating server from seeing individual updates) provides multi-layered privacy protection. Blockchain's role in this architecture is to provide governance transparency: the privacy parameters, the aggregation protocol, and the participant roster are all recorded on-chain, enabling external verification of the system's privacy properties.

Split learning, a related technique in which a neural network is divided between the client and the server so that each processes different layers, has gained attention in healthcare settings where even gradient updates are considered too sensitive to share. Blockchain-based coordination of split learning pipelines enables multiple institutions to contribute to model training while retaining tighter control over their data's computational exposure.

Edge AI and decentralized inference

The traditional model of centralized AI inference, in which user queries are sent to large cloud data centers running on powerful GPU clusters, faces environmental, latency, privacy, and resilience limitations. These challenges have driven substantial investment in edge AI, where inference is performed on devices located much closer to the data source, from smartphones and tablets to IoT sensors and industrial edge servers.

Blockchain provides essential infrastructure for distributed edge AI networks. When AI inference is distributed across many edge devices operated by different entities, coordination mechanisms are needed to route inference requests to available devices, verify that inference was performed correctly, compensate device operators, and manage model updates across the distributed fleet. All of these functions map naturally to blockchain smart contracts.

Projects like Gensyn (decentralized AI training) and Ritual (on-chain AI inference) are building blockchain-native infrastructure for distributed AI computation. The vision AI models that run on decentralized networks of consumer hardware, coordinated by smart contracts, compensating participants in tokens for their computational contributions, represent a potential shift in the economics of AI that could significantly reduce the concentration of AI capabilities in a small number of large cloud providers.

The technical challenges are substantial. AI inference on heterogeneous edge hardware is significantly more complex than inference on standardized cloud GPUs. Verifying that inference has been performed correctly, without running the computation a second time, which would defeat the purpose of distributed processing, requires cryptographic methods such as zero-knowledge proofs of inference accuracy. These techniques remain computationally expensive and are still in the process of maturing. However the trajectory of progress on both hardware efficiency and cryptographic verification techniques suggests that these barriers are surmountable on a five-to-ten year horizon.

Decentralized autonomous organizations and AI governance

DAOs are organizations whose rules and operations are encoded in smart contracts on a blockchain, have become an important governance model for decentralized AI projects. Rather than a conventional corporate structure where a CEO and board make key decisions about model training, deployment, and use policies, DAO-governed AI projects distribute these decisions to token holders who vote on proposals.

MakerDAO's governance of the Dai stablecoin and Uniswap's governance of its decentralized exchange protocol are among the most extensively studied DAO governance examples. AI-focused DAOs are earlier in their development but include projects like SingularityNET (which governs its AI services marketplace through AGIX token voting) and Ocean Protocol (which governs its data marketplace through OCEAN token voting).

The promise of DAO-governed AI is significant. Decisions about model capabilities, deployment contexts, and access restrictions made through transparent, on-chain governance processes in which any affected party can participate represent a fundamentally different relationship between AI systems and the communities they affect than the closed, proprietary decision-making typical of large technology companies. That said, on-chain governance decisions do not automatically carry legal weight in off-chain jurisdictions. In enterprise and regulated deployments in particular, the relationship between DAO resolutions and enforceable legal obligations remains an open and consequential question that governance designers must address explicitly.

The structural challenges are equally real: voter apathy (most governance decisions are made by a small fraction of eligible participants), plutocratic dynamics (large token holders dominate voting), and the difficulty of encoding nuanced ethical judgments in binary on-chain votes all limit the model's effectiveness in practice.

Several projects are exploring design approaches intended to address these limitations. Quadratic voting, in which voting power scales with the square root of token holdings rather than linearly, reduces the dominance of large holders. Delegation mechanisms allow engaged community members to accumulate voting power from less active participants, improving effective participation rates. Structured deliberation processes with mandatory comment periods and adversarial review requirements before a vote is called improve the quality of decisions that do get made.

Blockchain consensus innovation

The consensus mechanisms that underpin blockchain networks are not static. **Proof of work (PoW)**, which secured Bitcoin's early years, consumed extraordinary amounts of energy and imposed significant latency. Ethereum's transition to proof of stake in 2022 (the Merge) reduced its energy consumption by an estimated 99.95% while maintaining security properties comparable to PoW. The next generation of consensus mechanisms is addressing the remaining limitations: finality latency, throughput, and the tension between decentralization and performance.

For decentralized AI applications, the most relevant consensus advances are those that reduce transaction costs and confirmation times, enabling real-time AI inference coordination on-chain; those that support private computation verification, enabling AI inference proofs to be submitted and verified efficiently; and those that provide stronger security guarantees for high-value applications like financial AI and medical decision support.

Directed acyclic graph (**DAG**)-based consensus, implemented in networks like Avalanche and **Internet of Things Application** (**IoTA**), enables parallel transaction processing that dramatically increases throughput. zkRollup consensus aggregates many transactions into a single on-chain proof, reducing costs while inheriting the security of the base layer. These advances are directly relevant to the economics of blockchain-AI integration: as transaction costs fall and throughput rises, use cases that were previously impractical (real-time AI inference coordination, high-frequency data logging for AI training, micro-payment-based AI service marketplaces) become economically viable.

Regulatory developments

No technology of real consequence operates in a regulatory vacuum, and decentralized AI and blockchain integration, precisely because of its significance, has drawn sustained attention from legislators, regulatory agencies, and international governance bodies across every major jurisdiction. What makes this regulatory environment particularly challenging is not the complexity of any single framework, but the fact that multiple overlapping frameworks are evolving simultaneously, often at different speeds, from different institutional starting points, and toward differing policy goals.

Regulators responsible for overseeing AI must now grapple with systems in which decision-making is distributed across networks with no identifiable central operator. Those tasked with supervising financial markets must engage with protocols that carry out transactions autonomously through smart contracts. Data protection authorities must evaluate privacy risks in architectures where personal data never leaves its source institution, yet still contributes to AI models with substantial power and reach. These are not incremental extensions of familiar regulatory questions. They represent fundamentally new challenges that require fresh analytical methods, new enforcement mechanisms, and new forms of collaboration among regulators who have traditionally operated within tightly defined sectoral boundaries.

At the same time, the global regulatory landscape is not uniformly restrictive or uniformly permissive. Jurisdictions such as the European Union, Singapore, and Japan have shown that thoughtful, technically informed regulation can provide the legal clarity innovators need while still allowing the experimentation that drives progress. Understanding the trajectory of regulation and the reasoning behind it is essential for anyone building, deploying, or investing in decentralized AI and blockchain systems. It is a strategic imperative that will determine which systems achieve scale, which markets remain open, and which participants earn the institutional trust required to operate in the most consequential domains.

Global regulatory landscape

The global regulatory landscape surrounding decentralized AI and the integration of blockchain technologies is evolving quickly, though unevenly, across different jurisdictions. The primary regulatory challenge is structural: existing oversight systems were built for centralized organizations such as companies, exchanges, and banks that can be licensed, audited, and held accountable. Decentralized systems, in which responsibility is widely distributed and no single party exercises full control, do not align neatly with these traditional frameworks.

Regulators have responded to this mismatch in varied ways, ranging from innovative and adaptive approaches to more reactive and restrictive measures. For builders and innovators working in this domain, understanding this shifting landscape is not optional but essential.

European Union framework

The European Union has produced the most comprehensive regulatory framework for both blockchain (Markets in Crypto Assets, or MiCA) and AI (the EU AI Act) of any major jurisdiction. The interaction between these two regulatory frameworks is directly relevant to integrated decentralized AI and blockchain systems.

MiCA, which entered full effect in 2024, establishes a licensing regime for crypto asset service providers and issuers. Significantly for decentralized systems, MiCA includes a partial exemption for fully decentralized systems where no identifiable intermediary provides services, but the definition of fully decentralized has been the subject of extensive regulatory guidance and legal interpretation. Most real-world blockchain systems have identifiable developer teams, foundation entities, or validator sets that regulators have argued bring them within MiCA's scope.

The EU AI Act categorizes AI systems by risk level, with the highest-risk applications (including AI used in healthcare, critical infrastructure, and credit scoring) subject to conformity assessment requirements, transparency obligations, and human oversight mandates. The intersection with blockchain creates novel regulatory questions:

- If an AI system's outputs are executed by autonomous smart contracts without human review, does this satisfy or violate the human oversight requirements?
- If an AI model is governed by a DAO whose token holders are distributed globally, who is responsible for conformity assessment?

These questions are being actively litigated and negotiated between industry participants and the European Commission.

Jurisdictional fragmentation of the United States

The United States presents a more fragmented regulatory picture. Multiple agencies like the **Securities and Exchange Commission** (**SEC**), **Commodity Futures Trading Commission** (**CFTC**), **Federal Trade Commission** (**FTC**), **Food and Drug Administration** (**FDA**), **Office of the Comptroller of the Currency** (**OCC**), and state-level financial regulators have claimed jurisdiction over different aspects of blockchain and AI systems, often with conflicting interpretations. The SEC's aggressive classification of many tokens as securities under the Howey test has created significant compliance uncertainty for token-based AI systems whose tokens are claimed to have utility rather than investment characteristics. The CFTC has asserted jurisdiction over crypto derivatives and certain spot markets. The FTC has brought enforcement actions against AI systems that engage in deceptive practices or unlawful data collection.

Legislative efforts to create a coherent federal framework for digital assets have repeatedly stalled in Congress, leaving the US market to operate under an enforcement-driven regulatory regime that many practitioners argue is less predictable and more restrictive than the rule-based frameworks emerging in other jurisdictions. The 2024 FIT21 Act, which attempted to clarify the SEC/CFTC jurisdiction boundary for digital assets, passed the House but did not advance in the Senate, illustrating the continuing legislative gridlock.

For decentralized AI systems specifically, the US regulatory picture is similarly fragmented. The Biden administration's 2023 Executive Order on AI established cross-agency coordination mechanisms and safety reporting requirements for frontier AI models, but did not specifically address decentralized AI governance. The subsequent regulatory guidance from NIST, the FTC, and sector-specific agencies has focused primarily on centralized AI deployments.

Asia-Pacific approaches

Asia-Pacific jurisdictions have taken divergent approaches that reflect their different economic and political priorities. Singapore has positioned itself as a global hub for regulated blockchain and AI development, with the **Monetary Authority of Singapore** (**MAS**) providing detailed regulatory guidance for digital asset businesses and the AI Governance Framework offering a principles-based approach to responsible AI deployment. The MAS Project Guardian, a collaboration among the MAS, major financial institutions, and decentralized finance protocols exploring regulated DeFi, represents one of the most advanced regulatory engagement efforts with decentralized financial systems worldwide. China has taken the most restrictive approach, banning cryptocurrency trading and mining while simultaneously developing its own central bank digital currency (DCEP/e-CNY) and maintaining state control over AI development through regulations on the management of generative AI services. The Chinese approach represents an explicit rejection of the decentralization principle. Centralized control of both monetary and AI infrastructure is a deliberate policy choice, not a temporary regulatory gap.

Japan, South Korea, and Australia have developed their own licensing regimes for crypto assets and are actively working on AI governance frameworks. Japan's Financial Services Agency has been particularly active in developing forward-looking regulatory guidance for DeFi, and Japan's AI governance approach has emphasized self-regulation and industry standards rather than prescriptive legislation.

Regulatory trajectory

Several emerging regulatory trends are now clear enough to offer meaningful guidance for practitioners. Privacy-preserving AI computation, including federated learning, secure multi-party computation, and differential privacy, is increasingly supported by regulators in multiple jurisdictions as the preferred approach for handling sensitive personal data. Across sectors such as healthcare, financial services, and other high-sensitivity domains, regulatory frameworks are gradually converging on requirements that align closely with these technical methods.

Regulatory compliance infrastructure encompassing logs, audit trails, and governance records is also shifting toward blockchain-based implementations. Regulators are finding that the immutability and transparency of blockchain systems better satisfy oversight needs than traditional databases, whose contents can be altered by administrators. Authorities that were initially skeptical of blockchain are increasingly acknowledging its value as a compliance tool, particularly for cross-border operations and multi-party processes where no single institution's records can serve as a trusted source of truth.

Requirements for AI disclosure obligations to inform users when they are interacting with AI systems and to provide explanations for AI-driven decisions are expanding across many regulatory environments. Blockchain-based provenance solutions offer a natural foundation for meeting these obligations, and the C2PA standard discussed earlier in the entertainment section is now being adopted in regulatory contexts as well.

Future opportunities

If the earlier sections of this chapter have shown what decentralized AI and blockchain integration have already achieved, and what they have cost, where they have faltered, and what they have revealed, this section looks forward with deliberate ambition. The case studies, lessons, emerging technologies, and regulatory developments discussed so far are not final destinations. They form the accumulated foundation upon which a far more consequential next phase is now being built.

The convergence of maturing blockchain infrastructure, increasingly powerful AI models, privacy-preserving computation at a practical scale, and regulatory frameworks that are beginning to accommodate rather than resist decentralized systems has created a moment of genuine strategic opportunity. It is a moment that will reward those who engage proactively and thoughtfully and disadvantage those who wait for complete clarity before taking action.

The opportunities that lie ahead are not incremental upgrades to existing systems. They point to the creation of fundamentally new economic models in which the value generated by AI is distributed across the networks that create it, rather than captured by the platforms that control it. They open the door to cross-industry data collaboration at a scale that no centralized institution could authorize or manage. They include autonomous AI agents capable of conducting economic activity, managing organizational processes, and coordinating global resources with a level of speed, precision, and transparency that traditional institutions cannot match. They also extend to populations and regions that current AI and financial infrastructures have historically excluded, offering pathways into the global digital economy that do not depend on the permission of legacy gatekeepers.

This section charts these opportunities with the same analytical discipline applied throughout the chapter, grounding ambition in technical reality, economic logic, and institutional feasibility. The goal is to equip readers to engage with the future not as passive observers of unfolding trends, but as informed architects of systems that have yet to be imagined and built.

New economic models for AI development

The economics of AI development are currently dominated by a small number of large-scale compute operators whose capital advantages enable them to train the largest and most capable models. This concentration creates structural risks: a few technology companies control infrastructure that is increasingly central to economic activity, research, and communication. The question of whether alternative economic models can sustain competitive AI development is one of the most consequential open questions in technology policy.

Decentralized AI development, where the costs and benefits of model training are distributed across many participants through token economics, represents the most developed alternative model. The Bittensor network, which incentivizes participants to train and serve AI models by rewarding them in TAO tokens based on the quality of their outputs, provides a live test of whether token-incentivized AI development can produce models that compete with centrally developed alternatives.

Early results are mixed but encouraging in important ways. Bittensor's models are not yet competitive with frontier models from OpenAI, Anthropic, or Google on standard benchmarks. However the network has demonstrated that meaningful AI development activity can be organized through token incentives at a scale and diversity that no single organization controls. The quality gap stems partly from the resources available, since the network cannot yet match the computing power of the leading frontier laboratories, and partly from incentive structures in which reward mechanisms that encourage narrow optimization, such as maximizing benchmark scores, can overshadow the broader training goals needed to produce general capability. As both the resource base and the incentive design evolve, this competitive gap is likely to narrow.

The economic model also enables participation from AI talent and compute resources in geographies where access to centralized AI infrastructure is limited. A researcher in Lagos or Jakarta who contributes to a decentralized AI training network participates in the global

AI development ecosystem in a way that current centralized models do not facilitate. The geopolitical implications of this democratization are significant.

Cross-industry AI platforms and data marketplaces

One of the most promising opportunities in decentralized AI is the development of cross-industry AI platforms, shared infrastructures that allow applications to operate across multiple sectors by drawing on data and services from each. Blockchain provides the trust layer that makes this sharing possible: data contributors can participate with cryptographic guarantees about how their data will be used; AI model users can verify the provenance and training methodology of models they deploy.

The healthcare-finance intersection illustrates the potential. Patients whose financial behaviors are recorded on blockchain-based financial platforms and whose health records are managed through blockchain-based healthcare systems could, with their explicit consent, contribute to AI models that identify financial stress signals that predict health outcomes, enabling preventive interventions that neither sector could support independently. Privacy-preserving computation ensures that this integration does not require the aggregation of raw personal data in any centralized system.

Similar cross-industry opportunities exist at the intersection of supply chain and financial services (supply chain financing, where AI risk models trained on verified supply chain data enable more accurate credit pricing), between scientific research and healthcare (translational research where bench discoveries are applied to clinical contexts more rapidly through AI models trained on both types of data), and between environmental monitoring and industrial optimization (AI models that optimize industrial processes for both efficiency and environmental impact using data from distributed sensor networks anchored to environmental monitoring blockchains).

Autonomous AI agents and on-chain economic activity

The rise of AI agents, systems capable of taking multiple sequential actions to pursue defined goals while interacting autonomously with software tools and digital environments, represents one of the most transformative near-term developments in the field of artificial intelligence. When these agents operate in blockchain environments, holding digital assets, executing smart contracts, and interacting with other on-chain protocols, they become autonomous economic actors in a sense that has no precedent.

The implications cascade through every domain discussed in this chapter. Supply chains are coordinated by autonomous AI agents that negotiate contracts, arrange logistics, and resolve disputes through smart contracts without human involvement in each transaction. Financial markets are populated by AI agents that continuously optimize portfolios, provide liquidity, and manage risk, all on transparent, auditable blockchains. Scientific research consortia where AI agents handle data access requests, execute analysis protocols, and manage attribution according to pre-agreed smart contract rules.

The governance challenges that arise from this are profound. It brings us to the question: When an autonomous AI agent causes harm, responsibility becomes unclear: is it the developer who built the system, the organization that deployed it, or the DAO that oversees the protocol on which it operates?

Current legal frameworks, which assign responsibility to identifiable human actors, provide limited guidance. New legal frameworks for autonomous AI agents are beginning to emerge: Wyoming's DAO LLC legislation, which gives DAOs legal personhood, is one early step. The development of AI-specific liability frameworks that can handle the distributed responsibility structures of autonomous agent systems is an area of active legal and regulatory development.

Blockchain-powered AI marketplaces

The commercialization of AI capabilities through decentralized marketplaces, where models, datasets, computing resources, and AI-generated outputs are traded via smart contracts, represents a major near-term opportunity for the emerging AI economy. The inefficiencies of current AI commercialization models (where access to the most capable models requires subscription contracts with large technology companies, and where small AI developers have limited ability to monetize specialized models) create significant space for marketplace-based alternatives.

SingularityNET provides the most developed implementation of the AI marketplace vision: a platform where AI service providers publish their capabilities to a blockchain-based registry, charge for their services in AGIX tokens, and receive payment through smart contracts that execute automatically upon service delivery. The platform has attracted hundreds of AI services across domains, from natural language processing to financial analysis to drug discovery.

The next generation of AI marketplaces will incorporate more sophisticated matching mechanisms (AI-assisted selection of the best model for a given task), quality assurance mechanisms (blockchain-based attestations of model performance on verified benchmarks), and composability (smart contract-mediated pipelines that chain multiple AI services to accomplish complex tasks). The ability to compose AI capabilities from multiple providers, with clear attribution and compensation for each contributor, enables an AI development ecosystem where specialization is economically rewarded and where small, specialized AI developers can compete with general-purpose platforms.

Climate and sustainability applications

One emerging application domain that warrants particular attention is the intersection of decentralized AI, blockchain, and climate change. The scale of the climate challenge requires coordination across an extraordinary range of actors, governments, corporations, civil society organizations, and individuals in ways that no single authority can mandate. Decentralized systems provide the coordination infrastructure; AI provides the analytical and optimization capabilities; and the combination enables interventions at the scale and complexity that climate solutions require.

Voluntary carbon markets, which allow companies to offset emissions by purchasing carbon credits from projects that sequester carbon or avoid emissions, have been plagued by transparency and integrity problems: credits have been sold for emissions reductions that did not occur, monitoring has been unreliable, and double counting has been endemic. Blockchain-based carbon registries with AI-verified satellite monitoring represent a potential solution: satellite imagery analyzed by AI models quantifies actual carbon sequestration; the results are committed to a blockchain, creating a tamper-evident record; smart contracts issue carbon credits only when verified sequestration is confirmed.

Regen Network, Toucan Protocol, and several other projects are building this infrastructure. The opportunity extends beyond carbon markets to real-time grid optimization (AI models that balance renewable energy generation and consumption across distributed grids, with blockchain managing the financial settlements between participants), climate risk assessment (AI models trained on climate data secured and shared through blockchain-based research consortia), and supply chain decarbonization (AI optimization of logistics and manufacturing processes, with blockchain verification of the resulting emissions reductions).

Recommendations

Across the diverse stakeholders engaged in decentralized AI and blockchain, actionable guidance is essential to translate technical potential into sustainable impact. This section distills strategic priorities for technology developers and startups, established enterprises, and researchers and academics, highlighting the pathways that maximize value creation, mitigate risks, and advance innovation.

Technology developers and startups

The greatest opportunities lie at the intersection of specific, high-value problems and the technical capabilities that decentralized AI and blockchain uniquely enable. The urge to build broad, general-purpose platforms should be resisted in favor of cultivating deep expertise within specific vertical domains where you thoroughly understand users and their challenges. Focusing on interoperability, creating systems that integrate seamlessly with complementary infrastructure rather than attempting to control the entire stack, is not only a strategically sound approach but also one that reflects the decentralized principles that make these technologies unique. Invest in governance design from the beginning. The governance architecture you establish in a project's early stages will shape its trajectory for years. The choices made in founding documents, smart contract logic, and token distribution are difficult to reverse. Seek expertise in governance design with the same urgency you seek expertise in cryptography and machine learning.

Established enterprises

The path to decentralized AI and blockchain adoption that delivers the most value runs through consortium participation, not solo deployment. The network effects that make these systems powerful require participation from multiple stakeholders; a blockchain system with one participant is just a database. The enterprises that will derive the most value from this technology are those that convene and participate in industry consortia, contribute to open standards, and engage with regulatory processes constructively.

The risk of regulatory non-compliance is real but manageable. The regulatory landscape is developing, not static, and early engagement with regulators tends to produce more workable outcomes than adversarial postures. The enterprises that have built productive relationships with financial regulators, healthcare authorities, and data protection agencies are able to move faster and with greater confidence than those that treat regulation as an obstacle to be avoided.

Researchers and academics

The intersection of decentralized AI and blockchain is extraordinarily research-rich. Fundamental open problems span cryptography (efficient zero-knowledge proofs for AI inference, practical multi-party computation at AI training scale), distributed systems (Byzantine-fault-tolerant federated learning, incentive-compatible gradient aggregation), economics (token mechanism design for AI marketplaces, governance dynamics in DAO-governed AI systems), and social science (governance outcomes of different DAO structures, adoption dynamics of decentralized AI infrastructure).

The DeSci infrastructure emerging in this space provides new mechanisms for funding and coordinating research that may be more accessible for work in this area than traditional grant mechanisms, which have often been slow to fund genuinely novel interdisciplinary research.

The decade ahead

Looking forward across the next decade, the trajectory of decentralized AI and blockchain integration points toward several transformations that seem increasingly inevitable as the technical, economic, and regulatory foundations mature.

AI will increasingly operate as a layer of intelligence woven into decentralized networks rather than as a set of discrete applications. Just as the internet moved from a network of static documents to a substrate of real-time dynamic experiences, decentralized AI will move from a collection of discrete AI services to ambient intelligence embedded in the protocols that govern economic activity, data management, and organizational decision-making.

The distinction between on-chain and off-chain computation will blur. The advances in zero-knowledge proofs that make it possible to verify AI inference on-chain without reproducing the computation, and the advances in rollup technology that make it possible to process thousands of AI interactions per second at costs approaching zero, will gradually dissolve the architectural separation between the AI layer and the blockchain layer. The two will become, in effect, a single computing environment where intelligence and trust are co-located.

New forms of economic and organizational life will emerge. The combination of AI that can autonomously manage complex tasks and blockchain that can autonomously execute contractual commitments enables organizational structures that do not require human oversight of each individual transaction. The first generation of these structures, including DAOs that oversee decentralized finance protocols and AI agents that manage investment portfolios, is already in operation. The next generation will extend much further, managing supply chains, coordinating research consortia, governing public infrastructure, and potentially taking on roles that have traditionally been the sole responsibility of human institutions. This last possibility raises the most profound questions of all: questions about accountability, legitimacy, and the appropriate scope of autonomous systems in human social life. The technical possibility of autonomous AI-blockchain systems that manage significant economic and social functions does not settle the normative question of when such autonomy is appropriate, to what purposes it should be directed, and through what processes it should be governed. These questions, which are fundamentally political and philosophical rather than merely technical, will determine how the next decade of decentralized AI and blockchain development unfolds.

Conclusion

Across the industries and applications examined in this chapter, several fundamental truths about decentralized AI and blockchain integration emerge with consistent clarity. The combination is more powerful than either technology alone. Blockchain without AI provides transparency and immutability for data that humans cannot process at scale. AI without blockchain provides intelligence that operates on data whose provenance and integrity cannot be verified. The integration of the two creates systems that are simultaneously intelligent, trustworthy, transparent, and resilient, properties that are individually achievable through other means but extraordinarily difficult to achieve together in centralized architectures.

The technology is necessary but not sufficient. Every successful deployment in this chapter involved not just sound technical architecture but thoughtful governance design, genuine stakeholder engagement, sustainable economic incentives, and regulatory cooperation. Projects that overlooked these essential dimensions, no matter how technically advanced they were, either failed completely or achieved only minimal impact. The lesson for practitioners is that the design space of decentralized AI and blockchain systems extends well beyond the technical, and that design expertise in governance, economics, and law is as important as expertise in distributed systems and machine learning.

Privacy-preserving computation is foundational. The most impactful applications in healthcare, finance, and scientific research depend on collaboration between actors who cannot or will not share their raw data. Federated learning, secure multi-party computation, differential privacy, and zero-knowledge proofs are not advanced features of decentralized AI systems; they are the prerequisites for those systems to access the data they need to provide value. Practitioners who do not invest in privacy-preserving architecture are building systems that will be blocked by regulatory requirements, institutional reluctance, or both.

Index

A

B

C

F

G

H

I

T

V

W

Z

Made in United States
Orlando, FL
04 November 2026

90207787R00240